SUSAN ISAACS

SUSAN ISAACS

A Life Freeing the Minds of Children

Philip Graham

KARNAC

First published in 2009 by
Karnac Books Ltd
118 Finchley Road
London NW3 5HT

British Library Cataloguing in Publication Data
A C.I.P. for this book is available from the British Library

ISBN: 978–1–85575–691–5

www.karnacbooks.com

CONTENTS

ACKNOWLEDGEMENTS

I should first like to thank Barbara Tizard who suggested Susan Isaacs as a subject for a biography.

I should like to thank Jane Ridley, my mentor during the whole of the time I was conducting research and writing this biography.

I should like to thank Karina McIntosh, Susan Isaacs's niece by marriage, who knew Susan and her husband well during her child-hood and adolescence and who shared many of her memories with me over numerous interviews. Bridget Williamson, Karina's daughter, gave me access to the collection of books owned by the Isaacs and to additional papers and photographs. I should like to thank Rothamsted Research for permission to reproduce the photograph of William Brierley, to Taylor & Francis Books UK for permission to reproduce the photograph of Susan Isaacs at 10 years, and to Mrs. Janet Pyke for permission to reproduce photographs of the Malting House School.

I should like to thank Professor Jack Pole, a pupil of the Malting House School in the mid-1920s for granting me several interviews and to Dr. Susannah Elmhirst-Isaacs for sending me her recollections of her time at the school.

I should also like to thank the following who have provided a great deal of assistance in many different ways: Arnon Bentovim, Malcolm Pines, Juliet Hopkins, Robin and Inge Hyman, Jonathan Miller, Lucy Rickman-Baruch, Hannah Steinberg, John Munsey-Turner, David Birchall, Colin Leese, Kenneth Robinson, Liz Roberts, the late Willem van der Eyken, Jeni Reilly, Hanna Segal, Yvonne Connelly, Jill Barton, Moira Taylor, Brenda Maddox, Mary-Jane Drummond.

I should particularly like to thank the following who generously gave me large amounts of their time conscientiously reading and making most useful comments on complete, penultimate drafts of the book: Linda Lefevre, Juliet Hopkins, Jane Ridley, Barbara Tizard, Polly Shields and Robin Hyman.

I should like to thank the staff of various Library Archives, but especially Sarah Aitchison at the Institute of Education and Allie Dillon at the Institute of Psychoanalysis.

Finally I should like to thank my wife, Nori, for her encouragement and support during the writing of this book.

PREFACE

When Susan Isaacs died in October, 1948, the obituaries in the quality press were unanimous not only in her praise but in the top ranking they gave to her importance in the fields of education and psycho-analysis. *The London Times (13 October 1948)* enthused:

> ... her teaching has probably influenced educational theory and practice in this country more than that of any living person. Her contribution to psycho-analytical theory, especially to the analysis of children, has also been notable.

Shortly afterwards *(3 March 1949) The Times* published a letter from various prominent individuals, headed by R. A. Butler, a former Conservative Minister of Education and soon to be Chancellor of the Exchequer, announcing the launch of a Susan Isaacs Memorial Fund and asking for contributions.

The leading science journal *Nature (4 December 1948)* was more precise in its compliments:

> Dr. Isaacs's gifts were based on a combination of intellectual and emotional factors ... her outstanding intellectual characteristic was an extremely rapid grasp of the matter in view and an ability to classify and summarise it, to present it with remarkable clarity and to discuss it from various angles. Her exceptional capacity for instantly translating her thoughts and

impressions into verbal expression served as a powerful instrument for all her other gifts.

There were numerous similar eulogies in both the educational and psycho-analytic professional journals. For example, John Rickman (1950), a leading psycho-analyst, wrote a seven-page obituary in the International Journal of Psycho-analysis in which he referred to Susan Isaacs as "an intellectual delight" pinpointing her "supreme contribution to her times" in the way she acted as a psycho-analytic bridge between the two professions of medicine and teaching, "interpreting the one to the other".

Nor did Susan Isaacs's status among informed commentators decline with time. Adrian Wooldridge (1994) reviewing the whole field of psychology in England from 1860 to 1990 refers to her as the most influential English-born child psychologist of her generation. Her entry in the Oxford Dictionary of National Biography, proclaims her to be "the greatest influence on British education in the twentieth century" (Pines, 2004).

Yet her name, let alone the nature of her contributions to education, psychology and psycho-analysis is so little known that when I have been asked whose biography I am writing the name usually elicits polite disbelief that anyone could write about someone so obscure. Mary Jane Drummond, a leading expert in nursery education, writing about her, comments, after listing her achievements— "It is not the least remarkable aspect of Susan Isaacs's unique contribution to educational progress that it remains so undocumented by other educationalists in this country" (Drummond, 2000). A few teachers trained in the nineteen sixties recollect having to read her books; to a few psycho-analysts the name produces a flicker of recognition, but no more. There has only been one previous account of her life. In 1969 Dorothy Gardner, her pupil and successor as Head of the Department of Child Development at the Institute of Education, London, published a book entitled "Susan Isaacs: the First Biography" (Gardner, 1969). Clearly Dorothy Gardner adored her teacher and the book is more of a hagiography than a considered appraisal of a woman's life and work. As well as suffering from its reverential tone, some of the information it carries is inaccurate in important detail and much is misleadingly incomplete. Nearly twenty years later an American educationist, Lydia Smith, wrote an account of Susan Isaacs's work "To Understand and to Help" (Smith, 1985), but this did not add to the already published biographical material.

When I began this biography, some sixty years after Susan Isaacs's death, re-consideration of someone so widely and over such a long time period thought to be such a significant figure seemed clearly desirable. Though the concept of child-centred education had been around for many years, it was she, the first Head of the Department of Child Development at the London Institute of Education and the author of key textbooks in teacher training from the 1930s to the 1960s who forcefully introduced it into mainstream British education. The approach continues to elicit violently conflicting ideas and emotions not only among educationists but among all those who take an informed interest in educational matters—and who does not?

Among those in the child psychoanalytic field and those mental health professionals who mainly look to psychoanalysis for their understanding of child behaviour, Melanie Klein's influence remains paramount. Yet who realises that Melanie Klein might very well have been extruded from the British Psycho-analytic Society but for the intervention of Susan Isaacs who, during the nineteen thirties and forties Klein regarded as her closest friend and associate? Andre Green, a leading French psychoanalyst, has described the record of the so-called Controversial Discussions that decided Klein's fate as "the most important document of the history of psychoanalysis" (Perelberg, 2006). The discussions held by members of the British Psycho-analytic Society were spread over ten sessions of which the first five were entirely taken up by a key paper on phantasy written by Susan Isaacs and the following three by an article on regression of which she was co-author.

If asked to name the first British pioneer of direct observational studies of children in schools, now common place, no psychologist today would be likely to give the name of Susan Isaacs, yet she it was who, in the 1920s long before ethological observation became a recognised approach to the study of children's relationships and behaviour, first recorded, minute by minute, the speech and actions of schoolchildren in their natural setting. Who knows that it was she who first formulated serious criticisms of the studies of Jean Piaget, the foremost child psychologist of his time, forcing him to re-consider his approach? It was not until the nineteen seventies, over forty years later that developmental psychologists re-discovered the objections she had been the first to raise.

Not only was her work groundbreaking in the fields of education, psychoanalysis and psychology, but as an "agony aunt", answering readers' questions in the Nursery World, she had a strong influence on the way middle-class mothers brought up their young children in the pre-Spock era of the nineteen thirties in Britain. In 1937, in the United States, her extremely successful baby book won the Annual Award given by Parents Magazine, the most popular periodical for parents published in the world, for the best book for parents published in the previous year. Finally she was deeply involved in controversies, no less active today than they were in her time, around the quality of parenting, children's rights, physical punishment, the care of deprived children, and the capacity of lone parents.

Her historical significance in the fields of education, psycho-analysis, child psychology, child welfare and upbringing can thus hardly be exaggerated. As I made progress on this book I was repeatedly struck by the contemporary importance of an under-standing of her ideas. My sense of the relevance of this biography grew rather than diminished as her story unfolded.

There is an important sense in which I might be regarded as doubly disqualified from writing a life of Susan Isaacs, for I am neither an educationist nor a psycho-analyst. I can, in defence, plead a number of compensatory advantages. As an academic child and adolescent psychiatrist, my professional work has brought me into close touch with the fields of both psychoanalysis and education. I have worked, happily I think, with psycho-analytic colleagues from the Kleinian, Freudian and Independent groups. I even once had the chairman's responsibility for introducing Anna Freud to a vast audience of psychiatrists eager to hear what she had to say. On the educational side, my research has taken me into many mainstream schools as an observer both formally interviewing schoolchildren about their lives and informally listening to teachers in their staff rooms. I have worked with educationists on various committees including one (chaired by Mary Warnock), on children with special educational needs. At one time I served on the Management Com-mittee of the Institute of Education, London, where Susan Isaacs had earlier pioneered the teaching of child development. So my double disqualification is, I hope, tempered by some relevant experience.

Further, the fact that I do not, by virtue of my professional work belong to any particular school of thought either in education or in psychoanalysis does, I hope, allow me to take a more dispassionate view of her ideas than might otherwise be the case.

Knowing as little as I did about Susan Isaacs when I began researching for and writing this book it turned out that I had been extremely fortunate in my choice of subject. Not only was it a learning experience in more ways than I care to admit, but I was lucky to discover that there was much original material that had not been available when Dorothy Gardner wrote her biography in the nineteen sixties. Sadly this did not include any previously undiscovered diaries kept by Susan Isaacs herself or any letters written by her. But Nathan Isaacs, her second husband, was a prolific letter writer, many of his letters casting an indirect, though unexpectedly piercing light on his wife's personality and the life they led together. These letters that I discovered, partly held in recent years at the Archive of the Institute of Education and partly privately owned, have enabled me to make much more sense of the personal reasons why Susan Isaacs embarked on her various crusades than would otherwise have been the case. Further, the courage in recent years of the British psycho-analytic establishment in making available for general consumption verbatim accounts of the extremely bitter exchanges between the rival schools of psycho-analysis before and during the Second World War has enabled me to describe the historically significant part Susan Isaacs played at this time. All these advantages were not available to Dorothy Gardner when she wrote the first and only previous biography. They alone amply justify another book about this intriguing woman, the worlds in which she lived and the influence she exercised in so many different spheres of life.

INTRODUCTION

In psychoanalytic terms for a boy or young man the death of his father represents his final victory in the "oedipal" struggle for the exclusive love of the son's mother. For a girl or young woman her father's death represents the loss of her very first sexual love. William Fairhurst, a devout Methodist, and the father of Susan Isaacs, the subject of my biography, died on 2 May, 1909 and was buried three days later according to the rites of the Christian church. From the considerable amount we know of the family, who was present or absent at the funeral and their very different feelings towards William, the scene before the funeral (Litten, 1991) can be reconstructed. It must have been something like this:

As the family gathered in Bromley Cross, a suburb of Bolton, Lancashire, on the morning of 5 May, 1909, in the large, book-lined living room of the family home, Monks Field, it is likely that it was twenty year old Alice, the youngest daughter, who was the most obviously distressed. She might well have sat sobbing on one of the large armchairs, both her hands held by her married older sister Bessie, who had come over alone from her own house a few hundred yards away early that morning. The oldest of the brothers and sisters present, Enoch, or Eny as he was known in the family, had come up from London by rail to Bolton in the last hours of William's life and had taken responsibility for the funeral arrangements. He was outside checking the number of carriages, the drivers and their horses. Annie, William's second wife, was in the kitchen, where she had been most of the previous day, preparing food for the guests who were to come after the funeral.

Meanwhile Susie Fairhurst, later to be better known as Susan Isaacs, twenty three years old and the next youngest sister, sat in her room upstairs, reading a book that she frequently put down to reflect on the past, on her turbulent relationship with her father and on whether his death would mean that there was no longer sufficient money for her to continue her studies at the University of Manchester, where she had spent only part of one academic year.

Gradually, other relatives would have arrived. Three of William's brothers, one accompanied by his wife, came from their homes in Ormskirk and from nearby in Bolton. A brother of William's first wife, Miriam, who had died eighteen years previously, came from Manchester. Assorted cousins arrived from Liverpool and Southport. They chatted quietly, sipping the tea that Annie brought in. Susie came downstairs, dutifully feeling she needed to share in the hospitality, however confused her own feelings might be. The talk would have been about William's last illness. He had been ill before with stomach trouble, but had previously always recovered well. In his final short illness, he had suffered a burst duodenal ulcer that had caused peritonitis. His friend, former neighbour and family doctor, Andrew Cosgrove, had brought in a medical colleague and they had both fought to save his life, but the condition was inevitably fatal. Acutely painful and unpleasant, the illness had lasted less than a week. They would have talked too about how the news of their father's death was to be conveyed to the two oldest sons, William and Archie, and to the other sister, Miriam or Mirrie, all of whom were abroad.

Just before two o'clock Eny came in to usher everyone into the carriages. In front was an open landau carrying the coffin and filled to overflowing with wreaths and other floral tributes. Then came the carriage carrying Annie and her grown-up step-children, followed by further carriages with the rest of the family. The sedate horses, black plumes fixed to the backs of their heads, resplendent on this fine spring afternoon, were led by bearded men in black top coats and black top hats. The procession would have made its way slowly down Grange Road, with open country to the left and large houses, mostly screened by trees, to the right, into Turton Road, built-up on both sides and then on for a further couple of miles to the vast, recently completed Methodist King's Hall in Bradshawgate where the service was to be held.

As the members of the family entered, they must have been surprised by the size of the congregation. They were greeted at the front of the Hall by Herbert Cooper, the Minister who conducted the service. Susie would have sat with her sisters, Alice and Bessie, next to their stepmother, in the front row. As the service unfolded, it must have raised in her feelings of great ambivalence, if not downright hostility and anger. For agnostics or atheists such as Susie a religious funeral service inevitably elicits conflicting emotions, especially when it is a parent who has died. The talk of everlasting life is contrary to everything an agnostic leaning towards atheism believes, yet the temptation to entertain the possibility of life after death is almost irresistible. Whether, as Psalm 130, the hymn that had inspired John Wesley on the afternoon of his conversion, was sung, Susie sang the words "I wait for the Lord, my soul waits, And in his word I hope" or kept her mouth tightly shut, the service must have been difficult for her as religious funerals always are for non-believers.

Hardly less emotionally difficult for Susie must have been the experience of hearing the Minister, Herbert Cooper lavishing extravagant praise on her father, the man who ten years earlier when she was only fourteen years old, had cut short her education and refused to allow her to proceed with it because she had voiced agnostic views.

For the rest of the events of that day we can turn with greater certainty to the obituaries in the local papers. In his funeral oration, Cooper was extravagant in his praise. William Fairhurst, journalist, sportsman, but above all Methodist, had been an active member of numerous Methodist chapels, an esteemed editor and sub-editor of local newspapers, as well as prominent in local and national football and other sporting organisations. Represented at the funeral, as well as the publishers of his newspapers, were the Bolton Mission Committee, the King's Hall Brotherhood, the Egerton Wesleyan Trust, the Birtenshaw Wesleyan Trust, and the Birtenshaw Wesleyan Society. From the sporting world came representatives of Bolton Wanderers Football Club, the Lancashire Football Association and the Bolton and District Cricket Association. In his address, the Minister referred to the dead man as "a real Christian gentleman, the true soul of chivalry, quite fearless in advocacy of the right, and singularly unselfish. It would be impossible to associate him with . . . anything mean or ungenerous or unworthy of a Christian gentleman. He was broad-minded and large-hearted, and, in his public work, had a high sense of his responsibility, living in his daily work in the fear of God. He was intolerant of all that was wrong and his passion for righteousness never failed. . . ."

The claim that her father was "broad-minded and large-hearted" must have struck Susie as preposterous, while the frequent references to his Christian beliefs and values can only have confirmed her religious scepticism. After the service closed with the Lord's Prayer, the bearers of the coffin of panelled oak with silver mountings carried it to the waiting carriage outside the Hall. The vast congregation of several hundreds of people, led by the members of the family, walked behind it to nearby Tonge cemetery. After a short interment service, the coffin was lowered into the ground ". . . in sure and certain hope of the Resurrection to eternal life", a hope that Susie will not have shared however sure and certain others may have been.

In May, 1909, when her father's funeral took place, Susie Fairhurst was nearly twenty four years old and could fairly be seen as a New Woman. She would have been regarded with approval by George Bernard Shaw, H. G. Wells and all the luminaries of the new thinking that marked the beginning of the twentieth century. As well as her atheist beliefs, she was socialist in her politics and a member of the Fabian Society. A supporter of the suffragette movement, her commitment was to a career and not primarily to marriage and motherhood. She was coming to the end of a year's training to be an infant school teacher at the University of Manchester. She had so impressed her teachers that, even before the academic year had ended, she had been recommended to enter for an Honours Degree course in Philosophy. She was ambitious and had already conceived the idea of a career in a University Department of Education. For her the death of her father meant the personal loss of a parent. It was also a small milestone in the passing of an era.

Though it took place eight years after the death of Queen Victoria, William Fairhurst's funeral, with its heavy formality, had been a Victorian occasion, marking the end of the life of a locally eminent Victorian. His daughter was part of the early twentieth century movement that rejected Victorian values and beliefs. The Victorian way of life was typified by the Victorian paterfamilias and the patriarchal family he headed in his own autocratic fashion. Arnold Bennett in his novel, "Anna of the Five Towns" (1985) describes Anna's father, Ephraim Tellwright, a late nineteenth century Staffordshire businessman and Methodist lay preacher in such terms:

The women of a household were the natural victims of their master: in his experience it had always been so. In his experience the master had always, by universal consent, possessed certain rights over the self-respect, the happiness, and the peace of the defenceless souls set under him, rights as unquestioned as those exercised by Ivan the Terrible. . . . He belonged to the great and powerful class of house-tyrants, the backbone of the British nation . . .

Like all stereotypes associated with the Victorian age, the Victorian autocrat has been overdrawn. Some have suggested that the nurturant, companionable side of the Victorian father and husband has been neglected by those who have written about the period (Tosh, 2005). But the subordinate role of women, and the treatment by Victorian men of their wives and children as their property to deal with as they wished, kindly or brutally, is not in doubt. At school, though again there were exceptions to the stereotype, the Victorian schoolmaster inculcated knowledge by rote learning and depended on the cane to ensure obedience. After school, for most people, paid work meant long hours in manual or clerical drudgery in jobs lacking safety or security with holidays the privilege of the few. Apart from teaching, as Susan Fairhurst was to discover, the professions were virtually closed to women, so there were firm limits to the realistic career expectations of intelligent girls.

The early 1900s saw a dramatic acceleration in the journey away from Victorianism towards a new set of beliefs and values (Quinton, 1972). Susan was well aware of all these currents of change. As an atheist she was an active participant in the increasing secularisation of life in Britain. As long ago as the early 1880s, after a long and bitter struggle, Charles Bradlaugh had been allowed to affirm rather than take the oath of allegiance on election as Member of Parliament for Northampton. He had been partly responsible for the formation of the National Secular Society. According to Eric Hobsbawm (1987), ". . . intellectually western religion was never more hard pressed than in the early 1900s, and politically it was in full retreat".

In 1884, the Fabian Society, to which Susan Fairhurst belonged, had been founded with the support of the Webbs and George Bernard Shaw as a middle class socialist group aiming to "transform the country not by radicalism or revolution but by permeation", as

Sidney Webb put it (Cole, 1963). Out of their conviction that there could be a science of society, they founded the London School of Economics to act as an academic centre for such an endeavour. Later, in 1913, they were to be largely responsible for the publication of the New Statesman, a weekly political magazine intended to stimulate wide discussion of socialist ideas.

The Labour Party had emerged as a political force for the first time in the 1906 General Election when it had won 29 seats. Much of their support lay in the north-west of the country and Bolton had elected a Labour Member of Parliament in that election for the first time. In the Westhoughton Division, where William Fairhurst was a member of the Liberal Party, the Labour candidate, with Liberal support had beaten off the Conservative challenge.

While the Webbs and the Liberal politicians focused on the most deprived sections of the population and the reform of the Poor Law, social injustice was also widely felt among the middle classes when it came to the position of women in society. Frustration at the inferior status of women was nothing new, but in the second half of the nineteenth century the sense of injustice sharply increased and boiled over into direct political action in the first decade of the twentieth century.

By the early twentieth century the New Woman, determined to make a career for herself regardless of her role as wife and mother, had firmly arrived. Increased openings for their employment had opened women's eyes to the negative discrimination they experienced. Reduction in family size and the abundance of servants gave middle class women more time for activities outside the home. The political activities of the New Woman and the efforts of the men who supported her crystallised in the campaign for votes for women (Fulford, 1957). The early pioneers of the suffragist (later suffragette) movement, Richard Pankhurst, his wife, Emmeline and his daughter Christabel, lived and agitated in Manchester, only a few miles from Bolton where Susie lived. Christabel Pankhurst was one of the first women graduates of Victoria University, Manchester where Susan was just completing her first year. By 1909 the movement had become more desperate in its activities. This was the year when suffragettes were first imprisoned for civil disobedience. Susan was a member of the Women's Suffrage Movement though she was not involved in any militant activities.

Psychology and, in particular, educational psychology was slow to develop in Britain, but there was no hostility to the subject. This was not the case for the more disturbing psycho-analytic ideas put forward by Sigmund Freud. By 1909, Freud had mapped out the main features of his new theory of the mind. The importance of unconscious mental activity, the various defence mechanisms the mind used to defend against unconscious emotions that were unacceptable to the conscious mind, the importance of sexual erotic pleasure in early emotional development, the development of the Oedipus complex and incestuous fantasies in the 3–4 year old boy and of penis envy in the girl of this age, and the ways in which mental disorders in both adolescents and adults arose from dysfunction that was readily explained and indeed treatable using this framework, had all been described.

Although Freud's ideas had originally been developed as an attempt to explain and more effectively treat mental disorders in adults, they had implications not only for the treatment of children with such problems, but for teachers and parents educating and bringing up normal children. Indeed it was in 1909 that he published his account of his analysis of Hans, a five year old boy, who was suffering from phobias Freud thought to be due to unconscious sexual feelings for his mother. Freud had previously, in 1907, published an article on the sexual enlightenment of children.

Round about this time Freud attracted a teacher, Hermine Hug-Hellmuth, to his psychoanalytic group. Eventually Hermine gave up teaching and became a psycho-analyst, but in the meantime her presence stimulated much discussion of the possible role of psycho-analysis in educational practice. Freud himself was cautious, saying that he wanted to avoid drawing conclusions, even less to give directions about education on the basis of current psychoanalytic knowledge. However at a meeting of his group in 1909 he suggested he would welcome a paper from Hermine on the impressions a teacher might have on the subject.

There was considerable controversy as to whether psycho-analysis, into which Susan Fairhurst later in life put so much of her energy, could be considered a science. Freud himself was not totally consistent on this matter. In 1900 he wrote to a colleague "I am actually not at all a man of science, not an observer, not an experimenter, not a thinker. I am by temperament nothing but a conquistador, an adventurer. . . ." But later in life he was much clearer that psychoanalysis was indeed a science. It is, he wrote, in "The Future of Illusion" (Freud, 1927) in reality a method of research, an impartial instrument, rather like the . . . calculus. Psychoanalysts are and remain objective and to be objective was to be scientific; hence psychoanalysis was a science.

Whether scientific or not, in the early years of the twentieth century the reception of Freud's ideas by the scientific community and by the relevant medical specialists such as neurologists and psychiatrists was largely sceptical. It was therefore important to Freud that he should receive some recognition from the academic community. This happened quite unexpectedly in 1909 when he received an invitation to give a series of lectures at Clark University in Worcester, Massachusetts and to accept an honorary law degree at that University. The occasion went off extremely well and his lectures were well received. His citation for the Doctorate of Law read "Sigmund Freud of the University of Vienna, founder of a school of pedagogy, already rich in new methods, leader today among students of the psychology of sex, and of psychotherapy and analysis, doctor of laws". So 1909 is the year when psycho-analysis achieved respectability and status and was recognised as a new school of pedagogy.

Psycho-analysis was to play a major part in Susan Fairhurst's later life, but it was for educational innovation that she was to be mainly known during her lifetime and for some time after she died. The early 1900s were a time of change not just for the organisation of British education, but for the introduction of new ideas into the field. Though there is not a single example of a sympathetic teacher in the novels of Dickens, the rote learning and rod-driven discipline of Victorian education, so characteristic of schools of that era, were not universal. The first infant school in Britain was established in 1816 by the mill-owner Robert Owen in New Lanark, in Scotland where his son continued to run the school after Robert died. A little later David Stow described his infant school in a book published in 1836, "The Training System adopted in the Model Schools of the Glasgow Educational Society". He contrasted the ordinary infant school of the time which tended to stress repetition and "the old rote work" with the teachers he trained whose task was to help children to acquire ideas, show kindliness to one another, and gain experience through play. Other exceptions to the rule were the nursery and infant schools run along lines advocated by Friedrich Froebel, a disciple of Pestalozzi, who himself had been directly influenced by Jean-Jacques Rousseau. Froebel had a mystical view of child development and regarded the teacher's task as to foster harmonious development, best achieved through self-discovery. The Froebel child-centred education movement was especially strong in Manchester where there was a Froebel Training College. Nevertheless the approach of what Stow had described as the "ordinary infant school" largely prevailed throughout the rest of the nineteenth century.

By the last decade of that century if not the wind of change, at least a gentle breeze was blowing down school corridors into a small number of staff rooms bringing new ideas. This came from two directions. From the United States a fresh approach was pioneered by John Dewey. In 1894, at the age of thirty five, he went for ten years to the University of Chicago to the Chair of Pedagogy. Here and at Columbia, New York, where he was for the next decade, his best work was done and he developed his ideas on education. In 1895 he opened the Laboratory (Lab) School which was founded on his radical ideas about the purpose and process of education. He defined education as "the art of giving shape to human powers and adapting them to social service". Education must begin with "a psychological insight into the child's capacities, interests and habits". Knowledge best emerged from setting children problems and getting them to think. He was thus an early protagonist of "child-centred education". In contrast to some progressive educators, Dewey accepted the need for a certain amount of repressive discipline, though he saw this as a minor feature of the running of a school.

In his educational programme Dewey placed emphasis on the need to associate academic learning to real-life experience. Thus he linked cooking to chemistry, and meteorology to the passage of the seasons and to the rhythms of working life. He believed that singing, drawing, and manual training, play and dramatisation should permeate the school not just in the infant years but right through from school entry to school leaving. The children in Dewey's laboratory school were closely observed and their progress carefully monitored. While it would be misleading to suggest that the students formed part of any sort of controlled experiment, it is clear from the use of the term "laboratory" and from the fact that the school formed part of an academic department of Pedagogy that here was an attempt to introduce a scientific approach into the study of education. Dewey's work became known in England largely through the efforts of John Joseph Findlay, one of the two newly appointed Professors of Education at the University of Manchester, whom Susan Fairhurst had recently heard lecture.

The second direction in which new ideas were detectable in the early years of the twentieth century was from the first wave of the progressive school movement. The founders of this movement shared a belief that education had more to offer than classics, games, chapel, and the prefect system. Education was required to be more practical, to harness the imagination and to be alert to the need for social development through co-operation and problem solving. These progessive schools rejected memorising and rote learning and promoted learning by doing. They discarded competitiveness and the acquisitive spirit, rejected authoritarian approaches and tended to be libertarian and socialist in their philosophy. Although they were seen as experimental, their founders did not make any attempt to show scientifically that they suited the needs of children better than traditional schools. There was, all the same, an implicit assumption that they would come out well in any sort of comparison with traditional schools.

Early examples of these schools in Britain were Abbotsholme, founded in 1889, Bedales founded in 1893 and King Alfred School, founded in 1897 (Stewart, 1968).

The children who attended these schools often had emotional problems and tended to have parents who were professional or in creative occupations. The fathers had often had unpleasant experiences at traditional boarding school themselves. They were obviously a selected group, but the new, pioneering philosophy of the schools became widely known and influenced teachers and other educationists such as Susan Fairhurst herself.

While these progressive schools and the Froebel schools largely catered for middle class children, child-centred education for poor children was pioneered by Margaret McMillan and her sister Rachel in the very early years of the twentieth century. Margaret was an activist in the Independent Labour Party (ILP). She campaigned for nursery schools for the poor in Bradford and later founded such a school herself in Deptford, Kent, a seriously deprived borough in south-east London, soon providing care for the under-fives. She "developed a theory of the regenerative and political power of children made healthy, clean, and beautiful by good nutrition and a physiological education that paid equal attention to their physical and intellectual development. By seeing the potential of their own children thus revealed, working-class parents would be moved to embrace socialist principles and vote for the ILP". Susan was greatly attracted by this combination of socialist principles and progressive education.

Thus in 1909 at the time of her father's funeral, with religious belief in slow decline, the new field of scientific psychology was rapidly expanding. Findings from the social sciences were being deployed in the arguments about the reform of the conditions in which the poorest sections of the population lived as well as in the debates on votes for women. At the same time, though much more slowly, scientific approaches were nosing their way into education. Psycho-analytic ideas, scientific or pseudo-scientific, were beginning to be used to bring insights into the process of learning.

At the time of her father's death in May, 1909, when she herself was, at the relatively late age of twenty three, Susan Fairhurst had nearly completed a year's training to be an infant school teacher. She was about to start a university degree course in Manchester, with the world in which she lived in the process of rapid change. Contrary to popular belief, Edwardian England was not the staid, comfortable, self-satisfied country so often portrayed as embodied in the person of its overweight, pompous king (Hattersley, 2004). Instead the rapid decline of religion and widespread acceptance of the theory of evolution, the growth of socialist thinking, the emergence of the Labour Party as a political force, the strong push towards the emancipation of women, the expansion of educational opportunities, and the beginnings of a psycho-analytic movement that would revolutionise the way people thought about how their minds worked—all these made the end of the first decade the most exciting period of the twentieth century, a time in which to be young, intellectually bright and alert to what was happening in the world was the most exhilarating experience. Susan was all three of these and would take full advantage of the circumstances at the point she reached mature adulthood.

CHAPTER ONE

Damaged roots

Susan Isaacs, born Susan Sutherland Fairhurst, on 24 May, 1885, spent the first twenty-three years of her life in Bolton, a Lancashire mill town in the north-west of England. Although not very different in the size of its population, about a quarter of a million, the Bolton into which she was born in the 1880s was a very different place from the Bolton of today. Most strikingly, it was a manufacturing town in which the pattern of employment was dominated by the cotton industry. The majority of men, women and children over the age of thirteen worked in the mills for low wages. Although family size was reducing, the average number of children in each family was around four to five and most people lived in cramped accommodation with no inside toilets or hot water. Hygiene and medical care were poor; about one in six children died before their first birthday; now the figure is more like one in a hundred. Then the middle classes were largely made up of mill owners and their managers, together with shop keepers and others engaged in trade. The small number of professional people such as doctors and solicitors were a cut above the rest of the middle class socially, while teachers and nurses, though still seen as middle class, were generally poorly paid and lived in more modest circumstances.

The town may have been materially poor, but there was a much stronger interest in politics and religion than is the case today. Thousands of people would cram into the town hall to hear a visiting cabinet minister talk about tariff reform, a topic of great significance to a town whose prosperity was already threatened by the import of cheap manufactured goods. There was similar lively interest in proposed reforms of the education system, with strong beliefs about the role of the established church in governance and in the curriculum. Correspondingly, church attendance was high with around 60% of the adult population going to church every Sunday, mostly to Church of England services, but also to a great variety of nonconformist chapels.

Looking back in her fifties at the town in which she had been brought up, Susan saw beyond the ugliness and squalor, providing an idyllic perspective on the surrounding countryside and seeing this as somehow permeating the town itself with a certain dignity and even beauty. She wrote (Gardner, 1969, p. 15):

> The streets of the town *were* grey and grimy, with their long rows of slate-roofed cottages, uniform in pattern, the doors opening straight on to the street without a green leaf of a space between . . . yet there was a certain dignity in the very bare-ness and stark simplicity of the streets. They belonged to the bare moors with which they were surrounded. . . . They clung together with a neighbourly warmth, and their solid grey stone and slate, and stark lines, were not so alien to the moorland heights. . . . From a hillside, it was of course the mills and chimneys which dominated the landscape. The little houses clustered round these great square buildings whose tall chimneys pierced the smoke and mist, each belching out its own addition to the general grime. But what sunsets, what silvery light the smoke and fog would bring to these moorland views.

When she returned in the nineteen thirties to visit her home town, she found her memories of the moors had not exaggerated their beauty. She went on (Gardner, p. 16):

> In the time between, I had seen many mountains and valleys, many lovely landscapes in other parts of England and the continent of Europe. And the brightness of these experiences had dimmed my memories of my native county, had led me to think of it always as of mills and chimney, of grime and smoke, of machines and hurrying workers. I looked again on these—not so grimy now, not hurrying so fast. But I saw also

that it *was* here that I first learnt what a good landscape was. I saw how noble these moors are, what grand open lines they show, what dignity and breadth their dark heather has. And as if for the first time, I saw how pleasantly the valleys turn, how charmingly they are wooded, how much in keeping the little stone houses appear. . . . I could see again the countryside as I knew it as a child—and see that it *was* good, in spite of the factory chimneys and the crowding streets of the towns, and that it *was* here that I first learnt to love noble hills and space and freedom.

Susan came from an upwardly mobile family, whose parents had achieved middle class status from a mainly working class background. Her mother was, christened Miriam Sutherland at her birth in November, 1847. Although Susan's sister, Alice, believed she came from Sale in Lancashire, and a family friend thought she was Scottish (Sutherland is indeed a Scottish name), she was, in fact, born in Southwark in south-east London, though then in the County of Surrey. Her mother's maiden name was Susan Hawkins so Susan Fairhurst was named after her maternal grandmother. At some point Miriam's family must have moved to the north-west of England where she was brought up and educated. At the time she married she was living in Hulme, a suburb of Manchester. Her father, called William like her husband, was a painter and decorator. She and Susan's father were married in December, 1870, in the Union Chapel, Chorlton, a parish neighbouring on Hulme, in a Baptist ceremony when she gave her age as 22 and he was 23 years old.

After marriage Miriam moved with her husband to Bolton, where he was working as a saddler. She herself worked as a milliner. The young couple lived in Duke Street, in the centre of Bolton, near his place of work. Soon after marriage she became pregnant with her oldest child, William, born in 1872, followed by Enoch in 1875. She had eleven pregnancies, of whom eight survived beyond their first birthday, Susan being the seventh. Of the surviving children, after William and Enoch came Archie, born in 1876, then Bessie in 1878, Miriam in 1881, Harry in 1884, then Susan in 1885 and after Susan, four years later, came Susan's younger sister, Alice, in 1889.

By the time Susan's older sister, Miriam, was born in 1881, the family had moved to a larger house, 238, Turton Road, on a main road in the northern suburbs of Bolton. Then, a little later, they moved closer to the centre of Bolton to a still larger house, 32 Bradshaw Brow, where Susan was born. Both these houses were quite large, with four to five bedrooms, situated on busy roads into the town. At the time the family lived in them, the houses faced open country, though that is no longer the case.

Susan's mother was known as a highly energetic person, an efficient, well-organised woman, capable of doing several things at once (Gardner, 1969, p. 17). This was a necessary skill for a woman with a large family in the days before labour-saving machines when even home-loving men did virtually nothing to help at home. In the early years of her marriage when the children were young, she had very little help around the house. In 1881, when she had five children under the age of ten, the family had one servant, compared with two living at the house next door where there was only a doctor, his wife and their one year old child.

Susan's mother obviously had "presence". Her daughter, Bessie, recalled her (Gardner, p. 17) as "a very dignified woman, not too tall, always immaculately dressed even at the very beginning of the day", and as "an exceptionally fine, intellectual and helpful companion to her husband". She was musical, playing the piano well, a talent she passed on to her daughter.

Much more is known about Susan's father, William Fairhurst, who became a prominent citizen of Bolton. He was born in 1847 in Ormskirk, a small town to the north of Bolton. The son of a book-keeper, he was educated at Ormskirk Grammar School. At the age of 18 years he left Ormskirk for Bolton and found work there with a Mr. Abraham Entwhistle, who ran a saddlery business. This was a large firm that expanded while he was working for it. It is not clear whether he worked making saddles, fitting and selling them or keeping the books.

While working for the saddlers, he taught himself shorthand and, equipped with this skill, when he was 25 years of age, a year or so after his marriage, he obtained a job as a journalist on the Bolton Evening News. Tillotson and Son, the publishers of this daily newspaper also owned the Bolton Journal and Guardian that came out on Saturdays, so he worked on this as well. Around 1880 he was appointed sub-editor, later senior sub-editor, to both these newspapers and worked as such until his death in 1909.

The job of a provincial newspaper sub-editor is distinctly more limited today than it was in the late nineteenth century. Nowadays sub-editing consists largely in proof-reading, processing copy, correcting spelling and grammatical mistakes and designing page lay-out. As his obituary published after his death in 1909 makes clear, William Fairhurst's position on the Bolton Evening News and Bolton Journal and Guardian was much more demanding, and today would be performed by a deputy editor or an assistant editor.

As a journalist he possessed keen perception, and the faculty of rapidly selecting everything of interest to newspaper readers, gifts invaluable to all engaged in the profession of catering for the reading public. The task which confronted him every morning of making choices from a wilderness of material of items of varied information, embracing the most important incidents in the national and world-wide events of the day, and preparing telegraphic, telephonic and other intelligence in fitting form for publication was a very heavy task, and he discharged it with conspicuous ability, as our columns have borne testimony over many years. His prescient judgement, mastery of detail, ready facility for assimilating new ideas, and power of efficiently carrying out purposes and plans have impressed themselves upon the issues of the paper from day to day. (Bolton Evening News, 3 May 1909)

Further, at the time William Fairhurst was employed as a journalist and sub-editor, provincial newspapers were not merely, as they largely are today, indeed as the Bolton Evening News is today, almost entirely purveyors of information about local news. They carried substantial information, opinions and views about the great national issues of the day. Debates in both the House of Commons and the House of Lords were described in some detail. Editorials commented on matters such as tax reform and proposals for changes in tariffs in goods imported from overseas. Foreign news was also covered, including accounts of the more sensational murder trials in France and Germany.

When Susan Isaacs was asked later in life where she got her considerable energy from, she replied that without doubt it was from her mother. If that was indeed the case, her mother must have been a remarkably dynamic woman, for not only was her father responsible for the sub-editing of a daily evening newspaper and a large weekly that appeared on Saturdays, but in 1884, the year before Susan's birth, he founded, established and anonymously edited until his death, a sporting newspaper entitled "The Football and Cricket Field". A natural sportsman, as a boy and young man he had played a great deal of both football and cricket, so he already had a strong interest in sporting matters.

Sporting newspapers, selling at a penny, had begun to proliferate after the repeal of the stamp duty on newspapers in 1855 (McIntire, 2000). Penny Bell's Life and Sporting News, soon to become "Sporting Life", began publication in 1859. To begin with the content of this and other sporting newspapers was confined to racing news. In the mid-1880s new sporting papers were founded that included football and cricket. Some were published in London, but a good few emerged in the provinces. Many had a short life. For example, London's Athletic Record ran for only five issues in 1886. The Birmingham news-sheet "The Sporting Eclipse" ceased publication after six months in the same year.

William Fairhurst's newspaper was one of the first of its type and, according to his obituary, had many imitators. It was a 16 page weekly, costing one penny, published by Tillotson and Son, who also published the Bolton Journal and Guardian and Bolton Evening News, on which Fairhurst worked as sub-editor. As time went on, Fairhurst began to contribute a regular weekly column called "Olympian's Corner". Usually this was an account of a football or cricket match he had seen that week, but sometimes it covered wider issues such as the status of professionalism in sport. His editorial nom de plume "The Olympian" doubtless embodied his belief in the amateur sportsman as the ideal in sporting activities. He was not however opposed to professionalism, providing payment was open and above board.

The paper he founded, the Football and Cricket Field, covered all the major sporting events, both national and international, were covered in racy style. In addition, the paper carried a number of regular features on a variety of sporting activities. There was an article on cycling by "Pathfinder", on Liverpudlians by Richard Samuel, Racing Reflections, and Our Chess Column, as well as briefer, sometimes gossipy items in columns called Nuggets and Whispers.

Fairhurst obviously loved sporting gossip. A lengthy account of an article in The Melbourne Punch, accusing English cricketers of cheating by wasting time and then querying the width of the bats used by the Australian cricketers in a test match is followed by a denial of the truth of any such accusation by a Major Wardill, the manager of the Australian team.

The paper ranged outside strictly sporting activities giving, for example, in Footlight Flashes, information about theatrical events in the north-west of the country. Sometimes too there was coverage of national politics such as the formation of Lord Salisbury's new administration in 1886, with the inclusion of Lord Randolph Churchill as Chancellor of the Exchequer.

Tillotson and Son, the publishers, must have made a fortune from advertising revenue. At least half the space was taken up with advertisements for items catering for every possible material male need—wine and spirits, beer, dining facilities, men's, youths and boy's suits, footwear, patent boot studs, cricket bats and pads, bicycles, billiard halls and so on. The gastronome might have been tempted to buy for his wife "The Latest Invention", a Fried Fish and Chip Cooking Apparatus, the complete outfit including potato chopper and cooking utensils with stove piping for one room (No Smell, No Waste, No Removing Fires or Boilers) for sale at £6.

When Fairhurst died, the whole of the front page of the Football and Cricket Field (8 May 1909) was dedicated to an appreciation of the founder and editor for 25 years. Unlike many of its predecessors and imitators, The Football and Cricket Field had a relatively long life of over thirty years from 1884 when Fairhurst started it to 1915, six years after his death. Those who wrote about Fairhurst at the time of his death laid emphasis on his integrity and the high moral tone of his journalistic contributions. He believed in "Christianity which aims to provide a sound and well-developed body as the fitting basis of a vigorous and joyous soul". Unlike today, in the late nineteenth century there were strong links between chapel and association football. For example, In 1874 Aston Villa Football Club was founded by members of the Wesleyan Chapel in Aston, Birmingham.

Fairhurst played roles in sport other than through his journalism. In his youth he had played for Bolton Cricket Club. He was frequently invited to referee major football matches and games of cricket at a time when referees were selected on the basis of agreement on a name between the two teams a few weeks ahead of the game. A few weeks before he died he was honoured with an invitation to present the Palatine Trophy, played for by Lancashire clubs, to the Captain of Blackburn Rovers, the victors in the 1908/9 season.

The newspapers that Fairhurst edited had very high standards of grammar, spelling and punctuation. Reading the three newspapers for which Fairhurst was responsible today over a hundred years after they were produced, one is struck by the quality of the product. No matter what the subject, the literary style is lively and interesting without being vulgar or condescending. Typographical errors are undetectable; the proof readers' attention seems never to have wandered. Evidently these high standards were also evident in Fairhurst's behaviour towards his children's speech and writing. Alice, Susan's younger sister, recalls many meals of bread and water after the detection of grammatical errors in her speech. Particularly heinous grammatical crimes were sentences ending in prepositions. Doubtless Susan suffered similar punishments for grammatical misdemeanours.

Although not active in politics, Fairfield was a member of the Westhoughton Division Liberal Association. As well as his participation in football and cricket, he was a keen cyclist, though how he found the time to pursue this activity is unclear. All in all he must have been a formidable father, his energy and high standards setting an example it was difficult to emulate. Alice, his youngest daughter found him lovable, but his sons and Susan herself found him to be authoritarian and much less sympathetic.

William Fairhurst came from a Methodist background as did many with his social background in the north of England. He was a lay preacher at the local Methodist chapel and Sundays were dominated by chapel activities of one sort or another. He was an associate Trustee of the local Egerton and Burtenshaw Chapels. Her father's religious beliefs and adherence to the Methodist church had very significant consequences for Susan's education and upbringing.

Methodism had come early to Bolton (Turner, 2005). John Wesley, its founder, had visited the town to preach in 1748. Initially he had a rough reception; in his diary he referred to the Boltonians as "utterly wild". When he began to preach at the Market Cross, they threw stones at him, trying to knock him down from the steps on which he stood. The following year he again visited Bolton, when his reception was no less violent. He recalled that "the lions of Rochdale were lambs in comparison with those in Bolton, such rage and bitterness I scarce ever saw before . . ." One of his followers was badly knocked about but Wesley managed to silence the crowd and "spoke to the people with such effect that he was afterwards able to walk through every street without molestation and to preach to receptive gatherings in the open air". The first Methodist meeting house was built in 1751, and only forty years after Wesley first preached in Bolton, there were a thousand Methodists attending just one meeting house there. By 1851, 5.8% of the population of Bolton was attending a Methodist chapel each Sunday, and the number continued to increase.

In many respects, William Fairhurst was a typical member of the Methodist church. Most were artisans, the cream of the working class, upwardly mobile, hard-working and thrifty. Politically they tended to subscribe to the beliefs of the Liberal party, as did he. They were regular church-goers and their social activities centred round the chapel they attended. These included talks from visiting preachers and missionaries, followed by questions and discussion of the talks that had been given. But there were also musical events, organised outings for children and their parents and later, Sunday football and cricket for the young men. The Methodist "class" was an important setting in which debate, mainly but not entirely on biblical subjects, took place. Such "classes" were originally centred in the home where discussion was led by the spiritual leader, always the father, but in Fairhurst's time such classes more often took place in the chapel or school linked to the chapel.

Fairhurst did not have narrow religious interests. He was a highly cultured man who placed great value on literature, art and music. Through his publisher employers, Tillotson and Son, he obtained a number of literary and political periodicals, including the Review of Reviews, founded by W. J. Stead. The walls of the Fairhurst home (Gardner, p. 31) were lined with books, not just on revivalist religion, but on politics, the arts, history, travel and, of course, sport. Methodists sometimes have a reputation for living a culturally sterile life focussed entirely round methodical study of the bible. Of course, some Methodist families such as that headed by Alderman Roberts, in which Margaret Thatcher was brought up fifty years later, fit this stereotype. But some Methodist families of which Fairhurst's was one, managed to combine deep, uncompromising religious belief with a lively, secular cultural life.

At the time of Susan Fairhurst's birth, all her older brothers and sisters were still at home. The nearest in age to her was her brother Harry who was only about 18 months older than she. She was breast fed and her infancy was unremarkable until, when she was eight months old, Harry caught measles that was complicated by the onset of pneumonia (Gardner, p. 18). Measles was a serious illness then, as it can be now, and he died on 10 January 1886 after a few days illness. This was not an uncommon family tragedy at the time, but Harry had been a particularly happy, affectionate and much loved child. Susan's mother became depressed and the breast feeding came to an end. This sudden weaning took on great significance when Susan underwent psycho-analysis later in life. Over the next four years, with now only one child under five to look after, her mother was able to give her a good deal of attention. Afterwards, Susan recalled happy times with her mother and felt guilty that she had deprived her dead brother of such care.

Perhaps in reaction to their authoritarian father (though exactly how authoritarian is, as we shall see later, open to question), two of her older brothers, William and Archie, now became troublesome (Gardner, p. 22). The older of the two, William, of whom she was very fond, suddenly left home at the age of eighteen when Susan was three years old to join the Merchant Navy. Later Susan said that she experienced the loss at his departure as a bereavement. She recalled that she had felt responsible for his leaving home, sensing, as she recalled later, that she had in some way driven him away. In reality it is much more likely that he left home because of the oppressive family atmosphere and difficulties with his father.

Shortly after William's departure from home (Gardner, p. 19) Susan's mother became pregnant with her younger sister, Alice who was born four years after Susan. The birth was normal, but immediately after it her mother became physically ill, probably with a progressive form of arthritis, and after a few months, was permanently confined to bed. At this point much of Susan's care was taken over by her older sister, Bessie, whom she sometimes subsequently referred to as her mother/sister. Her mother's illness resulted in a well-ordered household becoming chaotic and unpredictable.

Susan now saw very little of her mother who, by the time she reached the age of six years, had become a permanent invalid, looked after by a succession of housekeepers and eventually by an Irish nurse, Annie. Alice, in her recollections of her childhood, recalls that one of the housekeepers was particularly unsuitable. This particular lady (Gardner, p. 19) had a drink problem and on one occasion was picked up by the police when she had become noisy and disorderly in the town. She told the police that she was Mrs. Fairhurst. Two policemen called at the house to tell William that his wife was being held in the police station and he should come to collect her. Susan's mother heard what was going on, got out of bed and, when she heard what the woman was claiming, shouted down from the top of the stairs "That you have not. That is my drunken, good for nothing housekeeper and *I* am Mrs. Fairhurst". Annie, the successor, proved more reliable.

After two years of chronic illness, Susan's mother's condition took a turn for the worse and the children, including Susan, were called to her bedside to say goodbye to her (Gardner, p. 21). They talked, and Susan, in all innocence, told her mother of the signs she had noticed of the growing affection developing between her father and Annie. Her mother did not believe her and told Susan she must ask God to forgive her for telling such a wicked lie. Susan knew that she had told the truth and felt powerless to do what was right. Then, according to Susan's later recollection, someone came and led her away from her mother's bedside. Her last memory of her mother was of her mother's white face wearing an expression of deep distress that she herself had caused. Shortly afterwards, on 11 July 1891, her mother died. From her death certificate it is not clear exactly what had been the matter with her. The cause of death is given as "rheumatism, 18 months, abscesses". It sounds as if she might have had a form of septic arthritis, a dangerous and, before antibiotics, an often fatal disease.

A further separation occurred shortly afterwards (Gardner, p. 22). Archie, now 16 years old, ran away and joined the Army. He regretted this step and tried to get his father to buy him out, but his father refused. Subsequently, he rarely returned home. Again, the most likely inference to be drawn from his sudden departure is that he had quarrelled with his father.

Annie stayed with the family,[1] now reduced to Susan's father, Susan, the older brother Enoch (Eny), who was now partly living in London where he was attending art college and beginning to establish himself as an artist and illustrator, and Susan's three sisters. Now no longer acting as a nurse but as a housekeeper, Annie cooked the meals, looked after the children and developed an even closer relationship with Susan's father. In December, 1892, eighteen months after the death of Susan's mother, she and Susan's father married. Miriam, Susan's mother, had been a lively, energetic, cultured person, with some musical talent and widely read. Annie, whom the girls now called Ma, was more rough and ready. Her family was further down the social scale than the Fairhursts. On the marriage certificate her father is described as having been an "officer's servant in the army". At 36 years of age, about nine years younger than her husband, she had been a nurse in a number of city hospitals and was evidently tough, rather thick-skinned and insensitive. Neither Susan nor Alice, the two youngest daughters, liked her.

Shortly after his wife died, William Fairhurst was promoted to be senior sub-editor on the Bolton Journal and Guardian and the Bolton Evening News. This was a better-paid job and, with the extra salary he earned as editor of the Football and Cricket Field, the family were able to move from 32 Bradshaw Brow to an altogether grander house, Monksfield, in the village of Bromley Cross situated in the northern suburbs of Bolton. Monksfield was and indeed remains an imposing house with a fair-sized garden and an attractive, uninterrupted view over fields and hills.

Alice, Susan's younger sister, provides a vivid description of an event occurring during the move that illustrates both her step-mother's insensitivity and perhaps Susan's over-sensitivity as a child (Campbell, 1953).

> Bessie (who was then 12 years of age), pushed my little child's carriage, with Susan walking beside me, and of course, when we reached the house, she and I began to investigate the garden. In the backyard was a drain with one of those removable grids and Sue, to whom it was new, let her foot go down one side and into the drain, and Ma just laughed and laughed. I can still see the hurt, puzzled expression on Sue's

face, an expression I was to see very often from time to time, and it must have been quite incomprehensible to Sue; her memories of Mother and her instinctive knowledge of what Mother would have done at the mishap, compared with Ma's attitude, must have immediately raised a barrier between Sue and her step-mother.

According to Alice, she and Susan were often in trouble for misbehaviour. The most common punishment was to be given bread and water instead of their usual meals until they apologised. When this happened, Susan would direct Alice to go into the kitchen and raid the larder where there was always plenty of food. On one occasion, when Alice reckoned that she had been falsely accused of some form of misbehaviour, she refused to apologise. By this time, the larder had evidently been put more effectively out of bounds. Eventually, as she was about to go off to school, her father realised she was looking unwell and hungry and asked his wife what was the matter with her. When her stepmother explained this was a punishment for bad behaviour, he tried to intervene, saying that she mustn't be allowed to go to school on an empty stomach. The punishment continued nevertheless for four days at the end of which time, Alice reports, "a visitor saw me and was aghast at my condition, whereupon Ma for the first time really looked at me and became troubled at her punishment. Again she tried to make me say I was sorry but my only reply was 'You'd be sorry to be hungry.'" Alice continues "whereupon she produced a very lavish dinner".

Susan herself later recalled an occasion when she was sent off alone to the dentist to have a tooth extracted and afterwards, sobbing with pain, returned home on foot over the railway bridge (Gardner, p. 22). Family friends do not seem to have been particularly sensitive either. One man, an old friend of the family, had sometimes jokingly asked her if she would like to be his wife one day. A little later, round about the age of six or seven, she got into trouble at home, so arrived on his doorstep and said she would like to marry him now. He took her in and sent a message to her home letting them know where she was and why she had arrived. Ma then sent back a package with a message saying that if she was going to get married she would need some clothes. But when she opened the package it was filled with newspapers. She realised she was being mocked both by her family and by the adult friend and went home deeply humiliated (Gardner, p. 23).

Like many stepchildren, Susan and Alice fantasised that their father had remarried someone more to their liking. Alice recalled that Sue would sometimes insist that they visited a shop in the High Street owned by two pleasant looking women. According to Alice, the two of them would peer into the shop, looking particularly at one of them and "conjecturing what type of stepmother she would have been instead of the ogress we thought we had".

The children were clearly mourning the loss not just of their mother, but of the different sort of marriage William had had with his first wife and the better care they had had when she was alive. Miriam had been a more cultured, better educated woman than Annie. His first marriage had inevitably been more companionable, with Miriam, an accomplished pianist, also able to play her part in conversation about books and music. The two had worked together from very modest beginnings to achieve a much more comfortable way of life. Such a companionate marriage was not at all unusual in Victorian times, especially towards the end of that era. In contrast, the second marriage sounds as if it were more patriarchal, indeed more conforming to the classic image of a Victorian marriage, with the father, mostly too busy to participate in family life, but when he intervened, taking most of the important decisions with little consultation with other members of the family. All the same, according to Alice, Annie was a loyal and helpful wife. Alice reports "She was a very good, willing hostess to all the friends of the family and surely no one could ever have been ashamed of her. She quite wisely ministered to the physical needs with good food, beautifully prepared and arranged, leaving the conversation to the others".

Although Susan had only been six years old at the time of her mother's death, despite her experience of psychoanalysis, she remained attached to her idealised picture of her mother throughout her life. At University she made sure that she signed herself Susan Sutherland Fairhurst and she continued to use her mother's maiden name of Sutherland as a middle name throughout her married life. Her behaviour became difficult during the years after her mother's death, especially at school, but also probably at home where she remained troublesome and disobedient, especially to her step-mother.

All the indications are then that from the time of the death of her mother when she was six years old to round about the age of eleven years, Susan was a difficult, naughty child both at home and at school. Her unusual level of disobedience probably arose as a reaction to the bereavement, her anger with her step-mother for having taken her mother's place and the change in the quality of care she received. At any rate at this time on the surface she seems to have been a thoroughly angry little girl (Campbell, 1953).

If Fairhurst's week was spent in frantic activity to ensure the publication of the daily Bolton Evening News and the two Saturday weeklies, the Bolton Journal and Guardian and the Football and Cricket Field, Sunday, though far from a day of rest, was dedicated to religious observance. The day was well described by Alice, Susan's younger sister. After breakfast the children attended morning Sunday school and then went on to the morning Chapel Service at which their father might preach. They returned home to a heavy Sunday dinner with roast beef and Yorkshire pudding before they went back to attend afternoon Sunday school. After a return home for high tea, they went back to the chapel for a prayer meeting, evening chapel and then a final prayer meeting which might take the form of a series of "testimonies" by visitors, sometimes missionaries, or members of the congregation who had undergone experiences that made them feel they had been in direct contact with the Lord.

The children did not take all these activities seriously. Alice reported (Campbell, 1953) "I think the testimony meetings really gave us the greatest pleasure, because Sue and I always knew what to expect in advance. There was one woman with her husband sitting alongside, who would time and again repeat the same exhortation to the Lord to bring her husband to 'see the Light'. She would kneel with the pew seat in front of her, thump it with great thumps, and say 'Lord, make him miserable, until he sees the Light!' . . . and it was well known that the poor man was the most harmless of creatures."

Although the children respected and admired their father's role in the chapel services, they lost no opportunity to ridicule their stepmother's behaviour. Again, according to Alice (Campbell, 1953), "father always finished the meeting with the most dignified of prayers, which apparently affected Ma so much that she would gently weep. Sue and I would watch through the fingers over our eyes and try to control our giggles".

Round about the age of eleven, Susan began to identify with her father's faith and engagement in preaching the message of the gospels. She went through a strongly religious phase. Alice records (Campbell, 1953) how at one stage Susan wanted to become a missionary. She would stand on a garden box or roller and deliver fiery sermons to the surrounding cabbages that would serve as symbols for a crowded congregation. If the two girls managed to get an empty compartment on the way to school or on return home, Susan would persuade her younger sister to kneel on the floor, eyes closed and hands together, while she, Susan, delivered a sermon. Alice commented "Surely no preacher ever outdid this would-be evangelist in fervour." This religious phase seems to have been quite short-lived for within a short time she was expressing quite different beliefs.

Fairhurst Sundays do not sound much like days of rest, but they brought all the family together in a way that, mainly because of Mr. Fairhurst's extraordinarily busy life as a journalist and editor, could not happen during the week. Alice later wrote a vivid description of an occasion when the family returned from Chapel after a special Methodist celebration (Campbell, 1953).

I well remember one bitterly cold but brilliantly starlit New Year's Eve we were returning over the snowy fields from the Watchnight Service at Chapel, Father and Ma and we four girls. Mirrie (Miriam) made up and sang a little doggerel,

"The Fairhursts came home two by two,
Mirrie and Alice, Bessie and Sue,
Father and Ma brought up the rear,
And *that's* the way we do up here!"

Bearing in mind the significance of Susan's contribution to educational practice in the following century, the details of her own schooling are of particular interest. The school she attended, the Mawdsley Street Board School, was situated near the centre of Bolton.[2] It was a Congregational School, now closed, to which most of the Methodist parents who could not afford a private school sent their children. One might have thought, given her father's social position and income Susan would have been sent to a private school, but evidently this was not the case.

The school was overcrowded, unsanitary and had low standards of teaching. The unhealthy atmosphere may be gauged by the fact that during Susan's first year at the school the school keeper reported that he had found eight rats in the cellar. Attendance by the pupils was highly variable, but in general around 90% of the 319 children on the roll of the school were present. Excuses for non-attendance seem to have been unconvincing. Examples characterised by the head teacher as "trumpery" include "went to have his hair cut", "locked in the house to mind it", and "the clock was stopped and they did not know when it was school time".

The school inspectors took a poor view of the quality of some of the infant teaching. A commentary on the infant class at the time Susan was there reads "The results of the teaching in elementary subjects are good with the exception of the reading of the first class. The children do little more than spell and show little power or efforts even to form syllables".

Some of the teachers found it difficult to keep order. In January, 1892, it was reported that a Mr. Hall "does not seem to have made a favourable impression upon the upper standards. He seems to have only a small power of command and the class has found that out". By the next day a couple of the classes had "got into an extraordinary state of disorder" and another teacher was put in charge. In early February Mr. Hall "sent word to say he was ill" and by April the poor man had left.

Later that year Her Majesty's Inspectors reported on the failure of the infant class to progress. "The infants who come to the school at a later age than usual are somewhat behindhand in discipline, intelligence and attainments. I cannot doubt that with good management more considerable progress might be made." On this occasion the school's budget was cut until the time that "the Infant's class had a certificated teacher of its own", so clearly Susan was taught by unqualified staff.

The following year the HMI's report was hardly more complimentary for the higher classes into which Susan had by now moved. "The children are orderly and do their exercises with creditable neatness on the whole, but there is considerable weakness of Reading and Arithmetic in the upper Standards, where the work in other respects falls below a satisfactory point. Neither of the specific subjects has been very profitably taught. Success in these can hardly be looked for until a better style of teaching has made the children quicker of perception and more interested in the full exercise of their powers." Overcrowding was still impeding progress in the infants' classes.

Such negative reports were by no means invariably made of Bolton schools. For example, a report on the Eagley Mills School, an elementary school serving the children of employees of a cotton mill rather nearer Susan's home than the one she attended reads

Mixed School: "The order is excellent, and musical drill is smartly done. The writing is neat and well formed; spelling is very accurate and composition neat and intelligent. Reading is clear and well expressed, and the children answer intelligently on the matter contained in the lessons. Arithmetic, both written and oral, has been well taught. Needlework, singing by rote, English and Geography are excellent. Altogether this Department is in a most creditable state of work and order."

Infants' School: "The infants continue to be taught with the same kindness, vivacity, method and intelligence, as in former years."

The Eagley Mills School report then gives the names of the three qualified teachers and their subjects they teach. They have a broad remit. E. A. Mather (sex unknown but probably female), for example, taught Handwriting, Arithmetic, Grammar, Geography, and History. The Report finishes with the amounts of the grants to be made to the schools for the following year; for the Mixed School the sum of £296.2.8 and to the Infant School £94.9.0. The linking of the grants to the Report on the schools was not fortuitous. At this time schools were paid according to results and a less satisfactory report would have resulted in a smaller grant and thus lower salaries for the teachers. Clearly this is what happened at Susan's school.

The general health of young English children at this time was poor and their resistance to infection particularly weak. On one occasion in 1892 a number of children were reported to be absent for quite long periods with measles and a little later a child is reported to have died of pneumonia, possibly as a result of a measles infection. His classmates "sent a wreath to place upon his coffin".

A teacher at the Eagley Mills School reported at one point in 1890, the year in which Susan started at the Mawdsley Road School: ". . .

many of the children who have been ill with measles seem not to have recovered properly. They look pale and listless and take very little, if any, interest in their work". A month or so later she wrote "... we have noticed during the week that many of the children are suffering from deafness and seven children are at home with gathered ears. . . ."

In January, 1893, when she was eight years old, Susan's own school was closed for three weeks on account of an outbreak of measles. The effect of these infections is likely to have been greater because the children were poorly nourished and clothed. At this time, the children wore clogs and, when it was very cold, their clothing was unable to protect them adequately.

When difficult behaviour occurred, there was a heavy emphasis on punishment rather than understanding. Children who used bad language would have their mouths washed with soap and water. Other punishments included standing in the corner or being kept in after school. The cane was probably not used frequently, but was always feared by the children. Behaviour resulting in the use of the cane included truanting, disobedience, smoking in the boy's toilets, and bullying.

Unfortunately we know little about how Susan herself fared in her elementary school. Alice reports (Campbell, 1953) that her sister's memories of the school were "always very bitter to her". Susan did remember that when she went to the infant school she was very keen to learn, but that her enthusiasm was dampened rather than stimulated by her teachers (Gardner, 1969 p. 19). She remembered a teacher she would have loved to please "looking at her sewing and telling her to 'make her stitches smaller', but being bewildered how she could possibly do that as the stitches were already there. Further, she stood out as being dressed differently as well as being more intelligent than most of the other children. Alice reports that she and her sisters were always 'abominably dressed.'" Susan was on the small side, and it seems quite likely that she was bullied, but we have no firm evidence for this. We do know however that she later recollected that she was a very difficult child in school and there is independent corroboration that this was the case.

In an article entitled "Rebellious and Defiant Children", written in her late thirties but only published later in a collection of her articles entitled "Childhood and After" (Isaacs, 1948b), she paints a picture of a child that is almost certainly herself. When she was six years old this girl's mother has died "after a long and severe illness during which the home had become disorderly and unhappy". This girl "throughout her school years was characterised by obstinacy, noisiness, insubordination, seeking after boys, occasional stealing". At seven years "she ate chalk. . . . She used in school to blow her nose very loudly in order to annoy a woman teacher whom she much admired and loved". In confirmation of the picture she drew of herself a friend is quoted (Campbell, 1953) as saying "My word! She *was* a naughty girl at school—she used to play in class and the teacher would pounce on her and ask her questions, but she always knew the answers". This description suggests she was under-stretched and bored as well as reacting to the stress of an unhappy home; her later academic career indicates this may well have been the case.

Susan's older sister, Miriam, was appointed a candidate pupil teacher at her primary school in 1894 at the age of thirteen years. At this time if they had reached a certain standard the more able pupils were appointed to such positions at the end of their school careers usually at the age of fourteen years. Miriam's progress as a pupil teacher was regarded as unsatisfactory to begin with, but after being given a "serious talking to" and it had been pointed out to her "what would be the consequences unless there was a considerable improvement next month" her performance improved and there were no further complaints about her.

When she was twelve years old, though in theory she could have stayed on until she was thirteen or fourteen years old, Susan left the Mawdsley Road School and, in 1897, was sent to the new Bolton secondary school, the equivalent to a present day grammar school. Probably at the same time Miriam transferred to the same school.

Even though she was unhappy at her elementary school and going through a religious phase, the period from 10 to 14 years old had its happy moments. Her home life was more settled at this time. Her step-mother may not have been sympathetic to her, but, according to Alice, when the children returned home from school, she produced "sumptuous teas". They were also rapturously welcomed by the family collie, Fritz. The children clearly had a great deal of fun together. Again, according to Alice, Mirrie (Miriam) would often "perform a laughing nigger act which reduced the girls and even the stepmother to uncontrollable mirth". In the evening, Alice remembered "the talk of books and writers . . . surely never were people so fully alive". On one occasion, a Fairhurst uncle turned up with ten of his children, all of whom played a musical instrument, and gave a concert in the drawing room. At about this time too, the two younger girls, Susan and Alice started to go regularly away for a two week holiday with their stepmother and father. At first they went to a farmhouse near Morecambe Bay, and, after three summers there, they went to Whitby Bay and then to Barmouth in north Wales. Alice remembered these holidays with great pleasure.

On entering secondary school (Bolton Library Archive), Susan and Miriam were two of the 843 pupils who entered the new Central Higher Grade Board School in Bolton on 6 September, 1897. The children who entered all came from other Bolton schools and most probably had to pass an examination to enter. For the 843 pupils there was a qualified teaching staff of seventeen (a second master and sixteen certificated assistants. There were also five pupil teachers. Pupil teachers, one of which Miriam became, had to be at least 13 years old and to have reached a required level in reading, arithmetic and geography. If they passed a further examination, they were eligible to be given Queen's Scholarships that gave them free places in a teacher training college and paid for their maintenance.

The log books of the school provide rather little information about the curriculum, but clearly all the main subjects were covered. In the light of subsequent events, it is interesting that Scripture and Religious Instruction feature little in the curriculum, although there were Scripture Examinations in November, 1890. Like her primary school, Susan's secondary school was overcrowded from the start, with class sizes of about 50 in each class. An Inspector who visited in 1898 pointed out that several of the classes were too large.

In 1899 another Inspector visited and gave a favourable Report. He wrote "The children appear to be proud of their work and exert themselves well, on the whole, to profit by the instruction which is commendably exact and liberal". He noted that M. Fairhurst, almost certainly Susan's sister, Miriam, who had been previously been appointed a pupil teacher at Susan's primary school, had obtained a first class in the Queen's Scholarship examination. This gave Miriam a place at teacher training college and would have supported her maintenance while she was there but her father did not allow her to take up the teacher training scholarship she had been offered.

Like many men of his time, he felt it was inappropriate for girls to be trained for a career.

Miriam's success was the highest academic achievement possible for children at this school. In the year she obtained her scholarship, it is noted that, of the pupils who left, 30 (4 boys and 26 girls) became pupil teachers, 36 (34 boys and 2 girls) went into commercial life, 43 (33 boys and 10 girls) entered industrial occupations and none went on to University. The little information we have about Susan's life at this school suggests that, once again, she was teased because of her clothes. Alice reports (Campbell, 1963):

We were always abominably dressed—children were in those days, with always our best tight laced-up boots and frocks with ghastly high collars. There again, Sue was much more affected by the hideous dresses than I was. She used to plead with Ma for something more attractive, and as she grew older and was in a school class containing boys as well as girls, her distress became acute when Ma would not let her have longer frocks, and she became an object of derision to the boys. Where I would merely start a fight, she would suffer in dignified silence.

When she was fourteen years old, her school career came to an abrupt end (Gardner, 1969 p. 30). Apparently under the influence of her brother, Enoch (Eny), who was eleven years older than herself, she lost the religious faith that had been so powerful beforehand, and became agnostic or atheist, holding these views with the same fervour as she had previously been attached to her religion. Her father was deeply upset and decided to remove her from school. His attitude was "If education makes women Godless, they are better off without it". For two years he refused even to talk to Susan, so she stayed at home and helped her sister, Bessie and her stepmother, with whom she had a strained relationship, with the housework. This account of the reasons why she did not pursue her education at this point is not supported either by a family friend, Dorothy Rogerson, or by the account given by her younger sister, Alice, who attended the same school. Alice does not give a reason why Susan left school at 14, but Dorothy Rogerson wrote "Susan was educated at the school, which is now known as the Bolton County Grammar School, but in her day pupils left at 16 years . . .", thus giving the impression that Susan did not leave school until she was 16 years of age. This account fails to take note of the fact that, on her own account she left school at fourteen or, at the latest, fifteen years, nor does it tally with her sister, Miriam's success in obtaining a scholarship to go to teacher training college at the age of seventeen or even eighteen years.

It seems most likely that the version that Susan Isaacs gave to Dorothy Gardner was nearer to the truth. It is perhaps more likely that her sister and family friend omitted to mention the episode because it might have seemed too painful or embarrassing than that Susan fabricated it. Later in her life, as we shall see, Susan was to insist most forcefully that psychological reality was as "real" as material reality. Whether we agree with that view or not, it seems as if, for whatever reason, her mid-and late adolescence represented for her, at least, a dark, perhaps the darkest period of her life. She described herself as having developed "over-seriousness" at this time, and having lost her "characteristic sparkle and humour". This is confirmed by the description that is almost certainly of her own early adolescence in the lecture on "Rebellious and Defiant Children" mentioned above. She wrote ". . . in early adolescence she became an intellectual rebel against everything her father believed in and had frequent feelings of utter despair, with strongly marked suicidal tendencies". She has a tragic, rather emaciated appearance in photographs taken of her at this time and this suggests she may have gone through an anorexic phase, associated with depression. Given her relationship with her father, it is clear that she was deeply angry with him for having terminated her education. It is likely that she took to controlling her food intake as a means of exercising control in an area of her life over which he could not prevail.

Childhood, the formative period of life, is always important in understanding the life history of an individual. In the case of someone who, in adult life, dedicated herself to education and to professional understanding of the life history of others through psycho-analysis, it assumes even greater significance. What then does the childhood of Susan Isaacs tell us about the person she became and the ideas she championed? Clearly she suffered many losses in the first few years of her life. Her slightly older brother died when she was eight months old and she was abruptly weaned from the breast. When she was three, William, her oldest brother, to whom she was greatly attached, left home. At four years the birth of her younger sister, Alice, meant she lost the exclusive attention given to the youngest child. Then, almost immediately, perhaps the most serious loss of her life occurred when her mother became ill and died after two years of chronic illness. A year after her mother died, another older brother, Archie, left home to join the Army. Shortly after this, her father remarried and she became a less important person in his life. Instead he became taken up with her step-mother, whom she found, to say the least, unsympathetic. Finally, at 14 years, her loss of religious faith meant that she lost the good opinion of her father and became deeply estranged from him, at least partly cut off from the talk of music and books that stimulated her mind.

Even for a Victorian family living in an era of high mortality and the frequent early departure of children from home, Susan does seem to have suffered the hammer blows of misfortune to an unusual extent. One might have hoped that for a child suffering so much grief at home, school would have been a compensating experience. This was certainly not the case as far as her elementary school was concerned; here she was teased and found no pleasure in learning. This school was, by comparison with others of the day in the same city, poorly run. The teaching was regarded as of low quality and some of her teachers found difficulty in keeping order. Her secondary grammar-type school was more demanding and stimulating, but even here she was not happy. She remained a difficult and troublesome girl.

With this dreadful background, it would have been surprising it she had not suffered from depression, both in her adolescence and in her adult life? How did Susan Isaacs avoid serious emotional problems later in life? In fact, as we shall see, although she does not seem to have been depressed in early and middle childhood, her behaviour at that time does suggest she was a troubled girl. She was a highly intelligent, actively inquisitive child in a school with weak, unimaginative teachers and little to stimulate her imagination. Her rebellious behaviour in school arose from the boredom that comes with lack of stimulation.

Her relative immunity from depression in late adolescence and adult life is likely to have emerged partly from her personality and partly from the close, affectionate relationships she enjoyed with her sisters. Her older sister, Bessie, whom she later referred to as her mother/sister took a large part in looking after her, mainly because

Susan found her step-mother so unsympathetic. She herself must have found rewarding the responsibility she took upon herself for looking after her younger sister, Alice. Her older sister, Mirrie, who attended the same schools, was also a bright girl with a great sense of humour. The four sisters seem to have functioned like a close-knit group of intimate friends. Because Bessie stayed at home to look after their father, the group of sisters was not split up until Mirrie left home, by which time Susan was almost through her adolescence.

Then, as Alice makes clear in her own recollections (Campbell, 1953), home was an exciting, stimulating place to be. Other relatives, friends of the family, visiting preachers, all contributed to make the home emotionally warm and lively. Until her rift with her father, he was a man Susan looked up to and admired. Her gifted, older brother, Enoch or Eny, later recognised nationally as a gifted artist, was also musical and had strong religious and political views. Susan was much influenced by him ultimately to the detriment of her relationship with her father.

Susan's childhood experiences provide ample explanation for the fact that, when later engaged in psycho-analysis, she chose to become a member of a group of analysts that put the greatest emphasis in the explanation of psychological problems on early relationships, anger, hostility, envy, guilt and loss. Her experience of not being listened to as a child, either at home or at school, surely provides some explanation for her later insistence that teachers should spend most of their time listening to children and answering their questions rather than imposing unasked-for and often unwanted information upon them. All the same, there were probably tens of thousands of British children who, at that time, suffered multiple bereavements and who were not listened to at school. What made Susan Isaacs different? For the beginnings of an answer to this question we have to turn to her later adolescence and University days.

Notes

1   The account given here is based on a variety of sources. Most derives from information sent to Nathan Isaacs in the nineteen fifties by Alice Campbell in an autobiographical essay she wrote called "A Family Life" that she sent to him in October, 1953 (IoEd S1 A1).

2   Details of Bolton schools provided here are in the Bolton Library Archive.

CHAPTER TWO

Our star student

At the time Susan left school at fourteen or fifteen years, it was not unusual for girls of this age to stop their schooling in order to help out at home. Out of the 81 girls who left the Science Department of the Bolton Municipal Secondary School in her year, 25 or about one in three left either to help out at home or in the shop their parents owned.[1] Monks Field, the house the family lived in was large and there were no servants. According to Mrs. Dorothy Rogerson, a family friend, the "kitchen was spotless, gleaming with brass" (Gardner, p. 31), and doubtless the rest of the house was regularly cleaned and dusted. It may be difficult today to see how cleaning and cooking could have taken up the time of Annie, Susie's stepmother, Bessie, her older sister and Susie herself, but, in the absence of labour-saving devices, and with the high standard of polish required of silver cutlery and ornaments, a fire in every room to be lit daily, a large lunch as well as a substantial high tea to be prepared, most households of this size would have employed two full-time servants, so it is unlikely that Susan was idle because there was not enough to do. According to the later recollection of Alice, Susan's younger sister, it was Annie, William's second wife, who did most of the housework. Except when she had a job or was away, after she had spent the early morning helping with household tasks, Susan spent her time reading or, in the afternoons, going for walks over the moors alone, or more frequently, with one or more of her sisters.

There were now six people living at home. Susie's father, William Fairhurst, left home early in the morning and returned late at night six days a week. Annie, her stepmother, did not go out to work. Bessie, the oldest sister, did not have a job but was also a great reader. Mirrie, now 19 lived at home and worked as a unqualified teacher. As well as Susan, ten year old Alice was still at home attending elementary school. The three older boys had now left home. The only one who was still in regular contact with the family was Eny, twenty five years old at the time Susan left school, who was making his way as an artist and illustrator in London. He made quite frequent visits back home to Bolton before he married and settled in Peckham, in south-east London.

Eny was a strong influence (IoEd S1 A3) on Susan when he lived at home as he did continuously until Susan was about fifteen years old. Then he only returned home intermittently, bringing new ideas back from the metropolis. He, Susan, Mirrie and Bessie had frequent conversations about books they had read. As well as being a gifted artist and illustrator, Eny was well read, knowledgeable about modern art, a socialist, and a supporter of the suffragette movement. It was he who persuaded Bessie and Susan to give up their belief in God and to develop agnostic beliefs.

From the time she left school in 1900 at the age of fourteen or fifteen years until she went to Manchester in 1908 to train to be an infant teacher, the information we have about Susan is sketchy. She worked briefly as a photographer's assistant after leaving school (IoEd S1 A3), but did not enjoy it and left after a few months. Then she spent about a year tutoring a boy in delicate health who was not well enough to go to school. At about the age of 18 she went to Morocco as a governess with an English family who were living in Casablanca. Apparently she took up horse-riding there and had an enjoyable year. When she came back from Morocco she did not have a regular job until at the age of twenty two she eventually found work for a year as an assistant teacher (Archives of Durham County Council, E/Dar 9/1), at Heaton Village Club School in a relatively deprived part of Bolton about a mile from her home. Otherwise she does not seem to have had any paid employment from age of nineteen to twenty two. How did she survive financially? According to Dorothy Rogerson, a family friend, she and Bessie were both given five shillings a week pocket money with which to buy their clothes and any additional necessities. But Alice, Susan's sister, recalled that the young women had no pocket money at all (Campbell, 1953). Like others in their situation they made their own clothes. In order to have time to read they rose at 4 a.m. or, in the summer even earlier at 3 a.m. and had cleaned and dusted by mid-morning.

This meant that Susan had a great deal of leisure time and she used it to widen her knowledge by extensive reading. According to Dorothy Rogerson (Rogerson, 1957) the home was full of books, newspapers and periodicals. The drawing room, dining room and bedrooms were lined with bookcases and both Bessie and Susan were keen readers. It is clear that by the time she entered the University Susan was extremely well read. Dorothy Rogerson remembered (Gardner, 1969, p. 32) her and all her sisters as avid readers, with a wide range of interests. At that time the implications of the theory of evolution were being widely publicised in scientific works and they certainly read these. One example, now little read, is Winwood Reade's "The Martyrdom of Man". This was a history of the world from an entirely new viewpoint, and was a prominent freethinking text of the late nineteenth and early twentieth century. Divided into sections on War, Religion, Liberty and the Intellect, it provided a new and non-religious way of looking at history. Very popular on publication in the 1860's and long after, the book influenced the thinking of H. G. Wells and George Orwell. As an early socialist and member of the Fabian Society, Susan would have read "Fabian Essays" edited by Bernard Shaw, to which Beatrice and Sidney Webb contributed essays. The Webbs' weightier early books such as "Industrial Democracy" were also available to Susan at that time and her later speeches suggested she had read them. Although with their limited resources they would not have been able to see Bernard Shaw's early plays performed in Manchester, Susan and her sisters would certainly have had access to the radical political and social prefaces he wrote to plays such as Widowers' Houses (with its description of slum landlords), and Mrs. Warren's Profession, a drama about prostitution that scandalized much public opinion by treating the married state as legalized prostitution. As supporters of the suffragette movement and members of the Women's Suffrage Movement, the sisters read the pamphlets produced by the Women's Social and Political Union, founded by Emmeline Pankhurst before the Pankhursts moved from close by Manchester to London. Standard reading at this time also included the great nineteenth century Russian novels by Turgenev and Dostoevsky as well, of course, as the "social message" novels of Charles Dickens and George Eliot.

The sisters regularly read "The Review of Reviews" edited by W. T. Stead, one of a number of magazines that acted as a forum for political, literary and artistic issues of the day (Campbell, 1953). Their father subscribed to this popular review and, through Tillotson and Son, the publishing firm that employed him, he had the opportunity to acquire all new books that came on the market. The content of these books and the political and social issues of the day were discussed with other young people in the district. Dorothy Rogerson recalled that the Fairhurst sisters would regularly meet at her house on Sunday evenings after the evening service at the Birtenshaw Methodist Church to drink coffee, eat toasted tea-cakes and discuss "every subject under the sun in lively fashion". Dorothy Rogerson (Gardner, 1969, p. 32) remembers the sisters as being full of ideas for social reform, declaring themselves socialists, vegetarians, Unitarians, and finally agnostics. Putting one in mind of the intense "greenery yallery, Grosvenor gallery, foot in the grave young man" described in the Gilbert and Sullivan opera Patience, she recalls them clothed "in arty dresses of sage green that fascinated us". She remembers too the "whole day tramps" she took with the sisters "over the moors—armed with baskets laden with delicious sandwiches of brown bread, dates, bananas, tomatoes and lettuce, walking around Entwhistle, or to Rivington or Holdcombe Hill—there were no buses—and how we talked!"

There were also opportunities for the exchange of ideas at meetings of the local Birtenshaw Mutual Improvement Society. These were held in the Sunday School attached to the Methodist Church (Gillham, 1972). These meetings were intended to encourage adult members of the local community to enhance their education. Speakers on all types of subject would come from Bolton and Manchester to introduce a subject, after which there would be a debate. Susan, often with the rest of the family attended regularly and took part fully in the discussions from the time she left school at fourteen. She is recalled as having "all the self-confidence of a grown-up person". Mutual Improvement Societies, developed especially during the middle of the nineteenth century were sometimes but by no means always attached to Methodist churches, and were forerunners of the Workers' Educational Association movement, officially founded only in 1903 (Ratcliffe, 1997). Susan's participation in these debates formed an important part of her preparation for participation in student debating societies in which she played so full a part once she arrived at Manchester University.

Thus Susan led the life of a privileged middle-class young woman. But she was acutely aware of the grim, impoverished lives of most of Bolton's population around her, most of whom were working in the cotton mills. Later in life she described their existence in moving terms (Gardner, 1969, p. 34)

When the six-o-clock hooters go, the dark valley will be starred with thousands of bright squares of light from those factory windows. The men and women, weavers and spinners, piecers and little piecers, foreman and hands, will be hurrying into those grim, cold, noisy buildings . . . the stone steps are worn hollow in the middle with the constant tread of the clogs, six times daily up and down the stairs. How those clogs echo in the grey stone streets, typifying the hard, unchanging grind of life in those grey industrial towns. At six o clock and eight o clock in the morning, at half past eight and half past twelve, at half past one and at half past five, you can hear the rhythmic clatter of iron upon stone . . .

When times were hard, she recalls (Gardner, 1969, p. 35):

I remember periods of pinching and even of famine among the cotton workers. . . . There was no unemployment benefit, no insurance, no general social responsibility for starving children, and skilled men could not find work. But fellow feeling was strong and direct . . . the chapel or the church called upon the lucky ones in half-time, if not in full-time work to pool their resources for the more needy. Many families who attended the Wesleyan Chapel in my own village deprived themselves for a week or a month of all butter on their own bread or sugar in their tea and paid the savings into the common fund for the help of their less fortunate friends.

Indeed, Alice recalled many years later (Campbell, 1953) that when she was twelve and Susan sixteen, there was a disastrous strike in the local cotton mills at which many of the Chapel members were employed. Susan decided to help and persuaded her sister to do without butter for months, if her stepmother would agree to put the money saved into the rebel fund. So they went without butter for several months. This was a particular sacrifice for them, Alice wrote, because the two were forced to eat dry bread without butter as a punishment whenever they were naughty and had to watch the rest of the family eating the appetizing dishes their stepmother prepared. If indeed Susan was going through an anorexic phase at this time, this might not have been such a terrible hardship for her as Alice later suggested.

Family life is portrayed by Alice as rich, warm, stimulating and apparently hugely enjoyable. There were musical evenings. One of William Fairhurst's brothers had a very large family, including ten sons, all of whom played a stringed instrument. With Eny or Sue accompanying they would give what Alice Campbell called "wonderful concerts, in the drawing room at Monks Field—secular music during the week with sacred music, mostly hymns, on Sundays". There was also a good deal of entertaining both of other members of the Chapel and of William's staff at work. Presumably he had especially close links with those who worked on the sporting newspaper as this was the paper for which he had overall editorial responsibility.

On occasions when the rest of the family was out, Alice and Susan would sit in front of the fire in the dining room, their father writing at his desk, their stepmother busy baking in the kitchen. When Eny was home from London he and his father would play chess in front of the fire. Their father and stepmother continued to go with Susan and Alice for family holidays every year by the sea at Barmouth or Whitley Bay or in the Lake District, in Silverdale when they all went for long walks and swam.

The only problem with this picture of cosy family togetherness painted by Alice is that is hardly compatible with Susan's recollection, reported to Dorothy Gardner (1969, p. 30) that her father was so angry with her that he would not even speak to her for two years after she announced herself to be agnostic in her religious belief. It is clear from the memories of all involved that the four sisters, Bessie, Mirrie, Susan and Alice, to put them in order of age, got on extremely well together, loved each other's company, went on long walks together over the Lancashire moors, and shared ideas. They did not always agree even on important matters (Gardner, p. 31), for example, Mirrie and probably Alice retained their religious faith, while Bessie and Susan did not. But this did not affect the loving and supportive relationships they enjoyed together. Further, while they had no contact with William and Archie, the two oldest brothers who had now left home, they all loved and admired Eny, the artist brother who was three years older than Mirrie. He not only influenced Bessie and Susan's religious beliefs but also encouraged them in their socialist ideas and in their support for the suffragette movement. He was the intellectual leader of the sibship in their childhood and adolescence. The sisters had a wide social circle, mainly consisting of young men and women of their own age with similar interests. They played an active part in this group, organizing parties and, because, like their father, they were quite athletic, sporting events like cricket matches. Indeed at one point, with the encouragement of their father, they made up a women's cricket team.

The tension between Susan and her father, which probably softened as time went on, was clearly painful to Susan and the pain remained with her for the whole of her life. It seems likely that this was particularly unpleasant for them both on Sundays, the day of worship, when Susan may have agreed to go to Church, but made it clear that this was under protest and that the religious service meant nothing to her. The other focus for continuing conflict was Susan's further education. Her father was not willing to allow her to continue at school and this meant she could not qualify to go to teacher training college to pursue the only professional career open to women at that time. Even though she had a good singing voice and would have liked to have taken singing lessons, he would not pay for these and so put a stop to this possibility. Her father's refusal to allow her to continue at school did not apply to Alice though he even needed to be pressured to allow Alice to continue her education. Two or three years after she left school, Mirrie went to South Africa where, shortly afterwards she married. In 1907, she returned at a time when Alice had also qualified to go to teacher training college and her father was just about to refuse to let her go. Mirrie insisted that he change his mind. She was firm with him and, perhaps because his will was weakened by poor health by this time, he was unable to resist Mirrie's persistence, and relented. So Alice went to

College in Manchester. Then, a year later, a few months before he died, he finally allowed Susan, who by now had some teaching experience behind her, to enrol on a course at Manchester University.

What sort of a girl was Susan during her teen years? In physical appearance Dorothy Rogerson found her to be "not beautiful in the accepted sense, but to have beautiful fair curly hair, fine teeth and a lovely smile. She had beautiful manners always and great charm". Photographs taken of her in her teens confirm Dorothy Rogerson's (1957) opinion of her appearance. However the photographs do also suggest a sad girl, indeed Dorothy Gardner, her biographer, found her expression in these photographs to be "grave and often tragic" (Gardner, 1969, p. 32). She adds that "the characteristic sparkle and humour of her later life did not, it seems, appear at all frequently at this time". Because of her knowledge of the greatly strained relationship with her father, and because Susan described herself as "over-serious" during her teen years, Dorothy Gardner may have been reading into Susan's teenage expression more than was there. The contemporary accounts of her behaviour at this age suggest, rather to the contrary, that she was lively and vivacious. Family photographs taken with her father in the picture however do make her look sad. This may have been part of the convention of such portraits at the time; the other members of the family do not look very cheerful either.

The inconsistencies between these various accounts of family life can be partly explained by the different experiences of the sisters. Alice, by all accounts, did have an affectionate relationship with her father whom she greatly admired. She was also able to find much to praise in her stepmother whom she saw as a great support to her husband. Contemporary research (Bifulco et al. 1997, Hardt and Rutter, 2004) on the recollections of sisters of a childhood they shared together has revealed that they often have memories that differ greatly. Another partial explanation probably lies in the fact that Susan's relationship with her father changed during her adolescence. Her bitter anger, frustration and depression at his refusal to allow her to continue her education was gradually softened when she found employment abroad. The photographs in which she appears so sad were all taken with her father in a family group when she was in mid-teens, so it is not surprising she looks miserable. When she returned home from Morocco she found work as an assistant teacher and a year later, with her father's financial help she was able to take up a place to train as an infant teacher, albeit only at the relatively late age of twenty three. Her mood improved, but in fact throughout her teen years and in her early twenties she had enjoyed a stimulating and enjoyable life, reading widely, engaged in discussion, argument and sometimes formal debate with her friends on the great issues of the day, and extending her knowledge of the natural world through going on long country walks alone or with her sisters.

So, in October 1908, Susan Fairhurst finally embarked on an academic course at Manchester University. The course itself was perhaps the least prestigious of any offered by the University. It was a two year, non-degree course leading to a Certificate in the Teaching of Young Children. Susan was one of the first twenty young women students on this course that had only been approved by the University a year previously in 1907. It was the first such course in a British University (Robertson, 1990) and was pitched at University intermediate level, in difficulty probably about halfway between "A" level and a first year University course today. There were components specifically about the development of young children and practical experience with infants and in the lower standards of elementary schools. As well as principles of infant education, Susan studied zoology, botany, singing, drawing and needlework. The students also attended core lectures, already available to teachers training to be elementary or secondary school teachers, in addition to lectures specifically about the development of young children. The students also obtained practical experience with infants in the lower classes of elementary schools.

The students who entered teacher training at Manchester University in the last decade of the nineteenth century and the first decade of the twentieth took a different course from those entering the teaching profession today. Prior to the 1890s and for some time afterwards, elementary schoolchildren of fourteen years who had reached the required standards in basic subjects could become pupil-teachers, assisting qualified teachers in classrooms, as well as continuing their own education. After five years, they were qualified to sit for the Queen's Scholarship, or (after 1901) the King's Scholarship. If they were placed high enough on the pass list they were entitled to a place at a non-University teacher training college. Most of those who took these courses were working class men and women. Manchester University now offered these students a true University experience. As well as lecturers who had been recruited specifically on these courses, they also had the opportunity to attend lectures given by staff of other Departments of the University. If identified as gifted, they could sit for an examination to transfer to a degree course at the University.

The responsibility for the administration of the Certificate Course lay with a woman called Grace Owen, a pioneer of teacher training in infant classes, and a strong advocate of nursery schools, who was later to become the Principal of Mather College in Manchester, a College that specialized in training infant teachers. Owen was imbued with the progressive ideas concerning the teaching of young children of Friedrich Froebel, the advocate of play in the teaching of young children and John Dewey, who believed in the importance of experience of the "real" world in educating children (Brehony, 2000). Susan greatly admired Grace Owen and wanted to have closer contact with her. She recalled years later (Gardner, 1969, p. 37) that, unaccustomed to the niceties of the social distance between University teachers and their students she asked her if she might come to tea one Saturday afternoon and discuss some of her ideas further. This was arranged and it was only towards the end of her course that Susan realized it might not have been appropriate to invite herself round in this way. She apologized to Owen who told her how much she had enjoyed their conversation.

Grace Owen was so impressed with Susan's ability that she spoke to John Findlay, the Professor of Education, about her (Gardner, 1969, p. 37). He asked to see her and proposed that she should leave the Certificate course at the end of the year and enter for a full Honours degree course in philosophy. Facing him, Susan was unable to control her tears but explained that her father would never allow her to take a degree and that she was financially completely dependent on him. Findlay wrote to her father who was impressed that a man so eminent should take a personal interest in his daughter. He agreed to finance her studies. In fact she obtained a small grant towards her expenses conditional upon her agreement to enter teaching subsequently, and so, by leading a frugal life, and with the help of a small legacy from her father, and some additional help from her sister, Bessie who gave her part of her own legacy from their father, she was able to get by for the next three years. However before she could be admitted to a degree course, she had to take an entrance examination. This meant learning sufficient Greek and German in three months probably to about a level equivalent to halfway between "O" and "A" level today. Susan had left school before the age of fifteen and had a long way to go before she could tackle the examination with any hope of success. With the help of her slightly younger cousin (Gardner, 1969, p. 38), William Sutherland, who had had a proper formal education, but mainly due to her own efforts, she managed to pass and entered, four or five years older than her contemporaries at the age of twenty three, on an Honours degree course in philosophy in October, 1909.

Her father's death in May, 1909 was not unexpected; he had had serious illnesses before. But it was an emotional event for Susan whose relationship with him had been both ambivalent and intense. She had hated him for the way he had prevented her from continuing her education, but, at the same time, admired his energy, intelligence and literary skill. When he died he left all his material possessions to his wife, and the remainder of his estate, amounting in all to a little less than £1,200 to be divided equally between his wife and his four surviving daughters in equal shares so that the sum each received was modest. Susan's share helped her to continue with her education at Manchester.

Her father's death did not result in any prolonged period of bereavement. Far from it; the intellectual stimulation provided by a University degree course released a flood of energy and ideas. Within just a few weeks of the start of her honours degree course she began to take an unusually active part in a number of student societies. By her second year she had established a position as the most outstanding woman student and perhaps the most outstanding student overall of her year. She first made her mark with her debating skills. After only a few weeks into her first term as a degree student, the Manchester University Magazine (MUM) (19 November 1909) reported on a "long expected debate between the Conservative Club and the Fabian Society", in which the Fabian Society was represented by Susan and four men. In the view of the rapporteur the outcome was "a triumph for the Fabian Society, which showed that it possessed men and women of great debating power who are capable of stating a case with fairness and restraint".

She was now one of the most prominent members of the student body, perhaps the best-known and popular woman student. She was not by any stretch of the imagination, a beautiful young woman. Her cousin, William Sutherland, later described (Gardner, 1969, p. 38) her as "being small and stocky, tough and wiry" with a pronounced nose. But she had the unusual combination of very fair curly hair and exceedingly bright brown eyes. She was easy to listen to in conversation or public debate as she had a musical speaking voice. But her most pronounced characteristics were her intelligence, her energy and her commitment to the socialist policies to which she had already become attracted before she went to University.

She rapidly became prominent in the Sociological Society. Manchester was only one of two Universities to have such a society at that time. Susan first reported in the student magazine on the content of the meetings of this society, then became its Secretary and, in her final year, was Chairman of the Society. Early in 1910 (MUM 13 January 1910) she took part in a debate on the provocative proposal "That Education is Useless and Harmful". The proposer attacked current educational practice as failing to meet the needs of children and suggested that "the child should do as much of the selection of the curriculum as possible". Susan's position, hardly accurate but interesting in the light of her later work, was that this was "exactly the present day tendency of educational reform".

At a meeting of the Sociological Society (MUM 19 March 1910) later in the same academic year, a Dr. Lapage presented data claiming to show that, if women went to work this was harmful to their children. Taking part in this debate that, of course, is still being vigorously pursued today, Susan "declaring herself to be jealous of the Feminist Movement" criticized some of the figures quoted and deprecated Dr. Lapage's condemnation of women's labour on "such small grounds", suggesting that "other causes might account for some of the results he deduced". Working women (a subject about which she had direct knowledge as in Bolton she had taught many children whose mothers worked in the cotton mills) was also the subject of a debate held in May, 1910. A woman speaker proposed that "when a girl accepted 'John', it was her duty to give up her career and devote herself to making 'John' comfortable". Immediately, reported the student magazine, "Miss Fairhurst was challenging any such dictum". This was "the old cry again". A career should be given up if the child needed it, but it was wrong for a woman to give up her career for which she was efficient, simply because "John" wanted her to. "Women" she claimed "are always being accused of being subjective, the remedy for this was definite work that must be done. . . . Women are struggling for individuality and any curtailment of this liberty is fatal . . ." The motion condemning the working woman was accordingly lost, with the rapporteur concluding—". . . and so closed the most successful debate in our new debating hall".

By the following academic year, Susan had become Vice-Chairman of the Women's Student Union (MUM 21 October 1910). Mrs. Sydney Webb was elected its President. In October, 1911, Susan again gave an address on the employment of women, this time focusing on "the professional and economic waste which seems to be incurred when a woman marries after a careful and laborious training for an outside career". While in her previous contributions on working women she had attacked the idea that, if a woman of whatever social class went out to work her children would be harmed, now she pointed to the loss to the state if resources were expended on the training of largely middle-class women for careers in which they would never be employed. Later in the academic year, Beatrice Webb, already with her husband, Sidney, the leading researcher in the social sciences in the country, gave a talk on "Methods of Investigation in the Social Sciences".

It is customary for the Chairmen of Student Societies to be responsible for the selection of topics and speakers for the year in which they hold office. Susan, not surprisingly in view of her later interests, arranged for Margaret McMillan, then the leading British protagonist of nursery education to be one of her speakers for the Sociological Society (MUM 11 November 1911). McMillan had spoken a few days previously in Manchester on the causes of illiteracy and generally low educational standards in young children living in poor areas. She advocated a focus on the needs of such children for a change of environment, better housing and a healthier diet. In her talk to the Sociological Society "The Effect of Monotonous Toil on the Adolescent" (MUM 1 February 1912) she claimed that only 5% of the children with whom she was then working in Deptford in south-east London were well nourished. Many, she said, go straight from school at the age of 14 into workshops and factories and do not have any adolescence at all.

Possibly as a by-product of her Chairman's address, Susan published a paper in the student magazine (MUM 19 March 1910) with reflections on the Sociological Society. In it she espoused a view of sociology as the high-water mark of self-consciousness, of the careful investigation of social questions with impartial judgement, free of sentiment and unsupported opinion, in the search for Social Truth. The notion of social truth that she idealized may seem fanciful nowadays, but at the time Susan was writing, the possibility that all social problems might be resolved by pragmatic investigation, as proposed by the Fabians, was popular and she was an enthusiastic protagonist. Her demons, those "bringers of darkness and confusion" she contemptuously described as "Generalisations from Insufficient Data and their night-loving brethren, Party-Prejudice, Jingo-Emotion, Ready-made Remedies and Universal Panaceas".

At the same time as she was preparing for her Final Examination, including the writing of a dissertation for which she was com- mended, Susie was not only President of the Women's Student Union and Chairman of the Sociological Society, but also continued to be active in the Fabian Society. At a meeting held in Manchester of the Fabian Societies of British Universities, she was elected onto the Executive of the Federation of Fabian Societies that was formed at this meeting. Politicians then, as now, took student political societies seriously and in March, 1912, Ramsay Macdonald, the Leader of the Labour Party and Prime Minister twenty years later, spoke to the Manchester University Fabian Society on "Some Problems of Socialism" (MUM 8 March 1912). He urged socialist undergraduates to throw in their lot with the Labour movement rather than with any of the competing political parties.

Susan did not just hold these positions in student societies—she carried them out with great success. In a report to the May, 1912 issue of the student magazine, Ellen Wilkinson, later to be Minister of Education in the 1945–50 Attlee government, wrote of a Women's Students Union debate "The Chairman for the session was Miss Fairhurst, who has brought tact to a fine art without being reduced to dull impartiality". Ellen Wilkinson, who came from a similar Methodist though much more materially deprived background, remembered Susan throughout her life. When, as a Minister, she was visited by a delegation pressing for an expansion of nursery educa- tion in 1946, Dorothy Gardner gave her a message of goodwill from

Susan Isaacs. She looked blank until she was reminded of Susan's maiden name. "*Not* Susie Fairhurst. Is *she* Susan Isaacs? Of course I remember her. She was our star student".

In June, 1912, Susan took her final examinations and passed with First Class Honours. This was a remarkable achievement given her lack of education prior to the undergraduate course and the extent of her involvement in student societies during her studies. She was awarded one of the only two first class degrees in philosophy that year. In discussion of her future career with her teachers she expressed an interest in pursuing a career in psychology. Although Sam Alexander, the Professor of Philosophy, had recently recruited T. H. Pear to pioneer a course in experimental psychology, both these men thought that Susan would be better off in Cambridge, where academic psychology was better developed. When Charles Myers, Professor of Psychology at King's College, London and Lecturer in Cambridge was in Manchester as an examiner, he was shown Susie's undergraduate dissertation and immediately agreed that he would find support for her to come to his Cambridge department as a research student. Her short-term future was therefore assured.

She could look back at her undergraduate career with both pride and thankfulness for her luck in the quality of the teaching she had received. For during her time in Manchester, she had been fortunate to have as teachers three remarkable men all of whom were, at that time, in their early fifties. When she first began the Certificate Course for Teachers of Young Children, the overall responsibility for teacher training in the University was held by John Joseph Findlay, the Professor of Education. Findlay, the son of a Wesleyan minister, was a graduate of Oxford University, where he had achieved first class degrees in Mathematics and History, an unusual feat then as now (Brooks, 2004). After graduation he gained practical experience teaching in schools, including two Wesleyan schools. He then visited North America where he observed the spread of the pedagogic methods devised by Johann Friedrich Herbart, who advocated secondary school and university education involving the development of many-sided interests, through a curriculum integrating different subjects. Finally Findlay visited Jena, in Germany, where he observed the use of the small-group seminar method of university teaching devised by Wilhelm Rein.

On return from his travels, Findlay obtained a post as Lecturer at the College of Preceptors, London from 1895 to 1898. During

this time he was deeply involved in the creation of the first progressive, avowedly secular school in Britain, King Alfred School in
Hampstead, London. The organization of this school was radically
different from others of its day, with exclusion of religion, absence
of preparation for examinations and the banning of physical punishment. These principles would profoundly influence Susan in her
own later choice of educational methods.

   After further experience gained teaching in Cardiff, and in curriculum development in Wales, Findlay was then attracted to the Chair
of Education in Manchester which he took up in 1903. During Susan
Fairhurst's time at the University he was a fiery innovator, full of
ideas and impatient with the administrative work with which he was
burdened. He was highly critical of the teaching that went on in the
schools of his day, and of the training of the teachers who performed
so poorly. Any change, he claimed, was opposed by those who desire

   to prevent young teachers from becoming, in any sense,
   students; they are satisfied with the past; they are afraid of
   crude reforms which shall disturb the wholesome traditions of
   an older day; frequently they themselves, although painfully
   industrious in working the machine, are afflicted with laziness
   of mind which resents the challenge of new truth.

The particular attraction of Findlay's ideas for Susan came from his
determination to study the educational process in the classroom.
In this he was influenced by the American educationist, John Dewey
(1899), who had created a "laboratory school" in Chicago for this
purpose. Findlay described his own first major book "Principles of
Class Teaching" as written "from the workshop instead of the lecture
room". In 1907, the year before Susan began her teacher training, he
had been able to create his own workshop in Manchester with the
foundation of the Sarah Fielden Demonstration School. During
its twenty five year life, this school acted as a crucible for new ideas
in education. Right from the start there were new approaches to the
teaching of reading, nature study and French to young children.
Investigations were also carried out into physical and psychological
development, highly relevant to Susan's later interests.

   The second remarkable man with whom Susan Fairhurst came
into contact was Michael Sadler, appointed to the second Chair of
Education in Manchester in 1906. He also took first class degrees

in two subjects at Oxford University, classics and literae humaniores (Lowe, 2004). At the age of 24, in 1885, he took up a post with the Extension Sub-Committee of the Oxford Examinations Board. This involved him in all aspects of extra-mural education provided by the University. There was a rapid extension of lecturing by Oxford dons to young men and women from outside the University seeking to improve their education. Extension summer schools were established. Sadler's contacts with young people who were the products of the English secondary education system convinced him that there was a need for radical reform. He was appointed Director of a Research Department working under Robert Morant, the senior civil servant in the Board of Education. Sadler traveled widely in continental Europe and North America to explore new ideas. This convinced him of the need for educational research to inform educational practice.

The Conservative government then in power with Arthur Balfour as Prime Minister had its own ideas about educational reform and the civil servants under Morant became deeply involved in working out how to implement them. Sadler was unhappy with this role, taking a more questioning view, critical of the centralizing policies the politicians wanted. He believed that the local authorities, recently given considerable financial responsibilities should be involved in the determination of the curriculum according to local needs and wishes. Morant accordingly starved his research department of funds and he resigned. He, like Findlay, was attracted to an academic post in the University of Manchester, becoming Professor of History and Administration of Education. Sadler was a superb lecturer whose wisdom derived particularly from his deep knowledge of educational theory and of methods used in other countries, as well as from his critical appraisal of the British educational system. He stayed in Manchester until 1912 when he left to become Vice-Chancellor of Leeds University, but by that time he had made a major impact on those, like Susan Fairhurst, who were interested in new educational ideas. She was not to forget the clear, analytical way in which he had pointed to the need for research to guide both educational policy and practice.

The third and perhaps the most remarkable man to influence Susan's life in Manchester was Samuel Alexander. Alexander was brought up in a single parent, Jewish family in Melbourne, Australia, where he went to a Wesleyan school. At the age of 18 years he sailed to England to further his education, won a scholarship to Balliol College, Oxford and took first class degrees in mathematics and classical mods as well as in literae humaniores (Laird, 2004). Appointed to a fellowship to teach philosophy at Lincoln College, he was the first professing Jew appointed to a fellowship at an Oxford or Cambridge college. During his eleven years at Oxford, he took a three year leave of absence to study experimental psychology in Germany. In England at that time psychology was a branch of philosophy and experimental work in the subject was virtually non-existent. Although he remained interested and lectured on experimental psychology, on his return to Oxford he returned to more purely philosophical topics, developing an evolutionary approach to ethics. He came to be regarded as the foremost British philosopher of the generation that immediately preceded that of A. N. Whitehead, G. E. Moore and Bertrand Russell. In 1893 he was appointed to the Chair of Philosophy in Manchester, where he stayed for 31 years and was probably the best known figure in the University both locally and nationally. His classes were small, with less than ten undergraduates entering the School of Philosophy each year, so Susan had a great deal of personal contact with him. He was described as acting "like a very kindly father to her" (Letter NI D10/1). It is likely that his interest in psychology was one of the influences leading Susan towards this subject in her future career.

What each of these three outstanding academics had to teach resonated with Susan's opinions and interests in different but equally important ways. From Findlay she absorbed a philosophy of child-centred education with a need to base instruction in classroom teaching methods on practical experience rather than lecture room theory. From Sadler, she took the need to look abroad and particularly to German speaking countries for intellectual stimulation and example. He was also the teacher whose emphasis on research most inspired her. Finally from Samuel Alexander she learned that philosophical enquiry could be combined with experimental psychology.

In contrast to her academic life, her teachers and her participation in student societies, there is much less information about her social life (Gardner, 1969, p. 39). Her contemporaries report that she was a popular student with many friends. She shared a flat with another philosophy student, Nan Griffiths and the two of them had sandwich lunches with Dorothy Rogerson, a friend from Bolton. She was able to afford cheap seats at the theatre and was a member of parties made up to see performances at the Gaiety Theatre. However she had no regular men friends. When she first went up to Manchester, William Sutherland, her cousin, was attracted to her and the two of them did discuss the possibility of marriage. They even went as far as obtaining a medical opinion about the possible genetic risks of cousin marriage for any children they might have (Gardner, 1969, p. 39). Sutherland, describing her and their relationship at this time recalled that she had absolutely no small talk and was "essentially serious, though having her own type of humour". She would at times though "chatter away unrestrainedly" to him. She was clearly not in the slightest degree flirtatious and her relationships with men at the University seem to have been based entirely on mutual interests in the social and political issues of the day.

Probably through the Sociological Society (MUM, 8 March 1912) she met William Brierley, a bright undergraduate in the Botany Department. He was four years younger than Susan, but because she was such a late entrant, he was only one year behind her in seniority at the University. He used to visit the flat which she shared with another student. She assumed he was pursuing her flatmate and was surprised to discover that she was the attraction. They remained in touch when she left Manchester, but do not seem to have had a particularly close or intimate relationship while she was there or indeed for some time afterwards. It seems likely that he was the first man with whom she had any sort of physical relationship, though improbable that this occurred before she left Manchester when she was twenty seven years old.

When Susan Fairhurstt left Manchester she could look with pride on a record of academic success, the achievement of great prominence in student societies and she could contemplate, for the first time, the possibility of an intimate relationship with a man. She must have felt her undergraduate career had been as fulfilling as she could have hoped for. Now she was off to Cambridge and postgraduate study.

Note

1   Bolton Library Archive. Log book of Central High Grade Board School, Bolton. SLB/8/1

CHAPTER THREE

An academic marriage

Susan did not take to Cambridge. In an article signed "A Manchester Girl" written after she had spent a year there and published in May, 1913 in the Manchester University Magazine (Fairhurst, 1912/13), she compared the two universities. Manchester came out better in virtually every respect. "In Cambridge", she wrote "it is easy to forget the world, to dream one's dreams, to see life as a pleasant wandering between the library and the study". But in Manchester it was not possible to forget the real world. Its University "exists amid the throb and turmoil and deep unrest of a great manufacturing city, with its ceaseless hum of desire, its dark curtain of smoke and fog, and its urging sense of the grim hard pressure of life". There was no doubt which Susan preferred as more conducive to meaningful study relevant to the problems that, in 1913, the world faced. Then there was the position of women in the two universities. "The Manchester girl sees things from the centre. She is less likely to become artificially intellectual or objectionably academic. She is more in touch with normal human pursuits . . . The danger for the Cambridge girl is that her detachment, so useful and happy during college years, should become habitual, and leave her high and dry on an artificial dyke—out of the muddy stream, it is true, but also out of the deeps and swift thrill of actuality." There was no doubt in her mind where women were more accepted. She put it politely. Manchester's university had been established in the late nineteenth century when women students could be taken as a matter of course. In Cambridge, with its long history of exclusively male possession, women are "essentially intruders" and their social life inevitably suffers.

When she arrived in Cambridge at the age of twenty seven she was attached to Newnham College and lived in college rooms where she noted with amusement, she was not even allowed to receive her brothers without a chaperone present (Gardner, 1969, p. 43). But it seems she had little contact with college life. Her supervisor was Charles Myers, then thirty nine years old. He was to play a significant part in her life for the next ten years. Myers was London-born, Jewish, from a wealthy, cultured family, who had studied Natural Sciences at Cambridge and medicine at St. Bartholomew's Hospital, London (Bartlett, 2004). However he developed a strong interest in anthropology and psychology. He decided not to practice as a doctor and instead, at the age of twenty-five, in 1898, joined the Cambridge anthropological expedition to the Torres Strait, in what is now Papua-New Guinea. The expedition was carried out by six young men all of whom were to make a considerable mark later in life Among them was William McDougall, soon to become one of the most influential psychologists of his generation and W. H. R. Rivers, a distinguished physiologist and psychologist, later immortalised in Pat Barker's novel "Regeneration", Myers was given responsibility for a wide range of investigations.

The aim of the expedition was to investigate the psychological competence of what were then called "primitive" peoples compared to those in "civilised" populations. Myers was told to study capacity for musical rhythm and tone, hearing in general, taste, smell and reaction times. Subsequently in 1902 he returned to Cambridge to assist Rivers in teaching as well as research into the physiology of the special senses. In 1906, at the age of only thirty three, he was appointed part-time Professor of Psychology at King's College London, but he retained a position in Cambridge. In 1907 he became the first Lecturer in Experimental Psychology in Cambridge and, resigning his post at King's, he, with Rivers, began to plan for a new building and expanded Department of Psychology there. He published prolifically; his *"Textbook of Experimental Psychology"* (Myers, 1911) was the first British textbook on the subject to be published.

Myers had a wide range of interests outside his subject, including ethnic music and mountaineering. A talented violinist and competent tennis player he had a warm, engaging smile. He carried out a significant amount of psychological research himself, but his main professional achievements involved helping the development of new academic departments and institutions. A happily married, family man with five children, with a genial personality, he might have been an ideal mentor for a possibly rather lonely Susan Fairhurst when she arrived in Cambridge. In fact, we have no information suggesting that he played this role in any active way or indeed that there was any sort of social relationship between the two.

It is likely that Myers was far too busy with other matters to give much time to the new research student from Manchester. He and Rivers had met much opposition in their efforts to develop psychology in Cambridge. The Department was then housed in an antiquated, ill-ventilated and rat-ridden cottage in Mill Lane. It was necessary to raise £4,000 for a new building and Myers, who was a wealthy man, anonymously donated three quarters of this sum. Research and teaching began in the new building in 1912, the year Susan arrived there, and it was officially opened a year later in May, 1913. In his address (Crampton, 1978), Myers revealed a broad view of this newly developed subject. "In its applications, psychology enters into relations with Biology, in the study of animal behaviour; with Education, in the study of the individual and general characteristics of the developing human mind; with Economics . . . with Anthropology . . . with Medicine . . . With Art . . ."

Myers' did not himself personally carry out any work in the field of educational psychology, but he was keen to foster it in the Cambridge department. Indeed in 1913, he recruited Cyril Burt, who had recently been appointed to the newly created post of psychologist to the London County Council, to work for two half days a week in his department. So it is not surprising that Myers who was enthusiastic about the application of psychology to education should suggest that Susan, with her background as a teacher, should carry out a study of spelling. All the same, in the light of her subsequent career as an educationist who promoted the school as a place where, above all else, creativity should be fostered, spelling was a surprising topic for her to embark upon. Although she never suggested that correct spelling was an irrelevance, and her own spelling was impeccable, progressive teachers promoting the idea of child-centred education for which she was to be the main inspiration in the United Kingdom and elsewhere, have tended, to the irritation of many parents and some politicians, to downplay the importance of correct spelling. If children can make themselves clear and if what they produce is interesting and creative, then, child-centred educators say, what does it matter if their spelling is a bit idiosyncratic? Indeed they have suggested that, if children are indoctrinated with the idea that, above all, their spelling must be correct, then they are likely to be inhibited from writing at all. They will only use words they know they can spell correctly and this will have the harmful effect of limiting the vocabulary they use.

Some explanation for Susan's choice of topic can be found in her career aspirations when she went to Cambridge from Manchester. Even at this point in time, she knew she wanted to be an educational psychologist, whose main focus was to be on research and teaching. Her lecturers at Manchester had encouraged her to believe there were many gaps in knowledge that remained to be filled. She admired her teachers, especially Findlay, who often pointed to areas of ignorance in the educational field. She was happy to mould herself on his example, as well as that of and Sadler and Alexander. Charles Myers, her supervisor, was, at the time she came to Cambridge, already an experienced experimental psychologist. He might well have thought that, while Susan Fairhurst's background in philosophy would equip her well for the study of theories of education; what she needed now was training in scientific methods, the nuts and bolts of scientific experiment.

In Britain, up to the end of the nineteenth century, psychology or the study of mental activity, behaviour and the emotions had been within the province of the philosopher. Advances in knowledge were achieved by introspection rather than by experiment. Alexander, Professor of Philosophy in Manchester, was an exception; he was aware of new developments in experimental psychology in Germany and the United States where scientists actually tested their ideas in the laboratory to determine whether they were valid, even rejecting them if they were not. Whereas most of his teaching was highly theoretical, Alexander did attempt to demonstrate experiments in psychology himself. But he carried out no original work using this approach. So Susan's transfer to Cambridge exposed her to new approaches to psychology that were now capturing the field.

There is another possible reason why Susan landed on spelling as her topic for study. As we saw in Chapter 1, her journalist father was a stickler for correct spelling and grammar. Alice, Susan's younger sister, in her recollections of childhood written many years later, recalled the bread and water punishment that was handed out in the family for minor misdemeanours. One of the sins for which William Fairhurst punished his daughters in this way was incorrect spelling and grammar. It seems quite possible that, consciously or unconsciously, Susan was attracted to the idea of studying spelling so that it could be taught more efficiently. Children who were taught spelling well might escape the punishment she had had to endure.

All the information we have about the experimental work that Susan carried out during her year in Cambridge is contained in the paper she wrote about it. This was published in an educational journal, the Journal of Experimental Pedagogy five years after she left Cambridge (Brierley, 1918). Perhaps the word "pedagogy" requires a brief explanation. It is likely to be unfamiliar to most British readers for whom it may sound old-fashioned and conjure up an image of a pedantic schoolmaster. This is not the case either in continental Europe or in North America where it is recognised to mean the study of child development, including the process of education. In many continental European countries such as Holland and Germany, pedagogues form a body of well- trained professionals separate from teachers, who take a broader view than teachers towards the upbringing of children, especially young children. Pedagogy in the nineteenth and early twentieth century was defined in Britain as the study of the upbringing and education of children; more narrowly it was the science of instruction.

Publication in 1918 means there was an unexplained five year gap between when the work was carried out in 1912–1913 and when it was published. Writing up research results, then as now, was often a slow and painful business, especially for someone like Susan, for whom this was the first paper she had to prepare for professional publication. All the same, the gap in time is surprising, especially as Susan was later to show remarkable facility and speed in writing up her work. Perhaps this study of spelling did not grab her interest and enthusiasm as much as did her later work or perhaps the upheavals in her personal life as well as the First World War delayed her progress.

Her study had little immediate human interest though the results do shed light on how the task of spelling is tackled when it presents difficulties. What she and presumably Myers were interested in were the thought processes that best helped people when they were faced with a word they had seen before but were unsure how to spell. In particular they wanted to know how much people used visual imagery or conjured up a picture of the difficult word they wanted to spell. They hypothesised that people who used such imagery would spell better than those who relied on auditory memory, hearing the word and remembering its spelling as a result of links previously formed in the mind between the sound and the appearance of the correctly spelled word.

In order to test these two possibilities, she devised an experiment involving the use of nonsense words whose spelling her subjects had to learn. They then reported to her the mental devices they used to remember the spelling of the nonsense words she had taught them. So the study combined introspective approaches with an experimental design. First she divided her subjects up into good and poor spellers. She did this by testing them on a list of 120 words people often find difficult to spell. In her article she does not provide a full list of the words she gave, but does give some examples: *idiosyncrasy*, *unparalleled*, *gauge*, *symmetry* and *vacillation*. For the purposes of the study, bad spellers were those who made more than ten mistakes.

Her subjects, not surprisingly in view of the difficulty of the words to be spelled, were what she called "educated adults of University attainments, including four trained psychologists". There were 29 of them. Her experiments were of two types. In one type at each session she gave two series of words, each consisting of one "real" or what she called "sensible" word and six nonsense words. These were shown to the subjects in three ways, first visually, then without sight of the word but just spelling it out and finally with a mixture of visual and auditory stimuli. In the second group of experiments she dictated or spelled the words out loud. The subjects either just listened to her, or wrote the words out while blindfolded, or finally, wrote the words out in the usual way.

Her subjects were then asked to recall the spelling of the words and describe what mental processes they used to achieve success. Although a number of subjects reported using a variety of techniques, two, both women, described relying entirely on visual images. One of these said how, when recalling how to spell *assassination* she visualised a headline in the *Times* in which the word might have been used. When spelling *pulmonary* she said she visualised it in a medical article. There were also five subjects, falling into the so-called image-less group, who did not use images at all. They seemed to learn correct spelling by memorising the arrangement of the letters. It was much more difficult for these subjects to describe how they remembered the correct spelling of the words they were given, but they mostly seemed to use mnemonics or verbal tricks making adaptations from more familiar words. Thus when asked to remember the spelling of the nonsense word *throidkurr* one said he recalled it as a variation of *thyroid.* Another remembered *rowbtpalm* by associating it with *ptarmigan.* These five subjects emphatically denied that they used either visual or auditory images.

The remaining 22 subjects used a variety of techniques, involving both imagery and the techniques of the imageless group. They fell on a continuum ranging from those who used quite a lot of imagery to those who used rather little, with most falling in between. Visual imagery was reported to be used more than any other type. The introspective reports of these "intermediate" subjects are quoted in considerable detail in the article. It seemed as if, in achieving correct recall, the use of imagery often reinforced the use of non-imaging devices such as mnemonics. Most subjects reported they used both techniques. They also tended to use both visual and auditory images, the latter conjuring up the sound of words to help with spelling them.

When it came to looking at possible links between the amount and type of imagery used and spelling competence, and this was the main purpose of the study, the results were completely negative. There was no correlation at all between the amount and type of imagery employed and how good the subject was at spelling. This might have been disappointing as clearly the results could not be seen as having any direct implications for the teaching of spelling. However it is likely that Susan took away from the study a lesson that was to play a central part in her later work, the fact that, when it comes to learning, people can arrive at the same satisfactory outcome via any number of different routes. It is the task of the teacher therefore to help the child identify which of these routes is right for him or her, not to insist on a particular pathway to success.

Susan never carried out an experimental study of this type again. Indeed she was later to be heavily critical of psychologists who carried out so-called laboratory work and drew conclusions from their results that they tried to apply to real-life situations. She also took very little or no further interest in spelling. In a book which she wrote for teachers twenty years after she carried out this study, she discusses backwardness in reading in some detail, but makes no mention at all of spelling.

Looking back at this study in historical context, there are a number of surprising features about it. The most striking is the lack of any attempt to use the so-called correlational methods that had been devised by Sir Francis Galton in the nineteenth century and refined by Charles Spearman over a decade before Susan carried out her study. These methods involve comparing two sets of data. In the case of Susan's study these would be spelling ability and use of imagery. On each of these ranking scores would be obtained. So instead of classifying spellers into good and bad, she could have ranked spellers according to the number of mistakes they made. She could also have ranked individuals according to the amount of imagery they reported using. Using a statistical technique for calculating a so-called Spearman correlation coefficient, she could have calculated whether there was a greater than chance probability that the two were associated, for example that visualisers were better or worse spellers. Had she used this method, well known at the time, indeed discussed in some detail in her supervisor's textbook (Myers, 1911) and well within her capabilities, she might have obtained a different result. It is not at all clear why she didn't use this approach. It must have been obvious to her, as it is to us, that it makes little sense to classify as a good speller someone who gets a score of 111 out of 120 spellings right and someone who correctly spells 109 as a bad speller, no different from someone who can't spell at all and gets them all wrong.

A second problem with her study is the fact that she used such a very atypical sample. Of course it must have been tempting to use a University-educated sample because they would be able to give more sophisticated accounts of the processes they used. Then, no doubt, they were the easiest group from whom to obtain co-operation, and the most articulate to explain how they achieved correct spelling. But it would have been obvious to her that it would be difficult to obtain results from such a sample that could be generalised to the population at large. Further if, as surely must have been the case in view of her career aspiration to become an educational psychologist, she was mainly interested in how children learned to spell, why did she not carry out her experiment with a younger age group? Finally, one may question why she went to such elaborate lengths to answer a question that is, after all, not all that complicated. If she wanted to know what methods people used to achieve correct spelling, why did she simply not ask her subjects what they did if they came across a word they were uncertain how to spell correctly. Answers such as "I try to imagine what the word looks like" or "I think about where I have seen it spelled before" would have been as illuminating as the results she obtained from a year's painful study. Perhaps though and this is an even more important consideration today, the work would not have been publishable.

We have no way of knowing the answer to these questions, but we do know that Susan later said that she was pleased to have had the opportunity to carry out this study. When she was asked later in life about the value of the experience to her, she said she did not regret it and had learned much about the "disciplines of research" (Gardner, 1969, p. 43). Her attitude to this sort of experimental work in later life suggests that the main thing she learned was that this type of study is arid and largely irrelevant to the problems of understanding learning processes.

Incidentally she made one acute observation during her study. She noted a tendency for "good or bad spelling to run in certain families". She may well not have been interested in investigating this possibility further, and, in any case, the tools to pursue her hunch were not yet available, but, in fact, she had identified genetic influences as a possible major cause of variation in spelling ability quite likely to be more important than whether imagery is used or not.

It is possible that Susan might have pursued her studies if Newnham College, to which she was attached, had been more accommodating. Myers was impressed with the work she had done in her first few months in his laboratory in Cambridge and encouraged her to apply for a Fellowship at her College. In March, 1913 he wrote to Samuel Alexander, Susan's Professor of Philosophy in Manchester, asking him to provide a reference with respect to an application to Newnham for a Fellowship (Myers, 1913). He said that she had already got some "very interesting results" and "promises excellently". Filling Alexander in so that he could write a more informed reference, he added ". . . probably it is enough for you if I now state that, to my knowledge, her work is of a very excellent character and that she ought to be encouraged to go on with it at all costs". Newnham have not kept records of applications for Fellowships at this time, so we do not know if the application was pursued. If it was, it was certainly unsuccessful. In any event, by the end of the academic year, Susan was out of a job and needed employment to support herself.

It does not seem as if her time in Cambridge was particularly happy or fulfilling for her. The account she wrote for the Manchester University Magazine suggests she found the almost exclusively male society oppressive. She wrote that "women are essentially intruders. . . . nor is it good for the women students to be constantly reminded that they are not merely students but also female ones". Cambridge then, as now, is largely a university for undergraduates. Susan, as a twenty seven year old post-graduate was indeed an outsider not merely because she was a woman, but because she was older and more senior than the undergraduates, yet hardly able to mix easily with the clannish dons, male or female. As it happened the Cambridge Department contained the most outstanding psychologists in the country at the time. Men like Rivers and Myers were broad-ranging in their approach, happy to encompass anthropological data and hypothesis-testing laboratory studies. Cyril Burt, whom she met in Cambridge, was already distinguished in educational psychology, yet Susan seems to have taken little away from her contact with them. She does not seem to have made any female friends at Newnham and was never in touch with the College again after she left. She was to return to Cambridge a dozen or so years later, but made no contact with any acquaintances she had previously made there.

Before she left Cambridge she obtained a post as Mistress of Method in the Infant Department of Darlington Training College (Durham County Archive, E/DAR 9/1). This meant that she was in charge of the training of women aiming to be infant teachers. However she also taught the theory and practice of education, psychology and handwork. Her salary was £120 per annum with free board and lodging calculated to be worth an additional £40. The College had been established as a Teacher Training College as long ago as 1876, but a new Principal, Freda Hawtrey, had recently been appointed when Susan arrived. She had progressive ideas and was an enthusiast for nursery education (Gardner, 1969, p. 44).

Susan would have felt at home both in her place of work and in the city of Darlington, despite the fact that it was in Yorkshire and she was a Lancastrian. Although heavy industry was less prominent there than in her home town of Bolton and it was more of a market town, there were many engineering firms manufacturing railway stock. It was also a centre for the production of newspapers for the north-east of the country, just as Bolton, where her father had worked as a journalist, had been for the north-west. Finally, like Bolton, Darlington was a centre for nonconformist religious belief, though dominated by Quakers rather than Methodists.

Asked about what Susan was like when she was at Darlington, Freda Hawtrey, who later became Principal of the better-known Avery Hill Teacher Training College in Greenwich, reported (Gardner, 1969, p. 44) "she was beautiful and gifted". She certainly made an impact on the lives of two of her students, both of whom became infant school teachers. They provided detailed, and, as it happens, rather different recollections of her when they were interviewed over fifty years later.

Elsie Shorter clearly adored Susan (Gardner, 1969, pp. 45–6). She wrote in her account of Susan:

Her lectures were outstandingly vital and stimulating. Her work was always thorough, and she made her students attack their work with the same thoroughness and stimulation. No student willingly missed one of her tutorials though perhaps we went up to her room with a slight feeling of dread—her criticisms were severe and searching, but never unjust or scathing. Her aim seemed always to make her students think and analyse and criticise for themselves. Moreover she had a knack of ending the discussion on a constructive note and finding for each one of us some good point in our favour so that we left feeling stimulated.

Elsie Shorter remained in touch with Susan and became a personal friend and confidant later when they both lived in London. The other student who remembered her fifty years later was less complimentary and sheds some light on Elsie's enthusiasm for their teacher. She wrote that it was not easy to make contact with Susan.

> She was immersed in her search for the true methods of teaching. One student, however, found contact with her. She was Miss Shorter. She was like Miss Fairhurst in her impersonal attitude towards others and quite dedicated to her work.

Despite these reservations Naomi Clough (who was not the last to comment on the impersonality of Susan's approach to her subject) found Susan an exciting teacher, who gave the students glimpses of how teaching would be in the future. Already she was promoting the idea of teaching as building on the child's own ideas, rather than inculcating knowledge. But, Naomi Clough noted ironically, there was a contrast between the freedom allowed to children and that allowed to teachers, even teachers learning their trade. Naomi Clough went on (Gardner, 1969, p. 45):

> We learnt, through experience how projects brought knowledge to the children in a practical and interesting way, as well as giving them the joy of creative activity. A group of children were asked to make a 'house' their centre of interest. Two of us were given the bathroom to furnish. My partner asked me if I thought her wash basin was big enough. I said 'I think it is too big', and was reprimanded by Miss Fairhurst for speaking.
> It seemed curious that, in spite of her vision of a new freedom for the children, she was quite strict with the students . . . Her attitude to students in general was rather remote.

This remoteness, detachment might be more apposite, was remarked on by some people throughout her life. Others, like Elsie Shorter, found her delightfully warm and sympathetic. When their beliefs are questioned, there is always a problem for those in authority who believe with great fervour and enthusiasm that people should be given maximum freedom to make their own decisions. Perhaps the politician who most closely reflected this dilemma was Margaret Thatcher, like Susan Fairhurst from a strongly Methodist background, who believed passionately in the decentralisation of power except when those to whom power was to be decentralised seemed to want to carry out policies with which she disagreed. Like many of us, Susan was able to show warmth more easily to those who admired her and agreed with her views.

During the year she spent in Darlington, Susan and William Brierley decided to marry. William, having taken his Finals in Botany at Manchester University at the end of the 1910–1911 academic year had gone on to do an M. Sc. Course that he completed a year later. He was then appointed to an Assistant Lecturership in Economic Botany. He had a most distinguished academic career, winning University prizes in botany, zoology, and geology, and being awarded the Robert Platt Biological Exhibition, the Leo Grindon Botany Prize, a first class Teacher's Certificate, a brilliant First in Botany and a Graduate Research Scholarship (Stoughton, 1963). After she left Manchester, he and Susan continued to write to each other and Susan visited Manchester at weekends. Though the rail journey from Cambridge to Manchester is lengthy and tedious, the two hour rail journey from Darlington was simple enough, though Susan's salary would not have allowed the cost of many visits.

Her Darlington Teacher Training College staff record (Durham County Archive E/Dar 9/1) has a section for "Post, if any, taken up after leaving the Institution", and in it is noted "None—married 11/7/1914 to Mr. William Brierley". Clearly those who left the employ of the College at that time to marry were not expected to continue employment.

Susan and William had a great deal in common when they married. Like Susan, William had arrived at the University after a tremendous struggle, though in his case it was poverty and a deprived background with which he had to contend rather than the prohibitions of a father unsympathetic to female education. William was born in 1889 and so was four years younger than Susan. He was brought up in one of the poorest districts of Manchester and, later in life, often said "I was born in a slum and brought up in a slum". At the age of 14, the brightest child in the class, he had become a pupil-teacher and taught in the elementary school in which he had been educated up to that point. He, like Susan, qualified to train as a teacher at the University of Manchester and then transferred onto an Honours Degree course in Botany. He supported himself financially through University by teaching evening classes in botany and nature study at schools and colleges. Again like Susan, he had a strong impulse to become involved in the education of the masses. Indeed, somewhat earlier than she, while he was an undergraduate, he began to teach classes organised by the Workers' Educational Association.

He was a sociable young man, active in student societies, succeeding Susan in the office of Honorary Secretary to the Sociological Society (MUM, 1911). He was in the year ahead of Susan at the University and they were taking different courses, but they had a great deal in common and many opportunities to meet. When Susan came up from Cambridge to visit him, she stayed with a friend in Didsbury, while he was living in Moston, a little distance away. They probably had little opportunity to get to know each other in any intimate way before they married in July, 1914. The marriage took place in Chorlton Registry Office with William's father and Susie's married sister, Bessie, as witnesses. Unlike most brides, Susan did not use her marriage to display her femininity. Her wedding "dress" was a "tramping outfit—heavy boots, rucksacks etc" and the honeymoon was spent walking the hills (Gardner, 1969, p. 46).

For the first year of their married life they lived in Levenshulme, a suburb of Manchester, about three miles to the south-east of the city, well-placed to go for walks in the Peak District. He worked as Assistant Lecturer in the Botany Department and she also found temporary employment at the University as Lecturer in Logic in the Department of Philosophy. Her job had probably become available as a result of a member of the University being recruited into the armed forces.

For within less than three weeks of their marriage, Germany had invaded Belgium and war between Germany on the one side and England and France on the other had broken out. In general, socialists like Susan and William, had, before 1914, been opposed to expenditure on armaments. They believed the armaments race was a capitalist conspiracy for the benefit of business interests, an avoidable catastrophe brought about by the balance of power, and that war was a remote possibility. Instead they were pre-occupied with domestic issues such as the improvement of education and obtaining votes for women. The outbreak of war posed difficult dilemmas for them. On 4 August, the day of the declaration of war, Ramsay Macdonald, the leader of the Labour Party, made a moderate anti-war speech in the House of Commons with the approval of his supporters, but within days, most Labour MPs swung into support of the war and Macdonald resigned. He and a small group of left-wing MPs remained opposed to the war throughout, but most of the country was swept with jingoistic fervour into supporting the war and eventually many young socialist men volunteered for service.

We do not know how Susan and William initially reacted to the outbreak of war. In all probability they first reacted, as most socialists at the time, by opposing the declaration of war but then, as hostilities progressed, accepted that the survival of the country depended on full commitment to the conflict. Their dilemma is well described by a contemporary woman novelist, Cicely Hamilton, herself a pacifist and active supporter of the suffragette movement before 1914, who worked as a nurse in France throughout most of the war. During and after the war she wrote short stories and a novel based on her experiences. She described in *Senlis* the inevitability of the participation of the civilian population.

Modern warfare is so monstrous, all-engrossing and complex, that there is a sense, and a very real sense, in which hardly a civilian stands outside it; where the strife is to the death with an equal opponent the non-combatant ceases to exist. No modern nation could fight for its life with its men in uniform only; it must mobilize, nominally or not, every class of its population for a struggle too great and too deadly for the combatant to carry alone.

William Brierley's thoughts probably led him to the same conclusion, namely that it was his duty to defend his country. However this transformation took time. In fact, he worked in the Manchester University Department of Botany for a year and then in 1915 obtained a more interesting post as a First Class Assistant in the new Laboratory of Plant Pathology that had just opened at the Royal Botanical Gardens in Kew, in west London (Stoughton, 1963). Here he began an intensive study of Botrytis, a fungus mould affecting vegetables. William and Susan moved to London and found a top-floor flat in Richmond overlooking Richmond Park.

But the war gradually impinged more and more on their lives. It became more difficult for a fit man in his mid-twenties to remain apart from the conflict and, after a few months in his new job, William enlisted in the Artists' Rifles. The Artists' Rifles sounds like an oxymoron. Artistry and military discipline do not seem compatible. Were these soldiers who carried a rifle in one hand and a paintbrush and palette in the other? In fact, the Artists' Rifles, as part of the London Regiment, had been formed as long ago as 1859 (Gregory, 2006). At first the regiment largely consisted of painters, sculptors, engravers, musicians, architects and actors. Over the years several outstanding artists served in the regiment including Everett Millais, G F Watts, Frederick Leighton, Holman Hunt and William Morris. During the First World War the regiment took in many people who were not artists, but their ranks did include Paul and John Nash, John Lavery, and perhaps most famously, the poet, Wilfred Owen.

These were no dilettante soldiers. They saw as much front-line action as any other infantry regiment and their casualties were correspondingly high. Paul Nash painted a scene in which the regiment was going into action. Wilfred Owen was killed, while serving in the regiment, in the last weeks of the war. The name of the battalion did, of course, sometimes raise a laugh in other battalions. There is a story that as they were replacing another battalion in the front line, one of the famished cockney privates they were replacing was heard to say "Artists' Rifles, eh. I wonder if any of 'em would paint me a plate of 'am and eggs".

Fortunately, William Brierley was spared, though not without injury. He was invalided out of the Army in 1916 and returned to Susan and to his work in Kew (Stoughton, 1963). Subsequently their life in London was as normal as was possible in a city at war. William was completely taken up with his work. This was not just of scientific but also of commercial interest. The fungus he studied could be devastating to the production of vegetables, a major consideration in wartime when they were an important source of nutrition for the population.

Susan's life for the remainder of the war was busy, but not greatly focused. She did not find full-time employment but instead taught psychology to adults in a variety of settings, places of higher and further education (Gardner, 1969, p. 49). She organised and ran several such courses for the London County Council, for the Kent Education Committee and for Morley College. She was enrolled as a Lecturer for London University Tutorial Classes. In addition, she taught courses in psychology on a voluntary basis for the Workers' Educational Association. Until the end of the war, when soldiers returned from the front and life returned to greater normality, the classes she taught were small and poorly attended. People had other matters on their minds. Her own research proceeded slowly, but she managed to complete the writing up of the study on spelling that she had carried out at Cambridge during the academic year, 1912–13. This study, described earlier in this chapter, required a great deal of background reading. The analysis of the data she obtained was highly detailed and must have taken up much of her time. In addition, she started to prepare for the writing of a textbook of psychology that could serve as a standard text for the type of students she was now teaching. The lack of focus in her working life may also have been partly due to the fact that those who, as a result of previous contact, might have involved her in professional work, were now themselves engaged in military duties of one sort or another. In particular, Charles Myers, her supervisor at Cambridge, had been appointed consultant psychologist to the British armies in France and did not return to Cambridge until the end of the war.

Her social life was also restricted. William worked very long hours. Susan had not lived in London before. Her work was mainly carried out in isolation on a part-time basis and this is not a good way to get to know people socially. Except when he was in the Army, William was on a reasonably good salary, and she was earning some money so they were not badly off. She spent some time furnishing the accommodation they had rented and Elsie Shorter, her student at Darlington, who had followed her to London to obtain a teaching post in the capital, visited her and noted that in around 1917

The flat was beautifully furnished with simplicity and good taste. Mrs. Brierley introduced me to the fabrics of Liberty's and curtains, carpets, bedspreads all came from there. She was a good housekeeper and cook and everything was marvellously organised and running smoothly.

In fact, Elsie Shorter seems to have been a significant person in Susan's life at this time. Elsie had decided after leaving College during the year before coming to London to take further teaching qualifications. Susan coached her by correspondence and went through her essays with great thoroughness. Elsie recalled later (Gardner, 1969, p. 47) "I wrote regularly on topics of her choosing, the criticism was always severe—often almost devastating, but by a later post would be a kindly letter telling me where and how much my work had improved and suggesting lines of development".

It was not just Elsie's essays on educational topics that came under fire. Her religious beliefs were also attacked by the still militantly atheistic Susan. When Elsie expressed her religious beliefs, Susan could not hold back. She wrote (Gardner, 1969, p. 47):

> Why oh why if the blessed souls really wish to give us proofs of immortality, do they not do it properly and convincingly? One can only think they leave their intelligence behind with their bodies or they would find some really useful way of proving their existence after death.

Clearly Elsie was not totally satisfied with this response but her protests only elicited another onslaught:

> My dear, it's a little cruel to suggest that I want to "explain away" anything. I only want to find the solid truth as distinct from mere subjective belief and cloudy surmise . . . Should you *want* to believe either way in particular? Surely you should want to get as near the truth as you can, but you mustn't first think what you would *like* to believe, and then try to find supporting reasons for this view. Our effort should be to discount personal desires although I agree is it very hard to do so.

We may note the imperious style Susan adopted when telling Elsie what she must or must not think. Again this might seem odd coming from someone so committed to letting people make up their own minds about what they thought about different matters.

Once she came to London, Elsie made contact with Susan who was kind and helpful to a fellow newcomer; the more necessary as Elsie was living on very little money (Gardner, 1969, pp. 48–9). Susan escorted her to her first teaching post at a school in a depressing part of east London, and tried to cheer her up when she looked crestfallen at the slum district in which she would be working. Susan took her along to some of her classes and they talked afterwards about the obvious intelligence and curiosity of some of the more dilapidated looking members of the class. Once a month Elsie was put up for the weekend in Richmond, a treat she still remembered many years later.

William's tenure of his post at Kew proved shorter than anticipated. In November, 1918, the month in which the war ended, the Institute of Plant Pathology was founded at Rothamsted Experimental Station. He was appointed be the first head of the Department of Mycology, the study of funguses. He was only just thirty years old at the time and his career ascent had been spectacularly rapid. Indeed throughout his life he was a leader in his field.

What did this promotion mean for Susan? Rothamsted Experimental Station was and remains in Harpenden, Hertfordshire. It is about twenty five miles away from and within easy rail distance of central London though less easily accessible from Richmond. The Brierleys could easily have moved together to Hertfordshire and Susan could have continued to work in London. It would have been the sensible thing to do as clearly William was not going to change his job again for some time. Indeed he remained at Rothamsted until 1932 when he was appointed to the Chair of Agricultural Botany in the University of Reading. The fact that this did not happen is symptomatic of the fact that all was not well in their marriage. Indeed it was at this point, some time in 1919 that they began to talk about separating.

Neither of them appears to have either talked or written about the reasons for their separation. One can only guess, but there are a number of pointers. In particular, there are various possible reasons that appear highly improbable. We have already seen how the location of William's new job could not be seen as realistically problematic. There was no lack of common interests. They both enjoyed nature and went for long walks in the countryside together. Susan had a strong interest in biology, indeed she shared William's main scientific interest in the classification of plants. She used examples from mycology to illustrate some of the points she made in her psychology lectures. Both socialists, they shared political beliefs and values. In particular, William was a strong believer in votes for women and in the rights of women to work on equal terms with men. There were no financial problems. They both had relatively calm temperaments and their later lives reveal that they were both capable of sustaining long-term relationships. They were both sociable people and had many friends with shared interests. What then remains? It seems likely that there was a major degree of sexual incompatibility. And, as we shall see, Susan's later life gives considerable credence to this possibility. The particular nature of the sexual incompatibility not surprisingly remains uncertain, though again Susan's later life provides a number of clues.

For whatever reason, separation occurred not too long after William's move to Rothamsted in late 1918. Where did this leave Susan? She became a free woman, but her personal, social and career achievements over the previous five years cannot have given her much cause for satisfaction. In 1919 she was thirty four years old. Given her brilliant academic record, her work was bitty and piecemeal and she was making little advance towards an academic career. She had not found a topic in psychology that really interested her and there was no sign of a permanent academic post becoming available. Her first marriage had failed for reasons that might well have been particularly upsetting for her. Because of their nature, there was no one with whom she could discuss them. She certainly could not confide in Elsie Shorter, who reports that it was at this point, because, Elsie conjectured, she was too ashamed to admit her marital problems that Susan broke off contact with her for many years.

Susan needed a new, intimate relationship. Perhaps even more importantly she needed a new ideology. Over the next couple of years she was to find both and her life would be transformed.

CHAPTER FOUR

Finding a place on the couch

The new set of ideas or the new ideology that Susan or Susie Brierley as she was then known, was to embrace was psychoanalysis. The first propositions made by the Viennese neurologist and psychiatrist, Sigmund Freud, signalling the birth of psychoanalysis, were made in 1893, twenty five years before Susan entered the field. In that year Freud and his friend and colleague, Josef Breuer published a paper entitled "The Psychical Mechanisms of Hysterical Phenomena". In this paper and in a book "Studies on Hysteria" published two years later, Freud first proposed his bold explanation of hysterical disorders, medical conditions in which physical symptoms for which there appeared to be no physical basis were present. He suggested that the mind dealt with thoughts that were unacceptable, too anxiety-provoking, too hot to handle by placing them firmly in a compartment of the mind, the unconscious, which was inaccessible to the individual. But according to Freud, you can't keep a bad idea down and these repressed thoughts surfaced, through a process called "conversion", as bodily symptoms, such as headaches, weakness or even paralysis of the limbs, all, in his view, signs of hysteria.

The suggestion that the unconscious mind played a major part in hysteria and perhaps in other neurotic conditions opened up a therapeutic possibility. If the unconscious could be made to give up its secrets, and the patient could be reassured or could discover for him or herself that the unacceptable thoughts could be safely experienced consciously, then the symptoms would disappear. Breuer and

Freud (1895b) were at first attracted by the notion that this would best be achieved by producing a hypnotic state, a state of heightened suggestibility, in which the patient would reveal secrets not previously disclosed. But between 1893 and 1895, Freud developed a new technique involving the patient being encouraged by the analyst to say things that came into the head automatically. Thoughts expressed automatically would escape the censorship imposed by the conscious mind on threatening thoughts in the unconscious. Such "free association" would lead the patient to discover and face, with the help of a sympathetic analyst, the unacceptable ideas that underlay the symptoms. The raison d'etre for the symptoms having been removed, the symptoms would disappear.

These were powerful claims and within just a few months of publication in German, the work of Freud and Breuer had been noticed by English philosophers interested in the workings of the mind. Frederic Myers, a Cambridge philosopher absorbed in spiritualism, telepathy and clairvoyance and with the possibilities of getting in touch with the world of spirits inhabited by the souls of the dead, was the first to notice and write about Freud's work. In 1891, Frederic Myers, not to be confused with Charles Myers, Susan's supervisor at Cambridge, had been a founder member of the Society for Psychical Research (Oppenheim, 1985). The members of this organisation, whose name sounds so lunatic fringe today, in fact included some of the most distinguished figures of the late Victorian era—eminent scientists like William Crookes and Oliver Lodge, psychologists such as William James, writers such as Arthur Conan Doyle and politicians such as Arthur Balfour. Myers used Freud's work to develop a theory integrating the findings from psychical research with those from scientific studies in psychopathology and abnormal psychology. In fact Freud later accepted an invitation to become a member of the Society for Psychical Research though he was never active in it.

Over the following decades Freud elaborated his ideas in a number of key psycho-analytic publications, including "The Interpretation of Dreams" (1900a) and "The Psychopathology of Everyday Life" (1901) that followed a year later. Soon afterwards he wrote about the development of sexuality, the sexual enlightenment of children and the possibilities of extending psycho-analytic treatment to children. In 1909 he brought his ideas together in the series of lectures he gave when he was awarded an honorary degree at Clark University, in Worcester, Mass (Jones, 1962).

After the philosophers and spiritualists, the next wave of interest in psycho-analysis in Britain came from medicine, especially neurology and psychiatry. Round about 1903, Wilfred Trotter, a young doctor recently qualified from University College Hospital (UCH), London, later to achieve great distinction both as a surgeon and as a sociologist, read a review in the journal "Brain" of Freud's "Studies in Hysteria". He mentioned to his close friend, another doctor, later to be his brother-in-law, Ernest Jones, that in Vienna "there was a doctor who listened to every word that a patient said". Jones, then 24 years old, had made a brilliant start in medicine, winning all the prizes as a medical student at UCH. However his career had run into serious problems a couple of years after qualifying when, on more than one occasion, he took a weekend off without getting proper leave from the children's hospital where he was working. A little later he had blotted his copybook with the medical establishment much more seriously when he was accused of sexually assaulting two mentally retarded girls at an institution where he was working. He was charged with indecent assault, and, although, when he was tried two anxious months later, he was acquitted, the case had attracted great publicity in national newspapers. It was clear he was not going to advance in orthodox medicine. Though Jones himself always denied the truth of the various allegations that had been made against him (Jones, 1959), the details of his trial for indecent assault suggest he might have been very lucky to escape conviction (Maddox, 2006).

Jones decided to pursue the possibility of a career in what was then and remains to some degree now the marginal medical specialty of psychiatry. He succeeded so well that he became a major figure in psychiatry and played the dominant role in British psychoanalysis for the next thirty five years (Brome, 1982). In 1907 he decided to travel abroad to find out more about the new approach to mental disorder that Freud had now been describing for some years.

That year he met C. G. Jung, Freud's most significant disciple at that time, at the First International Congress of Psychiatry and Neurology in Amsterdam. The following year he encountered Freud for the first time at the First Psychoanalytic Congress in Salzburg and was greatly impressed by him. Returning to England, not surprisingly in the light of his tarnished reputation, Jones found it difficult to establish himself and went to Canada where, in 1908, he obtained posts in Toronto. In 1909, when Freud came to the United States to receive an honorary doctorate at Clark University in Worcester, Mass., Jones travelled south to meet him and accompanied him during his stay, acting as his factotum. After having been involved in further accusations of sexually inappropriate behaviour with women patients in Canada, he returned to Europe in 1912 and became the only English-speaking member of Freud's inner circle. In 1913 he had an intense seven week analysis with Sandor Ferenczi, one of Freud's close associates, and thereafter practised full-time, most successfully and without further scandal, as a psycho-analyst in London, while at the same time leading the British psycho-analytic field.

By this time, 1912–13, psychoanalysis had also attracted much interest from the intellectual elite especially through James Strachey (Hinshelwood, 1995). He was a member of the Society for Psychical Research, and partly through his brother, Lytton, was in close contact with the coterie of artists and writers of the Bloomsbury Group. Bloomsbury was fascinated by the notion of an unconscious part of the mind in which ideas and images could frolic and play, to surface later, transformed by unconscious experience, as abstract or surrealist art. Novels and poetry could similarly emerge directly from the unconscious, truer to reality than work that had not been through this process because it would contain emotionally charged material that had escaped censorship. Lytton Strachey, as well as Virginia and Leonard Wolff were among those interested in the possibilities opened by an understanding of the unconscious part of the mind, though Virginia was fiercely hostile to psychoanalysis and, more particularly to psychoanalysts (Meisel and Kendrick, 1986).

But it was through the impact it was making on psychology that Susan was brought into most direct contact with psycho-analysis at the end of the First World War. The group of psychologists who had been most influenced during and after the war, were those who had been on the 1898 Torres Straits anthropological expedition. As we have seen these included William McDougall, who, with others, introduced experimental psychology into the English-speaking world, Charles Myers, Susan's supervisor at Cambridge, and W. H. R. Rivers, also a member of the Cambridge department of psychology where she had worked in 1912 (Crampton, 1978). During the First World War Rivers had pioneered methods derived from psycho-analysis in the treatment of shell-shock. Between them these men transformed British psychology from a subject in the province of speculative philosophy into the empirical science it had already become in Germany. Further, impressed with what they saw as the empirical nature of psycho-analysis, they attempted to absorb Freud's theories into mainstream psychology. Early on McDougall became sceptical of this possibility and withdrew from an interest in psycho-analysis, Myers was more ambivalent, but Rivers, though highly critical of Freud's emphasis on childhood trauma as responsible for all neurosis, continued to use psycho-analytic concepts in his writing and practice. Many academic psychologists, even if they did not accept all its principles, treated Freudian psycho-analysis with great respect.

Meanwhile Ernest Jones had been actively pursuing the idea of establishing psycho-analysis on an organisational basis on the lines of associations already established in Vienna and Berlin (Maddox, 2006). In 1913 he had co-founded the London Psycho-Analytical Society, but immediately after the First World War he became dissatisfied with the fact that some of its members had developed a greater allegiance to Jung than to Freud. Jung had been demonised by Freud when a split occurred between the two with a final break in 1913; Jones, by then a loyal member of Freud's exclusive inner circle, listened to and obeyed his master's voice. In 1919 he dissolved the London Society and formed instead the British Psycho-Analytical Society (BPAS 1919: Minutes of the Psychoanalytical Society). He informed Freud that he had personally analysed six of its eleven original members so orthodoxy was assured. One of the eleven original members was J. C. Flugel, a psychologist on the staff at University College, London. Flugel was, by all accounts, a delightful man, modest and humorous, who had trained as an academic experimental psychologist in Germany before the First World War (Richards, 2004). He had an interest in psycho-analysis since his undergraduate days at Oxford. In 1913, he had been analysed by Ernest Jones, from whom he had sought help for problems with his marriage. He had then become a founder member of the London Psycho-analytic Society. In 1919 he became not only a founder member of the British Psycho-analytic Society, but Secretary of the International Psycho-analytic Association. Susan knew Flugel through her attachment to University College Psychology Department, where she taught as an assistant lecturer. In 1920 she asked him to take her on for analysis and saw him four or five times a week for a little less than a year (Personal communication Dr. K. Robinson, Hon. Archivist, British Psychoanalytic Association, 2006).

In 1919 when Susan first began to take a serious interest in psychoanalysis, it was seen by many psychologists as part of a "New Psychology". It seemed to provide the only available form of psychotherapy for use in psychiatric disorders that was backed by a coherent theory. Pioneering educationists too had found in psycho-analysis a useful set of ideas from which to develop new teaching methods. Further, over the decade following the First World War, psychoanalysis became a craze among British intellectuals. When one thinks of the impact of psycho-analysis on intellectual life, it is New York between the nineteen fifties and the nineteen seventies that comes to mind. Yet long before the east coast of the United States fell in love with psychoanalysis, indeed in the nineteen twenties and thirties, British and especially London intellectuals had enjoyed a passionate affair with it (Richards, 2000; Ellesley, 1975; Rapp, 1988). D. H. Lawrence, who reflected the significance of unconscious processes in his novels, was ambivalent towards what he saw as the simplistic notions of the analysts and mocked those who swallowed its tenets. In 1923 he complained (Lawrence, 1923) that . . .

psychoanalysis had become a public danger. The mob was on the alert. The Oedipus Complex was a household word, the incest motive a commonplace of tea-table chat. "Wait till you've been analysed" said one man to another, with varying intonation. "A sinister look came into the eyes of the initiates—the famous and infamous Freud look. You could recognise it everywhere, wherever you looked."

James Joyce was another author influenced by psycho-analysis. Mocking of its pretensions; he referred to Freud and Jung as "the Viennese Tweedledee and the Swiss Tweedledum" (Gilbert, 1957) though the interior monologues he wrote in "Ulysses" and other novels are clear examples of Freudian free association or what

William James had described earlier as "stream of consciousness". Virtually all artistic endeavour was influenced by psychoanalysis, not just novels, but the cinema and theatre. Surrealist art expressed the incoherent, apparently meaningless but immensely revealing unconscious. Philosophy began to move into post-modernist celebration of the subjective world. Even theologians attempted to incorporate psychoanalysis into their world view. It was therefore not at all surprising that Susan Brierley should wish to become involved in and committed to it.

There was in fact a variety of other, more personal reasons why Susan should have wished to pursue an interest in psycho-analysis. To begin with, as we have seen psycho-analysis had captured the interest of psychologists, such as Charles Myers, her Cambridge supervisor. Now her colleagues were moving in the same direction. For example, Cyril Burt, the leading educational psychologist in England at this time and for decades afterwards, was elected a full member of the British Psycho-Analytical Society in 1919, at its second meeting. Burt was later to be critical of psycho-analysis, but at this point in time he had great, positive interest even enthusiasm for it. He had previously taught a course on psychoanalysis at the University of Liverpool a decade earlier (Hearnshaw, 1979). It is also possible that Susan felt she would gain from psycho-analysis valuable insights into the behaviour of children that would be helpful to her both in her academic research work and in her teaching. Finally, and perhaps most importantly of all, it may well have been that she saw psycho-analysis as providing insight into and help for her own psychological problems that her failed marriage to William Brierley had uncovered. For whatever reasons, and all of those I have suggested are likely to have played some part, Susan's analysis with J C Flugel was important to her, though the fact that she almost immediately sought a further analytic experience suggests she did not find it sufficient for her needs.

In 1920, Otto Rank, one of Freud's closest associates visited London to make contact with the British Psycho-analytic Society. A year later Susan travelled to Vienna, hoping to undergo analysis with Freud himself. He was unavailable, so she saw Otto Rank for a further analysis that lasted about three months before returning to England. Rank was a close associate of Freud, indeed at this point in time probably the closest of his colleagues. Initially he had been an apprentice mechanic and had worked for a year or two as a locksmith. Always a wide reader, by the age of twenty he had been attracted to Freud's ideas, had made contact with him and started to treat patients. Like all Freud's colleagues apart from Jung and Ernest Jones, he was Jewish, but, unlike all the others he was not medically qualified.

At the time he saw Susan, Rank was developing an extension of Freudian theory proposing that the trauma of birth was responsible for much neurosis (Lieberman, 1985). He assured Freud, who had been initially encouraging to his ideas but then became much more sceptical, that he could reach the deepest levels of the unconscious to relieve the disturbances caused by birth trauma in just a few months. Presumably this was his focus in his analysis with Susan. Three months of analysis is very short by present-day standards; since the nineteen thirties an analysis is expected to last at least three years and involve attendance four or five times a week. But early analysts were content with much shorter periods of treatment. At any rate, with these two experiences of psycho-analysis behind her, it was natural for Susan to wish to join and become a full member of the British Psycho-Analytical Society. She began to attend the fortnightly meetings and, as Mrs. Susan Brierley was elected an Associate Member in December, 1921.

Over the first five years of its existence, from 1919 to 1924, the members of the Society only discussed the possibility of child psycho-analysis two or three times and indeed, though some especially of the women members were interested in children, rarely discussed direct involvement of children in psychoanalysis. At their Wednesday evening meetings the members presented papers to each other on a great variety of subjects. These reflected the themes and especially the sexual preoccupations of Freudian psycho-analysis at that time. They included cases of premature ejaculation, homosexuality, the symbolism of flute playing, nymphomania, masochism, emotional factors in enteroptosis (sagging of the gut), adolescent masturbation, fear in an adult patient arising from circumcision at the age of six years, repression in industry, psychical eye symptoms in ophthalmic practice, sadism, psychoses, myth and dream, polyphallic symbolism and the castration complex, types of onanism (masturbation), the castration complex in snobbishness and the problem of matriarchy. Though about a quarter of the members were women, the discussions were largely dominated by the men in the Society; it is noteworthy that the issue of patriarchy in society, later a preoccupation of post-Freudians, was not discussed. Looking back at these meetings, Edward Glover, a founder member of the Society, felt that the presentations had very much followed orthodox Freudian lines and lacked originality but nevertheless the meetings were lively and the membership grew.

While embracing this new ideology, Susan had formed a new relationship, the most important in her life. Reading Nathan Isaacs's first letter to her in October 1920 must have been a startling experience for her (IoEd N1 D2). She had recently given a psychology lecture to her Workers' Educational Association class. In the class for the first time there had been a short, dark, highly intense, obviously Jewish young man in his mid-twenties, who had immediately started to dispute some of the statements she had made. He had shown himself to be extremely well read both in philosophy and psychology, but put forward his views quietly. Though she was the lecturer and he the student, in the points he was making he did not seem to have any doubt that he was in the right and she in the wrong. The young man had been sitting next to a friend, slightly younger than himself but several inches taller, who had brought him along. The friend had attended her lectures the previous year and had, with her help, obtained a place to read for a degree in economics at the London School of Economics.

Now a couple of days later she received a five page letter (IoE NI B2 1) that began:

It was a very pleasant surprise, the combination of Mycological paper—which, as you know, I very much appreciated, Abstract, and Positive Provocation to criticise. As though I hadn't been likely to take the first opportunity of doing something like it anyhow! But perhaps that was the point. At all events, I had already managed to secure a copy of the abstract, had already been very much impressed by it, was in fact already determined to turn impression into expression at some time. You open the door, you ask me to enter. Thanks very much, but that's just where I pause. Perhaps I'd sooner not. If I did so, at your invitation, I should feel under a responsibility. I should have to make sure where I was going to, and, above all, to mind the carpet. No, I'd sooner not, but one moment, since the door is open, I'll go in as I intended: as if I were unasked.

By this time she would have had no doubt that the writer of the letter had been the intense young man. The suggestion that she had invited criticism was accurate, though she hadn't expected such an onslaught. Further she didn't expect to be accused of creating such an effect on her students. It turned out it was almost as if he had been mesmerized by her particular way of putting forward her ideas. He went on to distinguish between the abstract she had provided before the lecture and the lecture itself:

It isn't criticism then, it's whatever it may choose to be. I don't know yet. So far it is merely a curious impression, not from the lecture, but from the abstract. For in fact, the two seemed to differ in spirit, in a way quite unwarranted by their relation as summary and expansion. A lecture is naturally personal with the personality of the lecturer. An abstract should eliminate this element and be quite impersonal. But yours is impersonal with a personality of its own. It had, at least for me, a distinct dramatic meaning. Of course, I'm specially responsive to the ghosts of dramatic meanings lingering among abstracts. But I think the spirit in yours might be manifest to anybody. It's a relentless spirit and as one watches it at work on its victim, one feels with a premonitory shiver, one's own turn to come. There is something like it somewhere in literature, I don't remember where. A sort of confessor–inquisitor is engaged in stripping, mortifying, cleansing and renewing his charge or subject. Every other moment the latter stops confessing, as though now everything has been brought to light. But no, the probing, purging spirit inexorably continues, you have not finished. You are still deceiving yourself, you are still holding something back, you still have something to surrender. This "needs to be made conscious". So over and over again; and when the penitent is not betrayed by reluctance, he is betrayed by enthusiasm. The victim dwindles, but so long there is any victim left the analyst is pitiless. For so long as it is more than mere surface, there is always something that needs to be brought to the surface. When it is mere surface, it will have

passed over into, and will only exist within, not its own, but
the analyst's consciousness

The writer, whom by now she would certainly have realized to be
her new WEA student, Nathan Isaacs, then went on to discuss
consciousness and psychoanalysis etc. He quoted Hegel ". . . to be
conscious of a limitation is to transcend it". Clearly he was not afraid
to parade his learning. And, it would turn out later he was not just
trying to impress his teacher. Given the slightest opportunity, his
conversation was always carried on at a highly intellectual level and
reflected his wide reading.

Nathan Isaacs was, at that time, twenty five years of age, ten
years younger than she. His parents were of Russian-Polish origin,
but the family had migrated westwards before his birth (Personal
communication, Karina McIntosh, 2005). He was born in 1895 in
Nuremberg, Germany, but his family had an itinerant, irregular
existence and most of his early schooling was in Switzerland, at least
partly in Basel. He was the middle of three children, with an older
sister, Lena, and a younger sister, Malvin or Mallie. His father was
an orthodox Jew, a learned intellectual, fascinated by philosophical
issues, but unable and, in fact, uninterested in earning a living.
He read and wrote large quantities of unpublishable material. The
young Nathan had a difficult relationship with his father because he
refused to learn Hebrew as his father wished. The breadwinner was
his mother, an itinerant saleswoman, often away from home, who
sold embroidered blouses and skirts manufactured in Eastern
Europe. She earned little. The children were greatly loved, but they
were often hungry; and all were small in stature probably as a result
of childhood malnourishment.

Nathan came to England with his Jewish family, one of many that
came to England at this time mainly for economic reasons, at the age
of twelve years. He went to school in London until he was 16 years
of age. He then joined Bessler Waechter, a British firm dealing in
ferro-alloys and pig-iron, as an office boy, gradually working his way
up to become a manager (IoE, NI/D/4). In March, 1917, he volunteered for military service during the First World War and served
as a private in the Royal Signals. He talked little about his war experiences, but, in a letter written many years later (IoE N1 D11/1) he
describes how he was sent, with other signallers "after the slaughter

of Passchendaele to fill the gaps in a previously undiluted Artillery Battery in the 51st Highland Division. They were practically all miners and a fine, comradely, unspoilt lot of men". Fine and comradely they may have been, but they were clearly very different from Nathan. He describes in the same letter how, at one point, it was rumoured that there was a prostitute in the nearby town of Bethune, whose services were going to be available. Most of his comrades went off to stand in the queue but Nathan made it clear he was not interested and was staying behind. He settled down to a volume of poems by Robert Burns. A soldier who had been a miner before the war asked what he was reading and then if he could borrow the book for the afternoon as he expected he might have to wait his turn. When the man returned, Nathan asked him what he had thought of the poems and was told that they had turned out to be the best part of the afternoon.

He was in fact gassed at Passenchendaele in October, 1917 and left the Army shortly afterwards. He rejoined Bessler-Waechter (IoE N1/D/4) where he was working when he met Susan. It was a large firm and he was employed in every department. When he became the senior manager, he was responsible for about half a million pounds annual turnover.

Although he had a full-time, taxing job, Nathan continued to read voraciously, especially in philosophy and psychology. Despite the fact that English was not his first language, he was unusually fluent and articulate in it. He also spoke excellent French, good Spanish and some Italian. Everyone agreed he had formidable intellectual power. The friend who brought him along to Susan's class was, in fact, Lionel Robbins, later Lord Robbins, who became one of the leading economists of his day, and, among many other major responsibilities, chaired the Royal Commission on Higher Education, whose report published in 1963 set the pattern for higher education in the United Kingdom for more than a generation. In a Memorial Service held for Nathan many years later, Robbins (1966) described him as a "true intellectual and one of very high quality at that". Although Nathan had never had a university education, Robbins said he would always think of him "as an academic in the best sense of the word—a Gelehrter alter Stil (a scholar of the old school). He loved argument—it fed some inner necessity of his nature. But he loved truth even more; and this meant that he was humble before facts and always willing to write off past intellectual investments no matter with what zeal they had been made".

He and Susan were well matched intellectually and he realized this immediately. In a letter to her sent shortly after the first one, he wrote (IoE NI D/4):

Perhaps because I don't dance, it very much seems to me that any properly conducted discussion should be a sort of Protean minuet. There should be advances and repulses, advances and embraces, advances and withdrawals and anything you like—even a dance in between but the character of the dancers should change, the rapprochements should become increasingly distant, and the end should be in their original positions, two bristling balls, straining spines in all directions, at one another and at the whole universe.

The imagery that he used in this passage of his letter is strikingly similar to that used by a psychoanalytic colleague of Susan's, John Rickman. In his obituary of Susan, Rickman (1950), after describing Susan's formidable intellectual qualities, wrote:

It is not possible to speak of her intellectual discourse without reference to her husband, Nathan. To listen to the two of them in discussion was an experience that may be compared without belittlement to the aesthetic pleasure in watching a fine exhibition of ballroom dancing. The movement of their minds was in such close touch that it seemed as if a single figure moved in the intellectual scene, she skilled in philosophical method, followed his sterner logic, he yielded to her more subtle psychological intuition.

Susan first found Nathan to be an exhilarating though exasperating student. The weekly class she gave on psychology became a dialogue between the two of them. This was clearly not a satisfactory arrangement for the rest of the class who were excluded from their interchanges. Towards the middle of the course they were arranging to meet outside the class. By this time, Susan's relationship with William Brierley had completely broken down. They were no longer living together, William having moved to Harpenden to be near his work at Rothamsted, and Susan remaining in London. In the summer of 1921, Susan went on holiday to the continent and Nathan joined her. They shared a love of the mountains, and both took pleasure in long walks in the Alps. Shortly after their return they began to share a rented flat in Hunter Street in Bloomsbury. On 13 November, 1922, the divorce between William and Susan on the grounds of Susan's adultery with Nathan was made final. Four days later, on 17 November, 1922, Nathan and Susan married at St. Pancras Register Office, both giving 53 Hunter Street as their address. She gave her occupation as University Lecturer though in fact she only had a number of part-time assistant lecturer posts in University establishments. He gave his occupation as metals merchant manager. They could hardly have come from more different backgrounds, yet as all their friends recognized, this was indeed a marriage of true minds.

It is notable that Nathan was a non-observant Jew. Indeed it was his through his religion that he first met Lionel Robbins. As a very young officer, standing outside the synagogue in Woolwich in 1917, Robbins, who was not Jewish, had been told to march some Jewish troops to their weekly service. He described (Robbins, 1971) how he had told them to file in, when "there stepped forward a serious looking young gunner who said very solemnly 'I beg to be excused. I am an agnostic.' Needless to say I excused him and, breaking all the regulations of the day, we walked back up the hill together and founded a life-long friendship".

Susan had already had much contact with highly educated Jews, though she probably had not met any Jews at all until she went to study in Manchester in 1908. The Jewish community in Bolton was small and largely consisted of small shop traders and market people. In Manchester, by contrast, Jews played a major part in the intellectual and cultural life of the city. Samuel (Sam) Alexander, her Professor of Philosophy, was an active member of the Jewish community in Manchester and was always particularly encouraging to Jewish students. In fact he played a vital part in the establishment of the state of Israel. In a letter written shortly after Alexander's death in 1938, Chaim Weizmann, a Zionist leader and eventually the first President of the State of Israel, described[1] how, when he was a very young lecturer in the Chemistry Department in Manchester University in 1906, Alexander had introduced him to Arthur Balfour, the then Prime Minister who was visiting the University. It took several years but eventually Weizmann convinced Balfour that the Jewish people had a right to establish their own state. The Balfour Declaration made in 1917 affirmed that "His Majesty's Government view with favour the establishment in Palestine of a national home for the Jewish people. . . ." Acccording to this account given by Weitzmann, Alexander had played a key role in the events leading up to this statement though in fact in his autobiography, published twelve years later when perhaps his memory was not so accurate, Weitzmann (1950), wrote that his introduction to Balfour had been made by Charles Dreyfus, the managing director of a chemicals factory.

Once she left Manchester, her supervisor in Cambridge was Charles Myers, another Jew, but this time from a wealthy, cultured, north London family. He was not religiously observant, but undertook philanthropic work for the Jewish community. Susan remained in touch with Myers after she left Cambridge and would have been well aware of his Jewish identity. Her analyst in Vienna, Otto Rank was Jewish, as indeed were all the members of Freud's inner circle apart from Ernest Jones who saw himself as an "honorary Jew" (Maddox, 2006). So Nathan Isaacs was, in a sense, the fourth Jew to play an important part in her life. His influence however far surpassed that of the three previous Jews she had encountered, important to her though these had been. Nathan's Jewishness was, for most of his life, unimportant to him. He was completely assimilated and non-observant. Nevertheless, later in his life, his Jewish identity would surface, as it always does with assimilated Jews, when he was exposed to anti-semitism, either directly or indirectly.

Because of her name, Susan Isaacs is often thought by those who have heard of her to have been Jewish herself. Her non-conformist religious background was far from Jewish, yet in her life she was not only to marry a Jew and thus acquire a Jewish-sounding name, but to enter the field of psycho-analysis in which Jews played a particularly prominent part. There are a number of characteristics shared by Jews and non-conformist Christians, perhaps particularly Wesleyan Methodists, the religious movement to which Susan's father was so strongly attached. Both are required to have strong and unquestioning faith in divine providence, but both are encouraged to enter into passionate intellectual discussion about the interpretations of the Bible which have been handed down to them, in the one case the Talmud and in the other the writings of John Wesley and his followers. Both Jews and Methodists have an unusual degree of respect for scholarship and the authority of religious teachers, and put much of their spare time and much of their financial resources into the education, including the religious education of their children. The Jewish chedar and the Wesleyan Methodist Sunday School have a great deal in common. For both Jews and Methodists education does not end when childhood ends. Both Jewish rabbis and leaders of Methodist classes teach adult members of their flocks and sometimes enter into fierce, intellectual disputation with them.

Further when both Jews and non-conformist Christians abandon their religious faith, they often retain their passionate interest in the education of children. When, as inevitably happens, new authority figures emerge to replace religious leaders, former Jews and former Methodists retain the questioning ambivalence towards their authority that their parents had felt towards their rabbis and non-conformist religious teachers. Susan's belief system included not only the rejection of religion, but its replacement by faith in science and continuing adherence to many of the values important to her father as well as to many of the Jews she met in both her professional and her social life.

It is interesting to note that both her husbands were quite a bit younger than she, William by four and Nathan by ten years. Interesting it may be but there are no obvious conclusions to be drawn, though her friend and successor Dorothy Gardner, thought that there may have been a connection with her rejection in adolescence by her father (Gardner, 1969, p. 32). In neither marriage did she play a particularly maternal role, nor did her husbands look to her for mothering. Her marriage to Nathan, about which we know a great deal more than we do about her first marriage, seems to have been one of equals in emotional and intellectual maturity. We have no reason to think that the difference between their ages was of any particular significance to either of them at the time they met and in the early years of their marriage.

While her relationship with Nathan was ripening, and she was undergoing analysis with John Flugel, Susan was busy completing a basic textbook of psychology for the benefit of non-professional people who were attending courses in psychology, especially those organised by the Worker's Educational Association. This book appeared in 1921 so she must have been working on it during most of 1920 and perhaps earlier. "An Introduction to Psychology" (Brierley, 1921) is a short book, only about 150 pages long, but she managed to pack a great deal into it. It was a successful publication, running to five printings, in 1923, when it was published, in 1925 and 1928, when it was slightly revised, and in 1932 in its final revised edition.

It is an extraordinary little book. One can readily see why it was so successful. It covers a large territory. She discusses amongst other matters, definitions of psychology, methods used in psychological studies, the various fields of enquiry into which psychology had entered at the time she was writing, theories of drive and motivation, the ways in which human beings interact with their environment and finally, in a chapter entitled "The conscious and the unconscious" psychoanalytic concepts and mental mechanisms.

The book is well researched and Susan is clearly familiar with the work of all the most prominent psychologists of her day, quoting widely, for example, from books and articles published by William McDougall and Cyril Burt, with whom she was to work later. She is familiar with the tests of mental ability that had recently been developed by Alfred Binet in France and Burt in England, so she is quite capable of discussing quantitative approaches in psychology, such as the development, uses and abuses of intelligence testing. She has some sensible things to say about the use of questionnaires, which she sees as valuable, but only in the preliminary stages of a serious enquiry—a standpoint sometimes sadly neglected today when results from questionnaires are often cited as firmer evidence than they have a right to claim.

Her approach to psychology is rooted in biology, so again from the perspective of twenty first century psychology, she is remarkably contemporary. Our understanding begins, she writes early on in the book, when we learn to regard man "as an expression of biological laws and, in particular, when we learn to apply to him the concept of evolution. The theory of evolution laid the foundations of the scientific approach to the study of human nature". This leads her to discuss the ways in which the human organism has adapted to fulfil the functions, nutrition and reproduction, essential for survival. Thus, she writes for example, ". . . it is clear that the lips and their movements are at first in the service of the nutritional impulses; but before long they are also involved in erotic satisfactions and the kiss, which is clearly a modification of those movements and of the application of the lips to the maternal breast, has become (among Western Europeans) the universal preliminary to the complete sexual embrace". Contemporary evolutionary psychologists would find much to agree with in this section and might indeed be surprised to discover how much she had anticipated the standpoint they take today.

She is quick to dismiss the idea that human behaviour is dictated by cold reason. In a section entitled "The Rationalist's Fallacy", she affirms that "our intellectual world is liable to be highly coloured by our emotional trends and inner psychological necessities. We have proudly said . . . man is a rational animal and so he is, but he is none the less an animal. His reason is not the source of his motives; it is rather one of the various means by which these are harmonical, regulated and controlled. We may picture reason as the guiding hand upon the reins, but never as the fiery horses that draw the human chariot".

She frequently illuminates her points with dramatic and unusual examples. Thus at one point she is insisting that while general tendencies, such as nest-building in birds, are inherited, the form such behaviour takes is determined by what is available in the environment. She describes how, in the watch manufacturing town of Soleure, in Switzerland, the local birds make nests out of the discarded mechanisms of watches. "On a woodland walk" she writes in another context, when discussing the importance of attentional behaviour, "we will be pointed to quite different things depending on whether we are accompanied by a man of science or a landscape painter". Discussing the importance of imagery of different types in memory, she writes:

I may recall in visual images, for instance, the walk I took yesterday or the scenes I visited on my last holiday. If I am asked whether I know a certain piece of music its melody may come floating into my mind in sound images, perhaps with a mental picture of a particular conductor and orchestra and hall of entertainment accompanying the remembered sound. I may similarly recall in imagination "the touch of a vanished hand", the melancholy odours of woods in autumn and so on.

A singular feature of the book is the way in which she tackles subjects such as love and hate that are of obvious psychological importance, yet are often shunned by academic psychologists because of their vagueness or apparent complexity. Instead of avoiding them, Susan accepts their complexity, and then demonstrates how such complexity has been described in poetry and drama as well as by psychological colleagues. In addition to Chaucer, Swift and Coleridge, she quotes Shakespeare's shepherd, who explains what it feels like to be in love:

It is to be made of all sighs and tears
All made of passion and all made of wishes,
All adoration, duty and observance
All humbleness, all patience and impatience;
All purity, all trial, all observance

Then, and surely the juxtaposition is intended ironically to demonstrate the obtuseness of psychological writing on such matters, she quotes A. F. Shand, a psychologist, writing on the same subject, the experience of love, in a book entitled "Character":

The compound feeling, so long as its composition remains unchanged, acts in all times, places and situations in the same way. However greatly the situation may change, it can only respond to this situation with the same behaviour evoked by its compound emotion. Such a theory cannot account for the great diversity of the behaviour of love in different situations. . . .

Finally her discussion of psychoanalytic concepts, expanded by the time of the fourth and fifth editions, is masterly. She draws examples both from her clinical experience and from literature (not the academic literature but from poets, novelists and playwrights). To illustrate the mechanism of repression, she cites a woman who "lost" her husband's new gloves, until she used introspection to remember that, wishing for new gloves for herself, she had been quite envious of her husband's acquisition. Once she had gained some insight into her feelings, her recall as to where she had put the gloves was almost instantaneous. Maggie Tulliver in George Eliot's "Mill on the

Floss" who beat her doll when frustrated by her family, is used as an example of the mental mechanism of displacement.

All in all, with its vivid and compelling style, its combination of quantitative and humanistic approaches, and its achievement of comprehensiveness in the small space of 150 pages, "Introduction to Psychology" is a little masterpiece. It is, of course, quite out of date now, but I doubt if there is anything comparable on the market for beginners in psychology today.

Before she could become a practising psycho-analyst, Susan had to be accepted as a full member of the British Psycho-analytic Society, and this would inevitably take some time. She would have to complete a personal analysis and show some evidence of original thought in the field through delivering an acceptable paper to the Society. In the meantime she continued with part-time lecturing in psychology, though not now for the Workers' Educational Association that had barred her from their list of lecturers because she had developed an intimate relationship with one of her students. At this time, late 1920 into 1921, her Cambridge supervisor, Charles Myers, was changing career. Frustrated by delays in developing a proper academic department of psychology in Cambridge University, he decided to leave and focus elsewhere on the application of psychology to industry. He became one of the founding fathers of industrial psychology. Even after his philanthropy in Cambridge, he remained a wealthy man himself, and, with help from commercial organisations he set up the National Institute of Industrial Psychology in London. Still in touch with Susan, he involved her in preliminary discussions on the form this new organisation should take. In addition he encouraged her to write articles about the contribution that psychology might make in the workplace.

Susan wrote two papers, one on "Science and Human Values in Industry" (Brierley, 1921) in a magazine produced by the Co-operative Society, and the other, first given to the inaugural meeting of the Industrial Psychology Section of the British Psychological Society, in the British Journal of Psychology. This second, more substantial paper (Brierley, 1920) was entitled "The Present Attitude of Employees to Industrial Psychology". In the first of these papers she contrasts the nineteenth century, the period of man's conquest of nature with the twentieth, the age of the study of *human* nature. Up to now, she proposes, people have "rarely considered whether the new world of great factories in crowded cities was really satisfactory to human beings". Now they have revolted against the tyranny of machines. It has at last been realised that a tremendous "waste of precious human energy" has resulted from evil conditions of work, with loss of happiness and civic usefulness of men and women, all this being the result of "fitting the human being to the machine and neglecting the needs of human nature in industry".

But this evil, which she was far from the first or the last to point out, is reversible. What is needed, and here her argument is much more original, is scientifically gathered knowledge to prevent such waste, for example by working out ways of overcoming or avoiding monotony. She then describes the organisation to which she belongs, the National Institute of Psychology and Physiology Applied to Industry and Commerce (soon to be called the National Institute of Industrial Psychology), that had recently been set up to advance knowledge in this area and spread the results of its findings.

The second article on the attitudes of employers and workers to psychology is one of a collection of lectures given to the new specialist sections of the British Psychological Society. It is noteworthy that she is one of only two women out of the thirty or so contributors to the volume. Her paper was read at a meeting of the Industrial Section to which Charles Myers gave the Inaugural Address.

In her paper she continues to consider the theme of her previous article, the contribution that psychology can make to improvement in the conditions of work. In this paper she considers especially why working men are opposed to psychological approaches. She suggests that workers think psychologists are "in the camp of the enemy" and accepts that perhaps some psychologists do permit the needs of management to increase production to predominate their work. But, although inevitably psychologists will wish to bear management's need for higher production in mind, as well as the worker's need for shorter working hours and longer holidays, they should and will in the future, she claims, take a broader and more profound view especially of the worker's predicament. The psychologist seeks to understand the significance of the worker's whole personality for his industrial actions and reactions and to what degree the conditions of labour "hinder the healthy and balanced expression of the deepest needs of a complete human being".

Inevitably workers are suspicious of management wishing to bring in scientific improvements. There is a fear that scientific methods will increase unemployment, especially of the less-skilled. There is a further real and legitimate concern that mass production will reduce the craft element and the degree of autonomy that the worker has in production. Workers, for example, fear an increase in monotony—increasingly a function of industrialisation. Psychologists can address such fears by studying the many unanswered questions relevant to the experience of monotony. How important are personality factors, level of education, the presence of outside interests? She cites the example of an "admirable student" of her own with a monotonous job in the Post Office who feels his work is having a "terrible effect" on him, making him feel he "must shout or punch somebody". Workers, she suggests, wish to find a true vocation for themselves. Indeed they speak of "vocational tests" with derision, as really just assessing suitability to carry out a mechanical operation. Such an attitude, she protests, is unhelpful.

This is a complex area in which psychology, ethics and economics are "inextricably interwoven". Across the board, in the analysis of social behaviour, of educational methods, and of psychopathology there is revealed the need for self-fulfilment. She cites in support the example of the work of Maria Montessori in the education of young children, in the understanding of crime and in what she calls the misdemeanours of adolescence.

She concludes by asking some big questions, "Is it psychologically possible to have docile, externally controlled workers in industry who are yet free, intelligent and responsible members of a democracy outside it?" She has found that student workers as well as students of politics and social conditions have put such questions to her. Psychologists must face and attempt to answer them.

"Workers" she concludes with stirring words, "come to psychology as to the human science, the science which, whatever else may be prostituted to meaner ends, will, of its essence consider the whole man, in all his relations. It is for us, more than for any other science to lend our knowledge for the re-creation, not only of industry but of human society. To do this we must see the lesser in relation to the greater, and keep our vision whole."

Clearly, Susan saw a future for industrial psychology, but it was not a future she saw for herself. Although she served on the Council of the National Institute of Industrial Psychology for a number of years and served on one or two of its advisory committees, she played no further part in the field. Instead, with her textbook out of the way, although she continued part-time lecturing in academic psychology, she became more and more involved in psycho-analysis.

In March, 1923 she gave a talk to a meeting of the British Psycho-analytic Society, and was elected a full member later that year. In this talk she discussed differences between boys and girls in their sexual development. A few months later, based on her talk, she published her first paper written from a psychoanalytic perspective in the British Journal of Medical Psychology (Brierley, 1923). The title of the paper was "A Note on Sex Differences from the Psycho-analytic Point of View".

There had already been much written on this subject, especially by Freud himself, for whom sexual development was, of course, one of the three or four central pillars of his theories. Indeed initially Freud believed that an understanding of sexual development in childhood and at puberty provided the only satisfactory explanations of human personality and its aberrations. Later, in the light of the occurrence of neuroses arising out of traumatic experiences in the First World War he needed to modify this view as clearly these could not be seen as primarily sexual in nature.

In Freud's view the infant's drive to search for pleasure in the first two years of life is first centred on the mouth (the oral phase). In the next eighteen months or so on the anus (anal phase), finally settling round about the age of three and a half or four on the genitalia (genital phase). During the first two years the child's primary love object is the mother, with the father a shadowy figure in the background. As the child, whether boy or girl, becomes aware of the father during the second year of life, a sense of rivalry for the love and attention of the mother develops. When the genital phase begins at the end of the fourth or the beginning of the fifth year of life, this feeling of rivalry turns into acute castration anxiety, centring round fear that the father will cut off the genitalia or, at least in the case of boys, the penis. Such castration anxiety was not only a normal part of development, but was essential for the emergence of creative, productive activity. The complex was normally dissolved when, after a relatively short period of time, the boy identified with his father instead of seeing him as a threat. If this dissolution did not occur there was a risk of sexual deviation and other personality problems.

Clearly this explanation does not make sense for understanding the development of girls and this posed considerable problems for Freud. He came up with various solutions none of them very satisfactory to him or, it has to be said, for many of his followers. Up to the time of Susan's dissertation, broadly speaking, he maintained that there was no or little difference in the sexual development of the two sexes until puberty. In his first full account of the Oedipus complex appearing in The Interpretation of Dreams (1900), he assumes a complete parallel between the two sexes "a girl's first affection is for her father and a boy's first childish desires are for his mother". He repeated this view as late as 1923 in The Ego and the Id, in which he says that the dissolution of the Oedipus Complex is "precisely analogous" in girls and boys.

Despite this insistence on the similarity of development in the two sexes, very early on Freud placed great emphasis on "penis envy" in girls. Early on he wrote (Freud, 1905) "It is easy to observe that little girls fully share their brother's opinion of it (the penis). They develop a great interest in that part of the boy's body. But this interest promptly falls under the sway of envy. They feel themselves unfairly treated. They make attempts to micturate in the posture that is possible for boys by their possessing a big penis; and when a girl declares that she 'would rather be a boy', we know what deficiency her wish is intended to put right". He saw penis envy in girls as normal and universal, leading normally to a feeling of inferiority, and responsible for a loosening of the attachment with the mother who is held responsible for the girl's lack of a penis. Eventually, he suggested, the wish for a penis is replaced by the wish for a child. But this is not just a feeling of inferiority. It is indirectly responsible for what Freud saw as the actual lack of achievement of girls and women in creative activities. Freud was, of course, not alone in discounting or ignoring the stigmatising effect of the widespread belief in the creative inferiority of women and lack of opportunity in explaining the fact that relatively few women achieve fame as composers or painters.

In a paper published in German only just before Susan Isaacs wrote her dissertation, Karl Abraham, a close associate and favourite disciple of Freud, described what he called "the female castration complex" in more detail (Abraham, 1920). For Abraham, the girl does not initially see herself as deficient, but later forms the idea that she once did have a penis, but it was taken away from her. She is "wounded" and in puberty, the sense of being wounded is confirmed by the first and succeeding menstruation as well as by the rupture of the hymen at first intercourse, both events being connected with loss of blood. This paper was not translated into English until 1927, but Susan spoke fluent German and was familiar with it.

She begins her own paper by pointing out that people writing about sex differences are bound to be influenced by what they would like to be the "true" answers to the questions that the topic inevitably gives rise to. Psychoanalysts are, she claims, in a better position than others to take a detached view precisely because of their awareness of this problem.

Sex differences, she suggests, exist in three categories. There are first inescapable anatomical differences, the male has sperm producing, the female egg-producing sex organs. Next there are secondary sexual characteristics—those occurring as a result of sex gland secretions, such as differences in growth, hair distribution, skin, and tone of voice. She suggests these differences occur on a continuum from extreme maleness to extreme femaleness, most people falling in between. This is a rather surprising idea and goes against common observation. Surely the vast majority of sexually mature men have to shave if they want a smooth face—the vast majority of women do not. Men and women may be more or less hairy, but, as far as facial hair is concerned, most people do not fall between the two extremes.

Susan Isaacs then goes on to suggest that the continuum of secondary sexual characteristics is also found in emotional and temperamental traits, with extreme maleness at one end and extreme femaleness at the other. She is mainly referring here to male levels of activity at one end and female levels of passivity at the other. Starting from the assumption, now regarded as questionable, that there are wide innate temperamental differences between men and women, she then goes on to explain how these differences arise by reference to the "castration complex". She suggests that the greater passivity of women needs to be examined from a developmental (she calls it genetic) standpoint if we are to understand it. A developmental approach is, she claims, precisely what psycho-analysts are able to contribute. She suggests too that the psycho-analytic approach is unique in its attempt to explain conative (or what we would call motivational) and affective (emotional) differences

Taking a developmental standpoint, she then goes on to make a number of what she regards as irrefutable statements about differences in sexual behaviour. There is "no doubt", she claims, that the "male impulse is from the nature of the case relatively active, the female relatively passive" and this complementary activity and passivity are, in part, expressions of the sado-masochistic components of the sexual impulse. It needs to be pointed out that Freud and other analysts used the term sado-masochistic in an idiosyncratic way. They used the term sadism to refer to activity, only the extreme form of which involves the infliction of pain and can be seen as a perversion. They saw masochism as passivity, and again only the extreme form would involve enjoyment of the experience of pain.

Susan acknowledges that individual sexual behaviour is often more complex than the above explanation suggests. However, she continues in confident mode, "we cannot doubt that there is an organic element in female modesty. . . . that can undergo various degrees of reinforcement and exaggeration" leading as far as an "entire unawareness of sexual desire and an entire ignorance of the facts of intercourse. . . ." More usually, modesty in girls arises, she writes, echoing Karl Abraham, from the "castration complex . . . the shame of having no penis, of having only the wound which is itself a sign of having been despoiled. . . .the menstrual flow, a confirmation of the wound theory . . . this shame is a powerful element in female modesty".

Differences in behaviour between boys and girls are not obvious in infancy. Indeed, she suggests there is no very great divergence between them in, for example, passivity and activity before the onset of adolescence. Some women, she goes on to suggest, fail to reach what she sees as normal passivity even in adulthood. "Indeed we know" she asserts, again very confidently, that it (passivity) is a condition which many women do not reach. These remain in the immature clitoral attitude of the girl child and are anaesthetic to vaginal stimulation. (It was this belief that women who could only achieve clitoral orgasm were in some way immature, whereas those who could reach vaginal orgasm had, so to speak, passed their sexual driving test, that so enraged the feminists of the 1970s. Their position was strengthened by strong evidence that clitoral orgasm was by far the most frequent route to female sexual satisfaction and that vaginal orgasm was much less usual and, in any case, was not linked to any particular evidence of maturity, sexual or otherwise.)

Susan Isaacs goes on to suggest that what she calls "ego activities" or productive activities, are always positive and energy-consuming whether performed by men or women. In men, however such ego trends are in harmony "in nature and direction with the sex impulse, whereas in the female they are in essential and perpetual conflict" with it. So for women ego or productive activity is more complicated, even (though she does not say this but infers it), unnatural.

She then discusses the significance of the "castration complex" in more detail. She makes an interesting observation that seems highly relevant to her own situation. Castration elements "undoubtedly" (that word again!) play a large part in the genesis of a state of total repression of sex interest and sex knowledge in highly educated women, where there is present a strongly marked ego development with a repudiation of even "the existence of sexual facts". It is surely likely (though I would not for one moment suggest it is *undoubtedly* true) that this observation might refer to Susan's own state before she entered psycho-analysis with J. C. Flugel and Otto Rank, when, following the breakdown of her first marriage, she was confronted with the need to consider her own sexuality. A close friend described her in adolescence as a late developer who "never indulged in flirtations" (Gardner, 1969, p. 32). "If she loved it was with intense seriousness. If anyone loved her she was almost bewildered by it."

The discussion of the details of her discussion of the different ways in which the castration complex affects the two sexes need not concern us too much. It is derived directly from the Freudian theory described earlier. Like him and other analysts at that time, she agrees that in both boys and girls the mother is the first love object. In boys this generally remains the case. However she elaborates on this position by insisting that the details of a boy's sexual develop-ment depend on the continued presence of the mother and their modification if the mother is absent. She describes the role fathers play if, for example, they are either absent or overbearing. She also describes the father's role in the sexual development of girls but does not touch on what happens if the mother is absent. This omission is particularly striking because it is precisely this situation that Susan herself faced as a child when her mother was so ill. While it is disappointing that she does not give us her views of the situation closest to her own, the omission perhaps tells us more about her continuing unwillingness at this stage of her life to face all the problems that the events of her own childhood and adolescence brought with them.

Her conclusions are largely drawn from the views I have already recounted. There is however one further "undoubtedly" that deserves quotation. One of her conclusions is that "the fact that, on the whole, women show a lesser degree of scientific curiosity is undoubtedly to be correlated with the greater degree or repression typically occurring as a general condition; and with the castration complex as a specific determinant". Where exactly this puts Susan herself, a woman whose sister attributed her success as a psychologist to her insatiable curiosity (IoE S1 A1) and yet who was herself apparently so sexually repressed, is puzzling. One wonders how she reconciled this statement with her own life and personality.

In the report of the meeting held on March, 1923 of the British Psycho-Analytic Society at which Susan gave her paper on sex differences in development it is noteworthy that there is no report of any discussion. In the account of meetings at which other papers were given, it was nearly always reported that, after the presentation, there had been an "interesting" or "very interesting" or "full" discussion, often with some account of the main points that had come up. Following Susan's paper there is no such additional information. This may have been because she left no time for discussion, but it is also possible that the members of the Society did not think there was anything very original in what she had said that was worth discussing. If this was the case, they were wrong. Although a large part of her published paper does indeed regurgitate orthodox Freudian views on the subject, she may have been the first analyst to emphasise the differences that arise if family structure is unusual or if the behaviour of one or both parents is unusual.

In reading this paper at the beginning of the twenty first century, one is first struck by its supremely confident tone. The idea, questionable to many, that psycho-analysts are, because of their awareness of the importance of the unconscious, in a privileged, indeed uniquely superior position to discover psychological truths was, of course, not new and has been repeated countless times since. It is nevertheless striking that Susan, whose academic writing otherwise is a model of caution, should have expressed herself in such, for her, uncharacteristically confident, not to be contradicted mode. One wonders why she felt the need to do this.

One reason might be that she felt that there was no theory other than the psycho-analytic that was making any attempt to explain sexual differences in development. It is indeed the case that psycho-analysis held an undisputed monopoly in this respect. But the fact that psycho-analysis provided the only available well-worked out theory of sex differences does not mean that it was necessarily valid and indeed it was only a very short time before it was seriously challenged from within psychoanalysis. In 1924, the year following the publication of Susan's paper, Karen Horney, a Berlin psycho-analyst who emigrated to the United States at the beginning of the 1930s, was among the first to do so. In a series of papers with titles such as the "Genesis of the Castration Complex in Women" (Horney, 1924) she criticised the concept of penis envy as a universal female phenomenon though she acknowledged its presence in some neurotic women. She, like Susan Isaacs, believed that female sexual development was much influenced by upbringing and by social circumstances. Her lead was followed by a number of analysts working in the United States such as Harry Stack Sullivan and Erich Fromm (Brown, 1963).

Susan Isaacs's suggestion that it is against their natures for women to have a career is surprising, indeed astonishing when one remembers the speeches she had given in support of female employment in student debates at Manchester University just over a decade beforehand. It seems that, while a strong proponent of equal rights for women in the work setting, she felt that women, to achieve parity, had to strive harder than men, not only, as would be thought today, because of the competing demands of maternity and the upbringing of children, but because their sexual development, if this were "normal", clashed with their need to be proactive in their career.

Finally in considering this paper, one is struck by the absence of any observations drawn from her experience as a teacher of young children. After all, though a small number of other members had worked as teachers, she probably had had more contact with young children than all the male members of the British Psycho-Analytic Society put together. Why does she not refer to this? The answer lies in the fact that, at that time, and the tendency has continued, though to a lesser extent, psycho-analysts regarded clinical observations and evidence derived from psycho-analytic interviews as the only type of evidence worthy of inclusion in scientific papers. Susan does give one or two case examples, for example of a little girl who showed serious behaviour problems, cut off her hair and announced she was now a boy. She was discovered at one point to be in the act of swallowing her brother's whistle, saying "I didn't like the noise, so I hid it in myself." Perhaps this is, as Susan suggests, clear evidence of the existence of a castration complex in this girl, but it would have been interesting to read of such evidence in less seriously disturbed children drawn from her teaching experience.

By the end of 1923, when she became a full-time member of the British Psycho-analytic Society, Susan was continuing to combine part-time lecturing in psychology with private psycho-analytic practice mainly with children and adolescents. Referrals were made to her by colleagues in the Society, from doctors sympathetic to psycho-analytic treatment and from friends who asked her to see their children. Treatment involved seeing patients for up to five times a week for fifty minutes, often for years at a time, so only a small number of patients could be on the books at any one time. Bearing in mind her other commitments, she was probably only seeing three to four children at a time. These activities were not bringing in substantial sums of money, but Nathan had a well-paid, responsible job in a reputable firm of metal dealers so the couple were reasonably comfortably off. They were able to afford the rental of a flat in Bloomsbury, go on continental holidays and think of moving to a larger flat. They were however not wealthy. For example, at one point Susan contemplated training to be a doctor (Gardner, 1969, p. 52) so that she could add medical status to her practice as a psycho-analyst, but she decided that this would place an unfair financial burden on Nathan and gave up the idea. All the same, life was settled and comfortable. It was not to remain so for long.

By 1923, thirty eight years old, Susan had now found in psycho-analysis an ideology that satisfied her. She was married to a man who fulfilled her need for intellectual discussion. Soon she was to be able to gratify a further wish; she was to find a mission in life.

Note

1   Chaim Weizmann in a statement dated 25 November, 1938. Archive, University of Manchester John Rylands Library, Alex/B/4/61.

CHAPTER FIVE

The Malting House School: a dream becomes reality

On 24 March, 1924 the following advertisement appeared in the *New Statesman*. Versions of the same advertisement had appeared in *Nature* and the *British Journal of Psychology*.

"WANTED—an Educated Young Woman with honours degree—preferably first class—or the equivalent, to conduct education of a small group of children aged two and a half to seven years, as a piece of scientific work and research.

"Previous educational experience is not considered a bar, but the advertisers hope to get in touch with a university graduate—or someone of equivalent intellectual standing—who has hitherto considered themselves too good for teaching and who has probably engaged in another occupation.

"A LIBERAL SALARY—liberal as compared with research work or teaching—will be paid to a suitable applicant who will live out, have fixed hours and opportunities for a pleasant, independent existence. An assistant will be provided if the work increases.

"They wish to obtain the services of someone with certain personal qualifications for the work and a scientific attitude of mind towards it. Hence a training in any of the natural sciences is a distinct advantage.

"Preference will be given to those who do not hold any form of religious belief, but this is not by itself considered to be a substitute for other qualifications.

"The applicant chosen would be required to undergo a course of preliminary training, 6–8 months in London, in part at any rate the expenses of this being paid by the advertisers.

"Communications are invited to Box No. 1."

95

The man responsible for placing this remarkable advertisement was a 29 year old speculator on the London metals market, Geoffrey Pyke. The mixture of creativity, imagination and arrogance that shone through the wording was characteristic of this young city trader (Lampe, 1959).

Geoffrey was born in 1894, one of the four children of Lionel Pyke, a successful and well-to-do Jewish barrister with political ambitions and his wife, Mary. Lionel stood for Parliament as a Radical candidate in 1895, the year after Geoffrey's birth. In 1899, when Geoffrey was only five years old his father suddenly and unexpectedly died. Geoffrey was the second-born child, but he was the oldest boy in a Jewish household, and after his father died, his mother told him that he must now act as the head of the household.

Money was tight, but there was sufficient for Geoffrey to be educated at boarding school, and Wellington was selected. This could not have been a more unfortunate choice. Geoffrey was tall and gangly, obviously Jewish in appearance, clumsy and bad at games, and, worst sin of all in the aggressively anti-intellectual environment of the English public school, extremely bright. His mother insisted that he observed the Sabbath and that his diet was restricted along kosher lines. Wellington was traditionally the school to which army officers sent their sons to be prepared for Sandhurst and then go on to commissions in the smarter regiments of the British and Indian Armies. It was probably no more anti-semitic than most upper-class English establishments at that time, but that was enough to make Geoffrey's life a nightmare. He was a victim of schoolboy pogroms, sometimes called "Jew Hunts" or "Pyke Hunts". Eventually, when he was fifteen years old, he was withdrawn from the school.

He was then tutored at home before gaining admission to Pembroke College, Cambridge, in October, 1912, to read Law. At Cambridge he did little work, but was a friend of C. K. Ogden, later well known as a writer and linguist, and Philip Sargant Florence, an American reading economics, later Professor of Economics at the University of Birmingham. Geoffrey left Cambridge after a year at the outbreak of the First World War in 1914 without sitting for his degree. He tried to obtain work as a journalist and eventually persuaded the news editor of the *Daily Chronicle* to allow him to get into Germany and send reports back from there. The news editor was baffled as to how he would enter Germany without being picked up as an enemy alien, but agreed to publish stories if they arrived. Twenty year old Geoffrey bought an American passport from a sailor in the East End of London, trained in a printing works and succeeded in getting into Germany in late September, posing as an American printing machine salesman.

Within a week he had been picked up by the German security forces and was placed in solitary confinement in prison. He expected to be shot as a spy. However one of his guards reassured him with the words "We don't shoot babies". After nearly four months he was sent to the civilian internment camp in Ruhleben, on the outskirts of Berlin. He and another inmate, a 40 year old clerk called Edward Falk, who had been trapped in Germany on holiday at the outbreak of war, determined to escape. After a daring breakout and journey by train to Bielefeld, followed by an eighty mile walk to the Dutch border, they managed to get back to England.

Arriving back home, Geoffrey discovered his escape was already big news. A despatch he had sent back from Amsterdam had been published under the banner headline "DAILY CHRONICLE CORRESPONDENT ESCAPES FROM RUHLEBEN". His was one of a very small number of successful escape attempts during World War One. He published a moderately successful book based on his experiences and then tried to obtain work in publishing, but achieved most success helping literary magazines, such as the Cambridge Magazine, edited by his friend, C. K. Ogden. His value to the magazines lay in the fact that he was able to work out ways to circumvent restrictions imposed by paper rationing. In 1918 he married Margaret Chubb, the daughter of a Hampshire doctor.

After the war ended Geoffrey began to speculate on the commodities market, at first with little success, but later, on the Metal Exchange, with much greater profit. He made a great deal of money and, by 1921, at the age of twenty seven, he was a rich man. In that year a son, David, was born to Geoffrey and Margaret. Geoffrey immediately began to worry how he would organise a better education for his son than he felt he had received himself.

He first approached Philip Sargant Florence, the economist friend he had made at Cambridge who had now married and had two young sons. Geoffrey proposed that one of these sons should move into the Pyke household to be company and provide intellectual stimulation for his own son, David. Florence regarded this as a ridiculous proposition and turned it down. Geoffrey then decided that the only way he was going to obtain for his son the sort of education he thought appropriate was to found a school himself, run along lines that he himself approved; hence the advertisement.

Why did Pyke wish to send his three year old son to school and why, as was clearly the case, did he think no existing school was good enough? Although he had made a great deal of money by his mid-twenties, and had entered into an apparently happy marriage, Pyke had a restless and dissatisfied spirit. At about the time David was born he had embarked on a psycho-analytic treatment with James Glover, one of two medical brothers, both of whom were founding members of the recently formed British Psycho-analytic Society. The analysis did not go well and was never completed. Apparently James Glover was so overwhelmed by Pyke's forceful personality that "he became almost an accomplice instead of a guide" (Lampe, 1959). But Pyke remained influenced by psycho-analytic ideas. He saw his son's education as a tremendous responsibility and read widely about the education of young children. His own family life had been unhappy. During his teen years he had fallen out with his widowed mother because she had tried to insist on his staying on at a school he hated. Unhappy both at school and home, he looked back on his childhood and adolescence with anger and disappointment. Increasingly, and in line with much psycho-analytic theory then current, he came to believe that his son must have a life free from trauma and repression.

When Pyke looked around he failed to find an existing school that could provide such trauma-free education. In the early nineteen twenties about one in seven children aged three to five years was in education provided by local authorities (Board of Education, 1933). Most of these were in infant departments taking children up to the age of seven years. These in turn were usually on the same premises as junior schools that took children up to the age of eleven years. In 1905 a Board of Education Circular had encouraged local authorities to set up nursery schools especially for those children living in unsatisfactory living conditions in areas of deprivation. But no state grants were made available for nursery schools until 1919, though a few were established by private enterprise. Some of these, such as the Rachel McMillan Nursery School in Deptford, London, were magnificent places (Bradburn, 1976). The Deptford school provided a healthy breakfast, and a two course dinner. There were opportunities for free play, music and games. A school nurse on the premises and a visiting doctor provided health checks. The teachers were all qualified and there was a flourishing mothers' club. But such places were very much the exception. More often nursery age children in local authority provision were educated in run-down premises in classes of 40–50 children with one quite possibly unqualified teacher and a fifteen year old helper. In around 1904 and there was little evidence the situation had changed since then, an Inspector had written about the activities carried out in such schools (Board of Education, 1933, p. 31)

> Kindergarten occupations are often distinguished by absence of occupation, for in effect it is not education that is offered, nor even instruction in anything but drill, the children being kept idle, silent and still for long intervals, while the teacher inspects the last little act that she has imposed upon the class by word of command.

Laurie Lee described in his autobiography the infant school he attended (Lee, 1962). In 1918 he went to the local village school, a small stone barn, at the age of four. He wrote later of the tiny whitewashed Infants' room as "a brief but cosy anarchy. In that short time allowed us we played and wept, broke things, fell asleep, cheeked the teacher, discovered the things we could do to each other and exhaled our last guiltless days". Clearly it was unlikely that state provision would provide the sort of education Geoffrey Pyke had in mind for his son.

Most middle–class parents did not send their children to school until they were six or seven years old. Then, if they could afford it and the cost was not great, they would send them to private preparatory schools, usually as day pupils but sometimes as boarders. The schools were usually strong in religious teaching, sometimes with clergymen as owners and heads. Obedience to rules and regulations was rigidly enforced with the cane always in evidence and often used. Once a boy could read he was rapidly moved on to rote learning of Latin and Greek. Games on wet and windy afternoons figure prominently in the memories of those who attended these schools. Alternatively there were the remnants of "dame schools" in which unqualified women teachers taught the three Rs in what was usually a highly unimaginative manner. Neither of these seemed likely to satisfy Geoffrey Pyke.

The advertisement quoted at the beginning of this chapter might have been written with Susan Isaacs in mind. In 1924 Susan was 39 years old. Looking at the wording of the advertisement, she met pretty well all the criteria. She had a first class honours degree in philosophy. Her approach to psychology was as scientific as one could wish, and indeed she had already written an introductory text-book on the subject; in no way was she a dilettante psychologist. She was firmly atheist in her religious beliefs. The advertisement specified that a teacher training might be seen as an impediment, but would not be a bar to appointment so Susan's thorough grounding in pedagogy did not disqualify her. Even the eccentric suggestion that the ideal candidate for this headship of a new school might have "hitherto considered themselves too good for teaching", with its implication that a touch of arrogance would not go amiss, might have appealed to Susan's elitist instincts.

Shortly after the placing of the advertisement, James Glover, who knew Susan through the British Psycho-analytic Society meetings and who, until fairly recently had been Geoffrey's analyst, spoke to Susan about this opportunity and a meeting was arranged between both the Isaacs and Geoffrey (Eyken, 1969). It is clear from a letter that he wrote to Geoffrey four years later, that Nathan was involved in discussions from the outset.

The three-way discussions were passionately conducted. There was much discussion of the educational principles that should guide the running of the school and here all were in agreement. This had to be a school that would draw both on psycho-analytic theory and on the experience of the most recent progressive child-centred schools. Much time was spent in establishing the boundaries between the roles of the owner of the school, Geoffrey, and the head of the school (Gardner, 1969, p. 71). Geoffrey proposed that the relationship should be equivalent to that of a constitutional monarch and his prime minister. The head, like the prime minister, should be responsible for all organisational and teaching issues, with the owner only stepping in for the equivalent of major constitutional issues. However the head would be expected to keep the owner informed on all important matters. Although probably not discussed, it was also clear that the analogy with monarch and prime minister did not hold as far as financial matters were concerned. There would be no Chancellor of the Exchequer responsible to the prime minister. Geoffrey would hold the purse strings and be responsible for the financial viability of the school.

Susan Isaacs was immediately sympathetic to the ideas Geoffrey Pyke had for his son's education and the sort of school he wished to found for his son to attend. Her own training as a teacher in Manchester and all her subsequent reading, teaching and practice put her in direct line with the leaders in progressive education over the previous hundred years. She was, of course, highly knowledgeable about both the history and recent trends in the teaching of very young children.

The earliest pioneer of such education for children of David Pyke's age was Friedrich Froebel, a German educationist, the first to realise the potential for learning of the child under the age of five. He founded the first kindergarten in 1837 (Lawrence, 1961). Froebel was much influenced by the child-centred ideas of Johann Heinrich Pestalozzi, Rousseau's Swiss disciple, who wrote (quoted in Silber, 1960) that, as "a little seed . . . contains the design of the tree" so in each child is the promise of his potentiality. "The educator only takes care that no untoward influence shall disturb nature's march of developments." Froebel designed balls, wooden blocks, tiles, sticks and rings to demonstrate that children learn by playing. Known around the world as the Froebel Gifts or Gaben, these objects were an important part of his kindergarten. He saw their value largely in their symbolism, in the way they represented different aspects of the wider society into which the child would grow.

These ideas were extended and modified by John Dewey, a towering figure in the late nineteenth and early twentieth century history of pedagogy who was the greatest influence on Susan's educational philosophy (Gardner, 1969, p. 163) This American philosopher and educationist supported Froebel's principle of the child learning by discovery but was critical of the methods Froebel used. Although he wrote relatively little about the education of young children, in one of his articles on this subject, Dewey wrote that he thought that the kindergarten teacher should avoid being "stuck" with Froebel's materials and instead should use whatever local materials kindled the child's interests. Dewey was also critical of

Froebel's idea of symbolic learning. Instead he wanted children to learn by carrying out activities as near as possible to the real world of his home and the wider environment. Dewey (1906, p. 53) wrote:

> There has been a curious, almost unaccountable, tendency in the kindergarten to assume that because the value of an activity lies in what it stands for to the child, therefore the materials used must be as artificial as possible, and that one must keep carefully away from real things and real acts on the part of the child. Thus one hears of gardening activities which are carried on by sprinkling grains of sand for seeds: the child sweeps and dusts a make-believe room with make-believe brooms and cloths . . . All this is mere superstition.

Dewey's work had influenced J. J. Findlay, the Professor of Education in the University of Manchester who had taught Susan Isaacs while she was an undergraduate there. Findlay edited a selection of Dewey's essays on education so that they became much better known in Britain.

Susan was also aware of another major influence in turn of the century education of the young child, Maria Montessori. This powerful Italian doctor, on the basis of her experience of what were then called feeble-minded children, developed apparatus to stimulate the young child's discrimination of length, size, weight, shape, colour, and texture. Her book, "The Montessori Method" was translated into English (Montessori1912). Her ideas were favourably viewed in the Board of Education that encouraged the development of a number of private Montessori schools. The method encouraged the idea of the child having the freedom to choose the means of educating him or herself, but this freedom was felt by some to be inhibited by insistence on the use of Montessori equipment. Just before Maria Montessori's book appeared in English, the educational establishment had been attacked by the recently retired Chief Inspector of the Board of Education, Edmond Holmes (1911). In "What Is and What Might Be" he harshly criticized traditional methods of education, relying on rote learning and the strict imposition of severe discipline. Instead he wanted to place much greater emphasis on education through the stimulation of children's own interests. He described a school in Sussex which ran along such lines at which the children actually enjoyed their education and made remarkable progress.

By the early 1920s then when Geoffrey Pyke and Susan Isaacs met, child-centred education had entered the mainstream of educational ideas but certainly not the mainstream of educational practice, private or state. This was not to happen until well after World War Two, a generation later. Just before and immediately after the First World War however, progressive education received consider- able impetus from another source, the theosophists. Their beliefs, stemming from the teachings of Madame Helena Blavatsky, a Russian mystic and Rudolf Steiner, were first taken up in Britain by Mrs. Annie Besant (Nethercot, 1961). This ex-vicar's wife with a penchant for good causes moved in the last quarter of the nineteenth century from devout Christian belief through secular socialism and Fabian Society membership to militant trade unionism and then to a firm belief in a highly spiritual form of theosophy. This was based on belief in "an immutable, all-pervading principle which pre-exists creation and from which the universe, spirit and matter, growth and decay, all flow". The theosophist's task is to deepen and extend his or her spiritual life. By the First World War there were hundreds of branches of the Theosophical Society, many in Britain.

In 1914, Mrs. Beatrice de Normann, later Mrs. Beatrice Ensor, founded the Theosophical Educational Trust which established or took over several schools (Jenkins, 1989). The aim of these schools was to form miniature communities—co-educational and run on democratic lines. They were taught to have a deep appreciation of nature. Eurhythmics provided physical exercise and brought the child into harmony with music and the arts more generally. In 1921, largely inspired by the theosophists, Beatrice Ensor set up the New Education Fellowship (NEF). Its principles were child-centredness, freedom, individuality and growth, self-government, co-operative learning and co-education. Over the next five years the NEF with its journal New Era became a powerful vehicle for the dissemination of progressive ideas in education. The theosophist influence was rapidly replaced by a more secular, indeed anti-religious stance but the principle of child-centredness remained all-important. The NEF was joined by a number of those who had earlier pioneered child-centred learning in progressive public schools for secondary age children, such as Abbotsholme, Bedales and King Alfred School, Hampstead (Skidelsky, 1969).

This progressive educational movement gradually came in contact with psycho-analysts and psycho-analytic ideas. Sigmund Freud had, in the early years of the twentieth century, advocated a more open, permissive, less harshly disciplinarian approach by parents to child upbringing than had been the rule in nineteenth century Vienna and Victorian England. He had however stopped short of suggesting that such permissiveness should form part of public education. Indeed, his daughter Anna who became the orthodox expert on child development and education in the psycho-analytic movement (Dyer, 1983), was vehemently opposed to any suggestion of full openness, for example in relation to sex education in schools (Freud, 1927).

Some teachers had however taken Freud's message to mean that educational methods needed to move towards approaches where children decided themselves when and what they were going to learn; it was the teacher's job to assist this process not to direct it. Logically this meant there should be more freedom and less discipline. The teacher who personified this approach most closely was Alexander Neill or A. S. Neill as he was known in the educational world or Neill, Neill, Orange Peel as his pupils later called him (Neill, 1972; Hemmings, 1973). Born in 1881, Neill, who trained as a teacher or dominie in Scotland before the First World War, rapidly came to the conclusion that schools, as then organised, did not meet the needs of children. He was wounded in the war and was admitted to Craiglockhart, the hospital where WHR Rivers was using psycho-analytic methods to treat war neuroses. Much influenced by Freud and more particularly by Reich and Stekel, the most libertarian of the Viennese psycho-analysts, he also became active in the NEF. For two years from 1920 to 1922, he was Assistant Editor of New Era. He then left to teach in Germany, before long establishing his own school, Summerhill, run along highly permissive lines, first near Dresden, Germany, then in Lyme Regis, Dorset and finally in Leiston, Suffolk. For the whole of the rest of the twentieth century and indeed up to the present day, Summerhill has represented an extreme form of permissiveness that has involved not just child-centred but child-directed education.

At first alongside, but soon to be closely integrated into progressive educational ideas, came a new, persuasive and confident voice from the psycho-analytic world to which Susan Isaacs belonged and with which Geoffrey Pyke was very familiar. This belonged to Melanie Klein whose ideas became almost immediately attractive to British psychoanalysts. Although she later modified her views, in the early nineteen twenties, Klein was very firmly in favour of the application of ideas derived from psycho-analysis to education. In 1921 she published a paper entitled "The Development of a Child", the first part of which was sub-titled "The Influence of Sexual Enlightenment and Relaxation of Authority on the Intellectual Development of Children" (Klein, 1921).

Klein begins by asserting that the idea of enlightening children on sexual matters was gaining ground, especially among those who realised that ignorance in such matters was dangerous. But enlightenment would not be necessary if only, as was clear from "the irrefutable conclusions (ibid., p. 1) to be drawn from psycho-analytic experience" children were protected from any over-strong repression of their natural impulses in order to prevent subsequent mental illness or distortion of character development. In every case seen by psycho-analysts, the cause of their problems could be found in "repressions of childish sexuality". In order to achieve this result, it was necessary to remove from adult society the "dense veils of secrecy, falsehood and danger spun by a hypocritical society" that currently do so much damage.

Removing the repression of sexual expression in children would (ibid., p. 2) lay the foundation of "health, mental balance and the favourable development of character" but as well as this advantage for "the individual and the evolution of humanity" there would be another significant advantage—improvement in the development of intelligence. She then goes on to describe a boy she had analysed, whom she called Fritz. (This child was later identified as her own son, Erich.) She claims that, as a result of honestly and fully answering his questions about God, existence, and about his own urine and faeces, his intellectual development had been enhanced. We should not therefore (ibid., p. 26) refuse expression to any child of his "awakening sexual curiosity and shall satisfy it step by step, even—in my opinion—withholding nothing". Physical punishment and threats are to be avoided, and obedience secured by occasionally withdrawing affection.

She then concludes (ibid., p. 45) with the sweeping claim not previously made by other psycho-analysts, certainly not by Sigmund or Anna Freud that "no upbringing should be without analytic help". She admits this drastic view is based on only one case, but feels supported by much additional observation and the experience of others. This does not mean however that already established "good and approved principles of education" should be discarded.

Later in the paper Klein concedes (ibid., p. 45) that there may be entirely healthy, excellently developed people and even children without neurotic traits who have not undergone psycho-analysis, but their numbers she calculates are "comparatively few". Finally (ibid., p. 53) she asks:

> How can upbringing on psycho-analytic principles be carried out in practice? ... I would like here to make a suggestion. ... I mean the founding of kindergartens at the head of which there will be women analysts. There is no doubt that a woman analyst who has under her a few nurses trained by her can observe a whole crowd of children so as to recognize the suitability of analytic intervention and to carry it out forthwith.

This final proposal must have sounded most attractive both to Geoffrey Pyke and to Susan Isaacs who was probably at that time the only qualified infant and primary school teacher who was also a qualified psycho-analyst. The idea, coming from such an authoritative source, that a person with this double qualification would be ideal to run a kindergarten, must have been extremely encouraging.

Susan Isaacs's own educational approach was probably best expressed in an unpublished paper she wrote in 1926 (quoted in Eyken, 1969, p. 39):

> "One of the most far reaching changes of thought in human history is the modern view of the freedom of children as the basis of education. This is the great experiment of our age. Merely to give a vague and general freedom is, however, not enough. We must also observe what children do under free conditions, and study the laws of growth, so as to be able to meet their needs in detail.

In her view children's own natural ripening and immediate discoveries come first and ability to profit by instruction only later (ibid., p. 40). Parents and teachers cannot do more than provide rich opportunities for early development, both because they have far less means of knowing what is going on in the minds of children in the earliest years than they have later, and because language, which is an essential part of instruction, is unsuited for the communication of knowledge and experience until these later stages are reached.

Essentially her view was that children learn best when their natural curiosity leads them in a particular direction. Because their curiosity is most likely to be stimulated by the real world around them, it is the educator's task to provide them with an environment that contains elements of this real world. Teachers should interfere as little as possible with the direction in which children's curiosity leads them but should facilitate their learning by being constantly available to answer their questions. Teachers should also ensure that as few constraints as possible should be put in the way of children that might limit their freedom to explore their environment

Geoffrey Pyke had very similar ideas to Susan but was particularly interested in the creation of outstanding scientists. According to Nathan (Eyken, 1969, p. 20)), Geoffrey

ranks the scientist, or correlator, as he is fond of calling him, highest among human types. He does not want to make scientists, because he does not want to do any "making" at all. He does not set up his idea of what a child should be made into against other ideas. He does not want to limit a child's future by his own any more than any other past. Moulds are wrong, whosoever they may be; and shaping is wrong, whatever it may aim at. That, at any rate, is the assumption of his experiment: he may hope it will lead in one direction rather than in another, but it is the experiment that must lead.

Geoffrey believed that children's natural curiosity was taken away from them in British schools, contravening the principle that learning best takes place when preceded by discovery. So he wanted the adults in his school to be "co-investigators", helping the children investigate and giving them the sensation that they were discovering a new world for themselves. He even wanted children to be able to question the names of things. Should one of them ask what a tree was, the answer would not be "That is a tree", but "Shall we call this a tree?" (Lampe,1959).

Once the discussions between Geoffrey Pyke and Susan Isaacs had reached sufficient agreement, Geoffrey rented the Malting House and moved into it with his wife, Margaret and his son, David, in the summer of 1924. It was, and indeed remains, a large rambling residence situated in Malting House Lane in Cambridge, a little to the west, but still quite close to the backs of Kings and Queens Colleges. It was owned by Dr. Hugh Frazer Stewart, Dean of Trinity College, whose wife had run morris dancing classes for Cambridge male undergraduates in the large hall.

Susan later described the way the building was adapted for use as a school (Isaacs, 1930a, p. 14). The teachers and children,

aged at the beginning between three and seven years, met in a large hall, from which easy steps ran to the garden, where there was plenty of room for running and climbing, for communal and individual gardening, and for various sheds and hutches for animals. The garden had two lawns and plenty of trees, many of them bearing fruit. The large hall had a gallery with stairs at each end, and a low platform, on which the piano stood. The horizontal framework supporting the roof made excellent bars for the children to hang on or climb up to.

Beside the large hall, there were four smaller rooms as well as a cloakroom and a lavatory. Part of the cloakroom was used as a kitchen by the children; the gas cooker and shelves and tables for crockery and cooking utensils were kept there. The large hall was used for general purposes as well as for music and dancing. In the first year, one of the smaller rooms was used as a rest room, and another as a reading and writing room for the older children of the group.

Later on, one of the rooms became a quiet room for the older children, with shelves for the school library, and the general reading and writing equipment. One large room was fitted up as a combined carpentry room and science laboratory. (The children at one stage called this the "cutting up room" as most of their biological work was done there.) The third was a handicraft room with equipment for modelling, drawing and painting; and the fourth, a quiet room for the smaller children, in which reading and writing materials suitable for them were kept as well as movable tables and chairs. The school was attached to a house, in which the children who were in residence lived. The cooking of the mid-day meal was done in the house (unless the children did it themselves), and handed through a hatchway to the schoolroom. During the third year, several of the children lived in another house, St. Chad's, about five minutes walk away, with a large garden of its own. Each living-in child had a bed-sitting room of his own.

The striking feature of this description of the school is the lack of any mention of classrooms, and in fact there were none. However there was plenty of space in the garden and an abundance of stimulating equipment whose use the children could explore for themselves. In the garden there was a sandpit with a water tap, a tool-shed, a summer house with roof and open sides, a see-saw (which had detachable weights hung at intervals underneath), sliding boards, movable ladders, and a "Jungle-gym" climbing cage.

The indoor equipment included (ibid., p. 15) paints, both artist's colours and "real" (housepainter's) paints with suitable brushes, rolls of thin coloured muslin; plasterer's laths for woodwork and, later on, pieces of small timber; hammers, pincers, nails, and other tools of the proper size and weight for carpentry (including a double-handled saw for cutting up logs), bricks for building (both a variety of wooden ones, and old "real" bricks of small size for building in the garden); small movable pulleys that could be screwed in where desired; maps of Cambridge town and county; an HMV portable gramophone and selection of records; a pendulum, with movable weight, fixed on the wall. The carpenter's room in the second and third years included a lathe with a variety of tools, a drilling machine, and such oddments as a spirit level and callipers.

After the first year, Bunsen burners were fitted to the benches both in the large hall, and in the laboratory for the older children, and there were tripods, flasks, glass rods and tubing to use with them. (The supply of gas was controlled by a detachable key for each burner, so that the burner could not be used by the children unless one of the staff was there to supervise.) In the laboratory there were dissecting instruments and dishes, jars for specimens, human skeleton and anatomical diagrams.

The living animals (kept mostly in the garden) included several families of mice and rabbits, guinea pigs, two cats and a dog, a hen and chickens, snakes and salamanders, silk-worms, a fresh-water aquarium and a wormery.

There was also some formal educative material, including some Montessori equipment. The reading material included a wide variety of the "look and say" type—pictures of objects with names attached, pictures with short stories, commands, labels and so on. Much of this was made by the staff and the children as required. The older children had a typewriter and a library of suitable books.

The richness of the material available to the children is surely remarkable. Perhaps even more remarkable to the contemporary reader is the ready accessibility of such potentially dangerous equipment. One is relieved to hear that the supply of gas to the Bunsen burners was individually controlled and their use supervised. All the same, one has the strong impression that a visit from one of today's health and safety inspectors would have rapidly resulted in at least a temporary closure of the school.

All was now set for the opening; all that was lacking were the children. The school began in October, 1924, with ten boys ranging in age from two years eight months to four years ten months (Eyken, 1969, p. 25). Gradually over the next three years, while Susan was at the school, they increased in number, but only to about twenty children. Their ages naturally increased, so that by 1927, they ranged from two years seven months to eight years six months. In its second year the school began to take girls, but there were always at least four times more boys than girls.

The children came mainly from professional and academic families, and some of their fathers already were or became eminent in their fields (Eyken, 1969, p. 25). The two sons of G. E. Moore, the Cambridge philosopher and ethicist, attended. Other pupils who attended were the daughter of Edgar Adrian, later Lord Adrian, a Nobel Prize winning neurophysiologist; the grandson of Lord Rutherford; the nuclear physicist; and Tony, the son of Philip Sargant Florence, at that time a post-graduate student and later a Professor of Economics. Some who attended were friends of the Isaacs's. Thus Jack and David Pole, the two sons of Joe and Phoebe Pole, the Isaacs's closest friends, were both pupils at the school, starting there when it began to take boarders in 1925. There were also the children of two lecturers in physiology, the son of a Cambridge tailor and another of a bank manager. There were one or two children from overseas.

Not surprisingly given their genetic inheritance and their privileged, often academic upbringing, the children were very bright, much brighter than average. Evelyn Lawrence, a psychologist, joined the Malting House School in 1926 and tested all the children's intelligence shortly afterwards. She had recently studied for an economics degree at the London School of Economics, and then been attached to the Institute of Industrial Psychology, where she had learned about intelligence testing and modern techniques of interviewing. The scores ranged from106 to over 140, with an average of 131. This means that they fell, *on average*, into the top 5% of the population (ibid., p. 27).

Reading about the behaviour of the children today, one is struck by just how disturbed many of them appear. Susan wrote (Eyken, 1969, p. 27) that "It was sometimes said that the ten most difficult children in Cambridge had been sent to us." Reading the descriptions of some of them, this is not difficult to believe. One child, the son of a Cambridge don, delighted in drawing, cutting out, building and modelling, but rarely sat long enough to complete anything. Instead he ran about the rooms, laughing to himself. When he hurt himself, he never sought comfort from an adult, or one of the children, but would run off, throw himself on the floor or the stairs, bury his face in his hands and sob bitterly. When recovered, he would come back with the others again, without a word about the incident. Today such a child would probably be regarded as showing autistic spectrum disorder. The descriptions of other children suggest that a number were extremely aggressive. One, for example, developed a habit of spitting at children and for an early period was quite unable to cope with communal life. Another delighted in smashing things, and one day broke four vases in succession, picking up the pieces and smashing them again. This boy also had a streak of viciousness, once biting Susan severely. Thus the children were, on average, highly intelligent, with some, at least, showing quite severe behaviour and emotional problems.

These bright children, many of whom were emotionally disturbed, some severely so, presented a major challenge to the teachers of whom, at the beginning there were only two, Susan Isaacs herself and one other teacher. All the same, even at the end of the first term, Nathan Isaacs felt able to write "The school is going well, and one only wishes one could hurry time, and see the children so free to choose; to see what large choice they will make at last; what they will have learnt to know, what they will elect to do, who they will elect to be."

Just how the school functioned in practice, how it was perceived by the children themselves, by its staff and by outsiders and what eventually happened to it will be the subject of the next chapter.

CHAPTER SIX

Rise and fall of the Malting House School

Once the school opened its doors to pupils it was time to put the educational philosophy that Susan Isaacs and Geoffrey Pyke had worked out together into practice. The descriptions of the school by Susan Isaacs herself, by former pupils, by staff and by outsiders make it clear that the teaching practice started and remained remarkably faithful to the principles that had been laid down when the school was founded. The most striking difference from other schools was that there were no lessons. The children were left to choose their own activities from the equipment and the books that were available to them and from the rich experience to be found in the large garden. Here there was a sandpit, trees, tools, a canoe, hen houses, gardening implements and watering cans (Eyken, 1969, p. 33). Inside the house the children enjoyed making things out of plasticine, using the carpentry sets and from all sorts of other excitements like working out how the grand piano worked (ibid., p. 32).

Education went on beyond the school boundaries. The children watched an aeroplane flying low over the garden and were disappointed to find that the pilot could not hear them when they shouted up to him (Isaacs, 1930a, p. 37). However one of them wondered what they and their garden would look like from the air and this led to much activity making a map of Cambridge themselves and checking out distances and the position of the river Cam. When later Susan Isaacs said she was going to cycle to some place she had never been to before, the children were concerned she would get lost, until one of them suggested she could always look at a map. The lesson of the value of maps had been learned (ibid., p. 34).

There was an emphasis on activity undertaken spontaneously, from where the children were at rather than from adult direction. This allowed the adults to learn that the children could do more if left to explore for themselves, though with adult support. This proved instructive to Jean Piaget, the influential Swiss child psychologist, when he visited the school in March, 1927. Piaget's work with children in highly structured situations (see Chapter 7) had led him to the conclusion that the concept of mechanical causality was not within the grasp of children under the age of eight years. He and Susan Isaacs were discussing this point when a 5 year 9 month old boy came by on his tricycle (Isaacs, 1930a, p. 43). The child was asked why the bicycle was not moving forward, and pointed out it was obvious—he was back-pedalling. But what happens to make it go forward. "Oh well," he said "your feet press the pedals, that turns the crank round, and the cranks turn that round (pointing to the cog-wheel) and that makes the chain go round, and the chain turns the hub round, and then the wheels go round—and there you are!"

It was fundamental (Isaacs, 1930a, p. 45), dear to both Geoffrey Pyke and Susan Isaacs's principles that competence in reading and number work should not be formally taught, but should arise out of the activities in which the children engaged. The children should learn to read without being taught to read. The skill of reading should emerge naturally from the child's curiosity about the meaning of the printed word, and the realization that reading was a gateway to fascinating knowledge about the external world. Consequently, reading and writing at the Malting House School were solely related to practical tasks that required written communication. For example, the children who could manage it wrote out the weekly menus and the lists allocating domestic tasks such as washing up. They wrote letters to order equipment, to each other, to members of their families and to Susan Isaacs herself. They wrote whenever they had some-thing to communicate and were helped by the adults when these situations arose.

A similar approach was used with the older children when learn-ing more formal subjects such as geography, mathematics and history. Again, as far as possible, the impetus for learning was expected to come from the child and to arise from the child's own interests. Geog-raphy grew out of their country excursions and weather observations, history from their wish to learn about the origin of everyday things;

arithmetic out of the need to calculate purchases and change. Susan Isaacs accepted that "the giving of information and of definite instruction had a bigger place with the older children than with the younger" (Isaacs, 1930a, p. 47).

A fundamental belief of Susan Isaacs derived, as we have seen, from Friedrich Froebel but reinforced by the writings of Melanie Klein, was that young children largely learn through play (ibid., p. 99). As far as nursery age children are concerned, this is now so widely accepted (though not always acted upon), as to seem almost banal, yet at the time it was little short of revolutionary to educators who were wedded to rote learning as the primary vehicle to academic achievement. Susan Isaacs noted that when, as was usually the case at the Malting House School, children were free to occupy themselves as they chose, one of their main activities was make-believe play. With girls this was usually unsophisticated "family" play, involving father, mother and babies; with boys it was more likely to be "heroic" play, with policemen, soldiers, engine-drivers, bus-drivers, or, less heroically, fathers in their offices. A favourite make-believe game was shopping with each child having a pretend shop that the others and Susan Isaacs herself visited. She observed immediate direct benefit in the way play often led to greater understanding of the world, for example of the physical properties of matter. Thus "children's play in sliding down loose boards which they arranged at different angles, in using the pulleys, in putting up and taking down the trestle tables for their games of 'house' etc and in modeling stairs for their plasticine houses, provided a full variety of direct experience of mechanical facts" (ibid., p. 43). The adults, of course, participated fully in these various play experiences, indeed, as Susan Isaacs pointed out, the adult-child relations were more as fellow-workers and playmates, accompanying them in their real and imaginary experiences than as teachers and pupils.

The equipment was also used by children for scientific exploration, again undertaken with adults but also, as the philosophy of the school dictated, on the child's own initiative. In the garden, each child had their own plot to plant and look after as they wished with no direct pressure being brought on them to keep their plots in order. As the children gained in experience of plant growth, they no longer pulled up the bulbs they had planted to see how they were doing, but were prepared to wait longer. They learned that plants cannot thrive without water, because if they did not water their own plots, no one else did and their plants died. Gradually older children learned a good deal about plants, and many of them had successful, colourful gardens (ibid., p. 41).

The greatest challenge to the teachers came from the behaviour of some of the more aggressive children. The belief that children should be constrained as little as possible was heavily tested. It was not that there were no rules. Right from the start there were rules around time-keeping, about preventing children putting themselves in dangerous situations and about the limits to physical aggression between children. But otherwise the children were free to do what they wanted.

Direct refusals to comply with a request were dealt with depending on the seriousness of the situation. If children's refusal to comply might lead them into physical danger, for example if they ran out onto the pavement outside the school which was on a busy road, the adults would physically carry them back. But less serious infringements, that put the child in no physical danger (such as not clearing up mess), would be dealt with by waiting until the child appeared readier to comply or, if the child was tired, by helping the child to clear up (ibid., 23 et seq.)

Meal-times were used (ibid., p. 23) both as a means of encouraging the children to exercise choice, and as a way of helping them to learn about time-keeping. After the first year the children took turns in choosing the menu at the beginning of the week. This gave the cook the necessary notice to go out and buy the ingredients. If the children failed to choose, then they had to be prepared to eat whatever the cook had the time to prepare in short notice. This does not seem to have worked out as well as might have been hoped. Mary Ogilvie, a junior housekeeper at St. Chad's, recalled some years later (Eyken, 1969, p. 38) that ". . . the staff believed that it was revealing of children's behaviour to try and make them order the meals themselves, and when they forgot, as they were bound to do, to give them only apples and oranges. This happened time after time, and, of course, being small children, they often forgot. I felt that the experiment went on for too long. . . ." Many years later, one of the former pupils (S. Elmhirst-Isaacs, personal communication) commented on this approach ". . . we had to choose the mid-day meals (we took it in turns). The children tended to choose the same thing over and over.

Mostly children chose chicken. It must have been monotonous for the adults." Teaching the children about time-keeping through an arrangement of regular meal-times was more rewarding. The children were always given a few minutes notice, as was the case with all interruptions to their activities. If they were late, they just had to have a cold dinner and, though this happened very rarely, if someone was very late, the tables were cleared away and the child was left to finish his meal alone.

Considerable emphasis was placed on the avoidance of commands; "you must do this" or "you must do that". Indeed the staff was encouraged only to consider the use of the word "must" in its causal sense. . . . "if you build a tower with bricks as high as that then it must fall over". The word "must" was never used in its moral sense. How then were the rules—for there were rules such as one that involved washing up dirty crockery—how were such rules enforced? The approach taken was to leave it to the child to learn by experience the effects of breaking the rule. Susan Isaacs describes, for example, how a child of four and a half would not wash his cup after he had drunk some milk. For the next two days he got no milk as all the other cups were in use and his remained too dirty to use. When he did go to wash the cup he found the dregs in "an advanced state of decomposition", and was both interested and disgusted. He needed no further reminders (Isaacs, 1930a, p. 29).

Evelyn Lawrence, the psychologist who was recruited to the school after it opened, described (Gardner, 1969, p. 64) other limits to the permissive atmosphere.

> . . . Discipline is very free. There is no punishment, and little admonition. Prohibitions, when unavoidable, are of particular acts, not of whole classes of conduct. It is not true, however, that the school is entirely run without rules. It is generally understood that material used shall be put away. If the user (as often happens) is reluctant to clear up at once after his game, he is allowed to wait until he feels more inclined. But the matter is not forgotten, and sooner or later he usually agrees to put back what he has used in its place. Another rule is that implements must not be used as weapons. If this happens, the weapon is gently but firmly taken away. No anger, however, is ever shown by the teacher. If the two participants in a serious

quarrel are unevenly matched, there is intervention on behalf of the one who is at a disadvantage, so that the weaker child can feel he can get just support.

Lawrence wrote (Gardner, 1969, p. 65) that there were three main advantages to the relative lack of constraint . . .

In the first place you can get to know your children. Under the old disciplinary methods, the educator knew his pupils only very partially and mistakenly. The child was forced to wear a mask of seemliness and respectability in the presence of grown-ups and behind that mask his own inner life bubbled unseen. Here the children's crudities, the disorder or their emotions, their savagery even, are allowed to show. Emotional troubles can then be dealt with scientifically, or allowed to straighten themselves out, as they so often do, given time.

Secondly, the danger of driving strong emotions underground to work havoc in the unconscious is avoided. The open expression of sexual interests is allowed, but where possible they are canalized by being turned into scientific channels. This freedom entails a certain amount of unpleasantness for the grown-ups. It is useless to expect children to be free at times, and at others to exercise discretion in situations where discretion is usual. But one cannot have it all ways, and it is time conventional parents learnt that their children are not the little angels they had believed. Hostility, another uncomfortable passion, is allowed freedom of expression. If the Malting House children hate a person, they tell him so. It is then possible to investigate the reason for that hatred, and probably to remove it. Fights and squabbles often occur, and if the fighters are fairly evenly matched, they are left to work out the adjustment themselves.

This brings me to the third advantage of freedom. With conventional discipline, the child is kept wriggling under the dead weight of adult disapproval and prohibition. Here, his position is that of a fencer, continually adapting himself to the shifting conditions of the group mood. This is what he will have to do in adult life, and it is surely a mistake to make all his social adjustments for him until adolescence and then pitch-fork him into the world to discover from the beginning how human relationships work. When you have fought with another person over a thing, you realize that his desires are as strong as your own, and also, eventually that fighting is not the best way of settling differences. The result of this policy in the school is not anarchy. I have seen several children combine to prevent conduct which they rightly considered unjust, and I have seen children of the most forcible character voluntarily submit to the leadership of a weaker-natured child.

Was discipline really so lax in the school? Sometimes the account of a school given by those who run it accords poorly with descriptions given by outsiders. However it does seem as if the account given by Evelyn Lawrence of the absence of authoritarian use of prohibitions is accurate. James Strachey, the psychoanalyst and translator of Freud, wrote to his wife, Alix, who was in Berlin, undergoing analytic training herself, on 17 February, 1925. He reported a conversation he had had with Lella Florence, Alix's sister-in-law, whose son, Tony, was attending the school at that time. Strachey writes five months after the school opened (Meisel and Kendrick, 1986) about a visit he had made to the school:

I must say I can't see the point of it. There seem to be about 8–10 children, of ages from 3 to 5 1/2. And all that appears to happen is that they're allowed to do whatever they like. But as what they like doing is killing one another, Mrs. Isaacs is obliged from time to time to intervene in a sweetly reasonable voice: "Timmy, please do not insert that stick in Stanley's eye". There's one particular boy (age 5) who domineers and bullies the whole set. His chief enjoyment is spitting. He spat one morning onto Mrs. Isaac's face. So she said: "I shall not play with you, Philip,"—for Philip is typically his name—"until you have wiped my face". As Philip didn't want Mrs. Isaacs to play with him, that lady was obliged to go about the whole morning with the crachat upon her. Immediately Tony appeared Philip spat upon him, and in general cowed and terrified him as had never happened to him before. That may be a good thing; but it doesn't precisely seem to be the absence of all repressive influences.

Strachey disliked Susan Isaacs intensely, and the tone of his report might be seen to betray a certain prejudice against her. Indeed he goes on to say "However I suppose all these accounts come from a highly resistant source" but his account does have a ring of accuracy.

Ironically, it was a visit to the school by Melanie Klein, whose writings had at least partially inspired the removal of constraint from the pupils that led to some modification in the approach to discipline. Klein visited the school in July, 1925, at the end of its first year (Grosskurth, 1985, p. 138). She was greatly impressed with the school, but reinforced increasing doubts that Susan Isaacs had been feeling about the degree of verbal aggression that was permitted. This appeared to be causing intolerable pain to some of the victims and guilt in the aggressor (Gardner, 1969, p. 68). Subsequently more firmness was exercised in this respect, though "the children were still allowed much more freedom of speech, of movement, of enterprise and of experiment that most schools gave them at that time" (Gardner, ibid., p. 68).

By the end of the first year, Susan was able to write positively about the effect of the disciplinary regime and the general social feeling among the children. "With the exception of B., the individual aggressiveness of the children has grown much less, the pleasure of co-operative occupation and the application of simple rules insisted upon very much greater, the most striking instance being the rule that one set of material must be put away before another is brought out. At the end of the first term all the children appreciated this and rarely refused to comply with it" (Eyken, 1969, p. 34). Evelyn Lawrence confirmed this positive account of the school. She wrote (Gardner, 1969, p. 61) in glowing terms:

> . . . the most striking difference between this school and any other I have known . . . is the happiness of the children. Not that I have not been in happy schools, but I have never seen such pleased concentration, so many shrieks and gurgles and jumpings for joy as here. Of course this joy is particularly apparent because its expression is not hindered. If you want to dance with excitement you may. . . . It is delightful to be in a school where the usual answer to the question "May we do so-and-so?" is "Yes" instead of the almost automatic "No" one finds oneself expecting.

In general later reports of children who had been at the school confirmed these positive impressions. One former pupil described (Eyken, 1969, p. 37) a conversation he had had with Geoffrey Pyke at about the age of five years. "It was an intensively enjoyable experience for me and I remember thinking as I left what a marvellous conversation it had been." Another recalled that "it all just seemed great fun at the time. I do remember climbing trees, and, in particular, helping pour molten metal into a cold bath and watching it turn into different shapes" (Eyken, 1969, p. 37). But there was one interesting exception. While up to this point children only attended on a daily basis, in its second year some children living outside Cambridge, mainly from London, were taken into the school as boarders. They lived at St. Chad's, a large house about five minutes walk from the day school. Some of the children who boarded were very young. A former pupil recounted to me nearly eighty years after he had been sent to the school as a three year old boarder from London where his home was, how terrifying the experience had been for him (Professor Jack Pole, personal communication). He told me he had never forgiven his parents for sending him away and, as he saw it, rejecting and abandoning him. Indeed he thought that the emotional effects of this traumatic separation had never left him. He still had in his possession the detailed notes that Susan Isaacs had made of his first fortnight at the school. He gave them to me and I noted that, surprisingly, they made no mention at all of any distress (or lack of it) at the separation this little boy had shown over this period. I asked him why he thought this was. Could it be that she had not noticed, or that he had covered his distress up, or that he had, in retrospect, exaggerated his emotional reaction? He said he did not know, but pointed out two observations that had been made of his behaviour eighty years earlier. "You are surely right" he wrote "that the distress I felt on being dumped at The Malting House is not reflected in the record of the next few days". But, he observed, the notes reveal his interest in means of transport, always deciding that buses cars, trains, have to go *backwards*. I suppose this has to be where they came from. The notes make no comment on the psychological significance of this need to regress- (or go home?). Both the demand and the absence of editorial comment on it seem to me significant of deeper things. When he read of his three year old self that he had thrown Geoffrey Pyke's jacket in the Cam on an outing, he reasonably concluded this might have been a sign of his aggressive feelings towards those who had taken him from his parents. Professor Pole, incidentally a historian and not a psychologist as one might have imagined from the acuteness of his insights into the situation, recalled that he had been depressed later in childhood and that Susan Isaacs had tried to arrange an analysis for him. He had refused, not wishing to have anything further to do with psychological treatment.

Not all boarders sent away at such an early age had such painful memories. Dr. Susanna Isaacs-Elmhirst (no relation), later in adult life to become a child psychiatrist and Kleinian analyst, boarded at the school from the age of four years. She wrote (Elmhirst-Isaacs, personal communication) that she remembered she had been pleased to get away from her parents whose marriage had broken up at about the time she went to the Maltings, and whose stepfather was unkind to her. She did not recall any ill effects of separation from her parents. However she added that her sister, Elizabeth (Timmy) had to be sent home from the school for "crying too much".

Considering that John Bowlby, who drew attention in the 1940s and 1950s to the importance of attachment and separation to later personality development, was himself a psycho-analyst, it is remarkable that so little attention was given by those running the Malting House School to the potentially damaging effect of separating such young children from their parents for as long as a term or three months at a time. In understanding this surprising fact, we need to bear in mind that, although Anna Freud was something of an exception, most analysts at that time, especially those like Susan Isaacs who were under the influence of Melanie Klein, were so focused on what went on inside the child's mind, they often neglected to give due importance to the emotional effect of parent-child separations. Indeed, Bowlby had great difficulty in persuading his psycho-analytic colleagues even in the 1950s that his concerns regarding such separations should be taken seriously (Bowlby, 1991). Further, in the first half of the twentieth century, middle class children were quite frequently sent off to boarding school at an early age, commonly at seven or eight, though rarely as young as three years.

Despite the apparent lack of concern regarding the effects of separation from parents on the boarders, the staff of the school had frequent and rewarding relationships with parents of day children. Mothers and fathers came to lunch from time to time, visited the school to see how their children were getting on and participated in some of their activities, mothers with sewing and fathers with constructing models. There were also frequent reports to parents describing their children's activities and reactions.

The school was visited by a number of outsiders. One, a freelance journalist, was highly positive but was struck by the unusual nature of the experiences to which the children were exposed (Eyken, 1969, p. 52). He wrote about the way children learned about animal biology. When one of the animals died and the children wanted to know why:

How could you tell them in terms they would understand? And what is the worth of all those answers which cloak ignorance and burke enquiry? Here the reply is "Let's find out" so that the children have grown used to looking for the answers to their questions. Thus, quite simply and naturally, the little dead creature was dissected. They learned far more than the cause of death. On one occasion when a calf's head had at last been successfully sawn open, one child's comment was "What a small brain!" to which a six year old scornfully added: "Well, he didn't use it much!"

While she was working at the school Susan Isaacs talked rather little in public about the school, but she did have what seems to have been a more ambivalent contact with a discussion group of Cambridge intellectuals. These had all had some psychoanalytic experience and met regularly to discuss related topics. They consisted of "two members of the Royal Society, three others clearly heading in the same direction, one literary person . . . all Cambridge graduates". They invited Susan Isaacs to talk about the school. She attended a number of times. John Rickman, a psychoanalyst, described her arrival at the group (Rickman, 1950).

. . . she came across the lawn . . . as the company assembled— a sturdy figure in tweeds, a robust Lancashire girl; there was that in the vigour of her gait which put aside the fact that she was forty; she had a pale complexion, a chubby face with a mass of fair hair and bright hazel eyes. She was rather short, and she tilted her chin, as she spoke to these distinguished people; there was a challenge in that tilt, perhaps there was also a little mischievousness in her manner but there was also a most visible friendliness; she was always ready for a chuckle. . . . she was full of gaiety and sparkle—here was an occasion she was going to rise to . . .

Rickman went on to describe the discussion when she put forward arguments for the important part that freedom played in the lives of the children and how this had to include erotic excitement as well as aggressive behaviour. One of the group questioned whether all this freedom might not reduce the later creativity of the children who would have no unconscious, repressed fantasies to drive their imaginations. Was not the school, in fact, a sort of "pre-genital brothel"? According to Rickman, Susan Isaacs was so offended by this implied criticism that she would never attend the discussion group again. James Strachey, who was present at some of the group's discussions, and who disliked Susan intensely, gives an account (Meisel and Kendrick, 1986, p. 270) of one of these meetings in a letter written to his wife, Alix:

La femme Isaacs was there and disgraced herself. In order to establish her superiority, she took the line of superciliously despising these young men who tried to explain things on purely physical lines, whereas you can really do nothing without taking into account biological factors and especially the ego-trends.

In a later letter he wrote (Meisel and Kendrick, 1986, p. 280) "I now go to Cambridge for the weekend—to Tansley's to hear Mrs. Isaacs read some notes on Child Life. I hope to be very rude to her". Perhaps Susan Isaacs felt defensive in this company and it showed. She had not felt comfortable in Cambridge when she studied there as a postgraduate in 1912–13 (Manchester University Magazine, 1912). She had disliked then the precious other-worldliness of some of the dons who had had so little experience of the sort of "real life" that one experienced in Manchester. It seems quite probable that she showed a touch of arrogance in the company of men whom she felt were so out of touch with what went on in schools for young children and was quick to take offence when they criticised her.

By the end of 1926, as it entered its third year, the Malting House School seemed well-established. The staff was stable and the number of pupils was increasing. Even the finances took an up-turn (Eyken, 1969, p. 35). Pyke was left £9,000 in a legacy from an aunt who had recently died. He decided to put this considerable sum towards the expenses of the school that was now his main interest in life.

From the time the school began, he had tried to entice Nathan Isaacs away from the metal trade in which he was engaged to play a part in the development of the philosophy of the school. Nathan's encyclopaedic knowledge and breadth of understanding of educational principles had impressed him greatly. Insofar as he understood them, Nathan's ideas were in tune with his own. He wanted the school to run on lines that were supported by an explicit philosophy and by modern concepts of the way the mind developed.

Nathan, who was passionate about the need to increase understanding about the intellectual development of children, had always been attracted to this idea, but had not wanted to commit himself, because he was unhappy about the financial basis of Pyke's dealings on the commodities market. But in the spring of 1926, Pyke made Nathan an offer he could not refuse (ibid., p. 35). On the understanding the money would come from the legacy, the two of them drew up a contract that was signed on 15 September of that year. Nathan was employed for four years to write a number of books on the theory of knowledge. In return he was guaranteed £500 a year for that period. For Nathan this was a golden opportunity. His heart had never been in the metals trade; he had always wanted to dedicate himself to philosophy. So he gave up his job in London, moved full-time to Cambridge and began to read around his subject and write. In a typically arrogant turn of phrase, Geoffrey later explained "Nathan was told to run away and read and write. He had to research for four years and if, at the end, he produced, let us say, something useful, all the better" (National Archive, Geoffrey Pyke).

Having secured Nathan for purposes of educational research, Geoffrey then decided to advertise for someone who could introduce science teachng into the school in an experimental manner. This he saw as the next step in the foundation of an Institute of Educational Research. He drafted an advertisement that spread over three columns of the Times. The advertisement or edited versions of it appeared in the New Statesman, Spectator and Manchester Guardian. It is unclear whether Susan or Nathan had any hand in helping to draft the wording; its verbosity together with the fact that Nathan had a strong interest in science teaching suggests he may have played a part. But it was probably mainly Geoffrey's work. Whoever wrote it, its insertion in the *Times* and in other newspapers must have cost a substantial sum. It is quoted at length because it provides a clear statement of the philosophy of the school.

"WANTED—A SCIENTIST of the first order, if necessary of senior standing, but as young as possible, with a knowledge of the theory of science, to investigate and conduct the introduction of young children, 41/2 to 10, to science and scientific method.

"The ability to absorb instruction depends on the emotional attitude of the child towards the process of being instructed, as well as on the inherited quality of the brain. But the discovery of the idea of discovery, and the ability to tolerate fact—which constitute the scientific attitude of mind—are the intellectual basis on which, together with the emotional factor, subsequent intellectual progress is likely to rest.

"Thus arises the need for a technique to utilize and develop the child's native curiosity in the way the wheels go round—his interest, for example, in mud and water and his pleasure in messing about—in such a way as, in the long run, to obtain the maximum conversion of these drives into a controllable instrument of organized thought.

"This involves the investigation by careful and delicate observation not only of what sort of activities are best introduced into the environment but what should be the order of opportunity for these activities. Much is done by leaving the child who prefers modeling with clay to heating mercury, or working a lathe to watching caterpillars or painting a table, to do so. But there is no such thing as absolute freedom, and the very nature of the opportunities very largely limits and dictates his activities. And it is always possible—and this cannot be decided by a priori argument, but only by observation—that to sip hastily at every flower may spoil the appetite.

"It will not be plain that this type of environment-arranging needs also the provision of specially designed apparatus. Apparatus for adolescents is too arbitrary and traditional often in the very irrelevance of its forms, is insufficiently diagrammatic, and being designed for illustration and the support of textbooks and teachers rather than for discovery, requires—as

experiments on intelligent but innocent adults will show—a pre-knowledge of its purposes . . .

"It is as yet uncertain whether there exist any special factors limiting or making undesirable the introduction of children of 4–10 to scientific knowledge and thought. That is to say, whether the apprehension of multiple and permissive causality which is painful to the human mind, with its innate tendency to accept and manufacture explanations in terms of unitary and magical causality, is in early life so much more painful that the forces— equally innate—of curiosity and intellectual aggression towards the external world would be stunted rather than stimulated. Or whether, on the other hand, it is not rather a quantitative question, as at present seems indicated— one of developing methods compatible with the child's childishness, with his need of phantasy, and of grading the demands of reality to his capacity.

"This is the main theoretical question.

"As it is hoped that the occupant of the post will, in addition to exercising and developing an art, make of the task a piece of scientific work and research, leading eventually to the publication of his result—negative as well as positive—he will need to make ample records. For this purpose the services of a shorthand-typist will be placed at his disposal.

"Certain preliminary work with children of 4–7 has already been done at Cambridge at the Malting House School successfully enough to encourage the directors of the school to make a full-time, long-period appointment specially for its development.

"They hope to make of the appointment the beginnings of a research institute into problems connected with education. Hence they are all the more anxious to obtain the services of someone of outstanding suitability for the work.

"He would need not only to be a specialist in his own branch but to have some little acquaintance with other sciences, the history of science and the history of religious beliefs. . . ."

This advertisement was also submitted to *Nature*, which initially refused to publish it (Eyken, 1969, p. 48). *Nature*, then, as now generally regarded as the foremost scientific journal, was at that time owned by Macmillan, the publishing company, whose owner, Sir Frederick Macmillan, then well into his eighties, had heard a rumour that the advertisement for the Principal of the school with which the previous chapter began (an advertisement that *Nature* had accepted for publication three years earlier), was in fact a cover for an attempt to attract young women into prostitution, or the white slave trade.

When he received the letter of refusal, Pyke was furious. He wrote letters to his solicitor and advertising agents and insisted on an interview with Macmillan himself. On his return from this visit, Pyke wrote a letter, considerably longer than the excerpt published below, to the publisher that is revealing of the extensive nature of his high-level contacts in the academic world, his family connections, the esteem in which the school was widely held, and his own remorseless energy (Eyken, 1969, p. 49).

"Dear Sir Frederick, I have to thank you for sparing me so much of your time. You will perhaps forgive me if I put into writing a reiteration of the statements I made to you, not only about the scientific standing of the Malting House School, but as regards my own personal integrity and moral position.

"The Malting House School was founded by me in 1924; the lady appointed to the position then advertised was a married lady, Mrs. S. S. Isaacs, formerly Susan Brierley, one of the Assistant Editors of the British Journal of Psychology, whose textbook on psychology is published by Messrs. Methuen; the advertisement now issued has no purpose beyond that which is carried on the face of it.

"I should like to refer you as regards my own position to . . . Sir Percy Nunn, Principal of the London Day Training College and Professor of Education at the London University. . . . In addition, I will, if you desire, ask Professor G. E. Moore, the Editor of Mind, whose two children are at the school, also to write to you about my personal standing, and, if you wish for yet a further reference on this particular point, I will explain the moral issue raised to Sir Ernest Rutherford, President of the Royal Society, whose grandchild is at the school, to give you similar reassurances. I write without previous reference to him, but I think it probable that both he and Professor Cyril Burt, Psychologist to the London County Council, would give you their opinion as to the probability of my being engaged in any improper course with reference to this advertisement.

"I may mention that Professor Nunn, who was curious as to why the advertisement had not appeared in Nature, has already offered of his own free will—since he has not had the pleasure of your acquaintance—to speak to Sir Richard Gregory. I should also be prepared to ask Professor Nicholson, Professor of Physics at Oxford, to guarantee my respectability. . . . This reminds me that I should also be prepared to refer you to Mr. J. R. Scott, of the Manchester Guardian.

"My reason for availing myself of your kindness in listening to what I had to say is the slight that its non-appearance in the pages of Nature puts upon me in the eyes of the scientific world. I may add that I have not met one of my scientific friends since the advertisement appeared who has not asked me the reason for its non-appearance in the only general scientific paper.

"I greatly trust, therefore, that despite the trouble to which I have put you, you will see your way to reviewing the decision of the Advertisement Manager.

"Should you, by any chance ever be in Cambridge at any time, I should be delighted to show you the working of the School and introduce you to the scientist for whose appointment the pages of Nature will, I trust, be responsible."

Not too surprisingly in the light of this barrage of supportive eminence, Macmillan changed his mind and Pyke received the following letter from him a couple of days later:

Dear Mr. Pyke, With reference to your visit here on Wednesday and the letters which have passed between us, I now write to say that we have decided to insert your advertisement, if you still wish it, in the pages of Nature. I am giving instructions to the Manager to insert the advertisement if it is offered again.

Regretting the inconvenience which you have been put to in this matter, I am, Yours faithfully, Frederick Macmillan.

At about the same time, Pyke decided to commission a film of the school that could be used both to attract parents to send their children there and to publicise the educational methods more widely. British Instructional Films Ltd., experienced in making natural history documentaries, were engaged. The producer, Mary Field, later described (Eyken, 1969, p. 55) the experience.

He told us exactly what he wanted and I got the impression that some of the activities had been laid on specially for us. For example, the children were dissecting Susan Isaacs' cat, which had just died, when normally they were working with frogs or dogfish. They all seemed to be enjoying themselves immensely, digging away at the carcass. Only the camera man and I were

present while this was going on and I can remember him
turning to me and saying: "It fair makes you sick, doesn't it?"
Then there was the bonfire. It was supposed to be an exercise
in free play, but it got a bit out of hand. The fire spread and
reached the apple trees, and then it destroyed a very nice boat.
Even Geoffrey Pyke was a bit upset about that and he seemed
a very calm man.

During the filming Mary Field was able to see how Susan and
Geoffrey Pyke interacted. "I got the impression that he was far more
influenced by Susan Isaacs than she was by him. He always spoke
of her with great respect, although she was often not there when we
were making the film. I personally thought Pyke was rather confused
in his thinking about children and mixed up ideas from Froebel and
Freud in a rather haphazard way. He paid for the film himself and
I don't think he ever gave a thought to how much it might cost him
or where the money was coming from." It was not an easy film to
make. One of the camera men said afterwards "In all our experiences
of photographing every kind of wild creature, not excepting cultures
of bacilli" he said, "the problem of photographing children in their
wild state proved the most difficult to tackle".

The film was shown to an invited audience of between 400 to 500
people at the Marble Arch Pavilion on 24 July, 1927. It was well
received. A journalist reported (ibid., p. 56) in the Spectator:

For a short half hour I watched children of from four to nine
years of age having the time of their lives, wading up to their
knees trying to fill a sandpit with water, mending a tap with a
spanner, oiling the works of a clock, joyously feeding a bonfire,
dissecting crabs, climbing on scaffolding, weighing each other
on a seesaw, weaving, modeling, making pottery, working
lathes—in fact, doing all those things which every child delights
in doing. At Malting House School children's dreams come true.
    The school is equipped with the most extensive apparatus,
which will stimulate the natural curiosity possessed of every
child. The system of education adopted here is precisely the
opposite to that suggested by the old moral tale of Harriet and
the matches. Not all readers may be familiar with the awful
tale of Harriet, one of the children whose misdemeanours

Heinrich Hoffman immortalized in deathless verse: *"It almost makes me cry to tell, What foolish Harriet befell"* Harriet played with matches and, in consequence, she and her clothes went up in smoke until *"She had nothing more to lose, Except her little scarlet shoes; And nothing else but these were found, Among her ashes on the ground."*

The journalist went on:

It is a system of education by discovery, aiming at the preservation of this precious gift of discovery. At present there are seventeen children at the school, some boarders and some day children, and it is hoped they will continue their education there up to university age.

No child is ever told anything he can find out for himself. For the very young children, at any rate, there are no set lessons. Reading, writing and arithmetic are learnt theoretically after their practical value has been realized. For instance, the cook would give notice if she were perpetually bothered with countless verbal requests for favourite dishes (she will only pay attention to written menus) and so the children must somehow learn to put their requests on paper.

There is no discipline. There are no punishments. Children may hit one another so long as they only use their hands, but I believe quarrels are rare and, though it seems almost unbelievable with the unending opportunities which must occur, there has never been an accident of a serious nature. The children are left to form their own opinions, tastes and moral codes. After having seen this film, I came away wishing with all my heart that my own dull schooldays had been as theirs were, and that education could be made such an adventure for every child.

The response of the audience for the film was equally enthusiastic (ibid., p. 57). Pyke and Susan Isaacs received numerous letters of support and encouragement, some enclosing donations.

Meanwhile Pyke proceeded with the recruitment of the "scientist of the first order". He claimed in an advertisement to prospective parents (ibid., p. 54) that he had received over 200 applications, including eight professors, thirteen workers in pure research, nineteen workers in industrial research, twenty-nine medical men engaged in public health and general practice, thirty-seven professional educators, forty with other qualifications and forty-seven without any qualifications. He was later to suggest, again with more than a touch of arrogance, that he had been unimpressed with the field. The man to whom the job was offered was, in fact, later to achieve considerable eminence in the United States as a child psychotherapist and a pioneer in group psychotherapy (website of New York University Archives: Guide to the S. R. Slavson Papers, 1905–1981).

Richard Slavson, also known as Samuel Richard Slavson, was a 32 year old American, born in the Ukraine, trained as an engineer, but with a strong passion for teaching science and mathematics to children. He had experience of working with children at Teachers' College, Columbia University, New York. A strongly positive recommendation from Professor Kandel, of the Institute of International Education at that College, clinched the matter. Slavson was engaged at £850 a year, a substantial salary at that time. He arrived in Cambridge in the summer of 1927 to begin work in October of that year. He was assigned, as promised, a secretary who took down verbatim his interactions with the pupils.

Some examples of these interventions have been preserved. The following interchange (ibid., p. 58) illustrates the educational approach:

10.05 am.

J. A. comes in, and goes to a middle bench where his aeroplane is resting.
"Ah, that's my aeroplane". Then he turns to Mrs. P. who has just come in.
"What are you making?" He looks about and says:
"I want to make a shelf for my Daddy, yes, that's what my Daddy wants for his stamps."
He then goes to the aeroplane and says:
"I can't imagine how this aeroplane breaks."
He feels back of aeroplane which is very insecure.
Jack comes in.
"Where's Mr. Slavson?"
He is told he is through the house side. He dashes out to find him.

J. A. fits a piece of wood which has been used before into a wood vice,
then takes a nail, and with a side stroke begins to hammer into this piece
of wood that he has fixed into a vice. He continues to talk:
    "Do you know what a nice aeroplane is?" He stops hammering and looks
about. "I'm, you see, I'm sort of making that hole, yes, that . . ." and he
begins to hammer nail in.
    Jack returns, pulling Mr. S. by the arm. "Come on, Mr. Slavson. I'm
the engine and you're the carriage" and runs around Mr. S. holding his
hand. Dillon comes in, and in a friendly way lifts Jack up in his arms, and
carries him on to the landing; the latter appearing willing.
    J. A. takes a piece of wood out of wood vice and puts it back in the wood
racking, saying: "I'm going to make something quite big. I want to . . ."
    Dillon and Jack return.
    Jack: "Mr. Slavson, I want to make a French monoplane."
    Mr. S.: "You start."
    Jack: "I know how to make it, quite easy."
    J. A.: "I'm going to make something quite big."
    Dillon leans up against middle bench with a strip of wood in his hand.
    Jack: "Mr. Slavson, have you got any long, square pieces of wood?"
    Mr. S. hands him a piece of wood with equal length and depth, and about
six inches long.
    Jack: "That's just right."
    Mr. S.: "What would you like me to do?"
    Jack: "I'd like to make an aeroplane, a huge one."
    Dillon: "I can't see a piece of wood like that. I want a piece of wood like
that."
    Mr. S.: "Do you want to come down with me and get some? John, do
you want to come down with us and get some?"
    J. A., Dillon and D. P. go down with Mr. S. to the cellar to fetch some
more wood.

11.05
    D. P.: "Mr. Slavson, the axle has come off"
    Mr. S: "Why do you think?"
    D. P.: "Because of that nail" (pointing to bent nail)
    Mr. S.: "What's wrong with that nail?"
    D. P.: "I don't know."
    Mr. S.: "Do you think it's long enough to hold that (axle) in place?"
    D. P.: "No, it's too short . . ."

It can be seen from this excerpt that Slavson faithfully follows the principle that learning should take place in the context of the spontaneous activity of the child, with the adult answering questions but providing no guidance and no information beyond that demanded by the child's question.

Whether this approach would have resulted in the production of a galaxy of creative scientists we shall never know, for it was at this point that the financial structure on which the school was founded collapsed, leading to its closure over the next couple of years (ibid., p. 61 et seq.). To understand how this happened, we need to look at the nature of Pyke's speculations, his personality, Susan Isaacs' personality, and, as we shall see, most especially the complicated relationship between Geoffrey and Susan.

Let us begin by looking at the financial issues, for it was these that delivered the coup de grace to the school's existence. Pyke made his fortune out of buying and selling tin and copper. He had a theory that the prices of these two metals were reciprocally related in a cyclical fashion, so that when one went down the other went up and vice versa. So, from a small office in Great Ormond Street, on the fringes of Bloomsbury, he and one or two assistants played the metals market to great effect.

Although at that time tin was mainly mined in Malaya, then a British colony, copper was mainly produced in South America. United States investors dominated copper dealing. At this point in time, a consortium of American investors, the Anaconda Group, determined to achieve a monopoly of the copper market, driving other speculative investment out of the lucrative trade. Pyke, who was a relatively large holder of tin, also held a significant amount of copper and was one of their targets.

In early 1927 Pyke had been hard pressed for cash because the Inland Revenue was pressing him for back payments of tax. To avoid the need to pay tax immediately, he had formed two companies, in each of which he was the main shareholder. The companies paid him a salary of £7,500 a year as "financial adviser" and empowered him to borrow sums up to £10,000 (about half a million in early twenty first century values). At this point the Anaconda group began to depress the price of copper artificially. Pyke, who had very recently bought very large quantities of tin (he claimed at some point later to hold a third of all the tin owned in Britain) needed to sell copper to pay for the tin he had bought. But the drop in price of copper made this an unattractive position. Further if he sold a significant amount of tin the price of that fell too. So he held on to both for far too long and, by the time he had to sell, the price of both fell even further.

By the end of October, 1927 both his companies had lost all their assets and the three brokers with whom he dealt were demanding payment of a sum of £70,000 (perhaps £3,500,000 in today's value) that he did not have. He was bankrupt, though he did not behave as if this were the case. Using the last of his assets, he sent £2,000 worth of cheques to Margaret, his wife, in Cambridge, instructing her to pay a year's salary in advance to all the staff of the school.

On 1 November, 1927, Margaret called all the staff together to tell them of the changed fortunes of the school. She told them that she and her husband were determined to keep the school going and would raise money from other sources to ensure it stayed open. She then handed out personal cheques: £300 to Evelyn Lawrence, £640 to Richard Slavson, £300 to Miss Clark, a teacher; £100 to Miss Irvine, another teacher; £100 to Miss Ogilvie, Matron at St. Chad's; and £40 to the cook, Miss Wilson.

It was at this point that Susan and Nathan Isaacs resigned from the staff of the school. It is not exactly clear when they left, but certainly they had departed by the end of the year. At any rate, Susan Isaacs' descriptions of interactions between pupils and staff in the books she published later, contain no entries after October, 1927.

Their resignation was the culmination of a love-hate relationship between Susan and Geoffrey that had been going on from a few months after the school had opened its doors to pupils. The best, though obviously a biased description of this mutually destructive relationship, lies in a 68 page letter that Nathan wrote to Margaret Pyke, Geoffrey's wife (IoE. N1 D2). Dated October/early November 1927, this extraordinary and at times not fully coherent document describes the emotional roller-coaster that characterized the relationship between Susan and Geoffrey in considerable and explicit detail.

It should be remembered that, after Susan contacted Geoffrey Pyke in answer to the advertisement for a Principal of the school that was inserted in March, 1924, Susan and Geoffrey had numerous vigorous discussions in the Isaacs's flat in Hunter Street in Bloomsbury, in which Nathan Isaacs was fully involved. These were highly intellectual, passionate and friendly and culminated in the agreement that Susan and Geoffrey made when she agreed to head the school. When Susan took up her post in September, 1924, in advance of the school opening in the following month, the Isaacs rented a flat in Hills Road, Cambridge, but Nathan remained most of the week in their flat in London, nearer to his work.

Susan and Geoffrey were therefore thrown together for most of the week away from Nathan in their passionately pursued joint enterprise getting the school off the ground. According to Nathan (the wronged husband)in his letter to Margaret Pyke (the wronged wife):

. . . The friendship became closer, Geoff turned more and more to Susie as a confidant, as to one who was more important to him than anyone else, as to the woman he had been looking for and hoping for all these years. Susie wasn't less drawn to him, let us say:—one can't hope in a matter of this kind to be accurate about a little more or a little less, when the feeling is in fact mutual and the relation reciprocal and that at any rate it very soon was.

So that, by Easter 1925, they were in full and open love with one another, with your blessing and active encouragement and I was told. I showed a great deal of distress, drawn from a large number of sources, some known to me then, some later on, and no doubt some not at all. At any rate an important part of the facts was that I was full of admiration for Geoff, felt myself to be quite naturally displaced, but for that very reason couldn't very easily promise to stay in the perpetual presence of this fact. Susie had to decide in the face of this state of mind of mine, whether to go on with the relation, to full completion or to arrest it where it was. Actual intercourse became the natural symbol for going on, as against leaving off. That it was only a symbol was brought out later on quite clearly, when Susie had decided to go no further, and of course I never dreamt of doubting that that decision would be kept, but was nevertheless greatly troubled to find by sign after sign that the draw they were exercising on one another was more powerful than ever. What mattered to me was the actual, irresistible turning away from me. Susie however succeeded in reassuring me about that also and in fact turned back enough to do this. But Geoff meanwhile kept pressing on and on for completion, which he made to appear essential and important for him, he acted on Susie's very real love for him, he appealed further to her on the very ground of the school (I had foreseen danger to the school in the development of the love relation as soon as I knew of it—but Geoff actually drew the school into the service of his desires). Susie had nothing to oppose except my unreasonable symbolism, she didn't feel any over-powering longing for intercourse, but she was quite ready for it and so she adopted the simple solution: she consented but withheld the unnecessary and absurd pain of knowing this from me! This was a piece of extraordinary folly (at the time I should have found bitterer names for it), as if I had found out by some chance what was happening I should have broken away instantly . . .

So by the end of 1925, Susan Isaacs and Geoffrey Pyke were in a full sexual relationship with the knowledge of Margaret, but keeping Nathan in ignorance. The sexual relationship does not seem to have lasted very long, and its cessation occurred without any immediate emotional trauma. The two continued to work together reasonably harmoniously during most of 1926. As Nathan put it:

When their love relation came to an end the school collaboration went on for a long time, successfully and satisfactorily, just to show how independent it was in source, nature and conditions from the personal affair. That went its own course, was born, grew, flourished, withered and died while the school went on like the stable objective enterprise it was. . . .

Then however, for reasons that are not altogether clear, according to Nathan, Geoffrey started to become more and more unreasonable in his behaviour towards Susan. He began to make allegations against her, suggesting it was she who had drawn him into the physical affair. He accused her of trying to keep him out of the school, taking all the credit for its success, and denying him any role. According to Nathan, these accusations were totally without foundation. How did they arise? Nathan suggests in his letter that the school had become Geoffrey's child, which he wanted to possess for himself.

(Susie) . . . dumbfounded by suddenly finding herself in the middle of a struggle for a "child", defending herself as best as she could when attacked, but long unable to understand how she came to be attacked, needing several successive unexpected attacks to understand, and several more before she saw that there would be no quarter and no mercy until she gave up her job,

which, during her normal performance of it, according to agreement and understanding, had by some witchery got turned into a lover-hater's stolen child.

There may have been other reasons. According to Nathan, on Geoffrey's own admission, he had not been a very satisfactory physical lover. Further, Susan and Geoffrey were both strong personalities. Nathan accepts that Susan could have her 'normal share of irritability', and certainly the two seem to have irritated each other immensely. However it sounds as though Geoffrey's allegations often verged on the incoherent. Again according to Nathan, Susan's attempts to understand him were mixed with 'pain and distress and old friendship and love and effort to understand in Geoff's terms, and self-blame, and so a new sense of the monstrousness of the accusation, and of the way in which it alike devastated and degraded everything'.

Clearly, Geoffrey was at times totally unreasonable in his management of his Principal. According to Nathan, if she did something of which he disapproved:

She would be given another chance if she promised never to do another thing without Master's orders. When the office boy in a city entrepreneur's office makes a mistake, he naturally says "I thought. . . .", but is at once stopped by the old entrepreneur who says: "Who told you to think? You're here to do as you're told". That was the position in which the boss was willing to keep this unruly employee on in his establishment! That was the place which Susie was graciously to be permitted, this one more time, to try to keep. . . .

In the end there was a final straw. It isn't clear from Nathan's letter what this was, though the outcome was clear:

Of course, Susie got out. There wasn't any doubt about it this time. Geoff had piled it on three tiers high to make quite sure. She didn't waste any time or any words, but at once sent him a plain, simple, one-sentence resignation.

Apart from the fact that Nathan's letter so clearly delineates the relationship between Geoffrey and Susan, it also casts light on

Geoffrey's personality and the way in which this, in all probability affected his financial judgement. The letter suggests that, from a psychiatric perspective, he had pathological swings of mood. From the autumn of 1926, perhaps triggered by the unexpected legacy from his aunt, he began to spend extravagantly and quite beyond his means. The contract with Nathan Isaacs, the cost of advertisement for the scientist, the film of the school and the commitment to pay Richard Slavson a sum equivalent at today's values to £70,000 a year for two years were all based on moonshine rather than solid assets. From a psychiatric perspective he was suffering an attack of hypomania. The prominent features of such a pathological mood state include irritability, unpredictability and delusions or at the very least completely unrealistic ideas of personal wealth. All of these certainly seem to have been present if Nathan's description of him is to be believed. Indeed, Nathan himself, in his letter to Margaret Pyke, makes the same point in lay language:

Your Geoff is unhappily somewhat insane. From an alienist's point of view, it is no doubt quite slight; but for that very reason, because it is so very near the border line of sanity, and because he moves about that border line, now on this side now on that, and because sane and sensible people have to go on living with him on a footing of presumed sanity on his part, he becomes so desperately difficult and impossible. That, I am sure, is the key to the whole story. . . .

At any event, by the beginning of December, 1927, he was bankrupt and the Principal of the school he had founded had left. Not too surprisingly and not for the first or last time in his life, he became extremely depressed. A characteristic feature of bipolar or manic-depressive disorder from which he clearly suffered is rapid change of mood from elation to deep depression. He left the management of the school to Margaret and traveled to Switzerland where he remained out of communication for two months.

On his return his finances remained in a completely hopeless state (Eyken, 1969, p. 63). He determined to make the survival of the school his first priority. One of the parents, a Dr. Edgar Obermer, a young London doctor from a wealthy family, had sent his sons to the school a few months earlier on the understanding that, if the school came under financial threat, he would have the first option to buy Pyke out. At this point, Pyke had little option. He sold the lease, furnishings and fittings to Obermer for £451.14s. Obermer borrowed some of the money from other parents and well-wishers, some of them well-known people such as Victor Gollancz, the publisher, and the writer, Siegfried Sassoon. Geoffrey Adrian, the Nobel Prize winning physiologist who later became Master of Trinity College, moved into St. Chad's to live there with his family, thus further reducing the burden of Pyke's overheads.

Geoffrey and Margaret were now tenants in what had been their home, owned none of the furniture or equipment, and had no money to pay the staff beyond the end of the current financial year. However Geoffrey did not give up. He applied to the Laura Spelman Rockefeller Trust in New York for a grant to enable the school to continue (ibid., p. 63). He drafted a lengthy memorandum to go with the application to be signed by a galaxy of eminent academics. Part of it read:

Of the value of the educational work and psychological research which are being carried out at the school, we as a body are not competent to speak— but what is clearly the first requisite of scientific work, to wit, a copious and careful record of phenomena, is being kept to a degree which, we believe, at any rate in this country, to be unique. Should these observations prove to be of the value they promise, they will provide a starting point for discussion by anthropologists, sociologists, educationists and psychologists. Clearly also, any technique that may be evolved from such investigation should render the school valuable not only as a centre of research work but also as a training ground.

The application was signed by Sir Charles Sherrington, Past President of the Royal Society, Professor Cyril Burt, Professor Jean Piaget, J. B. S. Haldane, G. E. Moore, and Percy Nunn, between them representing the most eminent figures in science, educational psychology, developmental psychology, philosophy and education. It was to no avail; the application was turned down for unknown reasons, but perhaps information about Geoffrey's improvidence had leaked out and, in any case, the school was much less viable in the absence of the Principal whose educational philosophy had guided its development. The school closed for good in July, 1929. The pupils went on to other schools, usually to progressive establishments such as Dartington and King Alfred's in London.

Geoffrey Pyke faced bankruptcy proceedings in 1929 (National Archive, G. N. Pyke Bankruptcy Proceedings. Document BT226/4520). In his examination he made fun of the lawyers representing his creditors, mocking their ignorance of educational matters and claiming all his affairs had been carried out with scrupulous honesty and transparency. This had clearly not been the case. In the end he developed a more overt psychiatric disorder and was admitted to a Nursing Home in north London on 5 May, 1929. At some point he became unconscious and, although this is not clearly stated, it is implied he made a suicidal attempt. The medical certificate submitted to the Bankruptcy Court dated 30 May, 1929, stated that Pyke was "suffering from paranoia (bordering on insanity), amnesia, fits of melancholia and incapability of severe mental effort, and that he will not be fit to attend to any business or legal affairs for at least twelve months". The closure of the school was followed by a flurry of litigation. Richard Slavson sued Pyke for money he believed was owed to him. Obermer sued Slavson for the return of papers he accused Slavson of removing from the school.

Susan and Nathan returned to London where Susan worked on the systematic records of observations she had made at the school in order to write two books that were to be the main influences on the education of young children for the next thirty years; in fact, in some respects, for much longer than this. Thus an experiment in education that lasted only five years in all and that had never involved more than twenty most unusual children at any one time made an impact far greater than Susan Isaacs herself can have expected and indeed one amazingly true to Geoffrey Pyke's own grandiose dreams.

CHAPTER SEVEN

Resurfacing

According to her husband, Susan emerged from her Malting House experience a broken and deeply humiliated woman. In his bitter, angry letter quoted in part in the last chapter to Margaret Pyke, Geoffrey's wife, dated October/November, 1927, Nathan had concluded (IoEd.N1 D2) by describing the devastating impact on her of the events of the last months she had spent at the school:

The upshot now of Susie's coming to Cambridge three years ago is that she is left with her health badly deteriorated, her economic prospects seriously prejudiced, even her professional status somewhat cut under, and driven out of the school she came to Cambridge to create.

Bitterly, Nathan had continued:

Forced out finally by a letter which gave her no choice whatever, she was then left, as a parting present, with another which informed her that her going out was an admission of her guilt, and which rubbed in, with a good powerful corrosive, how totally and stupidly.she had been to blame all along and how barbarously Geoff had been wronged. With that letter she was left to enjoy her work and all that she had so cruelly gained by it at Geoff's expense.

Geoff, the poor victim, was by a just dispensation of Providence left in the absolute control, power and glory of the school, in which he had been so precariously trying to maintain a foothold against the machinations of this ambitious, power-lusting, despotic, vindictive woman who was, all the time, encroaching him out.

Evidently Susan's predicament was dire at this point. She was now unemployed and seriously emotionally distressed. But she was a resilient woman and, from the point of view of employment, she had three assets. First, she had preserved and taken with her the detailed observations of the Malting House children that she had made over three years. Right from the start she had every intention of writing these up in book form to inform and improve the education of young children. Second, she had maintained her links with her psycho-analytic colleagues and could expect, now that she was living back in London to receive referrals of children and adults for treatment. It was not easy to establish a practice as a psycho-analyst however, and most psycho-analysts practising in London at that time had other sources of income. A few, like Ernest Jones, Edward Glover, and, a little later, Melanie Klein were so well-known that they could attract sufficient patients to earn a reasonable, even a comfortable living through analysis alone. But many doctors practising as analysts supplemented their income with non-analytic medical work, and women analysts were often married to men earning good incomes themselves. Nathan, having been employed by Geoffrey Pyke, was himself now out of a job, though he soon found one.

A third asset lay in her contacts with the academic world of psychology. These meant that, with her experience and academic qualifications, while she tried to establish her analytic practice, she could undertake lecturing in psychology to supplement her income. Because of the scandal of her relationship with Nathan, she could not go back to the Worker's Educational Association, but she soon found work as a part-time Assistant Lecturer at University College and as a lecturer at the Morley College for Adult Education (Gardner, 1969, p. 76).

Nathan rapidly re-established himself in the metals trading business, earning a good income. It might be thought that this would have removed any financial uncertainty from her position. But Susan's marriage at this time underwent a crisis and she cannot have felt confident her marriage would last.

In fact, Nathan's letter to Margaret Pyke, so accusatory of her husband, was disingenuous in the extreme. For his wife's mental distress must have stemmed at least in part from his own behaviour. At the time he wrote the letter, he had only recently begun a passionate affair with Evelyn Lawrence, the psychologist who had been taken on by Geoffrey and Susan to work at the Malting House School about a year earlier.

In 1927 Evelyn Lawrence, the daughter of a school master, was thirty four years old. After leaving Tiffin's school in Kingston on Thames, where she had been head girl, she trained as an infant teacher, one of the few professional occupations open to women in 1911 when she left school. While working as a teacher, she attended evening classes in Psychology at the London School of Economics. She obtained a first class degree and then worked at the National Institute of Industrial Psychology (NIIP), directed by Charles Myers, Susan's mentor at Cambridge and later the founder and Director of the NIIP, learning the principles of psychological testing (Archive of the Froebel Foundation, B9 1072/3). In September, 1926, only just over a year before Susan and Nathan left the school, she was taken on as a psychologist at the Malting House School. Evelyn was, according to those who knew her at the time, a very good looking young woman, tall and dark-haired. She was three years older than Nathan, who was thirty one years of age at this time. Susan was now forty-two years old, quite a bit older than both of them. Just less than a year after Evelyn joined the school, in August, 1927, she and Nathan became lovers.

As far as Evelyn was concerned, her relationship with Nathan was exclusive and monogamous. Nathan's position was clearly more complicated, bearing in mind that he was married to Susan. Susan, however, knew about the sexual relationship between Evelyn and her husband from the start. In his letter to Margaret Pyke, Nathan had reproached his wife for not having told him about her own sexual relationship with Geoffrey. So, though it is not unusual for spouses to expect different levels of secrecy regarding extra-marital relationships depending on whether it is they or their partners who are involved, he made sure from the outset that Susan would know about his affair with Evelyn.

In the summer of 1926, before starting at the Malting House School, Evelyn had been on holiday in France, in Provence.[1] Here she had had a brief, but intense affair with a married Englishman living in the United States. In February, 1928, this man, whom I shall call Alan, not his actual name, wrote her a letter that reveals a great deal not only about his own relationship with Evelyn but about her relationship with Nathan at this point in time. Alan's affair with Evelyn had been accepted, even approved of by his wife, whom I shall call Anne. She had apparently not just tolerated his affair, but approved of it. He had clearly not seen Evelyn since the time they had spent in Provence together sixteen months previously, after which he had returned to the United States with his wife.

From a letter to Evelyn it is clear that he had suggested that they now resume their relationship. "I have been getting more and more in love with you for some time". But Evelyn made it clear that this is quite impossible because she has become committed to Nathan. She had clearly confided in Alan that Nathan's wife knew about the relationship and was acquiescent in it. Alan writes ruefully:

When the tolerant, acquiescent and sweetly reasonable wife was Anne, I had many approving, even extolling words for the new woman. Now I am less certain. For a few passing moments I have thought that perhaps Susie too lightly kicked over the institution of monogamous marriage, an institution indubitably established by god in his vision and for the good of man and posterity (for which as you know I have great concern). But very soon I admit finding myself back in the middle of the preceding paragraph and confessing that these Isaacs who have come into my ken with such a crash must be rather nice people.

He continues in a more generous, sympathetic vein:

That remark brings me to Nathan. I do not know what is my proper reaction or indeed if there is any reaction proper to my situation. I can hardly claim the right to reach for guns or battleaxes and in fact I find myself much more pacific. It may be that the lily liver has come to have a survival value. My main feeling is that you have just become monogamous in a new direction and, sad as I am about it for myself, it is the change in you that has made all the difference, and looking for exterior causes is a pursuit that friendliness dictates but one that gives no reasonable basis for taking umbrage. Here I feel the ice thin under my feet because you may feel I had some rights over you and that is of course completely untrue. I should, of course, have been very interested in meeting Nathan if your last letter had never been written for you pretty well know that anyone with whom you could be so friendly would interest me but now that the last letter has come its description of him makes me more interested than ever . . .

The situation led Alan to reflect on the possible uniqueness of the pattern of the relationships that she has revealed:

You have given rise to a new figure in the geometry of human relations, replacing the pentangle for the eternal triangle. I am afraid it is a move in the direction of greater complication but the latter part of your letter cheered me up greatly for it promised good things from the pentangle.

He goes on to reveal that Evelyn has written that she has told Nathan about the affair she has had with him, Alan:

Your telling Nathan about our holiday in Provence was obviously demanded by the circumstances and I have nothing to complain of in the disclosure (that was a badly selected word, for it makes the affair sound like a newspaper scandal). Gentlemen, as far as I know the books are not supposed to have any feelings on this subject; they are tight-lipped; but on second thoughts, I think the books do not even contemplate the present situation. But of course I will know that if you fell in love with anyone you will tell them. Equally well you may rely on my complete silence (and of course Anne's as well) with regard to your letter. I do not know whether Anne will write to you. She is as glad as I am to know that you are living through a fine love affair but she is also so faithful a wife that she said last night that she felt quite a deep disappointment that her two best friends were now unlikely to have that love affair that she had thought at least possible. She and Susie (you will note that I now claim a pentangular relationship with Susie sufficiently close to entitle me to use her Christian name; Susie sounds like a person while Mrs Isaacs sounds like a member of society with legal rights) ought to get together for they seem to have an uncommon idea in common.

Alan concludes his letter by wishing Evelyn "very much love and happiness, my dear", and subsequently disappears without trace from this story. In fact the the pentangle that Alan described rapidly collapsed into a triangle.

Correspondence between Evelyn and Nathan leaves no doubt about the intensity of feeling on both sides. In the earliest dated letter between them, written on 12 September, 1927, a few weeks after their affair began, written on a train from Bristol to Ilfracombe where Evelyn's family lived, she wrote

> I want to come back. I find myself looking forward most tremendously to next term. I wonder why ... the last two stations have been Morebath and Bishop's Nympton. Now I can see possibilities in Bishop's Nympton. Do Bishops have carnal desires? And, if so, do they have them for nymps? I should like to see a nymp fooling a Bishop. . . . I wish I could find a letter from you darling when I get home. I want some support for this mild and chaste and domestic life I'm going to lead for the next fortnight. . . .

In an undated letter probably written at about the same time, in response to a letter from Evelyn in which she had described how she had the fantasy that she could take her love out and look at it as if it were a real object, but then not be quite sure it was he who was still there, Nathan reveals the depth of his physical feelings

> Darling, what a lovely letter. Of course, it is only your love you are taking out and looking at, and that's really you, just like you. But I hope, I do hope, I'm in it enough to be able to go on seeming like the one you love. You won't say, as soon as you see me again "but you're not the right person"? You won't find me out just yet? You'll let me go on putting my arms round your shoulders, as if I were he? Because, you see, it will be real for *me*. I shall really be holding you close and kissing your lips, and your cheeks and your eyes and your lips and oh, what a long time before I can have my arms all round you and have you altogether.

The couple were occasionally separated from each other. On one occasion, probably in early 1929, it was arranged that Evelyn would travel to the United States to do some research work for six months. Nathan took her down by train to Southampton to catch the boat. After he had left her to return to London, she wrote to him:

> Sweetheart, I wish you were here to share this silly game with me. I'm back on the ship and fully installed . . . I rather fancy that if I post this now it will be taken off at this end, and you may get it tomorrow. So I'll send it just to surprise you, and to let you know that I didn't slip on a banana skin in Southampton and get taken off to hospital. I hope your train wasn't too late.
>
> Oh darling—if only I could have you back for one more hug it would be better than nothing. But I have some compensations —in the newness of it all and you haven't any. Sweetheart don't be too miserable I love you so very very much. There's half a day off the six months anyhow. I mustn't stop or this won't get posted at this end. I'll write again later in the evening when I've had a chance of seeing the people at dinner. No thrills so far . . . Give my very best love to Susie. I'll write to her soon. Yours E.

The reference to Susie in this letter makes it clear once again, if indeed there had been any doubt after Alan's letter to Evelyn, that Susan was fully aware of what was going on between Evelyn and her husband. But the affair, it is also clear from the correspondence, was known about by very few people. In a letter to Nathan, dated 5 January, 1928, Evelyn, who is staying out of London with friends, responded to Nathan who had been concerned she was unhappy:

> No I hadn't been looking blue or cut up, or anything like that, over your letters, and I'd made up no stories about defunct cats or tom-tits. But I thought that perhaps we had better be a bit discreet. We shall have to be careful, you know, in town. If H. is going to meet the Poleshuks anywhere for heaven's sake warn them that she knows nothing. Are they the Ps coming to Olympia?

By the Poleshuks, Evelyn was referring to Joe and Phoebe Pole. Joe was a friend Nathan had made in the Army during the First World War, and he and his wife were Susan and Nathan's closest friends, people who, at one stage of their lives, they met up with regularly every Saturday evening for dinner. H. refers to Hilda, Evelyn's sister, with whom Evelyn later shared a flat for some time in Elsworthy Road, situated in Primrose Hill in north London, only a few hundred yards from where the Isaacs lived at that time. It is clear that Hilda was not in the know and it was intended that she be kept in the dark.

Very occasionally, Evelyn and Nathan were able to spend a few days together out of London, in what they clearly regarded as blissful anonymity. After one such interlude, Nathan wrote:

It *was* wonderful, Evelyn sweetheart and I've been living it over and over again in recollection. It seemed a miracle that everything came off just as we had dreamt it, for that marvellous moment of your opening and my shutting of the house door onward. (Even the absence of the phone was a most valuable addition to our safety.) I was supremely happy. Having one another like this completely to ourselves and sleeping and waking, moving and living in that full self-contained communion, is to me the most perfect thing I know.—Like you, darling Evelyn love, I want it back and want it again and I can't help already hoping for it again. But anyway, I've still a lot, an immense lot left of the happiness that a kind fate did vouchsafe to us, and I'm still re-enjoying every moment of it and every one of its thousand phases and forms and aspects with a joy and gratitude far deeper than I can ever express.

Although we know from their correspondence something of the relationship between Evelyn and Nathan, and we know that Susan knew of their affair, there are many unanswered questions here. Did Nathan begin the affair when and perhaps because the physical relationship between him and Susan had broken down? If they had stopped having a sexual relationship, why had this come about? Assuming they had had one beforehand, did Susan and Nathan continue to have a sexual relationship after the affair began? If, as seems likely, the intensity of the Evelyn-Nathan relationship precluded any continuation of a sexual relationship between husband and wife, how was this perceived by the couple? Did Susan have any extra-marital relationships herself? Why did Susan not seek a divorce? She was already a divorced woman and had nothing to lose socially.

We do not know the answers or even have more than the faintest glimmerings of answers to any of these questions. What we do know is that Susan was sexually inexperienced before she met her first husband at about the age of twenty-six. We know that the relationship between her and her first husband had not broken down because of any incompatibility of interests or attitudes. We know that, after her first marriage to William Brierley broke down her first husband subsequently married and lived for forty years with his second wife in an apparently happy marriage. His second wife, Marjorie, was also a prominent psycho-analyst. They too had no children. We know that, after she had married a second time, Susan had a brief and unsatisfactory affair with Geoffrey Pyke, though we do not know why it was so unsatisfactory. Finally we know from his long and happy relationship with Evelyn that Nathan was himself capable of sustaining a full sexual life over many years. Both her husbands were regarded as sociable, attractive, highly intelligent men of a type with whom Susan got on well. So, by exclusion, it seems likely that Susan had a serious psycho-sexual problem that prevented her from ever experiencing a satisfying, full sexual relationship over a period of time. We do also know that, throughout her married life, Susan enjoyed an intense intellectual relationship with Nathan from which she clearly obtained enormous pleasure. For this reason alone, the question of separation or divorce may never have arisen.

*   *   *

With her marriage in difficulties Susan turned her attention immediately to harvesting the fruits of her work at the Malting House School. For Geoffrey Pyke and Susan Isaacs, the Malting House School experiment had been a great deal more than an attempt to run a successful school along new lines. For both of them the point had been to demonstrate that letting young children discover things for themselves was the best way to stimulate their intelligence and improve their intellectual development.

Susan Isaacs wanted to use the observations of the records of the Malting House School that she had salvaged from the wreck of its demise to do more than confirm the success of her educational methods. Given her background in philosophy and psychology she felt she could contribute to understanding how young children learned. In particular she wished to examine the most recent theories of child development (genetic psychology as it was then called) to see whether her own findings supported or refuted them. The scientific questions that were in her mind were of great practical importance. How did children acquire knowledge? What were they capable of at different ages as they developed? To what degree did the acquisition of knowledge depend on the type of stimulation they had from teachers and parents? How great was the influence of parents and teachers compared to the physical maturation of the brain as the child developed? The fruits of her work at the school were published in two major texts, of which the first "The Intellectual Growth of Young Children", published in 1930, was by far the most influential.

She began with the premise that the best place to gather data systematically about how children acquire knowledge is where a great deal of children's learning takes place anyway, namely the school. But not just any school and, in particular, not a conventional school in which teachers play a large role in deciding what activities children undertake. Children must be left free to decide what they will do. Given such freedom, they will demonstrate their competence to maximum effect. Of course there must be plenty of equipment around for them to experiment with and there must be teachers available to answer the questions that arise in their minds as they use the equipment.

The routes that had been used previously to investigate children's cognitive development were, for Susan, limited in their scope or misleading in their findings. Some psychologists, such as Charles Darwin (1887) in England and Wilhelm Stern (1924) in Germany, had studied their own children in their own homes. Their results, especially those of Stern, had made a great impact, but Susan was deeply critical of this approach. When, as was inevitable and natural for them, parents were imposing standards of personal behaviour and morals, to some degree at least controlling their children, they could not, at the same time study the behaviour of their children with any degree of impartiality. Stern had come to definite conclusions about the emotional development of children and infantile sexuality on the basis of his observations of his own children; but surely, she felt, such generalizations must be founded on unsafe ground. Others, such as the American psychologist, Arnold Gesell (1928) had carried out surveys using questionnaires filled in by parents about the development and behaviour of children at different ages. These, though valuable for establishing norms of development, did not attempt to provide information about the processes involved in the maturation of children's intelligence.

While Susan Isaacs had been developing and testing her ideas at the Malting House School, a new and impressive figure had appeared on the scene. Inevitably when she began to write up her data she was greatly influenced by the very recently published books and articles of the Swiss psychologist, Jean Piaget. Indeed much of what she wrote was in direct response to his ideas and experiments. Piaget was born in the canton of Neuchatel in Switzerland. Showing great scientific talent at an early age, by the time he was eleven years old he had published an original observation on a partly albino sparrow he had studied in the local park (Piaget, 1973). At fifteen years in 1911, he published a monograph on molluscs and these were his abiding interest for a number of years. He studied biology at university, but then rapidly broadened his interests to philosophy and psychology. He became interested in epistemology, the study of knowledge and in the way children acquired knowledge. Still in his twenties, after some experience in psycho-analysis and in the standardization of intelligence tests he decided that his focus was what came to be called developmental epistemology, the study of knowledge and the way children develop the competence to acquire it. In his own words, genetic (developmental) epistemology deals with the "formation and meaning of knowledge and with the means by which the human mind goes from a lower level of knowledge to one that is judged to be higher".

So, in the nineteen twenties he began to carry out experiments on the thinking processes of young children. While from the start Piaget was aware of the relevance of his work to educationists, his main aim was to advance knowledge of the way in which children's concepts developed from the earliest ages through to adolescence. What, he asked himself, were the processes governing such development?

He rapidly came to see the growth of knowledge as arising from a progressive construction of mental structures. Less powerful logical means were superseded by higher and more powerful ones up to adulthood. Therefore, children's logic and modes of thinking were entirely different from those of adults. He reached this idea through careful and detailed experiment.

Piaget's experiments involved him in the ingenious development of a number of tasks for children of different ages, usually from four to twelve years of age, and then asking them questions to elicit their level of thinking and knowledge about the tasks. For example, in his investigations into the growth of relativity of ideas in the child (the way the child could go beyond immediate reality to understand how matters are seen differently from different perspectives), he investigated the way children of different ages could converse about brothers and sisters. To begin with (Piaget, 1928) he asked "How many brothers have you? And how many sisters? If the child had a brother A and a sister B, he would go on—And how many brothers has A? And how many sisters? And how many brothers has B? And how many sisters?" He found that 19% of children aged 4–5 years could answer these questions correctly, 24% of 6–7 year olds, 55% of 8–9 year olds, 87% of 10–11 year olds and 100% of 12 year olds. So there was indeed evidence for a progressive increase in the understanding of the nature of relationships between siblings. The questioning would then go on to probe the understanding of the idea of a brother more closely. For example in conversing with an 8 year old boy about what a brother was he received the reply " '*why that's a boy, it is someone'*. Are all boys brothers? *Yes, and then there are cousins and nephews as well.* Has your father got a brother? *Yes.* Why is your father a brother? *I don't know.* What must you have to be a brother? *I don't know. That's very hard"*.

Piaget concluded from the conversations he had along these lines with hundreds of young children that those under the age of 7–8 years do not, to take the above example, realize that a brother must necessarily be the brother of somebody. They were in fact stuck in what Piaget called "childish realism", which he put down to childish egocentrism. By this he did not mean that children of this age are selfish, but that they are unable to go beyond their own point of view. Nearly all six year olds would know that a brother was a boy. They would know too if this were indeed the case, that they had a brother.

They would not however be able to say with any certainty whether their brother had a brother or who that brother was. Thus they were unable to take the perspective of their brother because of their egocentricity, a feature of their thought that could be shown to be a limiting factor in their knowledge of the real world in many other ways.

On the basis of experiments such as this, or, as he would put it, on the basis of the structured conversations he had with children, Piaget proposed clearly defined, if not sharp transitions from one stage of mental development to the next. Some readers, especially older teachers and students of psychology will doubtless have had to learn and memorise Piaget's stages of mental development; for others they will be unfamiliar. Some acquaintance with them is necessary to understand just how fundamentally Susan Isaacs differed from him in the way she saw children's minds develop.

In very brief summary, because the model he put forward was much more complex than I have space to describe here, on the basis of his experiments Piaget proposed that human intelligence began with a "sensori-motor period" lasting up to about 18 months to two years when the infant is profoundly egocentric, unable to make any distinction between himself and the outside world, responding initially in a reflex manner to the stimulation he receives from his environment. This phase is followed by a "concrete operational period". In the first phase of this period, lasting up to about 7 years, the child retains an egocentric standpoint, and is able to operate purely on the basis of what he can observe. Symbolic thought develops at this time in language and symbolic play. After roughly 7 years he can think about what he is doing. He becomes more capable of appreciating how the world looks from the point of view of others and can successfully tackle tasks that require this skill. From about 7 to about 11 years the child is able to succeed in more complex tasks requiring reflective thought and the ability to bring two pieces of information together so long as these do not require him to use abstract thinking. From about 11 years he enters the phase of "formal operations" when he can at last use abstract concepts, entertain hypotheses, deduce consequences and use his deductions to put hypotheses to the test. This brief summary of just one part of Piaget's model of mental development fails to do anything like justice to the richness of his ideas (for a fuller summary see Donaldson,

1978). Over a forty year period Piaget wrote over thirty books. His experimental work and contribution to theory represented a massive achievement. Most academic child psychologists would regard him as the most influential researcher into child development in the twentieth century. However this is not a book about Piaget and all I have tried to do is to provide a framework for understanding how Susan Isaacs differed from him as a result of her own observations.

Piaget's work was almost immediately seen to have importance for psychologists, teachers and indeed philosophers. In the late nineteen twenties a number of his books were rapidly translated into English. Susan Isaacs was given these to review both by the philosophy journal, Mind, and by the Journal of Genetic Psychology. She was immediately greatly impressed. "There is probably no single contributor to genetic (developmental) psychology within recent years whose work is of greater interest than that of Jean Piaget", she wrote (Isaacs, 1929a). Elsewhere she noted. . . . "The importance and interest of these contributions of Piaget can hardly be over-estimated. He has not only added greatly to our store of facts about the child's beliefs and ways of thought, he has gone far to show how these hang together as a coherent, psychological whole" (Isaacs, 1929b). But she had many reservations both about the way he carried out his experiments and about the conclusions he drew from them. Indeed, although she wrote that she greatly admired Piaget's contribution to the understanding of child development, the fact was that she could hardly have disagreed more with his methods and had doubts about some of his conclusions.

So it is not surprising that Susan Isaacs begins her own book "Intellectual Growth in Young Children" with objections to the methods Piaget used to obtain information about what young children could or could not do. It was her view that taking children into what might be called laboratory situations, giving them toys or other equipment they had never seen before and proceeding to ask them questions as one might in an examination, could not hope to tap the full potential of the children they were studying. Susan Isaacs (1930a, p. 3) quoted in support Frederic Bartlett, the Cambridge psychologist, who was deeply critical of psychologists, like Piaget, who tried to generalize from findings carried out in highly simplified settings. It is, Bartlett had written, "mere superstition" to believe that behaviour observed in such artificial situations would bear any similarity to that shown in everyday life.

She put down what she felt were Piaget's quite misleadingly low estimates of the ages at which children could perform various tasks largely to his method of investigation. What would you expect of children, she asked her readers, if you put them into an examination situation with an unfamiliar adult? Of course they won't perform as well as if you just see them going about their business, playing, talking to other children and to adults, interacting with the real world.

On the basis of her own findings obtained in very different ways, she also took serious exception to Piaget's framework of the developing mind. In place of the rigidly defined stages of growth he proposed, she saw children's minds as having the basic equipment for logical thought much earlier on in their lives and the improvement in their competence as attributable not to any acquisition of new mental structures, but very largely to their exposure to a wide range of experiences and their gradually increasing ability to handle more and more complex tasks. Thus, and while in other respects many psychologists today would agree with her, in this they would not, she believed that children's minds were not qualitatively different from those of adults; they were just less experienced.

In contrast to Piaget then, Susan did not carry out experiments. Instead she observed what children could do at different ages. She provided evidence to support her view that young children might indeed be egocentric in experimental situations, but they were a great deal less so in everyday life. For example, she criticized Piaget's conclusion drawn from his experiment asking children about their understanding what a brother was. Although this is not an example she gives, because of her experience as an infant teacher and in the Malting House School, she was well aware of situations that arise when groups of young children aged 4–5 years, including brothers, are playing together. If the brother X of another child Y hurts himself and begins to cry when Y is not present, other children go and fetch Y to comfort X, thus clearly showing their awareness of the special relationship of the two boys and indeed may well explain to Y how his brother has hurt himself.

Her conclusion, drawn from her wide experience, was that young children, even under the age of three years could, in the right circumstances, perform quite complex tasks. In this lay her main disagreement with Piaget. It will be recalled that when Piaget visited the Malting House School in March, 1927, he and she were together when a boy of 5 years, 9 months passed by on his tricycle, back-pedalling. One of them asked him why the bicycle was not going forwards, and the boy replied that it was obvious. "Oh well," he said, "your feet press the pedals, that turns the crank round, and the cranks turn that round (pointing to the cog-wheel) and that makes the chain go round, and the chain turns the hub round, and then the wheels go round—and there you are!" Now Piaget had published work suggesting that the concept of mechanical causality was beyond the competence of children under the age of 8 years. Piaget, in later years, referred to this experience at the Malting House School. He described the school "astonishing" in its approach and acknowledged that the children did indeed make very good progress. However, he wrote, "even these exceptionally favourable circumstances were insufficient to erase the various features of the child's mental structure, and did no more than accelerate this development".

On the basis of her own observations, Susan Isaacs proposed, in contrast to most of her contemporaries, to most psychologists today, and certainly in sharp contrast to Piaget, that after taking into account the immense difference in knowledge and experience, the behaviour and modes of thinking of little children were, in general, very little different from those of adults. Throughout the whole of life, she suggests, the essential act of knowing involves the "seeing" or drawing out a conclusion from an observation by linking it to another observation. Thus she describes (Isaacs, 1939a, p. 135) how, at 3.9 years, "Phineas tried to knock a nail into the metal handle of the door . . . When he found he could not do it, he said 'Perhaps it's made of stone.'" At the same age (Isaacs, 1930a, p. 84), Denis said "The bread's buttered, isn't it? so if we want it without butter we can't, can we?—unless we 'crape it off wiv a knife . . . and if we want it without butter and don't want to 'crape it off with a knife, we have to eat it wiv butter, don't we?" In each case, Susan Isaacs suggests, the child's cognitive act is similar in its most essential character (the linking of two disparate pieces of knowledge), to his acts of understanding throughout his later life even if he works in an intellectually demanding occupation, as a historian, a scientist or in business.

Now clearly older children can tackle difficult tasks more success-fully than younger children. Is this the case because older children have had more experiences or because they benefit from maturation of the brain and of their cognitive apparatus? Susan Isaacs (1930a, p. 57) was firmly of the opinion that one should not attribute the greater success of older children to maturation unless one has ruled out the possibility that the greater experience of the older child is responsible. If one assumes that younger children *cannot* carry out a particular task because their brain structures are too immature, this will lead parents and teachers to under-estimate their capacities. She concedes that there is a sense in which certain forms of competence depend on prior skills having been attained. For example, a child may not be able to grade five boxes in terms of weight at a time when they can easily grade five boxes differing in size. This is because size can be simultaneously appreciated, whereas grading weights accur-ately requires the child to hold in his mind different weights that he can only appreciate successively one after the other. It is not therefore that the younger child is incapable of the weight task because it cannot appreciate difference in weights. Rather it is the greater complexity of the weight task and its requirement that the child holds information in his head over time that defeats him.

She observed, to support her own views of cognitive development that the behaviour of even very young children reveals their capacity to link information from the past to deal with a current problem. She describes (ibid., p. 66) how Tommy, aged 2 years 8 months, was put out that he had been told not to fill his watering can and take it into the garden because it was too wet outside. He muttered to himself and then took some flowers out of vases inside the house, put the water in the vases into his can and walked out into the garden smiling and saying to himself "Tommy has some water now". She points out that, in order to be able to do this, he had to synthesise information from several different sources. He had to realize that he needed water to fill his can, remember that there was water in the vases that he had previously helped to fill (even though the vases were not transparent and he could not see the water in them), and understand that he had to remove the flowers before he could empty the water in the vases. This synthesis was carried out in a moment. He just saw what he had to do and did it. This, in her view, suggests that as children grow older, they do not develop new modes of perceiving and thinking; they merely improve in their competence as their experience of the world grows. Psychologists today (e.g. Tizard and Hughes, 1984) would agree with her that the mistakes made by young children are often due to ignorance of information they have not been told rather than from any lack of competence to understand the information if it is made available to them.

The importance of experience in the gradual improvement in children's competence is supported, Susan Isaacs suggests, by the fact that all studies of mental growth find that, on average, there is smooth and continuous development. There are no sudden jumps in ability at particular ages. This, she argues, goes against Piaget's model of mental development with stages that are distinct from one another. She further takes exception (Isaacs, 1930a, p. 73) to the explanation Piaget put forward for the reduction of egocentrism at the age of seven or eight years. He had proposed that round about this age, by reason of biological maturation the child becomes a more social animal and forms relationships with other children. Susan Isaacs not only rejected the idea that egocentrism dominated the under 8s, but also objected to the notion that children suddenly, as a result of maturation, became social beings when they reached this age. Friendships between children and the capacity of children to learn from each other, she had observed, were clearly present in children much younger than this. She backed her views with numerous verbatim examples of young children clearly revealing their competence in a whole variety of ways. One interesting example that she provides is relevant to a later conclusion made by Piaget and his collaborators that children under the age of eight years cannot, because of their egocentrism, take the perspective of other people. A plane passed over the house. Christopher at the age of 5 years 8 months said the man in the aeroplane would "see some little specks walking about" (ibid., p. 115).

A further set of criticisms of Piaget's work and conclusions comes in an Appendix to "Intellectual Growth of Children" (Isaacs, 1930a, pp. 291–349), written by her husband, Nathan. It will be recalled that towards the end of Susan's employment at the Malting House School, Geoffrey Pyke persuaded Nathan to leave his job in the import and export of metals to come to the school and study any aspect of the children's development he found interesting. Nathan chose to study the "why" questions asked by young children and came to very different conclusions from Piaget.

For Nathan, there are various reasons why young children ask "why" questions, including, but not limited to the need to obtain more information to fill in gaps in their knowledge. The main reason for the "why" question, he thought, is "epistemic", knowledge-related. The need to ask "why" questions arises when the child has to deal with an anomaly, deviation, contrast or difference that has stimulated a sense of unease or unsettlement. Examples of "why" questions he considers in this category are:

Why haven't little goats any milk?
Why do ladies not have beards?
Why do ponies not grow big like other horses?
Why do animals not mind drinking dirty water?

In each of these examples, he noted that an anomaly had been noticed by the child who wanted it cleared up.

When Nathan Isaacs looked at the "why" questions that Piaget observed, it seemed to him that Piaget's explanation for them was inadequate. Piaget regarded such questions as evidence of "pre-causal" thinking arising from psychological, intentional, mixed and confused expectations or beliefs about what were to adults matters of obvious physical causality. When Piaget tried to extend his understanding of children's "why" questions by asking them why questions himself, he assumed that children understood his questions in the way adults might; this, Nathan Isaacs thought, was an unwarranted assumption.

In contrast to Piaget, Nathan thought that you learn much more about children's "why" questions from studying the way children ask them when they are spontaneous and arise because the child has been struck with a new and puzzling situation rather than when they are subjected to a form of questioning designed to assess their existing knowledge. He believed that the way adults dealt with children's "why" questions was a matter of fundamental import-ance for their future intellectual development. Indeed the adult faced with children's "why" questions has a heavy responsibility to avoid pretentious tautologies, arbitrary selection of partial causes, imaginary and mythological causes, for the answers to "why" questions will determine the future general character and level of their intellectual life.

Throughout her career, probably partly as a result of her psycho-analytic training, Susan Isaacs took particular interest in the way young children learned about the basic biological facts of life: birth, reproduction, and death. A separate chapter in "Intellectual Growth of Young Children" is devoted to this subject. Her basic contention was (ibid., p. 158) that "an active, continuous and cumulative interest in animal and plant life—but particularly animal—develops easily and uninterruptedly out of the little child's impulses of curiosity and pleasure in these things, given certain conditions". Adults should, she felt, free themselves from prejudices and inadequate thinking as to the order in which animal and plant life should be dealt with. It was important to follow the child's actual direction of interest and day to day questioning and provide the situations and material which will answer his questions.

She proposed in her book that the then current preference for dealing with the sexual life of plants before animals was due to embarrassment and fear; children were much more interested in animals. Teaching about animals could inform the child about internal structure and physiology, and the facts of death. Adults try to protect children against the facts of death, but animal death is a part of everyday life, of what we eat, hunt, wear, fear, and collect. In her book and in a talk entitled "The Humane Education of Young Children" that she gave to the Annual Conference of Educational Associations in 1931 (Smith, 1985, pp. 273–6) in which she expanded these ideas she suggested that it was important for teachers to understand and accept the competing emotions that looking after animals evokes. "In all little children there are to be found impulses both of cruelty and tenderness, although one may show a readier tenderness and another a greater cruelty. . . . By building up a sustained interest in biology we can ensure the welfare of animals far more securely than if we content ourselves with the simple teaching of kindness." We should, she suggested, let children face the facts of animal death, while ensuring they are not responsible for avoidable hurt. This approach reduces the impulse to master and hurt, providing it is done in the context of caring for animals, feeding them and so on. She felt she had shown that this approach could be to the great benefit of children who experienced it. The opportunities that had been given to the Malting House children both to care for animals and to dissect them when they died had shown how educationally valuable such experience could be. There was far less of interest to little children in plants, whose functions were usually limited to gifts and decoration. Gardening too could be instructive and should be encouraged, but it was of less intrinsic value in the biological education of the young child.

Although she put great emphasis on the importance of experience in intellectual growth, Susan Isaacs was a strong believer in the hereditary nature of intelligence. In this belief she drew on work carried out by her psychologist contemporaries in Britain and the United States, especially Charles Spearman, Cyril Burt and Arnold Gesell. She also drew on a study carried out by Evelyn Lawrence (1931) that she knew well because she had given advice on its conduct. In this study children in institutions had been compared with those in an ordinary London elementary school. Evelyn had been able both to administer intelligence tests and to obtain information on the social class of the parents in both groups. She was able to show that, even though the institution children had often hardly been in touch with their parents since birth, the correlation between their intelligence and their parents' social class was as high as it was in the home-reared elementary schoolchildren. Assuming that the social class of the parents was closely linked with their intelligence (an assumption that Evelyn recognizes is far from solidly established) this surely means, she claimed, that genes and not experience determine the level of children's intelligence.

It may seem paradoxical that Susan Isaacs, who put so much emphasis on experience in the development of intelligence should be so convinced of the importance of genetic influences in determining the intelligence of children. In her view, it was genes that set the level of intelligence and experience that led to its growth. Thus, and this is my own example to illustrate Susan Isaacs's ideas, one might find three 5 year old children, one with an intelligence of an average 4 year old, one with that of an average 5 year old and the other brighter child with that of an average 6 year old. While genetic inheritance determined the level of intelligence, the experiences of the children would decide how their intelligence grew as they got older. If one tested them in a year's time at the age of 6 years however one would find that, if they had similar levels of experience, they would still differ in their levels of intelligence by the same amount. The difference would remain because of the influence of heredity.

The reviews of "Intellectual Growth in Young Children" in both the lay and professional press were strongly favourable. What mattered most to Susan Isaacs were the reactions to her work by psychologists. She need not have worried. C. W. Valentine, an influential contemporary psychologist, began his review in the British Journal of Educational Psychology (Valentine, 1931). "This book is beyond doubt one of the most important recent contributions to the psychology of childhood". He agreed with Susan Isaacs's criticisms of Piaget, especially her reservations about the existence of distinct stages of mental development. His own observations of the thought and behaviour of young children confirmed her view that they were far more competent than Piaget allowed. He was particularly admiring of Nathan Isaacs's Appendix on the "why" questions asked by children. J. C. Flugel, Susan's first psychoanalyst, was equally positive in the International Journal of Psychoanalysis (Flugel, 1931). An American psychologist, Raymond Willoughby, wrote in the Journal of Genetic Psychology (Willoughby, 1931) that the book provided the first evidence for the "child-centered" theory of education. He felt that, in her controversy with Piaget, Susan Isaacs had had "the better of the argument; Piaget's researches appear to have been carried out under the preconception that a structure would be found. . . . our author's positive findings indicate that true reasoning is present very early and that the incapacities noted by Piaget largely disappear when adequate experience for the formation of inferences has been obtained".

But the most penetrating, detailed and paradoxically in some ways the most positive evaluation of her work came from Jean Piaget himself. He wrote a twenty three page critical review of her book in French in the philosophy journal, Mind (Piaget, 1931a) and another nine page article in the British Journal of Educational Psychology (Piaget, 1931b). In his Mind review Piaget was far kinder to Susan Isaacs than she had been to him. He not only began his article, as she had begun hers, with compliments, but then, unlike her, detailed the many points in which he was in agreement with her as well as a small number with which he disagreed. He clearly took her disagreements with him extremely seriously. He began by expressing his admiration for the "remarkable talent with which Mrs. Isaacs

and her collaborators have collected important new data and interpreted them using systematic and original concepts" (my translation).
After describing the Malting House School in some detail he
recapitulates her criticisms of him. He then comments favourably on
Nathan Isaacs's Appendix on children's "why" questions which he
describes as "extremely subtle and penetrating".

He accepts all her criticisms of his "clinical method" and explains
that the five books he has so far written should really be seen only
as an introduction to the work he intends to pursue over the coming
years. The work he has completed may however, he suggests with
disarming modesty, nevertheless have some value. He then defends
many of his views robustly. He denies neglecting the role of experience, but he thinks the effects of experience are more complicated
than she suggests. There is, in his view, no maturation without
experience, but equally, there is no experience without maturation.
He is not put out by the example of the boy who could understand
the way a tricycle worked. He reasonably pointed out that all the
children at the Malting House School were above average intelligence
and most of them were well above average ability. Let us suppose
that the child on the tricycle was average in ability for the school, he
would have had an IQ of about 130. Now although it is not possible
to equate mental age with IQ in any very precise way, an IQ of about
130 in a boy of 5 years 9 months means that he had a mental age in
the region of 7–8 years. In other words, his mental age was about at
the point where Piaget would indeed have predicted that he would
understand mechanical causality in the way he demonstrated and
Piaget thought the boy's competence proved his point rather than
refuted it.

In order to explain his agreements and differences with Susan
Isaacs, Piaget drew a distinction between structure and function in
children's mental development. There are certain functions that all
organisms, of whatever level in the animal world and at whatever
level of development they may be, have to perform—digestion,
respiration, reproduction, perception. For these functions the Isaacs
model may be preferable. The structures that are developed to
perform these functions, including mental functions, will however
differ between species and within species at different ages. It is in
the description of the changing structure of the child's mind that he
feels his own contributions have more relevance. He concludes his

review in Mind (Piaget, 1931a) and expanded this point in great detail in his article in the Journal of Genetic Psychology (Piaget, 1931b) by suggesting that his approach and that of Susan and Nathan Isaacs were complementary rather than contradictory. He had examined the cognitive development of children at different ages by investigating the limits of their competence. The Isaacs had focused on the way children acquired new knowledge. This was an approach he planned to use in the future. It was indeed not only one of the approaches he used, but became, he claimed many years later, the main focus of his work. "My real concern is the explanation of what is new in knowledge from one stage of development to the next. How is it possible to attain something new? That's perhaps my central concern" (Bringuier, 1980, p. 19).

Perhaps the greatest compliment that Piaget paid Susan Isaacs was however not made explicitly. In a description of the development of Piaget's work, J. McV. Hunt (1969, pp. 4–6), an American psychologist and leading Piagetian, describes it as falling into three phases. The first phase covers the nineteen twenties, namely the period before Susan Isaacs's book had been published. The second begins with his observations of his own three children and involved following them around, not asking them questions but making observations of their spontaneous behaviour and expressions. This is precisely what Susan Isaacs had done. Why did Piaget change his approach?

In a series of conversations with a journalist, Jean-Claude Bringuier (1980, p. 53) Piaget quotes with approval a psychiatrist who had said of him "Piaget is much too narcissistic to have reacted to criticism and has gone peacefully along in his own way". In fact, this is, as we have seen, somewhat misleading. Two extremely lengthy defensive reviews and a shift in the direction of his work do not suggest that Jean Piaget had been in any way impervious to the critical views of Susan and Nathan Isaacs. They and, of course, others who had been critical of his early work had a significant influence on him that he had conveniently but understandably forgotten forty years later.

He had not however completely forgotten. At a memorial service for Nathan Isaacs held in June, 1966 a letter in French from the seventy year old Jean Piaget was read out. It included the sentences (trans. mine) "You know how much I loved Nathan Isaacs who, for me, was always a much valued friend and adviser. I recall with emotion the numerous scientific and friendly contacts we had over the years, in particular his participation in the group of at most ten people who met each year for the developmental epistemology symposium."

After the publication of "The Intellectual Growth of Young Children" Susan Isaacs, though still influenced by and indeed admiring of much of Piaget's work, took little further active interest in Piagetian psychology, though she remained conversant with it and indeed particularly praised later studies that Piaget carried out on moral development. Nathan, however, retained a strong interest in Piaget's work, corresponded and, at times, visited him. The link between the two men was only broken with Nathan's death.

Note

1   The account that follows of the relationship between Evelyn Lawrence and Nathan Isaacs was obtained from correspondence in private hands that was made fully available to the author.

CHAPTER EIGHT

Settled on the couch

When Susan returned from what must have seemed like losing a war at the Malting House School in Cambridge, she immediately picked up on her attendance at the regular fortnightly Wednesday meetings of the British Psycho-analytic Society (BPS). While she had been running the school her attendance had been infrequent, but now she began to attend much more regularly. She found the meetings to be very different from those she had attended when she had first become a member.

Before the end of 1924, with few exceptions there had been little consideration of child analysis at the regular Wednesday meetings of the Society. The members interested in children had given papers, but largely on subjects of significance to adult behaviour. For example in March, 1924, Susan herself at one of her unusual appearances between 1923 and 1927 had given a paper with Ella Sharpe, also a teacher, on "The Castration Complex and Snobbishness".

Then on 3 December, 1924, Nina Searl, who, like Ella Sharpe had previously been analysed in Berlin by a prominent German psycho-analyst, Hanns Sachs, gave a paper on "A question of technique in child-analysis in relation to the Oedipus Complex". This was followed by a short paper on a similar subject given by Sylvia Payne. Both papers discussed the differences between the analysis of adults and that of children under the age of six years. The discussion was evidently stimulating and vigorous for unusually it was agreed that the next meeting should be dedicated to a continuation of the same theme.

At this second meeting held on 7 January, 1925, Ernest Jones, the President, took a very active part. He thought that it was important to distinguish between the possibility of making a child aware of the full implications of the Oedipus Complex during infancy and the desirability of doing so. Nina Searl's paper, he considered, had demonstrated, presumably by providing material obtained in an analysis of a young child, that this was possible and he saw no reason why, in the course of time, one could not decide whether it was desirable. James Strachey then read an abstract of a paper that had been given by what was to most of the English group a new name in psychoanalysis, Melanie Klein, at the Berlin Psycho-analytical Society some weeks previously. This had been sent to him by Alix, his wife who, it will be remembered, was undertaking psycho-analytic training in Berlin. "Frau Klein", it was reported in the minutes of the meeting, "maintained that her experience showed that psycho-analytic treatment, in the strictest sense of the word, was applicable even to very young children, though a special technique was necessary".

Alix and James Strachey wrote to each other frequently, often every day. In his letter to Alix the day after the first "child-analysis" discussion in December, 1924, James had been scathing. He had written (Meisel and Kendrick, 1986, p. 136):

> The meeting last night was much livelier than usual. I must say the English are a minderwertig (intellectually inferior) set, especially the ladies. Miss Searl struck me as a mere jelly of sentimentality and prejudice. Mrs. Isaacs is conceited beyond words. Barbara's cracked. And though Mrs. R's morale is all right, her mind is decidedly enfeebled. Their arguments seemed definitely Jungian . . .

In this letter, "Barbara" is Barbara Low, Mrs. R is Joan Riviere and "definitely Jungian" was about the most powerful insult that the Stracheys used about their psycho-analytic colleagues in their letters to each other. (Carl Jung, originally one of Freud's closest colleagues, had split with Freud over fundamental disagreements relating to the primacy Freud gave to the sexual drive. Freud subsequently "excommunicated" Jung as he did others who rejected his ideas. Many colleagues left the Freudian camp at various points in time, but Jung was seen by Freud's followers as the prototype of disloyalty to the cause.)

Alix Strachey had only met Melanie Klein, a woman quite a bit older than herself, a few weeks earlier in December, 1924 at a meeting of the Berlin Psycho-analytic Society. The two had discussed psycho-analysis but also went shopping and to tea dances together. Alix immediately wrote about Melanie, whom she called "Die Klein" to her husband. He had returned to London after his own analysis with Freud in Vienna in order to set up in practice as a psycho-analyst. She was clearly much impressed with Melanie's ideas, though less with her dress sense. Alix described how she was relieved not to have gone to a ball with her as "she (Melanie) takes the high conventional line- a sort of ultra heterosexual Semiramis in slap-up fancy dress waiting to be pounced on, etc." Who then was Die Klein, this extraordinary woman who was soon to become one of the two protagonists in a major conflict in the psycho-analytic world? Her ideas, though they may seem outlandish to many non-analysts, were central to Susan Isaacs's views on the mental development of children and so need discussion in some detail.

From the mid nineteen twenties, through the nineteen thirties and the first half of the nineteen forties, psycho-analysts were sharply divided on the issue of child analysis. The two main psycho-analytic centres were in fierce and sometimes bitter disagreement with each other; Viennese Freudians squabbled and fought with the Kleinians in London virtually throughout this time. Susan Isaacs played a major part in the conflict, especially at the time of its denouement in the early nineteen forties, when she made what may have been a decisive intervention. The battles between these different schools of psycho-analysis therefore form an important part of her story as they do of the history of child analysis.

The conflict can only be understood with an appreciation of Sigmund Freud's relevant views of mental development from childhood to adulthood at the time that the arguments began in the early nineteen twenties. At this point in time, although Freud had retained most of his original views on the structure of mental activity, he had more recently developed new ideas. He believed throughout that in the first two or three years of its life an infant is entirely self-regarding, preoccupied with its own needs and only aware of the external world to the degree that this is necessary for its survival.

In this stage of self-absorbed "primary narcissism", pleasure is first derived from the mouth in a purely "oral stage" of development. Round about the end of the second year the mouth is replaced as a source of pleasure by the anus, which in its turn, at about the end of the third year, gives way to genital pleasure. During the fourth year of life, at the height of the infantile genital phase, the infant develops an exclusive love for the opposite-sex parent so that, in the boy, it is normal for an "Oedipus Complex" to appear. Intense rivalrous feelings of boys towards their fathers and of girls towards their mothers are universally found in normal development at this time. This was the age when, for the first time, the child formed a clear, distinctive picture of its two parents.

According to Freud, before the formation of the Oedipus Complex, the child's mind has been filled with confused and largely unformed feelings deriving from his primary drives for food, warmth and comfort. Gradual awareness of the external world is responsible for the differentiation of the ego, that part of the mind that is in touch with reality. At the end of the third year or a little later the guilt arising from the wish to do away with the same-sexed parent in the oedipal phase leads, in both boys and girls to the development of the superego, the largely unconscious conscience of the young child. The development of girls is further complicated at this stage by penis envy, the realisation experienced by all normal girls that there is something missing in their anatomy.

Deviations and distortions during this oedipal phase of development arise because the mind represses unacceptable desires that remain in the unconscious. Here they remain active throughout the life of the individual, giving rise to neurotic disorders unless or until they are released and understood through the process of psychoanalysis. The analyst's skill lies in detecting the clues in the patient's unconsciously driven behaviour, through free associations and through dreams, to what is going on in the hidden mind. But this is no easy matter. For example, unacceptable feelings for one person might be "displaced" onto another. A preoccupation with an unmentionable part of the anatomy might result in its being transformed by a process of "symbol formation" into an apparently innocuous non-sexual object.

The analyst's skill lies in penetrating the subtle deceptions of the minds of his or her patients. This process can be assisted if there is a development of "transference", that is if the various feelings, especially the negative feelings that the patient has for those in his immediate family, can be safely re-experienced and understood in a relationship with an analyst. To acquire the ability to handle such "transference relationships" the analyst has to undergo a period of prolonged and intensive training himself or herself. Through experiencing a "transference" to his training analyst, the trainee gains in self-knowledge to a degree that enables him or her to take the responsibility for becoming the focus of the transferred love and hate of those he or she analyses in the future. There is clearly a danger that the analyst might become personally involved with the patient during this process, but appropriate training enables the analyst to avoid this pitfall. Training is a lengthy procedure, but it is worth it; for in the hands of psychiatrists trained in psychoanalytic methods, psychoanalysis can cure "the most chronic psychoneurotic disorders". Moreover knowledge gained from psychoanalysis, if properly applied, might not only "diminish nervous and mental diseases", but would "establish new methods in our system of education".

This simplified account of Freud's thinking at the beginning of the nineteen twenties omits some important aspects of the rich theory he had developed by that time. In particular I have made no mention of the "life instincts" and "death instincts" that preoccupied Sigmund Freud and his followers after the First World War. However hopefully this account is sufficiently full to enable the reader to appreciate most of the doctrinal differences in child analysis so strongly engaging the intellectual and emotional energies of Susan Isaacs and her psychoanalytic colleagues over the next two decades.

The conflicting views of Anna Freud and Melanie Klein on the early development and potential for analysis of young children have led to the belief that these two women, often regarded as its pioneers, were the first to enter the field. This is not the case. Apart from Sigmund Freud's own brief foray with his analysis by proxy of 5 year old "Little Hans", published in 1909, a number of other analysts had contributed to the field. In particular, a Viennese woman teacher from an old Catholic family with aristocratic origins, Hermine Hug-Hellmuth wrote extensively on the technique of child analysis from 1911 until she was murdered by a neurotic and much-analysed 19 year old nephew in 1925. She described the use of play to reach the fantasy life of children; indeed many of her ideas were later taken up by both Anna Freud and Melanie Klein. In 1921 at the International Psycho-analytic Congress held in The Hague at which both Anna and Melanie were present, she gave an unpublished paper entitled "The Technique of Analysis of Children". Hermine was a shy, diffident woman whose self-effacement resulted in her fading from view, but her ideas lived on, mainly in the work of Melanie Klein.

Melanie Klein, whose influence on Susan Isaacs equalled that of Sigmund Freud, was born in Vienna in 1882, the youngest of four children. Her father, Moriz Reizes, a doctor born in Poland to an orthodox Jewish family, came to Vienna to improve his circumstances. He was relatively unsuccessful and for a time had to work as a dentist or even possibly as a dental assistant. Her mother, Libussa, originally from Slovakia, opened a shop that sold reptiles, presumably lizards, as well as plants. They had difficulties in making ends meet but eventually the family fortunes were rescued by Hermann, Libussa's younger brother, who made generous gifts to the Reizes family. Libussa was an overwhelming woman whose intrusiveness during Melanie's adolescence may have been one of the factors deciding her daughter to opt for an early engagement and marriage. Although originally intending to go to medical school, she gave up her studies when, at the age of 17 or 18, she became engaged to Arthur Klein, a chemical engineering student (Grosskurth, 1986).

The marriage took place in 1903. Melanie's first child, a daughter, Melitta, was born in 1904 and a second, Hans, in 1907. Her husband was often away for work reasons and there is reason to think that the marriage was unhappy almost from the first. Later in life, Melanie claimed Arthur had been unfaithful to her from their first year of marriage. The family moved around a great deal and, at one point, when, in 1907–8, Arthur obtained a job in Krappitz, in Slovakia, Libussa came to stay and took over from her the responsibility for running the house and looking after Melanie's children. For a period of about two and a half years, when her daughter was about four years of age and her older son just a baby, Melanie spent a great deal of time away from her children, mainly because she was so depressed. During this time she spent two and a half months in a sanatorium in Switzerland being treated for depression. At other times she was in an Adriatic seaside resort with a woman friend.

During this time her mother, Libussa usually took responsibility for the children. In 1911, Arthur found work in Budapest where there were a number of relatives, but Melanie, now nearly thirty years old, who moved with the children to be with him, still felt depressed, lonely and frustrated.

She began to read some of Freud's work and was intrigued by it. In 1914, the year in which her mother died and her third child, Erich, was born, she made contact with Sandor Ferenczi, a Hungarian psycho-analyst and one of Freud's closest associates. She started an analysis with him. He had an interest in the application of psychoanalysis to children and encouraged Melanie to undertake such work with children herself. Melanie's interest in working with children arose partly from feelings about her own childhood that had arisen in recounting it to Ferenczi and partly from guilt she was experiencing as a result of her difficulties mothering her two older children.

Perhaps partly in restitution she began in 1918 to psycho-analyse her own youngest child, Erich, who, by this time was four years old. Her five times a week analysis of Erich, intense and time-consuming, was described in a presentation to the Hungarian Psycho-analytic Society in 1919. A paper providing the same material was published in 1921 under the title "The Development of a Child". Melanie gave Erich the pseudonym "Fritz" and did not reveal she was describing her own child. Instead to explain why she knew so much about him, she referred to him as "the son of relations who live in my immediate neighbourhood".

Though it would be regarded as quite unacceptable for parents to analyse their own children today, in the early days of psychoanalysis, it was not at all unusual. Many leading figures in psycho-analysis, including Sigmund Freud himself and Carl Jung both analysed their own children. In 1919, as a result of a wave of post-war anti-Semitism, the Klein family left Budapest. Arthur went to work in Sweden and Melanie returned briefly to Vienna before spending a year with her in-laws in Slovakia. Melanie continued to take an active interest in psychoanalysis and the following year, in 1920, she went to the psychoanalytic conference in The Hague where she heard Hermine Hug-Hellmuth talk about child analysis and met Karl Abraham who was giving a presentation there. He was also a close colleague of Freud, practising in Berlin, who had analysed his own child.

It was at about this time that Melanie Klein began to conduct an analysis with her older son, Hans then aged thirteen years. In a paper published in 1926 entitled "A Contribution to the Psychogenesis of Tics", she describes the lengthy analysis of this son to whom she gives the pseudonym "Felix". She says he was "referred to her for analysis" and came three times a week for a total of 370 hours over a period of three and a quarter years. The interpretations she makes of her own son's dreams and play are interesting and, to a non-analyst, it is extraordinary that she could write of her own son in this way. One has to bear in mind that when Melanie Klein refers to Felix's mother, she is talking about herself. She describes his masturbation fantasies in great detail. *"He is playing with some little girls; he caresses their breasts and they play football together. In this game he is continually disturbed by a hut which can be seen behind the little girls"*. Analysis revealed (or she inferred from his play, from his dreams and from what he said to her) that "this hut was a lavatory which stood for his mother, expressed his anal fixation to her, and also had the significance of degrading her. The game of football was shown to represent an acting out of his coitus fantasies. . . ." One's wonderment that a boy of thirteen could confide the content of his masturbation fantasies to his mother is inevitably followed by conjecture as to how he must have reacted to the explanation his mother provided to him for them. At one point she attributed his "problems" to observation of intercourse at a time he had shared a room with his parents. Not only did she analyse Hans, but she intruded into his personal life, making him break off a relationship with a girl older than he because, as she interpreted the friendship, it led him to identify his mother with a prostitute. She later stopped a homosexual relationship in which he had become involved.

By 1921, Melanie Klein had become so impressed with Karl Abraham that she decided to move to Berlin to work alongside him. Her marriage was in the process of breaking down, and, although Arthur joined her for a couple of years, they finally separated and divorced in 1924–5. Melanie was a good-looking, vivacious woman in her early forties. She led an active social life in post-war Berlin both before and after her divorce. While still married, she began an affair with a married journalist C. Z. Kloetzel who was nine years younger than she, a relationship that continued for some years. Their correspondence makes it clear that she was in love with

Koetzel, but that he treated their relationship as one of many light-hearted affairs.

Now linking up with the Berlin Psycho-analytic Association that Abraham had founded in 1910, Melanie Klein concentrated on child analysis. Her daughter, Melitta, whom she had briefly analysed when she was in Slovakia, was now in medical school in Berlin and an independent young woman, but a significant amount of her time was spent in analysing her two sons. Erich, whom she had analysed as a young child in Budapest, had a relapse of his emotional problems with anxiety about going to school. This may presumably have been related either to the fact that he was taunted for being a Jew on the way to school or to the fact that he had to attend a new school and make new friends, but his mother focused on the road he took to school which was lined by trees. She thought these trees symbolically represented to him a desire for coitus. This had led, she decided, to the castration anxiety that lay at the root of his school phobia. Hans, her middle child, was away at boarding school until 1923 when, now sixteen years of age, he rejoined the family.

Once in Berlin, Melanie Klein began to analyse a number of children referred to her by colleagues and friends (Klein, 1975). In these analyses she exclusively used her play therapy technique to reveal to her what she saw as the underlying fears and anxieties of her patients. Once she had understood the source of their worries, she told the children what she thought their play represented. According to her, the children acknowledged the accuracy of her interpretations of their play through the appreciative looks they gave her. She was further confirmed in her beliefs of the truth of her observations by the way the children's problems disappeared once these interpretations had been made. For example, Peter, aged three years and nine months was very difficult to manage, He was unable to tolerate frustration and his behaviour was "aggressive and sneering". In his second session he bumped together engines, carriages and horses. Then he ". . . put two swings side by side and, showing me the inner and longish part that hung down and swung, said: 'Look, how it dangles and bumps.' I then proceeded to interpret. Pointing to the dangling swings, the engines, the carriages and the horses, I said that in each case they were two people—Daddy and Mummy—bumping their 'thingummies' (his word for genitals) together. He objected, saying: 'no, that isn't nice', but went on knocking the carts together,

and said: '*That's* how they bumped their thingummies together.'
... He now took another small cart and made all three collide
together. I interpreted: 'That's your own thingummy. You wanted
to bump your thingummy along with Daddy's and Mummy's
thingummies.' Peter had a total of 278 sessions, after which 'his
difficulties had disappeared and there was an extensive change for
the better in his whole character and disposition.' "

She told another child, Ruth, aged four years and three months,
that objects in her play, "the balls in her tumbler, the coins in the
purse and the contents of the bag all meant children in her Mummy's
inside and that she wanted to keep them safely shut up so as not to
have any more brothers and sisters". This interpretation produced
an "astonishing" change of behaviour. "For the first time Ruth
turned her attention to me and began to play in a different, less
constrained, way." Ruth's later play with a sponge in a session that
began with the girl tearful and screaming, prompted Melanie Klein
to interpret as follows: "I showed her in every detail how she envied
and hated her mother because the latter had incorporated her father's
penis during coitus, and how she wanted to steal his penis and the
children out of her mother's inside and kill her mother". This resulted
in Ruth changing her behaviour, leaving the session happy and
cheerful, and saying goodbye to Klein in a "friendly and even
affectionate way".

When she reported her methods and procedure at meetings of the
Berlin Psycho-analytic Association, her colleagues, apart from Karl
Abraham, reacted with indifference or hostility. Klein was greatly
admiring of Abraham, who was supportive of her ideas. She
persuaded him to take her on for psychoanalysis. She began this in
1924–5 and saw him five times a week for nine months until he
became ill in April, 1925, dying later that year. She always felt she
owed a considerable debt to Abraham whom she and many others,
including Freud, regarded as an impressive thinker and psycho-
analyst. Melanie felt she owed many of her ideas to him, in particular
her understanding of depression. He also encouraged her in what is
widely regarded by analysts as her single most influential contribution to psychoanalytic technique, the use of therapeutic play. Later
in life, Melanie recalled that, in 1924, Karl Abraham had said to her
in connection with a paper she had written on an obsessional child:
"The future of psychoanalysis rested in child analysis". After she had

given a paper summarising her work in Berlin, she arranged to go to Vienna to describe her work to the Vienna Psycho-analytic Society and meet Freud. To her disappointment, he and the other Viennese analysts took little interest in her work. In contrast, reaction among the London group of analysts was much more favourable.

After the meeting of the British Psycho-analytic Society in January, 1924 at which Melanie Klein's views that had been sent to him by Alix, had been reported by James Strachey, Ernest Jones became interested in hearing more first-hand about Melanie Klein's ideas. Some of her ideas fitted well with his own current psycho-analytic preoccupations with the origins of female sexuality. He had become convinced that infants experienced harsh aggressive feelings that they turned in on themselves before they reached the genital stage. He thought these early intimations of the development of a super-ego were incorporated into a later more mature super-ego and some of Klein's ideas resonated with this view. He might also have been influenced by observing the behaviour and play of his own children, Gweneth, now aged three and Mervyn, aged two, and might well have thought that what he was seeing fitted better into the framework that Melanie Klein provided, with its emphasis on aggression and sexual play in the early years than in the vaguer formulations of Freud, centred around the concepts of primary narcissism.

Encouraged by Alix, Melanie Klein wrote to Jones offering to come to London to talk about her work. He invited her to give a series of lectures in London to professional colleagues. Klein was unable to speak the language well enough to deliver her lectures in English and they were translated, probably rather freely translated to give them greater coherence. Klein could however handle questions and the discussion. The six lectures given in July, 1925, were enthusiastic-ally received, especially by Ernest Jones. While she was in England she visited the Malting House School in Cambridge and met Susan Isaacs who had heard her lecture in London before she returned to Berlin after her three week visit. There is no record of how the two women got on during this visit, but clearly Melanie liked what she saw of the school. The two women were similar in age; at the time they met, Susan was forty and Melanie forty three years old. They came from extraordinarily different backgrounds, though Susan, having visited post-war Vienna for her analysis with Otto Rank and having married Nathan, a Jew from continental Europe, was familiar with many features of the culture into which Melanie had been born and educated.

The death in December, 1925 of Karl Abraham, who had been a great supporter, meant that Melanie Klein became further professionally isolated in Berlin. Her marriage had now ended. Her daughter, Melitta, was a medical student in Berlin and her older son, Hans, now nineteen years of age, had begun to train as an engineer also in Berlin. They were both leading independent lives and, having been delighted by the positive reactions to the six lectures she had given there, she decided she could make a better life for herself in London. Her mind was probably made up by the fact that Ernest Jones whose children, by now aged three and four years were showing some emotional problems asked her if she would come to London and undertake the analysis both of his children and of his wife, Katherine. All the same it was a bold step to emigrate to England. She came alone in September, 1926, but her son, Erich, now 12 years old, followed three months later. She soon found a place to live in Notting Hill just to the west of the centre of London. Her daughter, by then married to another analyst, Walter Schmideberg, and a qualified doctor, moved to England later in 1932. From the end of 1926 Melanie Klein began to attend the Wednesday meetings of the British Psycho-analytic Society as an observer. Indeed at a meeting held in November, 1926 she gave a paper describing the analysis of a five year old child. By April the following year she had been elected a full member.

On her arrival in London, Melanie Klein immediately began to attract both patients and a small but significant following among psycho-analysts. Susan was among the most devoted and loyal of these; indeed her intellectual and professional life was never the same again. Perhaps the most important reason for Melanie Klein's influence and success was that she was felt to be extending the original psychoanalytic findings in an exciting way into the field of early infancy, a phase of mental life that both Sigmund Freud and his daughter, Anna, had painted in vague and uncertain terms. In contrast, Melanie Klein gave the first two years of life a meaning and a developmental significance they had not previously possessed. Klein's practice and influence grew at the same time as her ideas and techniques developed more and more independently of the Vienna, Budapest and Berlin schools where she had been trained.

The reaction in Vienna was far less positive. Indeed in 1926, the year of Melanie Klein's arrival in London, Anna Freud, Sigmund's daughter, launched a fierce attack on her. Anna, born in 1896 and so fourteen years younger than Melanie, was her father's favourite child. She, like Susan Isaacs, trained as a teacher of young children, but gave up teaching a year after qualification to train as an analyst (Dyer, 1983). She was analysed by her father, an experience which, as we have seen, was quite common for the children of analyst parents at that time. She soon became a prominent figure in the analytic world, specialising in the treatment of neurotic children. While she was still in her twenties, together with a number of other analysts and her life-long friend, Dorothy Burlingham, she was a leading figure in the loosely formed Vienna School of Child Analysis. In 1926 she, with others, founded a nursery school for a small number of children who were also in analytic treatment. Between 1923 and 1926 she undertook a number of long analyses with disturbed children aged between six and eleven years.

In 1926 Anna Freud gave a series of lectures dealing with aspects of child analysis that were published in 1927 in German and later translated into English. She began these lectures with a discussion of the indications for child analysis. Right at the beginning of her first lecture she expresses her disbelief of Klein's view that:

any disturbance in the intellectual and emotional development of a child can be resolved or at least favourably influenced by psychoanalysis. She (Melanie Klein) goes still further in maintaining that an analysis greatly benefits the development of any normal child and will, in the course of time, become an indispensable complement to all modern psychology.

In contrast Anna Freud maintained that analysis is only appropriate where a child has developed a "genuine infantile neurosis".

Also, unlike Klein, she believed that children differ from adults in their insight into their illnesses, their capacity to exercise voluntary consent to treatment and in their wish to be cured. Her strongest criticisms were reserved for the exclusively sexual or aggressive nature of Klein's interpretations. To begin with, Anna Freud did not agree that a child's play is equivalent to the adult's free associations as a gateway to the unconscious. She ridicules Klein's interpreting a child knocking over a lamp post or a toy figure in terms of an expression of aggression against the father or a deliberate collision between two toy cars as evidence of the child having witnessed intercourse between the parents. There might well, according to her, be much less loaded explanations of such play. Finally she disagrees with Klein's assumption that if a child shows hostility to the analyst this is a carry over of hostile feelings towards one or both parents. On the contrary, thinks Anna Freud, it is children who have the warmest and most affectionate relationships with their parents who are most likely to see a stranger as threatening. According to her, the analyst's job with children is much more educational than inter- pretative. But the analyst should not hesitate to intervene if the child's family is seen to be acting in ways that are harmful to the child's development.

These forthright criticisms soon reached the ears of the London analysts who were indignant at the attack on Melanie Klein by a colleague. At Klein's request, Ernest Jones organised a symposium to discuss Anna Freud's criticisms and give Klein an opportunity for reply. At this meeting Barbara Low read a translation of the Anna Freud lectures. Melanie Klein replied and a number of colleagues spoke in support of her views. The next year Klein gave a paper on "Early Stages of the Oedipus conflict" that provided case material indicating that the struggle for the affection of opposite-sex parent began in the first year of life, much earlier than the fourth year that had been the age proposed by Sigmund Freud when he had first described this conflict. The attacks from Vienna against her persisted. David Eder, an early member of the Society, is recorded as having expressed his disappointment at Anna Freud's criticisms of Melanie Klein. At a meeting of the BPaS on 6 April, 1927, he pointed out that the theoretical objections she had raised were a "replica of those with which we are familiar in the diatribes against adult analysis". He thought that some of Anna Freud's remarks sounded almost like "a despairing attempt against accepting Freud's account of infantile sexuality".

So Susan Isaacs's return to London in 1927 coincided with a turbulent period in the history of the British Psycho-analytic Society. She had no hesitation in taking Melanie Klein's side in the dispute. Although there had been no children under the age of three years at the Malting House School, she was convinced as a result of her experience with these young children that their fantasy life was rich in aggressive and sexual imagery. She was not alone in this. Most of the more senior figures in the British Psycho-analytic Society, such as Ernest Jones, John Rickman, and, early on Edward Glover, were already persuaded that Klein's new ideas were valuable and could be helpful in treatment.

Her return also coincided with a crucial point in the establishment of psychoanalysis as a respectable and respected profession. From the end of the First World War, psycho-analysis had certainly spread in popularity but it had also attracted great hostility and much ridicule, especially in the press. In January, 1921, The Daily Graphic, a popular newspaper selling at one penny with a circulation of about a quarter of a million ran what it called an Inquiry into Psychoanalysis. In pseudo-authoritative mode it appointed anonymous commissioners to its Inquiry who daily reported on its status as a fashionable craze. They found that women were especially drawn to it and, as women were notoriously susceptible to fashionable ideas, they were warned that "they should be on their guard against charlatans and quacks". The headlines in the Daily Graphic give some indication of the level of discussion: "The New Quackery", "Abuses of Psychoanalysis", "Charlatans who Prey on Women and Weak-Minded Men", "The latest fashionable cult". The paper published various anecdotes to support their claims. Sometimes its approach was more nuanced and, at one point a sentence describing abusive practice began

"While admittedly good work has been done by properly qualified practitioners of psychoanalysis. . . ." Indeed the paper put much emphasis on the need for qualified doctors to be involved.

Criticism from a more authoritative source came 21 months later in The Times. On 13 September, 1922, The Times published a letter from the Archdeacon of the East Riding calling attention to an alleged attempt at recently held meetings of the British Association to "establish the current methods of psychoanalysis in our schools". He questioned the validity of the theory, claiming its effects on pupils would "saturate their minds with pornographic material". He objected to a theory of psychology that traced "by far the greater part of the content of the mind, conscious or unconscious, to the sexual impulse". This letter stimulated an angry correspondence, largely terminated by a letter published on 23 September from Cyril Burt, who had been the Recorder at the debate held at the Psychological Section of the British Association, in which he denied that any "proposals of the kind indicated" had even been put forward at the British Association meeting and that "no exponent of the 'strict Freudian school had spoken in the debate.'" Undaunted, on 17 October 1922 a Times leader quoted a lecture given by an eminent doctor, Lord Dawson of Penn, in which he claimed that psycho-analysis in the hands of its almost innumerable "operators is becoming a public danger ... the necessity of 'transference' of the patient's affection to the analyst during the period of analysis constitutes in some instances a menace which needs no emphasising".

Disquiet about the possible abuse of psycho-analysis continued over the following years and finally, in March, 1927, a committee of enquiry into psycho-analysis was set up by the British Medical Association. Ernest Jones played a skilful part in the negotiations of this committee that finally reported in July, 1929. The Psychoanalysis Committee pronounced that Freud and his followers had the right to use the term "psychoanalyst" and no one else had such a right. The Committee made no attempt to examine the evidence for the claims for therapeutic value made by analysts, leaving it to them to carry out the necessary work for this to happen.

One of the reasons Ernest Jones had been successful in his negotiations with the British Medical Association was that he was able to point to the fact that the Institute of Psycho-analysis and British Psycho-analytic Society had recently introduced a more formal training procedure, thus establishing psycho-analysis as a professional discipline with a training that followed an agreed curriculum and led to a clear procedure for accreditation as a trained analyst. Susan Isaacs decided she would pursue the course and fulfil the criteria that had been laid down. The course involved a further personal psycho-analysis, the conduct of a full psycho-analytic treatment with an adult, a full psycho-analytic treatment of a child and attendance at a course of lectures given by Institute staff.

Although ostensibly her analysis was undertaken as part of her further analytic training, it may well have been the opportunity to discuss and, in the jargon, "work through" her difficult personal situation in a third analysis, following those she had had with J. C. Flugel and Otto Rank, that pushed her towards undertaking further training.

Joan Riviere, whom Susan chose to conduct her training analysis, was a colourful woman with a past to match (Hughes, 2004). At the time she began Susan Isaacs's analysis, seeing her four or five times a week for six years, she was 44 years old, just two years older than Susan. But they came to this prolonged and intensive encounter with very different experiences behind them. Joan was born in 1883 to a solicitor father and a mother who was the daughter of a vicar. Her uncle, Arthur Verrall was a distinguished classics don at Cambridge, where he was a key figure in the Society for Psychical Research. She had an unconventional schooling and went to Gotha to live in a family at the age of seventeen. There she learned fluent German. She was talented in dress design and, when she came back from Germany she worked as a court dressmaker for a couple of years. Married at 23 in 1906 to a barrister, she developed strong interests in social problems, becoming an active campaigner for divorce reform and votes for women.

At around this time Riviere also became interested in psychology and especially in unconscious mental processes. She attended meetings of the Society for Psychical Research at her uncle's house. Many years later, James Strachey recalled her as "standing by the fireplace at an evening party, tall, strikingly handsome, distinguished-looking and somehow impressive". It was already clear that she had a sharp mind and powerful intelligence. But in 1909 her life began to go wrong. Her father, like Susan's father, died in that year, but, instead of this bereavement acting, as it did with Susan, as an energising event, she became to suffer from "nerves". Although she probably suffered from anxiety and depression earlier than this, the first mention of "nerves" in her private, but remarkably unrevealing diary is not until March, 1915. At any rate, at least from this time, she began to suffer what were then called a series of "nervous breakdowns" and was admitted to different sanatoria on a number of occasions (Appignanesi and Forrester, 1993).

In 1916, because of these "nervous symptoms", she was introduced to Ernest Jones. She was in analysis with him from 1916 to 1921. True to his previous form with highly attractive women patients, Jones behaved in an inappropriate way in his relationship with her outside the analytic situation though on this occasion his behaviour was less reprehensible than it had been in the past. Around this time his own personal relationships were going through a traumatic period. He had earlier begun an affair with Lina, the maid of Loe Kann, his mistress or common law wife with whom he had been living for some years. However in 1917 he stopped the affair with Lina and married a Welsh woman, Morfydd Owen. She died a year later of appendicitis in a remote part of Wales, during an operation in which he had to assist himself in the absence of more skilled help. A year later, in 1919, he was married again, this time to an Austrian, Katherine Jokl, with whom he lived happily for the next forty years (Maddox, 2006).

Joan Riviere was well aware of these traumatic events, separations and deaths, occurring in the life of her analyst. She had fantasies, or perhaps not just fantasies, but realistic ideas, of marrying Jones herself. She fell in love with him, but he rejected her declaration of love. Foolishly, when she was in a desperate state, Jones lent her his country cottage for a week as she had nowhere to go for a holiday. Such close contact with Jones's personal life, when she was so frustrated in her love for him led to an angry reaction on her part and the analysis broke down. In desperation, Jones referred her to Freud in Vienna for further analysis.

Jones was reasonably, though not fully honest in what he told Freud about the predicament into which he had got himself. He admitted that her case was "the worst failure I have ever had". His loan of his cottage had "led to a declaration of love and to the brokenhearted cry that she had never been rejected before (she had been the mistress of a number of men). From that time on she devoted herself to torturing me without any intermission and with considerable success and ingenuity, being a fiendish sadist". Jones laid down a challenge to Freud. "The saying is that her visit to Vienna will be the final and most severe test of psychoanalysis and people are most curious to see if her disdainful way of treating other people like dirt beneath her feet will undergo any modification". Freud was not best pleased with his disciple's conduct. "You may imagine how little charmed I was by the prospects opened in your letter. I will spare myself any further remarks on the subject as you seem to have suffered sufficiently for your mistake. But let us hope all (sic) these adventures belong to the past".

Despite the unpromising start, this referral to Freud was a remarkable success. Freud liked Riviere and found her, as he wrote to Jones "not half as black as you had painted her. . . . In my experience you have not to scratch too deeply the skin of a masculine woman to bring her femininity to the light". (An element of sexual vanity can surely be detected here in the sixty year old Freud's words to the forty year old Jones!) In any event, under Freud's care, Joan Riviere became considerably less emotionally distressed, lost her vicious anger towards Jones, with whom she remained on good terms, and subsequently was able to work effectively until her death forty years later.

But her life was changed. Her previously chaotic relationships and somewhat empty emotional life were replaced by a strong commitment to psychoanalysis. Freud was so impressed by her and by her linguistic ability in German that he suggested to Jones that he appoint her to be the translation editor of the International Journal of Psycho-analysis. Jones resisted and this led to a tirade from Freud about how hard it had been to conduct Riviere's analysis because of Jones's behaviour towards her. Freud did not however minimise the severity of his patient's difficulties. He referred to her "narcissistic problem . . . a case of a character-analysis super-added to that of a neurosis". He felt that her conflict between "Ego and Ideal" which was unconscious, was the cause of her continuous dissatisfaction, "whenever it is revived she projects her self-criticism onto other people, turns her pangs of conscious into sadistic behaviour, tries to render other people unhappy because she is so herself". He added that "her sexual freedom may be an appearance, the keeping up of which required those compensatory attitudes as haughtiness, majestic behaviour etc".

Jones relented; indeed in the circumstances he had little option, and appointed her to the post Freud had suggested. Joan Riviere was now transformed from Jones's "worst analytic case" to a leading figure in British psycho-analysis. But many of the personality traits that Freud had noted did not, in fact, change. She remained hyper-critical, and many suffered from her biting wit. On one occasion later in her career when she wrote a positive report on one of her trainees, it was commented that this had only ever happened once before. She gave praise exceedingly sparingly. Her book reviews in the International Journal were often scathing. For example, she began a review of a book (Riviere, 1921) intended to provide a modern, including a psycho-analytic view of dreams and the unconscious, with the paragraph:

Nobody who wishes to acquire any information about psycho-analysis need turn his attention to this book, for there is none to be found in it; but on those who, like the author, have heard or read a little about it, and find it disagreeable and disquieting, it may have a soothing effect. . . . The vagueness and intensity of the whole book is indescribable.

Riviere's distaste for the "soothing effect" of the book she was reviewing is significant. What she appears to have found most attractive and exciting in psycho-analysis was its courageous attempt to face up to the destructive, sadistic and violently sexual elements in human fantasies and behaviour. These were anything but soothing. Perhaps it was this that led her to move from strictly orthodox Freudian psycho-analysis to an acceptance and later an enthusiastic espousal of the more exuberant theories of Melanie Klein.

Although they had previously met at the previous Congress at The Hague in 1920, Joan Riviere first developed a friendship with Melanie Klein at the Salzburg International Psycho-analytic Congress in 1924. As we shall see in more detail later, the main innovations that Klein brought to psycho-analysis were her ideas that the infant's mental life in the first two years of life was active and turbulent, that the infant experienced not only love for its parents but also terror of them leading to sadistic and aggressive fantasies towards them, that the way in which these fantasies developed affected the future mental life of the individual and that early psycho-analytic treatment, even before the age of five years, could have a beneficial effect.

Joan Riviere (1936) provided a vivid description of the inner fantasy life of the infant as visualised by the Kleinians:

Limbs shall trample, kick and hit; lips, fingers and hands shall suck, twist and pinch; teeth shall bite, gnaw, mangle and cut,

mouth shall devour, swallow and 'kill' (annihilate); eyes kill
by a look, pierce and penetrate. . . .

It is surely not too fanciful to imagine that, in Riviere's own fantasy
life, her previous sexual fantasies, played out in her earlier sexual
affairs, while she had been, in Jones's words, the "mistress of a
number of men", were replaced by this new Kleinian vision of the
infant's fantasy life as erotically sado-masochistic. Following her
analysis with Freud, Joan Riviere's sexual affairs ceased, to be
replaced by a passionate interest in the erotic, sadistic and aggressive
fantasies of infants. Of course the fact that Joan Riviere may have
had very personal reasons for embracing Kleinian theories does not,
in any way invalidate them. People often arrive at the "truth"
(whatever this may be) for reasons related to their personalities or
even their psychopathologies.

So this was the woman with whom Susan Isaacs chose to have a
further personal analysis in 1927. Because of many professional
contacts with her through the British Psycho-analytic Society,
Susan knew that she had placed herself in the hands of someone
who was highly intelligent, unusually critical and sparing in her
praise, and, perhaps most importantly and significantly, a committed
Kleinian in psycho-analytic orientation. Some idea of the themes that
emerged in her analysis with Joan Riviere are described in the almost
certainly autobiographical account of herself given in 1934, the year
after the termination of her own analysis in a lecture entitled
"Rebellious and Defiant Children".

In this article she gives an account of a girl whose behaviour,
throughout her school years, were characterised by obstinacy,
noisiness, disobedience, chasing boys and occasional stealing. This
child's mother had died when she was six years old. A later analysis
had revealed "earlier anxieties connected with her love of her mother,
her fear of her desire for her mother's exclusive love and attention
and thus of the envy and hatred of her older brothers and sisters;
and her still earlier anxiety that her own love and desire had
damaged the mother's breast by its greedy quality". At the time
Susan Isaacs was in analysis, Melanie Klein was developing a new
set of ideas about the causes of depression. These were only published in 1935 in a paper on manic-depressive states, but they were
discussed among the Kleinian group before they were published.

These laid emphasis on the universal experience of the first important loss in life that occurs at the time of weaning. The infant's hatred of the mother for withdrawing the breast conflicts with the love the infant feels for her, thus producing a profound and distressing sense of ambivalence, itself leading to the development of the "depressive position".

Susan's experience of abrupt weaning had been followed by the experience of her mother mourning for her dead son, Susan's slightly older brother. Not long after her mother, recovered from her depression, had become available to her again, she became pregnant and a rival sister was born when Susan was four years old. Her mother then became ill and once again Susan experienced a serious loss. Her guilt for her angry feelings towards her mother would have been intensified when she was reprimanded for telling lies about her father becoming fond of the nurse who was looking after her mother. The death of her mother would have been seen in psychoanalytic terms as a fulfilment of her oedipal wish to supplant her mother as her father's lover. From this perspective it is difficult to imagine a scenario more likely to elicit guilt in a six year old child with both immediate and long-lasting effects on her behaviour as well as her social and later sexual relationships. While she was a child this seems to have resulted in unusually aggressive, difficult behaviour, only resolved when she became reconciled with her father in her late teens. If, as seems probable, Susan later suffered from frigidity, it is likely that her Kleinian analysis would have pointed to unresolved grief for her mother, the reason for the lack of resolution lying in her guilt. Another element in the development of her frigidity that might well have been explored was her love for but also identification with her dominant father, giving rise to unconscious homosexual feelings interfering with normal heterosexual intercourse. Exploration of these themes would have given her an understanding of her sexual predicament (great love and affection for Nathan but absence of sexual feeling for him) that satisfied her both intellectually and emotionally even if it did not result in a change of behaviour.

Susan's previous two analyses had been carried out by men with a strongly Freudian orientation. J. C. Flugel, her colleague at University College, had been analysed by Ernest Jones, who had himself been analysed by Ferenczi, one of Freud's inner circle. We do not know the focus of Susan's two year analysis with Flugel, but he brought to the encounter a belief in the central importance of the Oedipus complex and of penis envy in girls, so it is highly probable that Susan's early relationship with her father in childhood and adolescence, the long illness and death of her mother, and the subsequent re-marriage of her father and her relationship with her step-mother would have been prominent issues, but would not have been related to much earlier, infantile experiences.

At the time she saw him in Vienna for her second analysis, Otto Rank, in many ways Freud's favourite disciple, had branched out in his ideas and had floated the notion, heretical to many of Freud's associates, but tolerated by Freud himself, that the basis of much neurotic anxiety lay in the traumatic experience of birth. We know nothing about the interactions between Rank and Susan Isaacs. Her own birth had, as far as we know, been normal. She might however have been impressed by the fact that someone so close to Freud himself was now laying emphasis on such early experience.

There were other reasons why Susan might feel particularly comfortable to have Joan Riviere as her analyst (though in passing it might be noted that clearly Joan Riviere regarded it as part of her job to make the people she analysed feel uncomfortable). In 1929 Riviere published a paper on the intellectual woman. In this paper "Womanliness as a Masquerade" she refers to the fact that, until recent years, women who pursued intellectual pursuits were usually overtly masculine. Now, she wrote, women in university life, in one of the professions or in business often seemed to fulfil "every criterion of complete feminine development". As well as successful in their occupations, they seem to be excellent wives and mothers, and to lead full social lives. She then goes on to describe one particular woman (certainly not Susan Isaacs who had no children) whom she has seen in analytic practice. This woman apparently fulfilled all these criteria and yet suffered from a constant need for professional and sexual approval from men. This fear arose from a fear of attack by men in response to her aggressive fantasies towards them. Her femininity was a mask disguising her hatred of men. This hatred is itself attributed by Riviere to frustration in her early feeding. The woman is described as having fantasies that she bites off her father's penis, and reveal fears that her mother would "mutilate her, devour her, torture her and kill her". Riviere concludes that "fully developed heterosexual womanhood is founded. . . .on the oral-sucking stage.

The sole gratification of a primary order in it is that of receiving the (nipple, milk) penis, semen, child from the father". She makes it appear as if the girl baby has an inner life in which fantasies of adult-sounding themes are incorporated and indeed need to be incorporated for normal development to occur.

There may be different views about the plausibility of the conclusions that Joan Riviere drew from this analysis, but she had clearly given a great deal of thought to the predicament of intellectual women in demanding positions who were often in competition with men and needed to work with and socialise with them, while remaining feminine in appearance and manner. She placed great emphasis on the satisfaction in the early feeding experiences of these women in the first year of their lives. To the intellectual Susan Isaacs, a woman with significant psychosexual problems, who had been abruptly weaned when she was between seven and eight months old at the time of the death of her older brother, it must have seemed fortunate that her chosen analyst had a set of theories so highly relevant to her own situation.

In another paper entitled "Jealousy as a mechanism of defence", Joan Riviere (1932) suggests that women who show sexual jealousy have psychological defences developed in early infancy, when they experience deep primal envy in which the "child's desire to despoil and ravage the mother—container of milk, breast, penis and children"—ultimately results in adulthood in a loved partner being unjustly suspected of infidelities. Again, Susan's predicament as the wife of a man who was conducting a passionate affair with another woman who had been a colleague and was still ostensibly a friend of hers must surely have raised issues of jealousy for which her analyst seemed well equipped to deal. At any rate, Susan was deeply grateful for the insights she felt she had gained during her analysis. She dedicated her important book on the social development of children to "Joan Riviere, who has taught me to understand my own childhood".

On her return to London and while she was undertaking her training, Susan Isaacs became a more active member of the Society. In March, 1927, she gave a paper about the school called "The Reaction of a Group of Children to Unusual Sexual Freedom". She made a number of general points. Very young children, she thought, do not constitute groups because each child is "working out his own imperative fantasies". One condition of friendship among children is their need for an outsider, an enemy. In many children, she thought, "it is only possible to love A if there is B to hate"—a pessimistic view, if true, which many today would doubt. She considered that the brotherly feeling within a group of children is most intense when "the group is united in hostility to an adult". Freud's picture of the relationships of a "group of brothers to the primal father" had been amply confirmed by her observations of the Malting House School children.

Increasingly, she quoted Klein's ideas in her own occasional contributions to the psycho-analytic literature. In 1927, for example, she published a short account of a six and a half year old girl in the International Journal of Psycho-analysis. The paper was titled "Penis-Faeces-Child". Despite this somewhat startling title, the paper provides a rather bland description of a "normal" child, X, who touched her pregnant aunt's abdomen and asked what was in it. Surprisingly we are not told how the question was answered. Subsequently X took considerable interest in the penises of a group of boys at school and, after seeing them, began to stick her tummy out. Then, after being told off at school, she ran to the lavatory and said she had fallen down it. She played a fantasy game with an older boy, pretending to marry him and have children. She made some egg-cup covers. She then asked her mother if she could defaecate in the drawing room and after being told that she must use the bathroom, her mother discovered an egg-cup in a corner of the drawing room that X must have put there. The case description ends with only the briefest commentary and it is not clear quite what one is supposed to learn from it. But in its focus on confusion between faeces, the unborn fetus, the penis and penis envy, faeces and defaecation, the laying of eggs etc, the paper seems to derive a good deal from Kleinian theory.

In another paper the following year, 1928, on "The Mental Hygiene of the Pre-School Child", Susan quotes Klein when she discusses the difficulties of developing mental health preventive strategies with the limited knowledge currently available. A central problem, she thinks, is the relationship between external factors and the inner workings of the mind. She quotes Klein as someone who is exploring "the fixations and the way and the time at which these fixations become connected with experience".

Finally, in her last contribution to the psycho-analytic literature for some time, a paper entitled "Privation and Guilt", published in the International Journal of Psycho-analysis in 1929, but written shortly after she began her analysis with Joan Riviere, Susan tackled the task of reconciling Melanie Klein's observations of young children with classical Freudian theory. She begins this paper by explaining that its aim is to set out some of the difficulties which appear to arise when the earlier formulas for the origin of the superego are set against the facts of mental history discovered directly by Melanie Klein's technique. She then goes on to suggest how a concept put forward by Ernest Jones might resolve these difficulties. Freud had put forward the theory that the super-ego or conscience developed as a result of the child's sense of guilt over his murderous fantasies towards his father, his rival for his mother's affections. According to Freud and his followers, the "Oedipus complex" that this triangular relationship (mother-father-child) reflected was only resolved at around the age of four or four and a half years.

Yet Melanie Klein had reported observations that suggested guilt was experienced by infants much earlier than Freud had proposed. According to Klein, the origins of guilt begin in the second half of the first year of life, at the point when the baby first experiences frustration. Around this time or perhaps even earlier than this, the baby is described by Klein in her paper "The Early Stages of the Oedipus Conflict" as responding to frustration in feeding by desiring "to get possession of the mother's faeces, by penetrating into her body, cutting it to pieces, devouring it and destroying it". This dramatic state of affairs is exacerbated at the time of weaning, when "the match of a fire of already prepared dissatisfaction" is lit. Over the next year, during toilet training, further matches are struck and fuel the fires of dissatisfaction. The infant experiences guilt over its own destructive urges at all stages of this process, through from the early feeding situation, at the time of weaning, during toilet training and then, only finally as Freud had proposed, during the genital stage when the Oedipal conflict is not, in fact, initiated but prolonged and intensified. Thus, according to Klein, "the earliest components of guilt belong to the least differentiated and graded levels of experience". This early onset at a time when the infant is only able to respond in the most primitive way accounts for the fact that guilt in infancy and early childhood is marked by its "all-or-noneness and automaticity".

It is clear that by this point, Susan Isaacs is committed to Kleinian theories to the extent that she now sees herself as able to make original contributions explaining the way they extend, in her view, knowledge about child development. She and her analyst are at one on the significance of Klein's theories for understanding human development.

During her personal training analysis with Joan Riviere, Susan Isaacs also fulfilled the other criteria to become a fully trained analyst for children as well as adults. She attended lectures by a range of prominent figures in the analytic world, including John Rickman, Melanie Klein, Edward Glover and Nina Searl. Supervised by James Strachey, she carried out the analysis of an adult, and Melanie Klein supervised her analysis of a child. In 1933, at the age of forty eight she was regarded as having satisfactorily completed all aspects of her child and adult psycho-analytic training. She was now fully qualified and, in psychoanalytic circles regarded as fully equipped to help children as well as adults in their own predicaments using analytic treatment.

CHAPTER NINE

The wisdom of Ursula Wise

For Nathan and Susan Isaacs the years after their return from Cambridge to London in late 1927 represented a period of stability. After returning from Cambridge, they were soon able to afford to rent 16c Primrose Hill Road, a flat in a large house situated opposite Primrose Hill, a small park in a leafy part of north-west London. After a few years they were able to move to 30a Primrose Hill Road, a slightly larger flat with a better view on the same road, in a house on the corner of Oppidans Road. They both led active lives. Nathan worked first for three years as a senior manager in a firm called Besser-Waechter to study the possibilities of plastics manufacture. Then he joined a firm called Murex, engaged in the import and export of metals. Here he was employed first as Export Sales Manager and then as Commercial Manager. Meanwhile Susan continued to lecture in various part-time jobs as a psychologist at the same time practising as a psycho-analyst, seeing both adults and children. Frustrated at not being able to continue to pursue the opportunity to write about psychology and education in the way that his work for Geoffrey Pyke had allowed him, Nathan looked around for more congenial employment. In 1928 he drafted an advertisement that reflects his restlessness:

> Advertiser, aged 33, wide interests in psychology, politics, education, literature and radical views: in short reasonably civilised person with concern in civilised things; hitherto employed in commerce, now seeks more attractive work. Linguist (French,

Spanish, some Italian)—specialised knowledge of philosophical sciences—perhaps some aptitude with pen—long practical experience in commercial and industrial affairs, and in general a fair prospect of being found useful in any one of a number of places, if he can hit upon one of them. Does not expect repaying work to be quite as paying as his useless commercial activities, but as neither a rentier nor a communist, decent salary indispensable. Permanency required. Useful industrial work would be far more attractive to the advertiser than his uneconomic branch of pure commerce, but he would prefer any non-competitive work with some cultural or social outlook to it. He does not doubt that there are many thousands with the same amiable wants and as good qualification, but takes the off-chance of one of them happening to be looked for. Offers to Box. . . .

It is not clear whether this advertisement was actually placed, but, in any event, Nathan was unsuccessful in escaping from the "commercial activities" he found so distasteful. His hours were long and, when he changed jobs he had a considerable journey to work as the offices of Murex were in Rainham, Kent. In a letter to a friend written in October, 1933 describing his work there he explained that he had to leave home at 7.40, getting back at 7.15 pm, occasionally working late and from time to time traveling abroad. He found some compensation in his membership of the Aristotelian Society, a London-based society allowing him the opportunity to debate philosophical issues. His contributions were seriously regarded. In 1931 he read a paper to the Society to which his friend, the economist Lionel Robbins, later the Director of the London School of Economics, responded with a paper, later to be turned into a book of major significance "The Nature and Significance of Economic Science" (1935).

As we saw in Chapter 7 the relationship between Evelyn and her husband began while Susan was detaching herself from the Malting House School in 1927. She must rapidly have realised its intensity for it was not hidden from her. She had already had experience of one divorce. Another divorce must have seemed very much on the cards. So it is not surprising that, in order to assure her own financial viability, she began to look for sources of income beyond her part-time lecturing and meagre fees from psycho-analysis, the latter just about paying for the training psycho-analysis she began with Joan Riviere at this time. She looked at the possibility of writing a popular book for parents.

Books of advice to parents to help them bring up their children have a long pedigree going back to classical times. The modern era of baby books begins with John Locke, philosopher of the Enlightenment and physician. In "Some Thoughts Concerning Education" published in 1693, he put forward his views on the child's mind as a blank slate. It was up to parents and then to tutors or teachers to write on this slate in order to form the character of their children. They needed to be firm in resolve to achieve the best results. Locke's book was popular and durable; it was reprinted 26 times, only going out of print in 1800.

Jean-Jacques Rousseau's "Emile: or On Education", published in 1762, sold less well, but was more influential in nineteenth century ideas on child upbringing. Rousseau was perhaps the first to write on child upbringing from the standpoint of a strong ideological commitment to child-centredness. His book, written for mothers ("It is to you that I address myself, tender and foresighted mother") begins with a cry to parents to allow the innate goodness of children to emerge with the minimum of interference. "Everything is good as it leaves the hands of the Author of things; everything degenerates in the hands of man. The great danger," he wrote, "is to repress the good nature of the child. Teacher and pupil should be equals in their search for knowledge". The activity of the child, he insisted, must be encouraged, not repressed, for it reflects his curiosity and this will motivate his learning. Indeed formal academic education should not begin until the age of 12 years.

The first half of the nineteenth century brought a mass of books and magazines for mothers providing great quantities of advice of one sort or another. These were written by physicians, society women who were also mothers and feminist authors, each writing from their own perspective. There was often a heavy emphasis on the acquisition of good manners that would identify a child as coming from a socially superior family. Advice was often tinged with moral religiosity, sometimes with a sentimental view of childhood, but usually the advice given was pragmatic and sensible by present day standards.

The scientific revolution in thought initiated by Charles Darwin in the middle of the nineteenth century arrested this flood of good advice. It was clear that his theory of evolution with its emphasis on the kinship between man and the animal world, and on inborn differences in the behaviour of individuals had implications for child-upbringing. But it was not so clear what these implications might be. In 1877 Darwin published his detailed observations of one of his own children in his "Biographical Sketch of an Infant". This stimulated a rush of imitators, James Sully's diaries of his own children's development in "Studies of Childhood", published in 1895, being the best known.

The prevailing ethos acknowledged there was much that was unknown about child development; parents, as well as psychologists and educators could contribute to closing the knowledge gap by making observations of their own children. This was the rationale behind the development of numerous Child Study Groups both in the United States and in Britain. Darwin's influence was not the only reason why parents began to look for a more scientific background in those giving them advice. By the turn of the century, improvements in child health were just beginning to result in a remarkable decline in infant mortality. Public health doctors, advocating better hygiene, balanced diets and the more effective prevention of infection were given the credit for these improvements. Parents became hungry for the views of men such as the American paediatrician, Luther Emmett Holt, on how to bring up their children. His simply expressed views in "The Care and Feeding of Children" first published in 1894, but revised many times, were popular on both sides of the Atlantic.

The status given to science and medicine meant that the stage was now set for the professionalisation of child care. This happened first with nannies or nursery nurses. In 1892 the first Norland Nursing School was established in Notting Hill Gate, in London. The students followed a comprehensive curriculum, involving the study of infant nutrition, hygiene and later child development. The teachers prescribed very closely how the young Norland nurse was to behave. These girls were to have superior social status to the common or garden nanny. The schools offered "a new career to gentlewomen by birth and education, and to girls of good education and refinement". This superior social tone gave further status to the work of bringing up children.

Such professional advice was soon offered to those lower down the social scale. In 1899 the first "milk depot" in Britain providing free, clean artificial milk was established in St. Helen's, in Lancashire. Such places began to be established throughout the country and, as well as free milk, began to dispense free advice to mothers on how to bring up their children. In an attack on infant mortality, the "milk depots", now called infant consultation centres, began to be staffed by trained or semi-trained health visitors. By 1916, a Local Government Board report laid down the numbers of health visitors that would be required to provide national coverage and in 1919, formal health visitor training programmes were established in Britain. By 1928, at the time Susan Isaacs began to write for parents, all health visitors were required for the first time to hold a Health Visitor's Certificate (Department of Health, 1976).

The professionalisation of nannies and the creation of the new nursing profession of health visitor led to the professionalisation of knowledge about the upbringing of children. After all, if a diploma was needed to practice as a nanny or health visitor, how could mothers be expected to do a reasonable job bringing up their children without special training? Middle class mothers had their own built-in professional in the trained nanny, but those a little further down the scale had only their mothers and perhaps older sisters or friends to turn to. Increased geographical mobility meant that mothers were less likely to live near their own mothers. So, not surprisingly, the need for books on child care and articles in magazines increased. Some baby books such as the popular "Common Sense in the Nursery" by Charis Barnett (Mrs. Frankenburg), first published in 1922, but reprinted several times, continued to be written by experienced and articulate mothers who were not afraid to question received wisdom—"The Gentleman in Whitehall", she wrote, "does not always know best . . . It is the parent's business to train children in healthy and active interests". But from now on there were going to be far more books written by professionals, especially drawn from psychology and the new specialist fields of paediatrics and psycho-analysis, than by parents.

Now if advice on child upbringing was henceforth to be based on the best scientific evidence, and all the baby books made this claim for their contents, it might be thought that the experts would speak with one voice. But in fact, this was far from the case (Hardyment, 1995).

There was a wide gulf especially between those behaviourists who drew their scientific evidence largely from the training of animals, often involving experiments using Pavlovian conditioning, and the psycho-analysts, whose knowledge they themselves regarded as equally scientific, coming mainly from intensive psychological probing of disturbed children sent to them for treatment. The theories and evidence from which the two opposing groups drew their knowledge were thus very different and, unsurprisingly, the advice they gave was very different.

Susan was not the first British psycho-analyst to write for parents. In particular, Hugh Crichton Miller, the founder and first Director of what has been for many years the best-known psychoanalytic establishment in the world, the Tavistock Clinic in London, wrote "The New Psychology and the Parent", published in 1922. This leading psycho-analyst tackled the task of writing a book for parents a few years before Susan Isaacs wrote her book from a similar perspective. All in all, Crichton Miller's book would be regarded today as a model of how *not* to write for parents. It begins with a firm condemnation of parents who are unfortunate enough to have a child with a "nervous breakdown". He confidently starts his book "The principal cause of all nervous breakdowns lies in the wrong treatment of the child by his parents". To avoid such "wrong treatment", he places great emphasis on the need for parents to have self-knowledge, preferably through having a psycho-analysis, if they are to avoid disaster in bringing up their children. While acknowledging that it is quite impracticable to imagine that psycho-analysis could be available to the entire population of parents, he gives no suggestions how self-knowledge is to be obtained in any other way. What is needed is for parents to rid themselves of unconscious motives; dreams provide a good guide to such undesirable thoughts. He then provides a number of classic Freudian interpretations of different dreams. He warns against amateur interpretations, so it is difficult to see why he provides these equations between dreaming about, for example, bulls and sexual libido or dreaming about moles and burrowing into the deeper recesses of the mind, if he does not want parents themselves to use dream content as a gateway to an understanding of their own minds. His use of psycho-analytic jargon (transference of the affect, compensation, projection and so on) makes his book even less user-friendly.

There is what would be regarded today as some good sense in Crichton Miller's book, but, reading the book, it is difficult to escape the conclusion that his own unconscious motivation sometimes gets in the way of the provision of helpful advice. For example, he has a horror of children developing homosexuality or masturbating. He warns "There is a constant possibility of the romantic friendships between girls developing into homosexuality" and later states that "the great thing for parents to remember is that masturbation is an indication that there is something wrong in the child's life and it is always wise to seek that something out and remedy it". Of course his views on these subjects must be seen in the context of the attitudes of his day, still influenced by Victorian attitudes and beliefs about "self-abuse". But it has to be said that despite the New Psychology in the title of his book and of which Crichton Miller is so strong an advocate, he seems to have had little new to say on these matters. This is surprising in view of the fact that, by 1922, strong links had already developed between psychoanalysis and the sexually sophisticated world of Bloomsbury.

Susan Isaacs brought a wider experience and indeed a unique combination of knowledge and skills to the business of giving advice to inexperienced or confused mothers. If she had been asked herself from where her most original ideas about child rearing came, she would probably have selected her psycho-analytic training and experience. This gave her confidence in discussing the emotional development of children, their moods, fears and anxieties, in ways that her competitors, usually more focused on the growth and stimulation of intelligence, found more difficult and challenging. Not only anxiety and misery, but love and hate, envy and jealousy, creativity and destructiveness—these are the psycho-analyst's bread and butter. This was a considerable advantage to her, for these were the issues about which readers of baby books most crave information. Her ideological commitment to psycho-analytic concepts, especially those of Melanie Klein, sometimes seem to have made her go overboard in dramatising the passions, especially the aggressive tendencies of young children and the complexity of their emotional experiences. But in most respects her psycho-analytic experience gave her an edge over her competitors.

Her professional training as a psychologist in Cambridge was also a significant advantage. The particular contribution of the academic mind is its fascination with and curiosity about areas of uncertainty and ignorance. Susan was well aware of the limitations of knowledge in the field of child development. Consequently she was able to claim not only scientific detachment for her views, but to indicate, with some justification, that if she did not know the answer to a problem a mother posed, then probably nobody else did. (Indeed, one attractive definition of an expert is someone who is able to say with confidence that not only does he or she not know the answer to a question, but that there is no one in the whole world who does either.) Only a few years earlier, she had written a textbook on psychology that had established her academic reputation. Further, psychoanalysis was, at that time, not universally but widely viewed as an empirical science, so it was not merely as an academic psychologist that she could lay claim to scientific expertise—psycho-analysis was equally important in this respect.

As a trained teacher of young children she had further credibility. She had not only founded and directed the Malting House School, but had previously taught nursery classes in Bolton before going on to Manchester University, where, as part of her teacher training, she had continued to teach children of nursery age. At Darlington she had been Mistress of Method or what would today be called Director of the Infant Section of a large Teacher Training College. She had taught children from all strata of society, both in very large and in quite small classes.

What was lacking and sometimes this showed, was the fact that she had never had any children of her own. She had, it is true, helped to bring up her younger sister, Alice, four years younger than she, and Alice's recollections of her childhood suggest that Susan played a significant part in her own upbringing. At the Malting House School Susan had watched the development of young children, some of whom had been boarders from the age of three years. Finally, from the time of her birth in 1928, she and Nathan took a good deal of responsibility for the upbringing of her niece by marriage, Karina. Karina's mother, Mallie, Nathan's older sister, had personal problems that meant that, from the start, she needed help in bringing up her daughter; Susan and Nathan were often involved in caring for her. But, all in all, compared to other dispensers of advice, Susan was lacking in the direct, personal experience of bringing up children of her own. It is arguable just how important this is. Of course, people writing from direct experience can describe with great feeling the despair that comes with that awful feeling of having failed as a parent. But there is also the danger of over-generalising from personal experience. Doctors and psychologists who have brought up their own temperamentally placid and easy to rear children will incline to give different advice from those whose children have been unusually fretful or irritable.

To compensate for her lack of children of her own however, Susan brought one very considerable advantage. She had a wonderfully lucid writing style, perhaps partly inherited from and certainly strongly nurtured by her journalist father. Always good at expressing her views, her experience in her teens at the Birtenshaw Mutual Improvement Society, at the Manchester University Women's Students Union of which she had been President and as a lecturer to infant teachers in training had all sharpened her ability to put forward her views in a succinct and forthright manner. She had an attractive way of addressing parents and nursery nurses, sometimes admittedly with a whiff of patronage, but always sympathetic, clear and practical in what she wrote. She was particularly good at reminding parents what it is like to be a powerless child. In a BBC broadcast she made in 1929 called "The Trials of a Child" she describes a three or four year old in a crowded railway carriage. What does it feel like to be him? Surrounded by strange faces, some of which smile at you while others don't. What does that mean? Wanting to move around but constantly being told to sit still. Fascinated by the cows in a field and wanting to see more of them but not understanding how to make more of them come; getting tired, irritable and weepy when the scenery doesn't change and then being told off for not enjoying the journey.

Susan Isaacs' most significant publication for parents was a short book "The Nursery Years" first published in 1929. The book was enlarged for a second edition in 1932 and then reprinted without further amendment nineteen times right up to 1971 when it at last went out of print. There is no information on the number of copies in each print, but, at a conservative estimate, it is likely that Routledge and Kegan Paul, the publishers, sold around 100,000 copies over this time. Forty three years is a long time for a book to remain in print, unrevised. Benjamin Spock's book on baby and child care which followed Susan's and out-performed it in popularity is still in print sixty years after its initial publication in 1946 (Spock, 2005), but it has undergone various major revisions over this time. Susan made a deliberate decision not to revise the book for later editions because she thought her advice had stood the test of time well. It still has contemporary relevance over seventy years after it was written.

She begins her book by suggesting that mothers and nurses are "turning away from mere custom and blind tradition, to science". Mothers need to know what to do, to be informed by science, and matters cannot wait until children go to school as "the main lines of their behaviour are by then firmly fixed".

She considers the difficulties that parents face, for example when they tell lies or ask questions about sex, when they are involved in biting, masturbating, throwing things on the floor, chalking on the walls, playing with fire or matches, in disobedience generally. Her approach lays great emphasis on the understanding of a child's behaviour. Obviously, she says, "we can only decide what we ought to do and what we should say when we understand what the children's behaviour means to them and know the actual effect of what we do".

Writing about individual differences between children and indeed between parents she admits that it is only possible to offer "broad guiding principles, and not . . . cut and dried practical advice. I cannot offer the latter, because parents differ, children differ and circumstances differ. What may be good advice for one may be unsound for another. It is, indeed, an essential part of intelligent parenthood to break away from rules of thumb, and learn to judge each situation for each child on its own merits in the light of a general understanding of the ways of growth."

After this general, introductory chapter, Susan moves straight into a discussion of play. She makes a telling point from a comparison with the animal world. The animals which are "able to *learn* more are also able to *play* more. Those with fixed and inherited instincts play not at all". Children learn, she claims echoing both Froebel and Robert Owen, largely through play. "Play is indeed the child's work, and the means whereby he grows and develops. Active play can be looked upon as a sign of mental health; and its absence, either of some inborn defect or of mental illness". Through play the child learns to use his hands, arms and legs to best effect. He explores and discovers the world around him. "No experimental scientist" she writes "has a greater thirst for new facts than an ordinary healthy active child". She expands on this theme in an article entitled "The Child as Scientist" published in The Spectator in 1931.

> The behaviour of intelligent young children in fact suggests that, at a very much earlier age than is usually supposed, they are actually reaching out themselves to a view of the world which, when it is fully developed and articulated, can only be called a scientific one.

But play does not just enable the child to learn about his body and the external world. It allows him the opportunity to develop *social* skills, through fantasies of being the mother, the father, the doctor and the nurse, as well as playing himself in different roles. She was the first to emphasise in a baby book the importance of imaginative play in rehearsing different social roles and in aiding the expression of repressed emotions.

In a chapter she calls "The Beginnings" she points to the need of the child for more than bodily care from the time of birth. "It would be the greatest mistake to think that the baby needed nothing but bodily care in his first year and that his mind only began to grow, say, when he began to talk". She goes on . . . "even the young infant has very powerful wishes and feelings and phantasies". She then discusses movement and space; touch (peek a boo); hearing; play and language; suckling, with the baby's development of the realisation that there are things to suck that are "not the breast". Then she begins to explain behaviour that seems unacceptable. The baby loves with his mouth and bites as a primitive form of love. It is normal for fear and rage to be expressed in the first few weeks of life. The infant gets pleasure from expulsion of faeces and sometimes from with-holding. He becomes aware of the feelings that his excretion pleases his mother or nurse so that he may see his urine and faeces as gifts and offer them in ways that upset those around him. They might be less upset if they understood why he behaved in this way.

This chapter on beginnings is followed by one on the norms of development. At the time she was writing, there was the begin-nings of a wave of interest in the creation of genius. Many mothers wanted their babies to be hyper-intelligent. Further, norms were becoming established giving average, above average and well above average ages at which children could perform different tasks. Susan's background enabled her to discuss this issue from first-hand experience. From the time she entered formal post-graduate education in psychology at Cambridge, she had worked on psycho-metrics, the science of the measurement of mental abilities. She had had a good deal of contact with Cyril Burt, the leading exponent of psychometrics in Britain, who had himself developed a number of mental tests. She quotes the work of Arnold Gesell, the American psychologist who had recently produced tables describing the levels that children should have achieved by particular ages. Just as there are norms for physical characteristics such as height and weight, so, she pointed out there are now norms for motor skills and for language.

She goes on to espouse the value of norms to determine whether a young child is advanced, average or behindhand compared to other children.

In a section on heredity and education she makes a distinction between the child's inborn abilities (the level of general ability that is constant through life) and "the actual use which is made of these native gifts by the education we provide for him". The fact that ability is inherited, she suggests, should not be seen as discouraging for parents, for they need to help the child make as good use of his gifts at whatever level these may be. In particular, gifted children should not be held back, but allowed to go at their own pace. Similarly, parents of backward children need expert advice. Only the highly trained psychologist can make an exact estimate of the child's intelligence. If the cause is unalterable, then at least it is good for parents to know this. But apparent backwardness may be caused by emotional inhibitions open to psychological treatment, or to special methods of training.

These are modern ideas and, to the contemporary reader, her views of the value of a developmental approach to parents of children from two to six years are remarkably similar to those of the present day. She describes how skills in movements of hands and legs come before the finer skills of fingers and hands. Parents who try to force children to perform delicate finger movements too early will only succeed in making them tired and irritable. The accidents that children have, for example, when they drop things they are carrying should be seen as part of learning and so not a reason for punishment.

Answering the questions that children of this age ask honestly and admitting to not knowing the answers is a vital part of helping children to understand the limits of the omnipotence they have assumed in their parents up to this point in their development. She then goes on to give advice on domestic furniture, the kitchen and nursery or what would now be called playroom design, always bearing in mind the child's need to learn through participating in "real" household tasks such as cooking and cleaning up.

Then, more directly from her psycho-analytic background, she describes the ways young children from two to six years experience violent emotions and express them in ways parents may find difficult and upsetting. Frustration and anger, jealousy and rivalry, guilt, these primitive emotions are, she indicates, completely normal. They need understanding and not suppressing. She describes a rather socially isolated little girl of two and a half, whose parents introduced another child as a playmate. At first this worked well, but soon the girl developed temper tantrums, became depressed and irritable, even went off her food and lost weight, just because her feelings of rivalry for her parents' affection were so intense. Sometimes, she suggests, the inner tensions these intense emotions bring about can be relieved by play, so it would be wrong to inhibit creative and imaginative play in any way.

After this chapter on the child's emotional life, she discusses how to handle problems parents may face in bringing up their children. How can obedience be reconciled with the need for freedom? How can the child be given real choice? Advice is given on phobias and feeding difficulties. In the final section on problems, entitled "masturbation", in a manner very different from her fellow psycho-analyst Hugh Crichton Miller, she discusses the whole issue of answering children's questions on sexual matters in an open and honest manner. Problems do not arise in sexual matters, she suggests, quoting Ernest Jones, from the child's own sexual behaviour, but from the angry or denying attitudes of those around the child. These are much more likely to create inner conflicts and tensions in the child than the behaviours themselves.

The final chapter is on playthings and here again her advice is practical and sensible. It is not possible in the early twenty first century, as she suggests, to have the climbing frame, light ladders and sliding boards made by a "local carpenter or ladder-maker", but her advocacy of simple, sturdy constructions, building blocks, clay and plasticine remains as valid today as it was seventy-five years ago. She encourages the provision of toys and dressing-up clothes suitable for make-believe play. The final page of the book is one of the few features of the book that dates it. Here Susan Isaacs provides fifteen "Don'ts for Parents". They are all quite reasonable, but they could all have been phrased positively as "Do's for Parents" and anyone writing for parents today would couch these suggestions in positive terms, not, for example, "Don't lie or evade", but "Do tell the truth".

In the same year that "The Nursery Years" was published Susan began writing a regular column for *The Nursery World*. This weekly magazine, then selling at twopence a copy, had been on the market for about four years when Susan began to write on "Childhood Problems" for it on 13 November, 1929. In the first issue of the magazine, published in December, 1925, the editor had written that, while "every new paper claims to 'fill a gap' and the claim is generally rather far-fetched *The Nursery World* claims not merely to fill a gap, but to be the *only* weekly paper in the kingdom devoted to the interests of the greatest profession in the world—the profession of the Nursery". The magazine was thus aimed specifically at the trained children's nurse or nanny, then almost ubiquitous in the British middle class household.

By the nineteen twenties, the college-trained nursery nurse, though relatively few in numbers, had grown in numbers. There were by then several training colleges, of which the Norland Nursing School was the best known, but there were many others. The 1931 National Census records over 1.3 million domestic servants in British households. Jonathan Gathorne-Hardy (1993) estimates that around this time about one-tenth of domestic servants were children's nannies, so there were probably between a hundred thousand and a hundred and fifty thousand potential readers of Nursery World, from the "nursery profession". Gathorne-Hardy quotes informants who suggest that a family could hardly qualify as middle-class unless there was a nanny, and preferably a trained nanny employed to look after the children.

The assumption that nannies were the principal readers of the magazine is clear in the first editorial. This concludes with the hope that the published material will appeal to all, rich and poor, to mothers as well as to nurses. A further hope is expressed that "a mother will read the paper herself before she passes it on to her nurse". As for those many homes where the mother is her own nurse, that is those not able to afford a nurse, The Nursery World "will be a never-failing friend". In fact, there is evidence from the correspondence to the magazine that there were far more mothers than children's nurses reading it. Letters to Susan Isaacs's children's problems column came about five times more commonly from mothers than from nurses.

Towards the end of the time when she was writing for the magazine, the availability of alternative employment for young women meant that the number of nurses employed looking after children in the home was rapidly declining. Indeed, only a little later, by the end of the Second World War, it was only the wealthier sections of the middle classes and the aristocracy who could afford to employ them. This affluent group has continued to employ nannies right up to the twenty-first century. The Nursery World even in the first decade of the twenty first century is still carrying weekly advertisements, almost entirely from the better-off south-east of the country, about twenty five for daily nannies and about fifteen for live-in nannies, but there were three or four times that number in the nineteen thirties. The target audience for Susan in the early nineteen thirties thus consisted of the whole range of middle class mothers of young children and the better educated among the college-trained nurses.

There had been a column called "Children's Problems" from the first issue of the magazine. Susan Isaacs wrote under a pseudonym and it is not clear why she should have chosen to do this. Medical contributors as well as various nurses writing on child health generally used their own names. Initially it was suggested that she used the pseudonym "Jane Strong", but Susan had rejected this on the grounds that it sounded too authoritarian and dogmatic. To me "Ursula Wise", the pseudonym she chose conveys mellifluous omniscience and perhaps this is what Susan Isaacs wished, though she was admirably prepared to admit when she was uncertain how to handle a particular problem.

Writing this column gave Susan financial independence. She wrote about 3,000 words a week and the magazine paid about 2 guineas a thousand, so she must have made at least £300 a year just from her journalism during the early and mid-nineteen thirties when she stopped writing her column. With a further small income from other writing, especially from "The Nursery Years", and with further small sums she earned for lecturing in psychology, she was probably earning around £500 a year. This was quite enough for one person to live on at that time. Nathan was himself in a well-paid job as a manager in a firm trading metals, so the couple did not strictly need her income. However in view of all she had written about the importance of employment for educated women and in the light of the possibility that Nathan might not remain with her, she must have felt relieved to be earning enough to keep herself should this become necessary.

The content of the advice given by Susan Isaacs as well as her tone are generally much more sympathetic to parents than that in Hugh Crichton Miller's earlier book, though this was also written from a psycho-analytic perspective. There is a much greater contrast when one compares her advice with that of the other most popular source of ideas about child-rearing: behaviourism. In the late nineteen twenties and nineteen thirties, the best-known and best-selling behavioural psychologist was John B. Watson. (Frederick Truby King, another very popular source of guidance, also wrote from a behavioural perspective, but his advice was especially directed towards the first two years of life (King, 1924).) Watson had started work as an animal psychologist, carrying out conditioning experiments along Pavlovian lines. From this he moved to carrying out similar experiments in children. He was soon able to show that he could first "condition" fear of rabbits in young children by linking a loud noise with the appearance of a rabbit and then, by gradually introducing the feared rabbit without the noise, he could "decondition" the child, who could then stroke and handle a rabbit without a qualm.

Watson's book "Psychological Care of the Infant and Child" published in 1928 was extremely popular on both sides of the Atlantic. It sold over 100,000 copies and was strongly recommended by Parents' Magazine (a copy ought to "stand on every intelligent mother's shelf"), and the Atlantic Monthly ("a godsend to parents"). Some idea of its tone can be gathered from some introductory remarks:

There is a sensible way of treating children. Treat them as if they were young adults. Dress them, bathe them with care and circumspection. Let your behaviour always be objective and kindly firm. Never hug and kiss them. If you must, kiss them once on the forehead when they say good night. Shake hands with them in the morning. Give them a pat on the head if they have made an extraordinarily good job of a difficult task. Try it out. In a week's time you will find how easy it is to be perfectly objective with your child and at the same time kindly. You will be utterly ashamed of the mawkish, sentimental way you have been handling it. . . . When I hear a mother say "Bless its little heart" when it falls down or stubs its toe, or suffers some other ill, I usually have to walk a block or two to let off steam.

Susan Isaacs was appalled by Watson's book as is apparent from a review she wrote of it in the International Journal of Psychoanalysis shortly after its publication. She hates his "habit psychology" that she sees as leading him, at least in some respects, to "depths of blindness, factual, biological and sociological", as well into what she calls "cruel blunders with 'rough handling of the mind.'"

Her own approach was a good deal more sympathetic. In particular, and here she differed sharply from both Watson and Crichton Miller, she well understood that the problems involved in bringing up children were often complex and difficult to understand and resolve. For example, in an issue of Nursery World, published on 11 December, 1935, she introduces an answer to a question from a parent about how to deal with a child born after a long time gap with the words "This is a very difficult problem in a rather difficult situation. . . ." In answer to the next question she begins "It is not at all easy for me to tell from your letter what the sources of the difficulty (crossness and irritability) might be". In answer to the next and last question dealt with in this issue, about sensitivity to shocks and disappointment, she begins "You certainly have a very difficult problem with this little child. . . ." In all her replies, this admission of uncertainly is followed by an easy to understand explanation of how the problem arose, followed by both general and very specific advice what to do about it.

Some idea of the different views of behaviourists and psychoanalysts can be gleaned by the contrasting advice given on a few key child-rearing issues. On the desirability of smacking both are unequivocal though in completely different directions. John Watson writes "I do not hesitate when children begin reaching for objects not their own to rap their fingers smartly, with a pencil. To get the right psychological conditions, the parent should always apply this painful stimulus just at the moment the undesirable act is taking place. . . . Unless negatively conditioned in this way how else will children learn not to reach for glasses and vases?" Watson does go on to say firmly that the application of pain should not be seen as punishment. Indeed "the word punishment should not appear in our dictionaries except as an obsolete word . . . Such things as beatings and expiation of offences, so common now in our schools and homes, in the church, in our criminal law, on our judicial procedure, are relics of the Dark Ages. The parents' attitude should be positive . . ." So rapping the fingers should be seen as "an objective experimental procedure, never as punishment".

In contrast, a mother writing to Ursula Wise in the Nursery World, who has given her three year old daughter a "good sharp slap on the correct place (it hurts me more than it hurts her, believe me. . . .)" is uncharacteristically but firmly told off by Susan Isaacs. "First of all let me say that I wish I could understand how it is possible for anyone seriously to claim that smacking a child hurts her more than it hurts the child. I confess that I feel that to be complete humbug. I have such vivid memories of being smacked when I was a child myself, and when I compare those feelings with my own as a grown woman when I have smacked children, it seems to me the sheerest nonsense to suggest that it hurts me now more to smack a child than it hurt me to be smacked when I was a child". She follows this with a discussion of the meaning of disobedience in terms of children testing out limits, learning to become independent and so on. In other words, she encourages understanding rather than punishment. So here we see a massive difference between Watson, who sees the child as a creature needing to be conditioned, and Isaacs, for whom the child is seen as needing understanding, with an emphasis on the need for prevention of situations in which disobedience is shown,

In an article titled "Corporal Punishment" published in New Era in July, 1929, Susan Isaacs goes further. Corporal punishment is far more likely to lead to delinquency than to prevent it. If the cause of the delinquency is "neurotic" in nature then corporal punishment is "certainly powerless directly and probably harmful directly". In other cases it "confirms and aggravates the psychological springs of delinquency . . . where bodily pain has itself an erotic value, corporal punishment at the hands of the father or his representatives enhances the wish to provoke it, and thus confirms the evil it seeks to uproot". She admits that even the best parents are sometimes so exasperated that they do lose control and smack children in their care. In disclosing the fact that she herself was beaten as a child and that it did her not the slightest bit of good, Susan Isaacs perhaps reveals at least one of the sources of her motivation in writing for parents; she wants children to have a better upbringing than she did herself.

The contrast between behaviourist and psycho-analytic views is also marked in discussion of children's fears. Watson vividly asserts "At three years of age, the child's whole emotional life plan has been laid down, his emotional disposition set. At that age, the parents have already determined for him whether he is to grow into a happy person, wholesome and good natured, whether he is to be a whining, complaining neurotic, an anger-driven, vindictive, over-bearing slave driver, or one whose every move in life is definitely controlled by fear". It is difficult to see how parent blaming could go further! In fact, Watson then provides some sensible advice on the overcoming of fears using so-called deconditioning methods (gradually helping the child overcome fear by slowly introducing him to the feared object or situation) that would, on the basis of some reasonably good scientific evidence, be widely advocated today. He also suggests, as would be the case today that a good routine will help to avoid the development of night-time fears, though his crude method of expressing how to achieve success cannot have been found attractive by many parents. Even after a calmly applied routine, some children cry when they are left, he admits, and in that case, "if he howls, let him howl. A week of this regime will give you an orderly bedtime".

In contrast, Susan Isaacs emphasises the child's own imaginings as the source of his fears. These phobias can spring up in little children, very often without any source in real events, "The child's parents may, in reality, be kind and temperate and gentle, but his own imaginings are more real to him than any external fact". She does not discount the possibly traumatic effects of real events. For example, she writes to one mother "I think you may be right in putting down the acuteness of your little boy's fears to the maid who frightened him but it is not necessary to look to her for the idea of biting. Such fear of things that may bite. . . . spring from the child's own primitive ways of anger". For treatment she advises letting him talk about the fear, but being firm about any "naughtiness" to which the fear may give rise. She ascribes night fears to some "difficulty in emotional development".

When it comes to the existence of innate temperamental differences between children Susan Isaacs's views are more friendly to contemporary ears. Watson does not believe in any innate differences between individuals. "If you start with a healthy body, the right number of fingers and toes, eyes, and the few elementary movements that are present at birth, you do not need anything else in the way of raw material to make a man, be that man a genius, a cultured gentleman, a rowdy or a thug." In contrast, Susan Isaacs makes frequent reference to individual differences. She writes to one mother whose child sleeps for only a few hours each night—". . . as I have so often pointed out, children differ so enormously in the amount of sleep that they can take. . . ." To another mother with two children who cannot understand why they behave so differently, she writes that evidently the little girl of two who is so difficult and strong-willed and her five year old brother, with whom the mother has never had an hour's trouble are of very different temperaments, and have responded to the same upbringing in different ways. Another little two year old girl who fights, kicks screams, bites when dressed in the morning "obviously has a very difficult temperament". Ahead of her time, she even puts forward a view very similar to those who today think in terms of gene-environment interaction. She sees behaviour arising as a result of inherited tendencies being exaggerated or minimized by the ways children are treated, with the way parents behave also being, at least in part, genetically influenced. For example, answering a question from the mother of a shy boy, she writes "I should almost be inclined to say that it is all the harder for a mother who has herself the same temperament to deal with such a child successfully, just because she knows so well what it feels like from the inside and can realize so vividly what the child is feeling."

Susan Isaacs and John Watson take a rather similar view when it comes to the sexual enlightenment of children. Both think this is important, though Watson thinks sex education cannot wait until the child asks the right questions. "It seems to me" he writes "that we should develop sex knowledge in our children as rapidly as they can take it in. The old theory was to wait until the child's own questions came naturally. I don't believe in this ... A mother who lets her daughters come to puberty or a father his sons, without telling them the facts about this subject are cruel in the extreme". Susan Isaacs, in contrast, notes the different ages at which children ask questions about where babies come from, and suggests the need to provide information honestly as the child's curiosity grows. When a child is seen to masturbate Watson sees this as a "problem" that begins at birth, calling for the need for constant guard against stimulation of the penis. He recognizes how commonly masturbation occurs after puberty, but nevertheless counsels the need for constant discouragement. Ironically, like Crichton Miller, the psycho-analyst writing before Susan Isaacs, he thinks—*"If it is persisted in too long and practiced too often it may make heterosexual adjustment difficult or impossible. This is as true for young women as for young men"* (italics in the original). Susan Isaacs is more sympathetic towards masturbation but even she finds it difficult to see it as part of normal development. What should we do "when we find the child of three or four playing with his genital organ? And the answer is—do nothing directly. For we can now see that this is but another expression of the intense inner conflict. . . ." She advises strongly against scolding or correction, as would, of course, be the case today.

Neither Crichton Miller nor Watson touch on the significance of play in the upbringing of young children, except occasionally as an unimportant diversion. In contrast, as we have already seen, in discussing The Nursery Years, Susan Isaacs here draws heavily on the ideas of Melanie Klein, by whom she had now become strongly influenced. Children not only develop their intelligence through play, their emotional well-being depends on them having opportunities to express themselves emotionally through play.

Perhaps the area in which Susan Isaacs differs most markedly from Watson is in their discussion of the relationships between parents and their children. Watson thinks about home life as a regrettable necessity. However imperfect it may be and, one gathers from him, it is usually far from perfect, we cannot get away from it. He writes "The home we have is with us—inevitably and inexorably with us.

Even though it is proven unsuccessful, we shall always have it. The behaviorist has to accept the home and make the best of it". He strongly advises against the demonstration of love. "A certain amount of love is socially necessary" he grudgingly concedes, "but few parents realize how easily they can overtrain the child in this direction. It may tear the heartstrings a bit, this thought of stopping the tender outward demonstration of your love for your children or of their love for you", but somehow you *have* to stop it. Indeed Watson dedicates a whole chapter to—"The Dangers of Too Much Mother Love", in which he advises parents never to hug or kiss children.

In contrast, Susan Isaacs, in her discussion of parent-child relationships, gives full measure, some might say over-full measure to negative themes of hate, jealousy, rivalry, anxiety and the complexity of feelings children have for their parents. And when she writes about the ways parents might show affection to their children she is sometimes, to say the least, cool in her approach. It is, she writes, "of the utmost importance that we should be in reality gentle and just, kind, temperate and reasonable". But she also acknowledges and approves of the passionate affection children and parents have for each other. Love means for children "the full-blooded sensory pleasure of caresses". Only slowly does it grow beyond this, and come to mean also the non-sensual pleasures of mutual devotion and service, talk and common interests. So the father's love, too, "means to the very little child the intense pleasure of being lifted in his firm, strong arms, and caressed with loving hands and voice".

A better idea of the contemporary nature of Susan's advice and the style in which it was given can be obtained from her responses to letters from mothers at their wit's end to know how to cope with difficult children. For example, in reply to a mother with a three year old girl who is showing really quite vicious behaviour towards a thirteen month old twin brother, who, unlike the other twin who has a crown of curly hair is bald, she writes:

You seem to be right in the reasons you suggest for your little girl's dislike of the younger twin. Such things as the loud scream and the bald head are so much more important to little children's feelings than to ours; and doubtless his great attachment to you makes her feel more jealous of him. I do not think it is helpful, however, to hurt her in the way she has hurt him. You found yourself it was unsuccessful, and I have never known this method to lead to any satisfactory results. Putting her alone in the room if she does hurt the child is a much more logical and humane method of dealing with her aggression, but you cannot expect that such strong impulses in a child of this age will be improved in a very short time. She is little more than a baby herself. It will take a period of growth and readjustment for her to tolerate the little boy who arouses so much dislike, and you will need to show a good deal of patience, and constant supervision, until she has achieved sufficient control and understanding. The fact that you play with her apart from the twins and that she has friends of her own age is extremely helpful. I would suggest that you make up your mind to recognize that you cannot change such an emotional attitude in the little girl all in a hurry, and that it will take time and patience. It would be advisable to try to avoid any situations of temptation, not to leave her with the younger one unless there is an adult close enough to prevent any serious harm. If she did really hurt him such as by pushing him downstairs she would only be the more wretched about it and hate him all the more for it. Careful supervision, affection and patience, will help her grow out of this attitude. Meanwhile the baby's bald head will improve naturally, and he will become a more interesting person to her as he leaves babyhood behind and becomes more of a boy.

Both Watson and Isaacs were widely read in the late nineteen twenties, but, by the nineteen thirties, though Truby King was probably the most important influence in infant feeding, when it came to the care of slightly older children, Susan Isaacs had the stronger influence on the behaviour and attitudes of parents In her time, Isaacs's influence spread beyond the United Kingdom. "The Nursery Years" was translated into many other languages. In 1937 the American edition won the Parents Magazine Award for the best book for parents published in the United States that year. Insofar as her book had been written as a reaction to the simplistic, mechanical approach to bringing up children advocated by Watson, time has surely vindicated her views in a most convincing manner.

Her book for parents and her advice column were not Susan Isaacs's only sources of advice to parents. Periodically she gave public lectures at the Institute of Psycho-analysis to public audiences. Those who attended were doubtless parents sympathetic to psycho-analytic approaches and it is notable how differently Susan communicated when she felt she could assume her audience would be open to ideas involving unconscious motivation. For example, in a lecture called "Rebellious and Defiant Children" given in 1934 (Isaacs, 1948b), she begins by suggesting that disobedience, lying, stealing, temper out-bursts in young children and aggression in adolescence may represent a temporary phase in the life of an individual or be part of behaviour that is lifelong with an outcome of adult criminality. (In making this distinction she was sixty years ahead of her time for it was not until the mid-1990s that Terri Moffitt (1993) on the basis of longitudinal studies put forward the distinction between "life-course persistent" and "adolescent-specific" antisocial behaviour.)

After giving examples of rebelliousness and defiance at different ages, she moves on to discuss the motivation underlying such behaviour. She rapidly dismisses in a few perfunctory lines the poss-ibility of external factors such as unreasonable levels of strictness by parents, illegitimacy and broken homes, before going on to the role of the unconscious. This can operate in many ways. Usually hateful behaviour is a defence against those feelings that often go with intense love of parents, the possibility that this love will not be returned or that the child might damage those whom he loves. Alternatively the child may feel anxious that all the good that he has had put into him by his parents may not be enough for him to reciprocate so his hateful behaviour may be a defence against his unconscious guilt. Yet another possibility is that he harbours in his unconscious mind phantasies of avenging parents, angry because of the damage his hateful ideas have done to them. Sometimes envy of older siblings may result in the demonstration of hateful feelings towards parents to show them just what a horrible child they have.

But at the deepest level, according to Susan Isaacs, in analytic work it is found that:

obstinacy, contempt, defiance and hatred are ultimately bound up with the anxieties relating to (these) earliest desires: the greedy love of the mother's breast as an ultimate source of pleasure and goodness, the wish to eat it up and incorporate it, the dread of the strength of such desire and the attributing of the same intense and uncontrollable wishes to the breast itself and to the mother. . . .

After this account of the motivation of rebellious behaviour, she gives a number of examples. One is of a girl who is angry and defiant when her mother is away looking after a sick relative and returns to her normal, delightful self when her mother returns bearing gifts for her. Another is a child with a chronically sick and disabled mother who is "utterly selfish and hard" throughout her childhood because, it is suggested, she feels she cannot fulfil the role of dutiful daughter that is expected of her. Finally she describes the most horrible child of all, which because of the similarity of the details given (death of older sib at eight months, birth of younger sister at three years, death of mother with subsequent disruption of home life at six years) can only be a description of Susan Isaacs herself as a child. I have used this graphic, autobiographical description in an earlier chapter when describing Susan's early life.

It is notable how differently Susan Isaacs communicates when addressing a general audience sympathetic to psycho-analytic ideas compared to when she is writing for parents in her baby book or "Nursery World" advice column. When writing for parents she is much more forthcoming about the possibility that aggressive behaviour may arise from the stresses and traumas children may encounter. All the same, it is surprising to the modern reader that, in considering the roots of aggressive behaviour, she makes no mention at all of the possibility that the child is imitating violent and aggressive behaviour by others, especially parents, in the home or by other children in the nursery school or day nursery. There is no word, for example, about bullying. No mention is made either in her account of motivation of the possibility of anger arising from frustration at the unresponsiveness of a depressed parent or as a reaction to physical or sexual abuse. Her preoccupation with the internal world seems to have blinded Susan Isaacs, as happened to other analysts of that day and for many years subsequently, to the very real traumas suffered by significant numbers of children. All the same much of what she had to say about difficult children continues to have great relevance today.

Turning her experience as an agony aunt to academic purposes, Susan Isaacs wrote up data she extracted from the letters written to The Nursery World for publication in a professional journal. In a paper she published in 1932 in the British Journal of Educational Psychology, she reported on the analysis of the contents of 572 letters from mothers and nursery nurses. The paper, titled "Some Notes on the Incidence of Neurotic Difficulties in Young Children" purports to be a scientific account of the rate of such problems in the general population. In fact it exposed her problem in making generalizations from groups of unusual children that the disagreement with Piaget had highlighted a couple of years previously.

As was already realized at the time Susan Isaacs wrote this paper there are three basic requirements for studies aiming to draw general conclusions from studies of the population attempting to establish the rates with which behaviour and emotional problems occur. They need to be carried out on subjects that are representative of the population; the problems studied need to be clearly defined, and the methods used to identify them need to be reliable. Susan Isaacs's article is disappointing on all three counts. The children about whom "Ursula Wise" received letters were entirely middle class and had mothers or nurses worried about their behaviour or development; these could hardly be regarded as representative of the general popu-lation. The paper contains no clear definition of a neurotic difficulty. Finally there is no attempt to use reliable methods to identify which of the children about whom letters were written did indeed have significant problems. Some will doubtless have had very serious problems, while others will have had mothers unduly anxious about quite trivial difficulties. The paper reveals Susan Isaacs was aware of these defects, indeed at one point she admits ". . . the mere number of these letters has no statistical value either way" but then obscurely adds that the letters "can be regarded as having a positive eviden-tial value in the hint they offer as to the probability of difficulties serious enough to lead parents to seek advice". Quite how the letters can provide evidence as to the number of problems existing in the general population as suggested in the title of the paper is not at all clear.

In order to understand why Susan Isaacs could have written such a weak paper even by the standards of her own day, one needs to examine what she was trying to achieve by writing it. Most studies of the rates of disorders in the general population, then as now, are carried out to investigate causes, to provide clues to the level of services required or to suggest what actions might be taken to prevent the disorders in question. She had little interest in any of these issues. She held the view that "the Freudian theory is the only theory of neurosis which offers theoretical illumination or practical help of a radical kind". This theory assumes that internal conflict is universally experienced. Her aim therefore was to show that "neurotic difficulties" were indeed experienced by all children because they represented "one of the ways in which the ordinary everyday child deals with the internal problems of psychological adjustment". She succeeded in doing this to her own satisfaction and, somewhat surprisingly, to the satisfaction of those who reviewed her paper for publication. But the obvious defects in the paper mean she can have persuaded few of her colleagues with any scientific training. Her conclusion that virtually all children show "neurotic" difficulties would not be acceptable today, except by those who use the term extremely vaguely nor, it must be said, would it have been found credible even in her own day. All the same, though Susan Isaacs was to some degree blinkered by her exclusive adherence to a psycho-analytic approach to child development, the insights that this approach gave her enabled her to communicate to parents an understanding of their children's behaviour in a manner more sympathetic and helpful than had been previously possible; indeed it has rarely been surpassed by those writing "baby books" since her time.

CHAPTER TEN

Teaching the teachers

D uring the nineteen thirties the turmoil of the economic depression and the increasing threat from Nazi Germany touched the life of the Isaacs hardly at all.[1] They had many friends, especially Joe and Phoebe Pole, whom they saw every Saturday evening. Joe was Nathan's closest friend, but the couple had many others, including Sibyl Clement Brown, a social worker who ran the mental health course at the London School of Economics and Percy Nunn, the Director of the Institute of Education.

Susan had an enormous variety of interests (IoEd S1 A 3). As a child and teenager, she had walked over the Lancashire moors close to her home. Then with her first husband she had explored the Lake District and the Derbyshire peaks. Now, in her forties perhaps her greatest pleasure was walking in the countryside, best of all in the mountains of Switzerland or Scottish Highlands. She loved hill-walking, mountain tramping and climbing. Knowledgeable about the natural world, she was an indefatigable bird-watcher and loved identifying rare species of mountain flowers in the Alps and in the Scotland.

Both the Isaacs went to as many concerts and plays as they could find time for. Susan also enjoyed the ballet and circus. Early in their married days, Nathan introduced her to chess and this became a "minor passion" to her, though because they were both so busy they virtually only played on train journeys and holidays. She was an enthusiastic player of demon or racing patience, revelling in the game when it was at its most furious pace and, according to Nathan, usually leading and winning the race.

She came from a musical family and, in her teens and early twenties had played chamber music with other members of the family and friends. An accomplished pianist, she enjoyed listening to virtually all classical music, Beethoven, Mozart and Bach above all, but Sibelius almost as much. As well as a great deal of poetry, from early English to contemporary poetry, she read and re-read the major French and Russian nineteenth-century novelists.

From time to time they saw her brother, Enoch, a professional artist and accomplished portrait painter who was elected a full member of the Society of Miniature Painters (IoEd N1 D10 2). He was an illustrator for *Punch* and *The Illustrated London News* and made a number of accomplished sketches for the Isaacs, including one of Nathan and his friend, Joe Pole, engaged in an absorbing game of chess. They saw little of Susan's three sisters. Bessie who had married and had children lived in Bristol and was rarely in London. Mirrie had emigrated to South Africa where, in the nineteen twenties, she was the first woman to be elected to the Cape Town council.[2] Not surprisingly, her particular interest on the council was in child welfare. She married and had two children. Her husband died and subsequently there were various business ventures that did not prosper. Finally she worked for a voluntary organisation, the Safety First Association, that promoted road safety. She eventually died, impoverished, in a nursing home in Cape Town in 1943. Alice married in Bristol and emigrated with her Australian husband to Sydney, where she also had two children, one of whom later died in a flying accident (IoE N1 D10 2). Nathan's younger sister, Lena, hero-worshipped him and, according to her own account, did not marry at least partly because she had problems following the experience of sexual abuse in childhood. Mallie, the older sister, divorced early shortly after she gave birth to her only child, Karina, in 1928. Nathan and Susan entertained both sisters in their home; both these women who largely lived alone were emotionally and, to some degree financially dependent on their successful brother and this did sometimes lead to arguments with them.

With Nathan's earnings increasing all the time, the Isaacs were able to afford to buy modernist paintings, including a Wyndham Lewis and a David Bomberg. At Christmas there were parties for the children of friends, at which charades, which Susan entered into with zest, were played and Nathan was able to indulge his love of clowning. They were also able to afford a living-in housekeeper who not only cleaned the flat but did most of the cooking. Susan is however remembered as a "very competent cook", and Nathan helped on rare occasions. He was "willing but not very competent at household tasks, partly because he wanted to hold intellectual conversations at the same time. So Susan preferred to get on with domestic tasks without being hampered by his 'help'" (Karina McIntosh, personal communication). Although they argued a great deal about intellectual issues, they were never heard to raise their voices to each other about personal matters, such as their financial arrangements.

The only unconventional aspect of this middle-class, "balanced" relationship lay in the rather substantial secret that Nathan and Evelyn Lawrence, unknown to all but themselves, Susan and the Poles, continued their sexual relationship. The Isaacs lived in Primrose Hill Road, about two hundred yards from the flat in which Evelyn and, after some time, her sister, Hilda, who was apparently not in on the secret, lived in Elsworthy Road on the edges of the St. John's Wood area of north-west London. Evelyn and Nathan met in a flat conveniently situated nearby. After leaving the Malting House School and a relatively short visit to the United States, Evelyn worked briefly as Chief Social Worker to the London Child Guidance Clinic, shortly after it opened in 1929 (Froebel Institute Archive, Roehampton, B9/1072–3). The following year she found a more permanent post as Lecturer in Psychology and English at the National Training College of Domestic Subjects, which was housed in a building in central London. Evelyn remained in this undemanding job for thirteen years until 1943, lecturing to girls aged around sixteen to nineteen years who were learning such subjects as needlework, cookery, child care and household management (National Archive, ED 164: National Training College for Domestic Subjects Records)

She was widely regarded as a "calm, tranquil, kind and generous" woman. Her life during the nineteen thirties, apart from her affair with Nathan, seems to have been relatively smooth, though she had a serious surgical operation in 1934 which meant that she had to be off work for several weeks (ibid., ED 164). She was a frequent social visitor at the Isaacs's flat and discussed Susan's work with her. In the Preface to "Intellectual Growth in Young Children", published in 1930, Susan Isaacs mentions Evelyn as one of three people who had been "good enough to read parts of the book and make a number of most valuable comments". In the Preface to "The Social Development of Young Children", published in 1933, she does not acknowledge Evelyn (or incidentally her husband) but thanks Evelyn's sister, Hilda Lawrence, "for her patient care in preparing the index". Secret affairs always bring complications, both practical and emotional, but Evelyn's involvement with Susan's work must surely have added to the complexities of this triangular relationship.

How did Susan, in particular, survive emotionally? Some clue might be found in a comment Alice made when she was asked what turned her sister into a psychologist (IoEd S1 A1). She replied "a constantly enquiring mind", but added enigmatically "on the other hand people who, when older, can be 'philosophical' as it is termed, seem to me very cold, very callous and quite indifferent to other people's feelings". This could be understood to mean that in addition to her enquiring mind Susan had a detached personality, able to compartmentalise her own feelings. Clearly her commitment to her work and her analysis with Joan Riviere must have played an important part in her capacity to cope with her personal situation. One suspects also from remarks made about her personality that although she could become passionately involved in intellectual discussion, she was an unusually cool and controlled woman in her personal relationships.

There were no children from either of her marriages. We do not know for certain why this was the case though Susan herself indicated (Gardner, 1969, p. 53) that she would have liked children but that neither of her husbands wanted to bring children into a dangerous and uncertain world. In the absence of any other reason for the breakdown of her first marriage, it seems likely that sexual incompatibility may have been the main or perhaps the only reason. The fact that Susan embarked on an apparently physically ungratifying affair with Geoffrey Pyke only three years into her marriage to Nathan suggests that there were sexual problems in her second marriage too. So it is quite likely that lack of sexual activity may have been the main reason for the fact that she had no children with Nathan either. While the experience of psychoanalysis was clearly immensely valuable to her with the sense it gave her of having her feelings of hate and envy understood and accepted it is unlikely that analysis would have resolved her sexual problems. Evaluation of the treatment of frigidity has revealed that psychoanalytic approaches in themselves are generally ineffective symptomatically unless they are combined with counselling to the couple on the quality of their relationship and on their sexual techniques, an approach not available at the time (Bancroft, 1989). In any case, by the time she had completed her analysis Susan was forty eight years old and virtually beyond the age when she might have conceived a child.

Although they had no children of their own, Susan and Nathan continued to find themselves with considerable responsibility for Nathan's niece, Karina, the daughter of his older sister, Malvin or Mallie as she was known. Karina was the child of Mallie and Eric Side. Although they did not divorce for many years, they split up fairly soon after she was born and although Eric remained in touch with his daughter and sometimes took care of her, Mallie largely brought her up alone. However Mallie was an erratic, temperamental and sometimes unpredictable character who found looking after Karina difficult, so Karina spent a good deal of time with Susan and Nathan during the school holidays. When she was still a baby they arranged for her to go to the Wellgarth Day Nursery in Hampstead and then, when she was only four years old, to board at the Caldecott Community. This was a boarding school in Kent under the direction of a formidable lady, Miss Leila Rendel, who ran the school for the benefit of working class children deprived of good, family care. Miss Rendel believed that it was helpful for such children to be exposed to a middle-class life style and this was provided not only by the gracious building in which the school was housed and by the teaching and care staff, but also by a sprinkling of middle-class children of whom Karina was one. Although in the nineteen thirties it was relatively common for affluent middle class parents to send their children, especially their sons, away to boarding school, it was most unusual for children to be sent away as young as four. It is surely paradoxical that while Susan was undergoing psychoanalysis with Joan Riviere, learning about how the traumas of her own childhood had affected her she should be instrumental in separating her niece by marriage from her mother, aunt and uncle and indeed all familiar figures. One must ask how someone known to be so sensitive to the feelings of young children could allow such a separation to occur, let alone play an active part in arranging it.

At the age of eleven years Karina moved on to Frensham Heights, a boarding school in Surrey run then as now along "progressive" lines. Susan was responsible for arranging for Karina to go to both these schools and the Isaacs paid for Karina's education throughout. Susan also encouraged her to learn the piano and again the Isaacs paid for her lessons.

While she was preparing her second book based on the Malting House experience Susan wrote a series of twenty four articles in The Teacher's World. These were brought together for teachers in a book called "The Children We Teach" (Isaacs, 1932). As in her previous books, there is a heavy emphasis, unattractive to most contemporary general readers, though since at least partly confirmed by much solid scientific data, on the importance of heredity in determining the level of intelligence. "Of all the differences between one child and another, inborn intelligence turns out to be the most stable and the most permanent. . . . The best teaching in the world may prove barren if it fall on the stony ground of an inherently dull and lifeless mind. And we cannot cater properly for the brightest and the stupidest children together in one class" (ibid., p. 27). The psychologist can use mental tests to "grade" children according to ability, so as to identify, for example, children like one she describes (ibid., p. 38) with an IQ of 77 who is "thoroughly stupid". All children should be tested at the beginning of their primary school life so that they can be put into appropriate groups or grades. (Today a child of this level of ability would be most unlikely to have his intelligence assessed, but if it was, a score of 77 would indicate a child in the low range of normal and not particularly remarkable from an educational point of view.)

The language used to describe academically less able children and the concentration on the influence on heredity apart, *The Children We Teach* provides an inspiring view of the way in which the best teachers can capture the interests of children and promote learning even in the less able. Susan Isaacs writes (ibid., p. 104), for example, of a dispiriting experience she had when visiting a low attainment group of girls in a city school near London. Each had a "mangled primrose" in front of her while "a formal lesson on 'pin-eye and thrum-eye' was being given". These children, she insists, need more than a flower in front of them to stimulate their interest. They need a "lively curiosity into the how and why of what one sees in the lanes and woods. And one needs the full context of experience in the garden or in the countryside. . . .before pin-eye and thrum-eye could be more than the teacher's sound and fury". Susan Isaacs believed that there was a need to change the emphasis in every part of the curriculum from the learning of facts to providing opportunities for children to show their natural interest in the world around them. Children, she asserts (ibid., p. 153) need the opportunity to speak and exercise their verbal reasoning. They should be allowed to talk about what they are doing so that they can put experience into words. If we offer children verbal teaching instead of encouraging them to speak, we deaden their minds. "What we have done is to 'shut the school door on conversation . . . We insist on a dumb tongue, but hope for an eloquent pen!' "

She has much to say on the social group as of increasing importance as the child moves through primary school and learns how to co-operate with others. As the child makes this progression, so his ideas of rules and of punishments that occur when rules are broken begin to approximate to the understanding of adults. In an article published in 1932 in a French journal "La Psychologie de l'Enfant" (Smith, 1985, pp. 276–287) she describes the way in which the social relationships of the Malting House children changed as they adapted to the staff and each other's presence. First they showed an unusual degree of calm and submission, followed by often quite severe aggression to each other and disobedience to the staff. Finally they settled into a socially cohesive group during which their behaviour to each other became more stable. She explains this progression with reference to the findings of Piaget, especially his concepts of changing levels of egocentrism. Despite her previous differences with him, in her articles for teachers she frequently quotes the findings of Piaget with approval. All in all, if one can ignore her over-deterministic bias based on her belief in the importance of heredity, "The Children We Teach" would be of interest to the teachers of young children today.

In 1932 she finally completed the second book based on her observations of the Malting House School children and this was published in 1933. Her original intention had been to publish three books, but the third that was to contain more verbatim accounts of the Malting House children, was never completed. Her second book *Social Development of Young Children* was superficially rather similar to the first, with large sections devoted to quotations from the children's speech, interspersed with commentary. But it was different in a number of important ways.

While the first book had dealt with the growth of intellectual understanding, the second was largely devoted to a description of the social and emotional life of young children. Susan Isaacs described intellectual growth largely without recourse to theory, except insofar as she used her observations to refute the theories of Jean Piaget. In contrast, in "Social Development" she leaned heavily on psycho-analytic theory, partly Freudian, but more particularly theories more recently advanced by Melanie Klein. Thus, while "Intellectual Growth" was, at least to some degree, a polemical tract countering Piaget's views, "Social Development" reads like a document providing strong evidence for the acceptance of Freudian ideas and, to an even greater extent those of Melanie Klein.

By the time Susan Isaacs was writing this book, many of Freud's theories were widely, though far from universally accepted. She, like many others at that time, not just in the world of psycho-analysis but outside it, found helpful the notion that the first five to six years of a child's life were taken up with the search for pleasure, first oral, then anal and then genital. Though like Klein she dated the Oedipal phase in the first year of life, much earlier than Freud, she accepted that, in their early years children formed a strong erotic attachment to the opposite-sexed parent, and developed rivalrous, even murderous feelings towards the same-sexed parent. Though she professed to be generally hostile to the idea of a fixed structure of the mind, she accepted that Freud's picture of the mind as consisting of id (basic, unconscious instincts), ego (conscious, directive) and super-ego (conscience, morality) was useful as pointing to the experience people had of possessing a "divided self". (She adapted this term derived from the writings of St. Augustine for psychology well before Ronald Laing wrote his best-selling book with this title). She was convinced that Freudian psycho-analytic techniques involving the painstaking revelation of unacceptable, unconscious thoughts and feelings provided by far the best means of healing the mentally ill and those who, if not ill, were disturbed in mind. She admired Freud for expressing his views in clear prose designed to convince the sceptical as well as the enthusiast.

Why was Susan Isaacs so captivated by the writing of Melanie Klein, an unorthodox extension of Freud's work? In many ways Klein's style represented the antithesis of everything that Susan Isaacs valued in her own writing: precision, clarity and elegance. Even her admirers agree that Melanie Klein's articles and book chapters are rambling and diffuse. To say they lack clarity would be an understatement. The idea of providing evidence that might convince others, more sceptical than herself of the truth of her theories, does not seem to have occurred to her. She is dogmatic in the extreme. So Susan Isaacs cannot have been attracted by the intellectual content of Klein's thoughts.

Those who, like Susan Isaacs, were impressed, indeed seduced by Melanie Klein's ideas were not swayed by the clarity of her thought, but by the ideas derived from her intuitive capacity to enter the mental world of children. They were convinced by their personal experience of her capacity, as they saw it, to empathise intuitively with the turbulent emotional life of infants and young children, helpless beings in a powerful world of terrifying giants and even more terrifying giantesses who sometimes met and then as the child perceived it, unaccountably frustrated their needs for sustenance, comfort and care. They admired her ability to elicit and "contain" the powerful, aggressive thoughts and feelings that children revealed in their play. They were, above all, amazed by her intuitive understanding of the child's emotional world and the power this understanding seemed to give her to reach out to young children, calm their agitation and apparently give a sense of meaning and coherence to their lives.

Susan Isaacs took two main messages from Melanie Klein. Very early on in her career when, in 1918, she was attempting to analyse her four year old son, Erich, Melanie Isaacs discovered she learned more about his inner world from observing his play than she did from talking to him, and that she learned more from his play if she avoided joining in his fantasies or talking to him about them. The other message she took on board, rightly or wrongly, is that the turbulent emotional life revealed in the play of disturbed children is not only experienced by children in difficulties, but is universal. Thus one might expect that all the children at the Malting House School, most of whom were not obviously disturbed, to reveal anxiety and fear as well as violence in their fantasies.

The attachment Susan Isaacs felt to Melanie Klein dated from the first time they met when Melanie visited the school in 1925. Clearly the school embodied many of the principles that Klein had advocated in her first full-length paper. There, in her missionary zeal for psycho-analysis she had suggested that all nursery schools should have psycho-analytically trained women available to detect and address developmental difficulties. Children, she had argued, should have the right to develop their own minds through their own endeavours by using their inborn gifts of curiosity and drive to learn. Forcing intellectual acquiescence could lead to "intellectual injury", producing life-long harm. The Malting House experience was thus a fulfillment of her dream for the future of education.

Susan Isaacs's observations of her pupils fully confirmed, in her view, Klein's theories. While the school did not contain children under the age of three years, it seemed to Susan that every day brought fresh confirmation of Klein's psycho-analytic views. When a little girl accidentally tore a card that had been sent to all the children, Dan, aged 4 years 11 months, said that he would "get a policeman to put her in prison" and "I'll kill her because I hate her". Paul, aged just 4 years, when Susan Isaacs told him to rest at a point when he wanted to go downstairs, was extremely angry and said "I don't think you are really kind, Mrs. I." and then added "I'll send you away and cut you up and eat you". When she called another child "darling", Benjie, aged 4 years 2 months, said "Why don't you call me that?" and then when she pointed out that often she did, he spontaneously remarked to another child "I don't like you, Cecil. I'll get a gun and shoot you dead". Theobald, aged 4 years 11 months drew a crocodile with a large mouth which, he said, would "bite Dan's legs off".

Oral fantasies often appeared sadistic. On one occasion a little three year old boy ran after Susan Isaacs in the garden and caught her. He said "I'll kill you" and called to two other children to "come and help me push her down and kill her and make her into ice-cream". Then to her he said "I like ice-cream! It will be pink ice-cream! I like ice!" At lunch that day there was talk among the children about cutting Susan up and "having her for dinner". Priscilla said she would "have her head", Christopher "her finger" and Dan "from her tummy to her bottom".

There was much sexual play and sometimes explicit sexual behaviour at the school. At one point when Susan Isaacs was leaving the school premises for the day, Priscilla and Dan made a fuss about her going and insisted on kissing her all over—face and hair and dress and shoes. After this Dan fidgeted about in a way that clearly indicated an erection and asked her to "lie down and be a motor bike" assuring her he wouldn't hurt her. She writes that, of course, she did not comply. However after leaving the school she needed to return and was standing at the bottom of the steps talking when Dan bent down and kissed her ankle, then suddenly thrust his hand up her leg. Priscilla tried to do the same which she firmly prevented.

So Susan Isaacs recorded many observations that appeared to her to confirm the existence of the sort of violent and sexual fantasies in children aged three and four years. These Melanie Klein had proposed, on the basis of her analysis of children aged as young as two years, appeared in the first few weeks and months of life. Neither of them, it should be noted, had made systematic observations of infants in the first year of life though many such observations have since been made purporting to confirm the existence of such fantasies in the early months as Melanie Klein claimed.

Although "Social Development" is thus very different from "Intellectual Growth" and received, as we shall see, much less enthusiastic a reception, it is, all the same, a remarkable chronicle of observations of a group of bright three to eight year olds in a quite exceptional setting. These observations form the basis for a thought-ful account of the social and emotional development of children of this age, to some degree written as a validation of Kleinian theory, but going well beyond a mere rehearsal of Kleinian ideas. In partic-ular, in contrast though not in disagreement with Klein, there is an acknowledgement that the ways adults behave towards children makes a real difference to their development.

There were three sources of information on which Susan Isaacs drew in the writing of her "Social Development" book. First and by far the most important, were the observations made at the Malting House School. Then there were the accounts given mainly by mothers but also by nursery nurses in letters written to Susan Isaacs in her role as the agony aunt, Ursula Wise, in *Nursery World*. Finally there is a prolonged account of the development of a little girl, also given the pseudonym Ursula, whose mother kept detailed records of her behaviour over a period of two and a half years.

The observations are followed by a discussion of the ways in which they substantiate psycho-analytic theory. Susan Isaacs points to the fact that observations in themselves are of rather little help in understanding the behaviour of young children. What is needed is a genetic (we would say developmental) theory to make sense of the observations. In her view only the psycho-analytic views of Sigmund Freud and Melanie Klein can satisfactorily explain the observations. The main body of the book is indeed organized along lines that follow first Kleinian and then Freudian concepts. After a brief section on egocentric attitudes, she discusses hostility and aggression. In a later section on sexuality she follows the Freudian scheme of development moving from oral eroticism and sadism, to anal and urethral interests and aggression, followed by exhibitionism, sexual curiosity, sexual play and aggression, masturbation, family play and castration fears. It is striking that in this 470 page book only one section is devoted to positive aspects of child development—nineteen pages on friendliness and co-operation.

After the case descriptions she begins an extended description of her theory of development by describing the very early behaviour of children. This she sees as profoundly egocentric, thus confirming Piaget's view, though of course denying that such egocentrism continues in the way he describes into the seventh or eighth year of life. For the young infant only the physical world exists. It is like a canvas on which he projects his own wishes and fantasies. Inner conflicts almost immediately start to be worked out in free dramatic play. She gives the example of a fourteen month old child whose mother describes him as constantly preoccupied with fitting things together, a lid onto a box, a stick into a hole. She considers such stereotyped actions to be best understood as a means of discharging the anxiety raised by certain fundamental fantasies, connected in the first instance with unsatisfied oral longings. His primary fantasies are stimulated by fitting his mother's nipple into his own mouth. As he gets older, this fantasy becomes less dominant so that, for example by the age of six years when he is playing with constructional toys, fitting one piece into another "his behaviour will still undoubtedly (sic) have a similar unconscious meaning, but its chief significance for his development then lies in the various problems it presents for skill and understanding".

She then goes on to discuss the more overtly sexual behaviour shown by young children. Some of the behaviour she describes, as, for example, the observation of Dan's erection and his request to her when it occurred to "lie down and be a motor bike", is clearly sexual. Sometimes however she considers behaviour to be sexual that is much less clearly so. As an example of sexual play and aggression she cites an episode when Paul "climbed on her back and put his arms round my neck". Another example came from Harold who spoke of "eating bogies" and, in a moment of hostility threatened to "push things up your nose". Susan Isaacs pours scorn on any who might dispute the sexual nature of children's feelings in favour of the theory that young children "do not and cannot have sexual feelings". She can, she writes, "leave the behaviour of children to establish this point for itself. He that hath ears to hear, let him hear". The notion that some, though perhaps not all young children do indeed have sexual thoughts, fantasies and behaviour but that perhaps this does not arise quite as frequently from elements of unconscious sexuality as she suggests is an idea she does not consider. Similarly she does not entertain the possibility that young children's talk of cutting up and killing has a very different significance in children who do not have a concept of the permanence of death.

Indeed one of the striking features of "Social Development" is that there is not a single occasion when psycho-analytic theory is questioned or when an observation is recorded that seems to run counter to such theory. For example there is a point in the book when Susan Isaacs astutely observes that young children who are "friendly and amenable when with one grown-up will become fractious and perverse as soon as another enters on the scene". This reaction, she notes, is not just the case with mothers and fathers, but with nurse and mother. Such irritability does not occur if the attention of the two adults is focused on the child. It is particularly noticeable, in contrast, when the two adults are engaged in some mutual activity, for example talking together in a way that excludes the child. Now all that is, of course, quite true, but one might have expected Susan Isaacs to describe situations in which children play very happily by themselves or with other children when two adults are conversing quietly or just getting on with whatever tasks they have in hand. That this does occur is a matter of common observation. Such behaviour is not explained by the Oedipal theory of rivalry with the same-sexed parent or any other part of psycho-analytic theory. It possibly doesn't need to be, but it is surprising that no such behaviour is recorded when all parents and teachers know that it occurs.

In the light of her twin role as educator and psycho-analyst, perhaps the most interesting part of the book deals with the relationship between the processes of education and psychoanalysis. She first describes the setting in which the analyst works. In a one to one relationship the analyst endeavours to allow the maximum of expression that can occur without the child hurting himself or the analyst. The prime task is the tapping of unconscious feelings of hate, rivalry, sadism, and the analyst must be capable of accepting these feelings, tolerating them, and understanding them. In contrast, to be effective the educator must attract to herself the forces of love in the child. The educator does not, if a child shows warmth or affection, question, as does the analyst, whether these positive feelings are but a cover for submerged aggressive ideas. While the educator mainly fulfils one role, namely that of an external super-ego or conscience, encouraging the child's moral tendencies and desire to learn, while ensuring clear boundaries are set to limit the child's behaviour, the analyst plays many parts, at one time representing a hated object, at another an object of love and affection; at one time as a receptacle into which all the child's sense of himself as rubbish are deposited, at another as an authority reminding the child that some types of behaviour cannot be permitted.

There are then very different functions performed by the educator and the analyst. Susan Isaacs strongly cautions against mixing the two. "An admixture of education and analysis tends to ruin both and can do little for the child but confuse and bewilder him". She warns against schools run along psycho-analytic lines where what she calls "real cruelty" is done through an "undesirable complex-hunting in everyday life". Indeed she complains that a reference to the Malting House School by Bertrand Russell as an "application of psycho-analytic theory to education" is misleading, though some might feel that Russell's phrase has more than an element of truth in it. In any event, she is clear by this point that although it is helpful for educators to have some awareness and knowledge of the unconscious, such material can only be safely handled by analysts.

In a final section to the main body of the book, she discusses some problems that arise in the development of children. She writes first about very difficult, antisocial children who appear to suffer from lack of conscience. This impression, she suggests, is misleading; in fact such children suffer from an overactive punishing conscience or super-ego and their behaviour arises from the fact that they are constantly testing out adults to find out how far they can go before they themselves will be deservedly destroyed. Such children need analytic help. In many middle class homes, she suggests, children are alternately subjected to extreme, unwise permissiveness and then, when this does not work, to harsh punishment. What they need is a "stable and ordered world of values". She describes how, when the Malting House School started, she allowed a good deal of bullying to go on in order to allow free expression of aggressive feelings, but she soon intervened when she realized how much young children valued a calm, controlling presence. There is therefore no truth in the idea that Susan Isaacs, at least after the first few months of running the Malting House School, advocated anything like a complete absence of control and discipline in the classroom.

Once again in this section she discusses the value of play as providing opportunities for imaginative creativity, the rehearsal in fantasy of skills that will be needed in reality and the opportunity for "sublimation", the artistic expression of unconscious thoughts, feelings and fantasies. She cautions against efforts by parents and educators to suppress erotic sexual behaviour unless it is "flagrant and persistent" in which case psycho-analytic help is required. Finally she discusses a variety of specific issues in development such as feeding and weaning, thumb-sucking, cleanliness, screaming and tantrums, and sexual behaviour. Her advice here is similar to that given in her "Ursula Wise" columns in The Nursery World, sensible, practical and generally tolerant. The only time when dogmatism creeps in is when she is using psycho-analytic concepts to explain particular sorts of behaviour. Thus when she is describing what to do about thumb-sucking, she interpolates—"if the child feels this strong and persistent need to get satisfaction from sucking, we can be *quite sure* (my italics) that he is suffering from great anxiety connected with oral destructive impulses".

"Social Development in Young Children" did not by any means receive the same level of praise as had "Intellectual Growth". Most enthusiasm came from her psycho-analytic colleagues. Ernest Jones (1934) described it as "an extraordinarily good book". Mildred Creak (1934), a general child psychiatrist sympathetic to psycho-analysis and at that time at the Maudsley Hospital was also fulsome in praise. However the educationalists and educational psychologists were distinctly critical. Mary Sturt (1934), in the British Journal of Educational Psychology and Dorothea McCarthy (1934) in the Journal of

Educational Psychology both praised the section of the book that drew comparisons between the approach of the educationist and the analyst. But they found much else to criticize. They vigorously attacked the emphasis on sexual behaviour or what they felt Susan Isaacs wrongly perceived to be sexual behaviour. They felt that a theory that had been derived from observations of deeply disturbed children was being applied to normal children without sufficient thought. It was, according to Mary Sturt, unnecessary to go into the "dark world of perversions" to explain what were really, in these young children's minds, no more than quite harmless "indelicacies". Why do engines have to symbolize a child's fantasy about parents and intercourse? The suggestion that an early sense of guilt stems from the oral sadistic state "strains the belief". She suggested that "a baby does not know he is hurting his mother any more than a puppy chewing a slipper". Dorothea McCarthy was more caustic. She began her short review "Unless the reader who has been attracted by the title of this book is an ardent disciple of Freud, he is sure to be disappointed by the author's narrow conception of the young child's social development, which is made to hinge entirely around problems of infantile sexuality". The review concludes shortly afterwards "The bibliography . . . is decidedly psycho-analytic and the excellent observational and experimental approaches . . . are conspicuous by their absence". Such robust scepticism was probably shared by many of their experienced colleagues, but nevertheless, the book remained a classic text in teacher training colleges for several decades.

Though few of them would have realized it, it is a surprising fact that the child psychology to which young men and women training to be teachers between the mid nineteen thirties and the mid nineteen sixties were to be exposed was largely derived from the ideas of Melanie Klein barely filtered through the writings of Susan Isaacs.

At around this time, in early 1932, Cyril Burt, the Professor and newly appointed Head of the Department of Psychology at University College where she was a part-time Lecturer, asked Susan Isaacs to collaborate with him in the preparation of a memorandum he had been asked to prepare for a Consultative Committee on Infant and Nursery Schools that the Board (now Ministry) of Education had set up. The Board had previously published two reports, on the education of the adolescent and on primary schools, and felt that it was now time to consider the educational needs of the youngest children in the education system. Like the previous reports, that on children and nursery age children was chaired by Sir William Hadow.

Cyril Burt (Hearnshaw, 1979) was the most distinguished and, in educational circles, the most influential British psychologist of his day. Susan Isaacs had first met him in her mid-twenties at Cambridge in 1912 when he was briefly attached to the Department of Psychology there. After this encounter Burt had worked as an educational psychologist first in Liverpool and then for the London County Council. In the early 1920s both he and Susan Isaacs had done work for the National Institute of Industrial Psychology set up by Charles Myers. In 1932 he was appointed Professor and Head of the Department of Psychology at University College, London where Susan had been working as a part-time Lecturer for some years.

Burt's output was prodigious—he wrote a number of classic texts, including "The Subnormal Mind" and "The Young Delinquent", developed tests of intelligence and aptitude that were widely applied, carried out fundamental psychological research on children and adolescents, was an indefatigable editor of psychological journals and acted as consultant to many government bodies concerned with education. He was a strong protagonist of the importance of heredity in determining the level of intelligence, a point of view to which Susan was sympathetic. Before the joint memorandum with Susan Isaacs, he had written evidence for the previous consultative committee on the primary school.

Burt was a dominating and self-opinionated character who, towards the end of his career, earned a reputation for deviousness in his determination to get his own way. Indeed one of his colleagues, parodying the title of one of Burt's best-known books referred to him later in life as "The Old Delinquent". After his death many came to believe that he had, at least in his final professional years, falsified data in order to bolster his view that intelligence is highly genetically determined, but the breadth and integrity of his earlier work up to and including the time Susan Isaacs worked with him has never been seriously challenged.

Chapter 3 (Mental Development of Children Up To The Age of Seven) of the final report (Board of Education, 1933) entitled "Infant and Nursery Schools" was largely based on the memorandum "The Emotional Development of Children up to the Age of Seven Plus", written by Cyril Burt and Susan Isaacs. In addition, another section of their memorandum was printed as Appendix 3. The chapter in the main body of the Report places great emphasis on the importance of heredity in various aspects of development. The hand of Cyril Burt is evident here, though Susan Isaacs would not have disagreed with his approach. The Appendix covering all areas of emotional and behavioural as well as moral development lays greater emphasis on the effect of the environment, on the "intense attachment of the child in the first two years to his parents, and on the emotional intensity of the young child's life that is thought to reach its zenith about the end of the third year" (ibid., p. 247). There is much consideration of the way children's relationships change with age as they develop from two to seven years. It is likely that Susan Isaacs played the greater part in the writing of this Appendix. Indeed Dorothy Gardner, her first biographer who knew her well, has suggested that in fact she was really the sole author of the whole memorandum (Gardner, 1969, p. 105).

The final recommendations (ibid., pp. 173–195) of the Consultative Committee were far-reaching. It recommended that the lower limit of compulsory attendance should continue to be five years, with transfer from an Infant Department or School to a Primary School at seven to eight years. Many of the recommendations would have met with Susan Isaacs's whole hearted support. Children "should be surrounded with objects and materials which will afford scope for experiment and exploration", and "scope should be afforded for 'make-believe' in the children's play. . . . The curriculum should be thought of in terms of activity and experience rather than of knowledge to be acquired and facts to be stored". There was a strong emphasis in the recommendations on the need to follow the learning pace set by the child. "The child should begin to learn the 3 Rs when he wants to do so, whether he be three or six years old . . . The principle underlying the procedure of the infant school should be that, as far as possible, the child should be put in the position to teach himself, and that knowledge that he is to acquire should come, not so much from an instructor, as from an instructive environment". It is suggested that "Freedom is essential for the child and only becomes dangerous when there is nothing to absorb the child's restless activity and provide an outlet for his experimental spirit".

There were recommendations for the establishment of more nursery schools than existed at that time. Such schools for children from two or three upwards should be set up in all areas "where the housing and general economic conditions are seriously below the average" and in some more advantaged districts too. The staff ratios recommended were not generous by today's standards. Children should be grouped in units not greater than 35–40 children, with a trained teacher and at least one untrained helper.

It is difficult to estimate the extent of Susan Isaacs' influence on the Committee's recommendations. One of the members of the Committee was Freda Hawtrey who had been the recently appointed Head of the Darlington Teacher Training College when, twenty years previously, Susan had joined the staff there. Hawtrey, who agreed with Susan Isaacs on virtually all issues, was now Head of the Avery Hill Training College in Blackheath. However she was interested in the education of the whole age range, whereas Susan Isaacs was a specialist in children aged three to seven years so it is likely that Susan was greatly influential in the formulation of the final recommendations. Many of these set the pattern for the structure and content of the education of young children for decades after the Report was published.

Susan Isaacs continued to take an interest in the promotion of primary schools. Indeed in late 1937, The Nursery School Association published a pamphlet written by her (Nursery School Association of Great Britain, 1937) on the educational value of the nursery school. In it she claimed that it was now established that "children in the nursery school learn more easily, play more actively and thrive better in every way than similar children who have not this advantage even if they live in good homes". The particular value of the nursery school lay in the opportunities it gave to study and understand the play of young children, especially play with other children.

When the ordinary school years come, Susan Isaacs suggested, the child who has not had the experience of play with others "is in a very different situation from those who have learnt, on the one hand, that it is possible to shout and run and sometimes be angry and jealous, without doing too much harm and, on the other, that other children are friends and helpers as well as rivals". Play with others can give children confidence and allow them to overcome problems such as phobias that might otherwise remain fixed and handicapping. Language development too is stimulated by nursery school experience. "It is only in the most intimate contact with activity and actual experience that (the child) begins to talk freely and to exchange ideas". This view of the positive effect of nursery education on language prevailed for fifty years until the mid nineteen-eighties when systematic comparisons between the language environment at home and in the nursery school revealed the much greater stimulating effect of the home, or at least most homes (Tizard and Hughes, 1984).

Children, Susan Isaacs wrote, need to have people around them who understand how real their feelings are and they need realistic experiences in which they are actively engaged. They need order and routine and rhythm in the plan of the day. Within a secure environment a child can take the opportunities provided for self-assertion and independence. Above all children need the chance to play with other children, not just their presence in a room in which they all sit at desks, but active social experience. Imaginative play alone and with others allows the child to "reap the full value to his intellectual life of his imaginative processes". Nursery school is not a substitute for a good home; it is a supplement to what a good home normally provides, a bridge between the home and the larger world. "It meets certain needs which the home either cannot satisfy or cannot satisfy in full measure, and it prepares the child for his later life in a way which nothing else can do".

In this pamphlet Susan Isaacs puts forward as good a case for the nursery school as has ever been made. It is ironic that a misunderstanding of the work of her psychoanalyst colleague, John Bowlby, on the harmful effects of separation of young children from their mothers contributed to delay in the universal availability of nursery schools in the second half of the twentieth century. It is perhaps only in the first decade of the twenty first century that the force of Susan Isaacs' arguments have become accepted, though even now the variable quality of nursery education makes the desirability of universal provision questionable.

Despite the adverse reviews for the second book, the publication of "Intellectual Growth" and "Social Development" established Susan Isaacs as the pre-eminent authority on the education of young children in Britain and indeed before long in many other countries as well. Whereas the Malting House School had been seen in its time as merely an interesting experiment, the two books, based on the work of the school, were seen as a solid achievement that established, for the first time, the education of young children as a subject with strong evidence to support it. The educational principles Susan Isaacs articulated were, from then on, widely accepted as the basis for the training of nursery and infant school teachers and remained so for the next thirty years, if not longer

Since they had returned to London from Cambridge in 1927, Susan and Nathan had become friendly with Percy Nunn, the Director of the London Day Training College which was transformed in 1932 into the Institute of Education. The Institute, a School forming part of the University of London was then, as it is arguably now, the foremost centre for the training of teachers and educational research in Britain. In December, 1932, Nunn spoke to Susan asking her to consider whether, if a proposal he was putting forward to the University to establish a Department of Child Development was successful, she would be prepared to accept an appointment to be its Head (Gardner, 1969, pp. 79–85). Although Susan Isaacs had not taken a university course leading to a doctorate, she had been awarded a Doctor of Science degree by the University of Manchester (Victoria) in 1931 on the basis of her published work. She was therefore academically eligible for such a senior appointment.

Nunn, who was knighted in 1930 for his services to education, was an engaging, highly cultured scholar whose book "Education: its data and first principles" had first appeared in 1920 and remained a standard text right up to its third edition published in 1945 (Aldrich, 2002) The book is highly favourable to progressive ideas in education. Indeed Nunn was elected one of the five permanent vice-presidents of the international movement of the New Education Fellowship in 1932. A contemporary colleague described his supreme position as "thinker, organizer, mathematician and teacher". His capacity to communicate complicated ideas in a simple fashion was widely admired by his peers; it was said of him by another colleague that "he could teach the calculus to a class of whelks".

The proposal made to Susan Isaacs, coming as it did, from such an outstanding leader of an outstanding institution, was obviously attractive, indeed almost irresistible (Gardner, 1969, pp. 79–85). Almost, but not quite! It turned out that she could not contemplate giving up the development of psycho-analytic ideas and practice. On 28 December, 1932 she wrote to Percy Nunn declining his offer. In many ways, she wrote, "the work you hold out to me would be.

... the fulfillment of all my previous hopes and efforts". But, she continued, taking up the post he had offered would "definitely mean my relinquishing analytic work altogether, not necessarily at once, but certainly within a year or so". Moreover, she added, understandably in view of the ideas she had expressed on the stark differences between educational and psycho-analytic approaches in "Social Development", the two are "not really compatible within one's personal life, since the latter demands a special attitude and a very special and continuous study of technique, even if one's time is not actually filled with patients. It involves quite a different mental attitude from teaching, lecturing, organizing. . . ." So, she concluded, "after more intensive heart-searching than I can convey to you, I have had to come to the conclusion that I cannot bear to give up the work of analysis".

The New Year however brought a re-consideration and a fresh thought. Suppose she could take up the post on a part-time basis. Would that be acceptable? So she wrote to Percy Nunn again, in a letter dated 6 January and told him that she had worked out that if she gave up various lecturing commitments, she could do the job on a part-time basis. She understood that the Institute might be better able to afford a full-time Head in three to four years time. Perhaps by then someone suitable could be trained up to take the post.

Percy Nunn wasted no time in accepting her proposal. Two days later, on 8 January, 1933, he wrote to say that he would now push on as rapidly as possible with his proposal to establish this new Department. Cyril Burt, the psychologist at University College who was responsible for some of Susan's work, was highly supportive. The fact that Percy Nunn could confirm that, if the Department were established, someone of Susan Isaacs's calibre would be prepared to head it, helped his proposals over the bureaucratic hurdles the University set up. He enlisted the support of the Board (Ministry) of Education, and this was enthusiastically forthcoming.

In his submission to the Board he referred to the two chief objectives for the new Department—to supply the demands of the new training colleges for people equipped scientifically to become lecturers in infant school education, and to create a centre of research in the field of child development and infant pedagogy. Susan Isaacs was appointed to the post in May, 1933. The original proposal for the Department involved her being given the title of Reader or Professor, a research assistant, and a grant to establish a nursery school with facilities for observation. In fact, despite all the enthusiasm, her salary was never more than £325 a year with an allowance of £100 a year for a secretary. Funds were never found for the appointment of a research assistant and the nursery school did not materialise.

From the time of her appointment until 1938, when the Institute moved into the North Wing of Senate House in Malet Street, her Department was located in cramped accommodation in the building the Institute of Education shared with the London County Council School of Arts and Crafts on the corner of Southampton Row and Theobalds Road, near Holborn underground station.

Dorothy Gardner, later her successor as Head of the Department and her first biographer, was taken on as a part-time student in 1933 shortly after Susan Isaacs took up her appointment. She has written a full account of the Department during the time Susan Isaacs was in charge (ibid., pp. 91–114). The Department was situated in one room that served as study, office and tutorial space. Indeed Dorothy Gardner had her tutorials with Susan Isaacs in the ABC teashop situated nearby. For many years Susan did not even have a phone in her room and had to walk down two flights of stairs if someone called her.

Susan's main activity was the running of an Advanced Course in Child Development. She also participated in an inter-collegiate course of lectures in child development attended by students from other schools in the University of London, especially King's and University College. In the first academic year the Advanced Course was attended by three full-time and twelve part-time students but by the 1938/9 academic year there were twenty full-time and ten part-time students. A number of the students, some of whom only attended for one or two terms, came from overseas. They came from varied backgrounds; some were teachers, others school inspectors, psychologists and training college lecturers. The inter-collegiate course of lectures in child development attracted large audiences of up to seventy students.

Much of the lecturing both for the advanced course and in the inter-collegiate lecture series was provided by Susan Isaacs herself. She gave a three term course of lectures on the psychology of infancy and childhood, as well as seminars on a range of topics including research methods, mental hygiene and mental testing. There were also lectures by other Institute of Education staff, including Percy Nunn on general principles of education and Herbert Hamley on educational psychology. External lecturers included Donald Winnicott, a paediatrician and one of Susan Isaacs's psychoanalyst colleagues. For the Advanced Course students the lectures were supplemented by practical work. This consisted of observation of children in nursery schools, and observation of and participation in work in Child Guidance Clinics. The students had the opportunity to discuss their observations with Susan Isaacs on a regular basis. The Advanced Course students who were qualified to do so were also encouraged to undertake a supervised piece of research. Alternatively they wrote a dissertation on some special topic. The research activity was modest, with three research students working for higher degrees and four engaged in other projects by 1939.

It had been hoped that the Institute would find the funds to set up its own demonstration nursery school. But funds were not forthcoming from the University, the Board of Education or the London County Council. Susan Isaacs did however make special links with the Chelsea Open Air Nursery School that had been set up by an American parent, Natalie Davis. Susan Isaacs took over the educational supervision of the school, to which she became a trustee. Students from the Advanced Course were sent to observe children at this and other schools. It was hoped that it would be possible to obtain funds to record observations systematically as had happened at the Malting House School, but again these were never forthcoming.

In a memorandum dated February, 1939 (ibid., pp. 179–84) to Sir Fred Clarke, who had been appointed Director of the Institute in 1936 in succession to Percy Nunn, Susan Isaacs listed her activities on behalf of the Institute. She was responsible for the full-time Advanced Course in Child Development, lectured on it and gave three seminars for it a week. She undertook all the tutorials and pastoral counseling and organized the visits to nursery schools. She was responsible for the research students of whom there were always between two and four. Since the Department had developed an international reputation, she now had a large number of visitors from abroad, especially from the United States, all of whom wished to discuss the work of the Department. She served on many committees and was on the Editorial Boards of the British Journal of Psychology and the British Journal of Educational Psychology. This entailed a significant amount of reviewing of manuscripts submitted for publication. She was involved in editing a significant number of pamphlets and handbooks for teachers. She gave several public lectures each year. She frequently reviewed books on children's issues for The Spectator, The New Statesman, the Times Educational Supplement and other similar magazines and journals.

A particularly notable activity (Smith, 1985, pp. 134–40) involved her in collaboration with staff of the Wiltshire Education Department in the development of a standard educational assessment form that could be used to record and monitor children's home circumstances, intelligence, educational achievements and behaviour. From 1936 when it was published this was widely used and can be seen as a prototype for subsequent forms developed for similar purposes.

As an authority on child development she was sometimes asked to be involved in legal cases. For example she gave written evidence (Gardner, 1969, p. 100) in the case of a Yorkshireman accused of murdering his two year old daughter by pushing her out of a railway carriage. The man maintained that he had left the compartment for a few moments and when he had returned the door to the line was open and his daughter had disappeared. Susan Isaacs testified to the fact that a two year old would indeed have been capable, as her father maintained must have been the case, of opening the carriage door herself. The man was subsequently acquitted.

It will be remembered that her appointment to the Institute of Education was part-time and that she was paid at a half-time rate. Clearly the Institute was getting good value for money. Much of her work for the Institute was carried out at home in the evenings and at weekends. Once a week she invited the overseas students to an informal gathering in her own home. In thinking about her volume of work one also has to take into account the fact that she was actively engaged in the world of psycho-analysis, seeing patients and attending scientific meetings at the British Psycho-analytic Society. She worked very, very long hours—in fact leading the life typical of a modern medical academic who has the well-nigh impossible task of combining teaching, research and clinical work with administrative duties.

The only account of her supervisions has been provided by Dorothy Gardner (1969, p. 97) who worshipped her and cannot be regarded as an unbiased observer. All the same she gives a most convincing impression that Susan Isaacs was a conscientious teacher whose personal influence on her students was considerable. Over the first few years her students feared her forthright criticism but later she mellowed and was held in less awe. In an article written shortly after Susan Isaacs's death, Dorothy Gardner wrote (Gardner, 1949):

> My most vivid recollections are of the many ways in which she led us to do our own thinking; of superb teaching, but also of wise silences until we had worked out a problem to a point when her help became essential and we could really assimilate it. A seminar to which students had come without adequate preparation could be an embarrassing situation and seldom occurred more than once in any one year! . . . She gave us so much, not only by her vivid speech, with its unerring choice of the perfect word to express full meaning, and by the artistry of her lecturing, but by the questions that set our minds working, by requests to be "more specific" when our statements became vague or ambiguous, and by a certain twinkle in the eye when we gave evidence of prejudiced thinking or willful disregard of evidence. She made us laugh at ourselves and face issues with honesty.

High praise indeed, and one might be suspicious of the accuracy of this description of such a paragon, but the praises were echoed by her colleagues at the Institute of Education. They described her as "homely, mothering, a much loved member of staff". Sir Fred Clarke (Dixon, 1986, p. 22), the Director of the Institute, said he wondered how "a strict, scientific temper can exist with such womanly sweetness and charm"—not language a man would use about a woman colleague today, but nevertheless conveying affection and warmth. One might expect a woman who, according to another colleague had carried out "work and writings on psychology and education that had made her a national figure" to be the object at least of some envy and certainly of some criticism, but these are remarkably absent from the contemporary descriptions of her. The worst that anybody could say was that she could often be a rather cool, detached person, but certainly she did not behave in this way to her students when they saw her individually or in groups for supervision or socially in her home.

Given her stature in the field of education, the quality of her publications and the extent of her teaching and administrative responsibilities, it is surprising that she was not promoted to a professorship. There is no correspondence to suggest this was even ever contemplated. A number of her male colleagues in the Institute of Education whose academic work was clearly less distinguished were promoted to chairs. It is likely that her failure to achieve promotion was due to a combination of the fact that she was part-time, that the Institute was chronically under financial pressure and perhaps most importantly that the "glass ceiling" preventing women achieving the highest academic positions was in powerful operation.

During the tenure of her position as Head of the Department of Child Development, there were two lengthy interruptions. The first occurred only three years after she took up the position when, at the age of fifty in 1935, she developed a cancer of the breast and had to take several months off (Gardner, 1969, p. 115). She was treated with radiotherapy, a much more physically damaging intervention then than it is today. She recovered but subsequently suffered a number of relapses partly caused by recurrences of the tumour and partly arising as complications of the radiotherapy. All the same, while working at the Institute she was otherwise able to function well, with just occasional weeks away for illness reasons.

Shortly after her convalescence (ibid., p. 116) over a period of about four months in the summer of 1937 she went as part of an international group of distinguished delegates to lecture on educational topics at conferences for teachers and others in the education field in New Zealand and Australia. The conferences were organized by the Education Research Councils of the two countries and sponsored by the New Education Fellowship. This was an organization founded in 1920 to promote modern ideas in education (Jenkins, 1989). It had a progressive stance, questioning the school curriculum, criticizing the examination system, and advocating less structured classroom teaching with more active participation by pupils. It was started in Britain, but branches were formed in many other countries. Susan Isaacs was for a time Chairman of the English branch.

She traveled by boat via the United States, first visiting New York where the Child Study Association had arranged visits for her. She went from there to California where at the University of Berkeley she visited, among others, Jean Walker MacFarlane whose classical studies of child development remain well known among child developmentalists today. From there she traveled with other members of the group to New Zealand, lecturing in Auckland, Wellington and Christchurch. The New Zealand Minister of Education, Peter Frazer, who was shortly afterwards to become Prime Minister, took a personal interest in the group. He was strongly supportive of early years education and so was especially keen on Susan Isaacs's contributions. In Australia she and the rest of the group attended conferences in Brisbane, Sydney, Melbourne, Adelaide, Hobart and finally Perth. In Adelaide she was awarded an Honorary Doctorate of Science at the University.

The group suffered from some tensions understandable in the light of the current political climate (Williams, 1994). Paul Dengler from Vienna, was suspected of having Nazi sympathies, especially when he spoke in positive terms of the German Youth Movement. Yasuke Tuurami, a Japanese Member of Parliament was strongly defensive of his country's invasion of China that most of the other delegates regarded as criminal. But there were lighter moments. At a ceremonial banquet in Fiji on the way home (Gardner, 1969, p. 120), the group that contained numerous distinguished and mainly elderly Professors and Directors of Education as well as Sir Cyril Norwood, President of St. John's College, Oxford, was entertained after dinner by a choir of magnificent-looking men, fearsomely made up in warrior paint. When they opened their mouths to sing, the expectation was for a series of battle cries, but instead they sang "Oh dear, what can the matter be?" and then "Baa baa, black sheep", evidently thinking this would be appropriate given the group's interest in children.

The conferences were attended by several thousand teachers in both Australia and New Zealand. Susan Isaacs's lectures seem to have been very well received. In New Zealand. Arnold Campbell, the National Director of Education spoke (Campbell, 1938) of the "great impact" of her lectures and noted that she "never met a hostile question with a hostile answer".

In New Zealand she gave seven lectures in different centres. Some flavour of her lecturing style can be gleaned from the opening sentences of her first lecture (quoted in Campbell, 1938), titled "The Principle of Activity in Modern Education":

The aim of modern education is to create people who are not only self-disciplined and free in spirit, gifted in work and in enjoyment, worthy and desirable as persons, but also responsible and generous in social life, able to give and to take freely from others, sensitive to social needs, willing to serve social ends and to lose themselves in social purposes greater than themselves . . . The principle of activity expresses the empirically discoverable truth that the child grows by his own efforts and his own real experience, whether it be in skill or knowledge, in social feeling or spiritual awareness. It is not what we do to the child or for the child that educates him, but what we enable him to do for himself to see and learn and feel and understand for himself and this is equally true for the young infant, the school child and the adolescent.

Some of the delegates, including Susan Isaacs, did not hesitate to criticize the educational system in the two countries and in both Australia and New Zealand a reform agenda, partly based on the recommendations of the international group, was carried out over the following twenty years. An article by John Godfrey (2004) published many years later describing the Australian conferences has a title, "Perhaps the Most Important and Certainly the Most Exciting Event in the Whole History of Education in Australia" that must not only break records for length and breathlessness but also conveys the impact of the visit. The main effect was on the examination system that, as a result of the influence of the group, became more relevant to the needs of the two countries. Susan Isaacs's international profile was greatly enhanced by her membership of this international group and she was subsequently visited in her own Department by many of those she had met during her travels.

In six years she had built up a Department with an international reputation and fulfilled Percy Nunn's dream of an academic centre for the training of those who could go forth as Lecturers to teacher training colleges well-equipped to teach about nursery education. But the threat from Nazi Germany and the armed conflict that ensued was to produce a dramatic change in the fortunes of the Department and in the life Susan Isaacs was to lead from now on.

Notes

1 In addition to information provided by Nathan Isaacs (IoEd S1 A 3), details of the family life of Susan and Nathan Isaacs as well as Susan's personality and interests were provided to the author by Karina McIntosh, Nathan's niece, who knew the couple well from the mid-1930s.

2 National Archive of South Africa, Cape Town, Minutes of Cape Town City Council, 1926–7: MOOC 6/9/10597, no. 89817

CHAPTER ELEVEN

Psycho-analysis in the 1930s: building up to war

W hile she had been building up a new Department of Child Development at the Institute of Education during the mid nineteen thirties, Susan Isaacs had remained actively involved not just in psycho-analytic practice with children and adults, but with the affairs of the British Psychoanalytic Society (BPaS) and the Institute of Psychoanalysis. She finished her training analysis with Joan Riviere in 1933 and completed her training as a child analyst in the same year (Ken Robinson, personal communication).

The requirements of psychoanalytic training and later practice meant that she had to be available three to five times a week at a regular time for at least three patients. It was laid down that she was not supposed to treat other patients using psychoanalytic methods while she was in training, but over this period she seems to have seen at least some adult and child patients on a short term basis for assessment and brief therapy. The papers she gave to medical and psycho-analytic audiences make it clear that she was treating children from as young as four years as well as adults in their twenties and thirties. She saw these patients either in a consulting room in Manchester Square, just north of Wigmore Street in central London or in her flat in Primrose Hill where she also had a consulting room. Visitors such as her niece, Karina, were expected to keep out of the way when patients were being seen.

At this time, the Medical Section of the British Psychological Society acted as a meeting place for doctors who, though not necessarily trained psychoanalysts were sympathetic to psychoanalysis. Psycho-analytic influence was dominant in the Section's journal, the British Journal of Medical Psychology. Susan Isaacs was one of the few non-medical members. She played an active part and gave a paper to the Section (Isaacs, 1934) partly based on material in "Social Development of Young Children", entitled "Property and Possessiveness". She introduces at the start of this paper the notion that a child's desire to own property always involves a "triangular relationship" between two people and the desired object. Other than perhaps food if a child is hungry, few things are wanted because of their intrinsic value. Instead, objects are desired because ownership gives a sense of power over another person. As soon as an object is seen to be of value to one child its value to others is increased. Only the "proved even-ness of a controlling adult" makes it possible for children to wait and "take turns". Children who receive gifts are grateful, not so much for the gift itself, but because it makes them feel "loveworthy" while those denied gifts are made to feel bad inside, to experience a sense of loss. The child who can give freely feels safe and good because to give is not to need. So it is misleading to think of the need to possess simply as a wish to own something one does not have; possessiveness is a more complicated matter.

She then goes on to describe a seven year old boy that she saw in analysis because he was slow to learn and had an inordinate craving for gifts. He stole in everyday life as well as from the analytic room. Analysis revealed that he had suffered from unsatisfied oral cravings after birth. He was constantly searching for the "good breast"; when he took things they became part of the "bad breast" and so valueless to him. His early disappointments at the breast led him to want to "attack and rob his mother of his father's penis". He constantly took toys from the analytic room to prove that his analyst still had good things to give him after they had been removed. He had violent wishes to separate his parents and gain his father for himself, this leading to a need to restore to his mother the things which had been taken from her, "whether the contents of her breast, milk and food, or of her body, the father's penis, her faeces and her children". At one point he asked Susan Isaacs if he could borrow a penny, but when she opened her cupboard to fetch her purse to give him one, he saw she did not have a coat and developed a delusion she did not possess one. He walked out without his penny, with a fantasy he would have to buy a coat for her. His slowness to learn, she believed, was caused by his belief that to know a thing was to want to possess it and thus, as far as he was concerned, to damage it. His reluctance to learn had arisen because at one point he had been taken into his parents' bed and had heard them having intercourse. He had wished to see them, and, as a result of his magical thinking, this wish had resulted in the separation of his parents.

Susan Isaacs concludes by suggesting that this case illustrates the need for co-operation between psychoanalysts who *really* understand the psychology of stealing with sociologists who are concerned with the "conscious sentiments of the adult, with large-scale behaviour and social institutions". Had Susan Isaacs really uncovered the true motivation behind this child's stealing? Many people, including myself, find her explanations involving the need to make restitution to his mother for having wanted to rob his mother of his father's penis etc. highly implausible. (I have not cited all the information Susan Isaacs provides to support her interpretations, and the reader will have to accept the additional information she gives does not add to their plausibility.) Of course all would agree that it is desirable for those studying the phenomenon of theft by adults or children to have regard to the underlying motivation of offenders (as well as other relevant information such as their upbringing, role models, and the criminal behaviour of those with whom they mix), but it is doubtful if the type of explanations provided by Susan Isaacs on the basis of clinical observations such as those described in this article would add a great deal to their understanding.

The British Psychoanalytic Society continued to hold scientific meetings on the evenings of the first and third Wednesdays of each month. These were opportunities not only for the presentation of scientific papers and discussion of difficult cases but also for networking, for exchange of views on training issues, and for the offer of new cases by those who were too busy to take on more to those who were still looking for work. Patronage and networking were then, as they are now, an important part of all forms of private practice; younger people were more likely to be given cases if their views were consonant with the more experienced, busier analysts. Bearing in mind all her other responsibilities and the fact that her husband was earning a good income, it is unlikely that Susan Isaacs was particularly interested in looking for work in this way.

She mainly attended meetings to share clinical experiences and scientific information.

At this time referrals to analysts were mainly made from general practitioners sympathetic to psychoanalysis. In addition, as had been the case when Ernest Jones had requested Melanie Klein to see his wife and his two children, Mervyn and Gweneth, analysts sometimes asked colleagues to treat members of their own family. Despite widespread advertisement, I have only been able to trace two of Susan Isaacs's patients. One, Jonathan Miller, the writer and opera director was referred by his father who was himself a psychoanalyst, at about the age of five years in the late nineteen thirties. He remembers little about his contact with her but thinks he only saw her on one or two occasions (Jonathan Miller, personal communication). The other, Lucy Baruch, a retired social worker, was referred by her father, John Rickman, also a prominent psychoanalyst, when she was sixteen years old at about the same time in 1937. Apparently the reason for her referral was that she had not started her periods and this was thought to have a psychological cause. For a year she went for an hour every weekday morning before school and lay on a couch with Susan Isaacs sitting behind her. She too has almost no recollection of what she and Susan Isaacs said to each other. She did remember that Susan Isaacs once used the word "masturbation" that she had never heard before and it had to be explained to her. She thought her analyst was probably a rather shy, inhibited person, but that there was some give and take in the relationship. About two or three months after the analysis began her periods started, but the analysis continued for several more months. At that point, in mid-1939, a place came up at Swarthmore College in the United States, which her mother had attended, and she went over to America to begin her college education. The analysis had to stop at this point. She does not think it made much of an impact on her, and indeed, looking back she sees her time with Susan Isaacs, about 250 hours in her seventeenth year, as "a bit of a non-event" (Lucy Baruch, personal communication). She contrasted her experience with Susan Isaacs with an earlier analytic experience with Melanie Klein, in about 1926 when she was five years old. Again her father arranged the referral, this time because of a fear of thunder. She has a clear recollection of playing with toys from her drawer, while Melanie Klein sat bolt upright, looked down on her from above and spoke in a loud voice with a heavy foreign accent. Melanie Klein introduced the word "Peter" to describe a penis which she found odd. Lucy Baruch recalls that Melanie Klein explained her fear of thunder to her as arising from hearing her parents having intercourse in the next room. When I asked her if she had found or now found that explanation believable, Lucy Baruch was sceptical. "Well", she said, "I was a very sound sleeper". She added charitably, "I suppose from her point of view I heard all this". But, in contrast to Susan Isaacs whom she recalled as pleasant and "sympatisch", she did not find Melanie Klein a likeable person. The fear for which she had been referred disappeared some time later, after she had stopped seeing Melanie Klein, when she got used to the barking of dogs and told herself if she could overcome this fear she could also stop feeling frightened of thunder.

Senior analysts also spent a good deal of time in analysis with each other, mostly for training purposes but also for help when a colleague was going through a difficult patch emotionally or when they wanted to enrich their knowledge through experiencing an analytic encounter different from that previously undertaken.

The scientific meetings covered a wide range of topics, but in the children's field, the ideas of Melanie Klein dominated the discussions during the early nineteen thirties. By 1934 she had contributed eleven papers or short communications to the Society. She was increasingly influential in shaping the ideas of other analysts, including Susan Isaacs. John Rickman and Ella Sharpe, both senior figures gave important papers using Klein's ideas as conceptual tools.

In the early nineteen thirties a new, distinctive voice began to be heard in child analytic circles. Donald Winnicott was a paediatrician who consulted Ernest Jones in 1923, aged 27, shortly after his marriage, probably for a sexual problem. Jones referred him to James Strachey who carried out an analysis lasting some ten years often at a frequency of six times a week. Winnicott gradually became interested in becoming an analyst himself and first attended a meeting of the BPaS in 1929. The first man to complete the training to be a child analyst, he was elected an Associate Member of the BPaS in 1934 and a full member in 1936 (Kahr, 1996).

During and after this long analysis with Strachey, Winnicott became dependent on, some would say addicted to the experience. Strachey had encouraged him to become familiar with Melanie

Klein's work and he immediately became attracted to her ideas. Winnicott continued to practice as a paediatrician during the nineteen thirties, and as a high proportion of paediatric work is with babies and very young children, so Klein's ideas were of immediate relevance to him, more so than those of Freud. He tried to persuade Melanie Klein to take him on for analysis, but she refused because, having seen him herself for two periods of analysis, she wanted him to take on her own child, Erich, then aged 20 years old, for a third analysis. So Winnicott approached Joan Riviere, Susan Isaacs's analyst and the next most senior Kleinian. She took him on two years after he stopped seeing Strachey, for another five year's analysis from 1935 to 1940.

Winnicott was a man of great charm and charisma. His appearance was elf-like and he had an engaging manner of speech, distinct but rather languid. He was a wonderful public speaker with a gift for choosing the unexpected phrase. After the Second World War he gave a series of talks for mothers of young children and these were brought together and published under the title "The Child, The Family, and the Outside World". He began his first talk "To begin with, you will be relieved to know that I am not going to be telling you what to do ..." In fact, for the rest of his talks he did little else! He went on "I am a man, and so I can never know what it is like to see wrapped up over there in the cot a bit of my own self, a bit of me living an independent life, yet at the same time dependent and gradually becoming a person". This gift for empathising with mothers and children endeared him to many paediatricians in training who remained influenced by him throughout their working lives.

Melanie Klein was initially happy to have Winnicott as a disciple, but when he began to develop ideas of his own about the nature of infantile anxieties, ideas that he himself saw as extensions of Klein's theories, though she did not, she rejected him and even forbad her trainees to go to his lectures. He found this extremely painful. In contrast, he got on well with Susan Isaacs. As we have seen, she asked him to lecture to her Child Development students on her course at the Institute of Education. In his foreword to Dorothy Gardner's biography (Gardner, 1969, p. 5), he described Susan Isaacs as "outstandingly superior, generous, and at the same time human, vulnerable, modest and humorously tolerant". He reported in his foreword that, as a family friend, he frequently heard the Isaacs in fierce but friendly disputation with each other. In view of this close contact it is not surprising that Susan Isaacs received a number of referrals for analytic treatment from him. One psychoanalyst who worked with Winnicott even believes that in his development of new methods of communicating with children he was much influenced by Susan Isaacs whose book whose book on "The Social Development of Young Children" he had read and admired (Judith Issroff, personal communication).

In the mid-1930s, while Winnicott was a relatively junior member of the psycho-analytic community, the Melanie Klein-Anna Freud battles continued. One way or another, mainly in the form of articles and book chapters, the artillery fire between Vienna and London with light and sometimes heavy shells lobbed from one capital city to another continued unabated.

The alignments between the different schools of psycho-analysis were complicated when strong divisions opened up in the mid nineteen thirties within the London camp. It was at this time that Edward Glover, Ernest Jones's lieutenant and the second most powerful figure in the British psychoanalytic world, originally quite sympathetic to Melanie Klein, became deeply antipathetic to her.[1] In 1935, Melanie published a paper entitled "A contribution to the psychogenesis of manic-depressive states" that many analysts regarded as a highly original contribution to the understanding of serious depression (Klein, 1935). It put forward for the first time the idea of the "depressive position" an attitude pervading the whole personality of an individual that arose during the second half of the first year of life from the guilt infants experienced arising from their desire to destroy the maternal breast. The "depressive position" was preceded by the "paranoid-schizoid" position in the third and fourth month of an infant's life. The phantasies the infant experienced at this very early stage of development arose, according to her, because of a sense of being attacked by an ungiving, frustrating maternal breast, in contrast to the other "good" giving, nurturant breast. Glover thought that these ideas represented not just an extension, but a major departure from Freudian psychology for which there was little if any supportive evidence. He also regarded Melanie Klein's explanation of serious mental illness as an incursion that trespassed into territory that belonged by right to the medically qualified psychiatrist. Despite being a non-medical analyst, Melanie Klein had attempted to contribute understanding into the causes of serious mental disorders and to suggest her own methods could help to cure them. Previously her publications had focussed on less serious problems in child development, as well as personality difficulties in childhood and adolescence. While he had originally found much of interest in Klein's ideas, Glover found these new thoughts of hers quite unacceptable. In contrast, Susan Isaacs found them stimulating and helpful in her clinical work, as the case described above in her paper "Property and Possessiveness" (Isaacs, 1934) makes clear.

There may well have been another, more personal reason for Edward Glover's hostility to Melanie Klein (Grosskurth, 1986, pp. 353–4). For some time he had been seeing her daughter, Melitta, in analysis. Either as a result of her analysis or for some other reason, Melitta had become deeply hostile to her mother and began to reject her mother's theories. Bearing in mind her experiences of Melanie as a mother, Melitta's defection is perhaps less surprising than the fact that up to 1934 she appears to have had a reasonably happy relationship with her mother. She helped her mother with various publications and received grateful acknowledgement. However her attitude markedly changed once she began her analysis with Edward Glover and it is not difficult to see why. Indeed, as she had had much previous analytic experience, it is puzzling why her hostile attitude to her mother took so long to develop. Psychoanalysis always involves recall of the past, and particularly of the person being analysed (technically the analysand). Melitta's life in childhood had been greatly affected by her mother's depression, the stormy nature of her parents' marriage, and the demands in time and emotional commitment that her mother's psychoanalytic training and subsequent career had made upon her. During much of Melitta's childhood and adolescence, her mother had left her for shorter or longer periods of weeks and months at a time initially in the care of her dominant grandmother, of whom Melitta was not fond, or with servants or at boarding school.

When Melitta was ten years old, her younger brother Erich was born, and, because of her newly developed interest in child development, it is clear that Melanie Klein spent much more time with him than she had with her two older children. She began Erich's psychoanalysis when Melitta was thirteen years old and so needed to spend several hours in what must have seemed an unusually private situation with him each week. In Melitta's mid-adolescence, the family moved to Slovakia to stay with her grandparents, but she and Hans were sent off to boarding school while Erich stayed at home. About a year later, the family moved to Berlin so that Melanie could work closely with Karl Abraham. It was at round about this time, when she was seventeen years old that her mother began, though only for a short period, an analysis of her daughter (Grosskurth, 1986, p. 95). She focused on Melitta's educational problems as she saw them. Among other matters she analysed her daughter's feelings about arithmetic in sexual terms. "The division of the big number by a smaller one was the coitus which she was to carry out with her mother in an ineffectual manner". In her published work, Melanie Klein gave Melitta the pseudonym "Lisa" and did not reveal she was writing about her own daughter (Klein, 1923) The analysis of their own children was, as I have previously indicated, not an unusual practice among the early psychoanalysts. It *was* unusual though for analysts to publish details of the analyses of their own children, even under pseudonyms. Further, however common it might have been for analysts to analyse their own children, one has to ask how Melitta must have felt about her mother talking about her maths problems in terms that involved sexual activity between the two of them. The pattern of intrusiveness that Melanie Klein had experienced from her mother seems to have been repeated with her own daughter.

When Melitta reached 18 years of age, she joined her mother in Berlin and, shortly afterwards, entered medical school there. Her mother, now permanently separated from Melitta's father, began to lead an active social life in Berlin, making a number of male friends and taking a lover. This might well have raised rivalrous feelings in her daughter. It is therefore easily understandable that the recall of her childhood and adolescence resulted in Melitta later developing a deep dislike of her mother. It is indeed remarkable that she had remained on such good terms with her mother while in her twenties. However, now as a 30 year old psychoanalyst, looking for ways of developing her own ideas and developing her own career, she began to attack her mother's ideas in public. She and her husband, Walter Schmideberg put themselves forward as allies of Anna Freud and guardians of the true Freudian faith.

Incidentally, the difficulties Melanie had in providing care for her own children has been known for many years but has never really elicited much comment from her colleagues. For example in their history of child psychoanalysis, Claudine and Pierre Geissmann (1998), having recounted quite accurately her behaviour during her children's early lives, conclude: "In her relationship with her children, Melanie Klein was neither better nor worse than other mothers." The neutral moral judgement the Geissmann's make of Melanie Klein's quality of mothering would not be shared by many non-analysts and one wonders whether their views on the average mother might not have been affected by the clientele they saw in their own clinical practice. In fact, Melanie Klein was, during much of the time her children were growing up, an unhappy and disturbed woman and it is not surprising that she was unable to provide a stable, happy home for them.

It is must be emphasised that it would not be in any way appropriate to judge the value of Melanie Klein's views on child development and child psychopathology on the basis of her behaviour towards her own children. Her scientific contribution must be appraised independently from such knowledge. As Susan Isaacs had very little, if any, knowledge of the early relationships between Melanie Klein and her children this is indeed what she must have done.

The conflicts between the divided London and Viennese schools surfaced in the International Psychoanalytic Congresses held each year. In 1938 Susan attended the Congress held that year in Paris. She played a prominent part in this meeting and read two important papers there. A paper entitled "Criteria for Interpretation" (Isaacs, 1939) is of particular interest to those who find far-fetched or even incredible the meanings for their dreams, their free associations and, in the case of children, their play that psychoanalysts gave to their patients at this time. For many non-analysts it is difficult to avoid asking the question—"how did analysts *know* that when the child or adult patient described a dream or, in the case of a child, played with dolls in a particular way that this meant what they said it did?" For example, in the other paper she read at the Paris meeting, Susan Isaacs (1943) describes a four year old boy called Jack who was suffering from what she called "acute psychotic anxiety". At one point Jack made a ship with chairs and asked Susan Isaacs to sit in it and be kept safe from floods and storms. To her the ship represented an omnipotent means of controlling his storms of hatred and disastrous floods of urine (he wet the bed). Later Jack pretended that all the toys and small objects in the drawer in which his toys were kept between his sessions with her were "coal" and he said he would "cart all the coal away" and "make it tidy". She regarded the pretend coal as "all the dead, dirty black things, the destructive faeces". How did she know so certainly that the "ship" was Jack's means of keeping her safe, and that the "coal" with which he played represented his faeces? (I have here deliberately selected an example of an interpretation that seems, at least to me, to border on the plausible, but to require some support for its confirmation.)

Fortunately in "Criteria for Interpretation" Susan Isaacs (1939) describes her reasons for deciding whether an interpretation was correct or incorrect. She first lists the sources of information the analyst uses in undertaking this task—the patient's behaviour observed by the analyst, free associations, dreams and waking fantasies, and behaviour in the outside world revealed by what the patient says about himself. She describes what she considers to be a plausible explanation of the apparently inconsistent words of a little boy. "A boy of five years of age, one day at a meal, addressing no one in particular, said in a very subdued way, 'I don't like dreams: they are horrid things'; and then, after a pause, 'and another thing— I don't have any.'" She goes on . . . "Now I find that every hearer, save the most obtuse, appreciates perceptually that in his denial the boy actually makes a positive statement, namely that his dreams are so horrid". Now although one may object to the suggestion that if one disagrees with her one is "most obtuse", most people would probably agree that her interpretation is convincing. But what of more problematic interpretations? Susan Isaacs suggests there is no essential difference between "analysing" this little boy's words from what happens time and again in the analytic hour. The only difference is that "the analyst is trained to perceive meanings which would be obscure to the untrained mind". The problem is that those without such training might reasonably be sceptical about the veracity of the more far-fetched interpretations that analysts make —perhaps especially sceptical of those interpretations made of the behaviour of infants and young children in the pre-school period when language and understanding are so limited.

Susan Isaacs lists a number of reasonable ways in which the analyst can confirm that interpretations are correct. These include when the patient finds what the analyst says to be revealing and when the patient's behaviour improves or at least changes after an interpretation. But she does not discuss the criticism most commonly levelled at this method of analysis, not least by non-Kleinian analysts about Kleinian interpretations. How does one know that the acceptance of an interpretation does not arise from the patient's suggestibility—the tendency to agree with someone in authority? How does one know that the changes in behaviour would not have occurred anyway, given the passage of time—an explanation that Susan Isaacs strongly endorses when describing elsewhere the findings of studies carried out by developmental psychologists? One method of convincing the sceptical (though by no means the only one possible) would involve using a technique commonly employed in psychological studies. A trained independent observer, with the knowledge of the subject or patient, is placed in the room or behind a one-way screen making independent interpretations that can be compared with those of the analyst. The two independent interpretations can then be compared. Susan Isaacs considers this possibility, but is uncompromisingly negative about it. "In analytic work this is quite out of the question, a serious handicap both for ourselves and for the general public. But we cannot alter this fact and have to accept it as a limitation for pure science, imposed on us by the very nature of the human mind". Grappling with the complexities of the human mind is certainly a difficult task. Psychologists and indeed psycho-analysts always find it necessary to simplify these complexities by reducing their data to manageable quantities. But it is surely sensible to assess the value of any psychological method by using whatever checks the human mind can devise. Since Susan Isaacs's time some psychoanalysts have accepted this point of view and have co-operated in experiments using independent observers. They have obtained rather mixed results. Many though, like Susan Isaacs, continue to find this approach unacceptable.

During the 1930s another outstanding entrant to the child psycho-analytic field, who was to have a number of professional contacts with Susan Isaacs made his presence felt. John Bowlby, like Susan Isaacs and Donald Winnicott, underwent analysis with Joan Riviere, starting to see her in 1929 when he was still a medical student with the aim of becoming a child psychiatrist. He was to become the psychoanalyst with the greatest influence on the understanding of child development during the second half of the twentieth century. His studies on attachment and loss have not only been of great theoretical and clinical significance for child psychologists, psychiatrists, paediatricians and social workers but have strongly influenced policies towards early child care and working mothers of young children all over the world (Bowlby, 1971).

In an autobiographical account, written in the 1980s but not published until 1991, a year after his death, Bowlby has much to say about the reception of his ideas by the Kleinian group at the Tavistock Clinic in the late 1930s (Bowlby, 1991). He provides an unusually frank account of Melanie Klein's personality. The members of her group (other than Susan Isaacs) were, he claims, hostile to him from the start. They tried to block his election first as an Associate and then as a full member of the British Psycho-analytic Society, telling him that what he was doing, namely investigating the family background of children who were behaving antisocially, was interesting but "not psychoanalysis". Only people who concentrated entirely on what went on within the minds of their patients could be regarded as true psychoanalysts. Bowlby was only elected an Associate member of the BPaS in 1938 and a full member in 1939. Interestingly, though he clearly saw Susan Isaacs as a member of the Kleinian group, he notes that she alone in this group was much more positive towards his work; he puts this down to her broader background as an academic psychologist. He later described her (BPaS, CBC/F09/006) as "one of a handful of members to be interested in his work on maternal deprivation and supported him when he presented it to the Society in 1939 and again in 1944".

Bowlby acknowledged that Melanie Klein had made an original contribution in revealing the infant's capacity to make relationships in very early life, but he was critical of other aspects of her theory. In the absence of evidence he felt it was important for all analysts to be tolerant of other views. He goes on:

> ... unfortunately tolerance was never part of Melanie Klein's outlook. Certain that she possessed the truth, she looked on those who did not share her views as deplorably blind. A very insecure person, she surrounded herself with disciples whose

role was not only to reassure her but to protect her against all criticism by means of strong attack. This made discussion impossible and also led to bad feeling.

Bowlby was also unfavourably struck by Melanie Klein's apparent lack of concern for the family lives of children in therapy. On one occasion he was seeing a difficult, hyperactive child under her supervision whose mother had very serious psychiatric problems herself. He was instructed to ignore the mother's needs. Eventually the mother required admission to a mental hospital and this meant that she could no longer bring her son for treatment with Bowlby. When he reported this state of affairs to Melanie Klein, she showed, according to Bowlby, an alarming lack of interest in the family. Her main concern was that Bowlby should be able to find another child to treat so that his psychoanalytic training with her should not be interrupted.

Her lack of interest in family relationships and, in particular, in the mothering of children in therapy, and her total preoccupation with their intra-psychic, mental existence, is extraordinary bearing in mind how sensitive she was to the suffering and anxieties of young children. She seems to have cut out all consideration of the quality of mothering from her view of the way children develop. Perhaps the whole subject of mothering was too personally painful for her to take on board.

To understand this wide gap in her understanding of child development, one has to turn again to her own very difficult relationship with her powerfully intrusive mother, Libussa. It was to escape Libussa's control that she abandoned her idea of studying medicine and instead, at the age of 21, fled into her unhappy marriage with Arthur Klein. There is good evidence too from her auto-biographical reflections that she had repressed her memory of the mothering of her own children. It is not surprising that a woman who, as we have seen, had so frequently left her own children for months at a time, while they were still quite young, should wish to put to the back of her mind the emotional damage that neglectful motherhood can do to children. Again one must emphasise that the fact that Melanie Klein had unattractive personality features does not in any way detract from the possible value of her ideas.

Although Bowlby excepted Susan Isaacs from his criticism of the Kleinian neglect of parental influence, her writings at this time showed little more interest in the influence of mothers and fathers than those of Melanie Klein. Her considerable interest in the importance of parents and in the social conditions in which children grow up came later, and Bowlby may only have remembered her later support and forgotten her earlier attitudes.

*   *   *

The rise of Hitler's anti-Semitic regime, the Anschluss and the imminent threat of a German invasion of Austria brought to an abrupt end the need for the long-distance exchanges of views for these tragic events meant that the two sides of this psycho-analytic conflict were soon living in the same city. Shortly after the Nazi occupation of Vienna, Ernest Jones had discussions with the British Society and the Home Office in London to pave the way for the evacuation of the Freuds and a number of other Jewish analysts (Jones, 1959). With the help of Princess Marie Bonaparte and the American Ambassador in Paris, through which the Freuds would have to travel, the departure was arranged (Maddox, 2006). On 6 June 1938, the Freuds arrived in London from Paris, and shortly afterwards settled in north-west London in a house in Maresfield Gardens, between Swiss Cottage and Hampstead. The spiritual centre of psycho-analysis had moved from Vienna to London, an outcome that gave much pleasure and pride to most British analysts, but was not at all to the liking of Melanie Klein.

On 3 September 1939 Britain declared war on Nazi Germany. The lives of all those in the combatant countries were profoundly changed for the next six years. Susan Isaacs was no exception. A year earlier her Department had moved with the rest of the Institute of Education into more spacious accommodation in the North Wing of Senate House in Bloomsbury, a vast, ugly building only a few hundred yards away from its home in Southampton Row (Gardner, 1969, p. 122). She had begun to make plans to use the considerable extra space to house a nursery class so that direct observation of children could take place on the premises. But before any such plans could materialize, war was declared. Accommodation in central London was required for expanded government departments involved in the war effort and most schools of London University were evacuated away from the city. The Institute of Education was relocated to Nottingham and it was suggested that her Department should be part of the move. But it was clear that there would be very few students and opportunities for academic work would be limited.

In September 1939 the Mental Health Course for Social Workers at the London School of Economics was evacuated to Cambridge. Sibyl Clement Brown, Susan's friend, who ran this course, had to find accommodation in Cambridge and Susan decided she would move too and they would share a flat (Gardner, 1969, p. 127). It would, in any case, be easier for her to continue to see some of her patients there. So she and Sibyl Clement Brown rented 30 Causewayside, a flat in a house near the River Cam not far from the centre of Cambridge.

The move to Cambridge turned out to represent pretty well the end of her University academic life. Giving up her academic work at the Institute of Education allowed her to commit herself much more fully not only to the parallel life she had been leading in psycho-analytic work for the previous twenty five years but also to embark on research in what was for her a completely new field.

Susan's move to Cambridge coincided with the massive evacuation of schoolchildren out of London to the countryside and to provincial cities that were thought to be safer (Marwick, 1976). Cambridge had been declared an "open city" where no weapons would be manufactured and, in return, it would be exempt from bombing. During September, 1939, over 800,000 school children, over 500,000 mothers with young children, over 12,000 expectant mothers and over 100,000 teachers and helpers left their homes in large British cities for safety reasons (Titmuss, 1950). When the bombing failed to materialise during the autumn and early winter of 1939/40, a trickle and then a flood of mothers and young children began to return to their homes. By January 1940 over 85% of mothers with young children and about half the unaccompanied school children who had been evacuated were back home again. But some remained.

When the evacuation began Susan Isaacs realised that a study of reactions to evacuation would provide invaluable data as to how children coped with separation. Such information would also have practical use for those wishing to ensure that evacuated children were not only safe, but that their physical and emotional needs were met as well as possible. The fact that so many children returned to their homes meant that a study of reactions to evacuation would have added value should, as indeed turned out to be the case, the phony war come to an end and German bombing of big cities begin in earnest. She set up a steering committee, including John Bowlby, Donald Winnicott, John Rickman and Melanie Klein to oversee the study (Isaacs, Clement Brown and Thouless, 1941).

Susan's contacts with the Cambridge authorities, especially the Chief Education Officer who was also appointed the Chief Billeting Officer, meant that she rapidly got permission to have access to the records of evacuated children. 3,000 had been evacuated to Cambridge. She decided to confine the study to those who had come from two London Boroughs, 373 from Tottenham and 352 from Islington. Between a quarter and a half of these children had returned home by December, 1939. As well as the information from the records, teachers in Cambridge filled in forms about the reactions of nearly all the evacuated children. The children wrote brief essays at school on the subjects "What I like in Cambridge" and "What I miss in Cambridge". Finally, psychiatric social workers carried out interviews in London with many of the parents whose children had been away and then returned.

The fact that the London School of Economics Mental Health Course for social workers under the direction of Sibyl Clement Brown, with whom Susan shared a flat, had been evacuated to Cambridge meant that there were plenty of volunteer interviewers. The Child Guidance Clinic in Cambridge had its staff considerably increased by students anxious to obtain experience in seeing disturbed children and their families. Susan had access to the records of children referred to the Clinic who had either been disturbed before they came to Cambridge or had become disturbed as a result of their evacuation experiences.

From an administrative point of view the evacuation scheme was a stunning success. The schoolchildren largely travelled with their classmates and home teachers. All the children were found foster homes or billets and the teachers were also all successfully billeted. Local people with rooms to spare also took in the substantial numbers of mothers with young children who were evacuated to Cambridge. Most children were happy in their homes and liked the schools to which they were allocated. Few of the foster parents found the children they took in to be too difficult for them. Indeed significant adjustment problems only arose in about 8% or one in twelve of the children (ibid., p. 53).

There was, all the same, a great deal of misery, unhappiness and homesickness among the evacuated children. Some evacuated children later wrote about their experiences that remained vivid and indeed unforgettably with them throughout their lives. Mel Calman, the cartoonist, wrote over 25 years after his evacuation to Cambridge (Calman, 1968):

I have an image of a small boy with a label tied round his neck. The boy has no features and is crying. . . . Even nowadays (he is writing in 1968) whenever I have to travel anywhere and have to say goodbye to my own children, I identify with that small boy. I remember the label and the gas mask and feel anxiety gripping my bowels.

The Cambridge team however concentrated their attention on the problems that arose from a misfit between the children and their foster families. A number of factors explained the difficulties that did arise. Maladjustment was greater among the older children, some of whom took matters in their own hands and took themselves off back to London without permission; it was not a complicated journey. As well as missing their families, these young people aged thirteen and fourteen years of age (then the compulsory school leaving age) often felt they wanted to return so that they could contribute to the family income especially if their father had been called up and finances were stretched at home. Among the younger children the rate of maladjustment was higher if brothers and sisters were split up or if parents did not visit. It was also found that children placed with foster mothers over the age of sixty years had a less successful outcome.

Unexpectedly mismatches between the social status and income of the evacuated children and their hosts did not affect the success of the placements though they did give rise to some surprises both ways. A boy of 14 years wrote (Isaacs, Clement Brown & Thouless, 1941, p. 82):

I live in a small four room house with no bath no hot water laid on only gas light where at home I lived in a nine room house bath hot water electric and all convenience should be in a house two of us have to sleep in a single bed. . . .

A girl of 13 years wrote (ibid., p. 80):

I like the maid who is not very old and we have good times together when the cook is not there . . . I do not like living in the kitchen of the house as the cook is very fussy. I do not like going to bed at half past seven.

In the children's essays easily most frequently mentioned among "what I miss in Cambridge" were parents and relatives. Second most frequently mentioned were friends not evacuated. This was the case for both boys and girls.

Of particular interest is the section of the book dealing those children who were referred for psychiatric or psychological help (ibid., p. 109–23). This was probably partly written by Sibyl Clement Brown and the children's problems were classified according to a scheme devised by John Bowlby for the purposes of the Survey. All the same, Susan Isaacs clearly contributed and probably wrote a good deal of this section.

What is striking about the children who are described is that their problems are only occasionally related to the quality of their billets or foster homes though sometimes this is indeed the case. These usually improved with a change of billet. The most frequently mentioned problems (ibid., p. 118) among children who were referred were bedwetting and soiling. Susan writes, surprisingly in view of contributions to the psycho-analytic literature, these symptoms were really more of a nuisance to the foster parents than a reason for anxiety. Most of the case histories about children with more serious difficulties provide ample evidence of chronic difficulties arising from the unsatisfactory nature of the homes from which they came. A few details (ibid., p. 114–6) are given in the book about nine cases.

Case 1. Girl, aged seven. "The reason for unhappiness appears to have been connected with the child's past home life, where she was the odd man out in a large and very poor family."

Case 2. Girl, aged thirteen. Lonely and homesick. "She was the middle child at home and apparently less well loved than the others."

Case 3. Girl, aged six. Anxious and unhappy. ". . . a child who had been distressed at home by scenes of physical violence between her own parents."

Case 4. Boy aged ten. Unstable and depressed. "This boy had experienced harsh treatment from his parents. His father was alcoholic. . . ."

Case 5. Girl of twelve. Hysterical, excitable and irresponsible. Her mother "deserted the home when the child was five years old. The father was left with three children and was himself very immature."

Case 6. Boy age eight. Unhappy, pining and peaky. No comments about his family of origin and improved when he was placed in an open air class.

Case 7. Boy aged ten. Over-dependent on his foster-mother's affection. "This boy's family had been unsatisfactory. His father was unstable. . . ."

Case 8. Two boys aged thirteen and seven who improved on being moved from one foster home to another more suitable one.

Case 9. Girl, aged ten. Fretful, poor appetite, sullen. Improved on being moved to a more suitable billet.

What is so striking in these accounts and in the other information that is given about the disturbed children is not so much what is mentioned but what is omitted. Thus there is no mention at all of early feeding difficulties and virtually nothing about sexual problems such as masturbation. It must have been felt by the psychiatrists and social workers who saw these children, by their foster families and by their home parents, that the adverse family circumstances or a mismatch between the billet and the needs of the child were quite sufficient to account for their difficult behaviour and emotional distress. There seemed no need to invoke Kleinian theories of complex intra-psychic disturbances in the first or second year of life.

The "Cambridge Evacuation Survey" reporting the results of the survey was published in 1941. The main recommendations (ibid., Appendix 2, pp. 196–204) were that much greater attention should be paid to the emotional needs of children if further evacuations occurred. Brothers and sisters should be placed together and parents should be strongly encouraged to visit their children even though this might cause immediate distress. The book was very favourably reviewed in *The Times*. By the time it appeared, the massive destruction of London, especially the East End of London, had begun. Evacuation was once again organised, but attitudes had changed. A footnote in the Introduction, clearly recognisable by its style to have been written by Susan Isaacs movingly states (ibid., p. 9):

> Since the bombing of London's East End, we have seen how this need to keep the family together and to cling to familiar home surroundings may override even the worst dangers. Among the simple and the poor, where there is no wealth, no pride of status or of possessions, love for the members of one's own family and joy in their bodily presence alone makes life worth living. So deeply rooted is this need that it has defied even the law of self-preservation, as well as urgent public appeals and the wishes of authority.

Even when bombing began with great force in August, 1940, many Londoners stayed in their homes with their children, though people from the most intensely bombed areas left in great numbers in a little publicised, unplanned and chaotic fashion. The lessons that the Cambridge Evacuation Survey had taught were not, in fact, translated into evacuation policy during the rest of the Second World War.

*   *   *

While Susan was in Cambridge for the year after war broke out, Nathan stayed in London. He was seconded from his firm to the Ministry of Supply to take charge of the government department responsible for dealing with the supply of ferro-alloys, especially tungsten and molybdenum, metals essential for weapons manufacture. Nathan and Evelyn were also separated at this time. In October

1939, following the outbreak of war, the National Training College of Domestic Subjects where Evelyn had worked as Lecturer in Psychology and English from 1930 was evacuated from London to Torquay in the south-west of England where it was housed in the Technical Institute.[2] Staff and students were billeted out with local families and Evelyn found lodgings in Torquay itself.

Susan returned to London in September, 1940, when the lease of her rented flat in Cambridge came to an end. She was intending to stay in London, but it was at just this point that the bombing of London began in earnest. Various ministries essential to the war effort were evacuated out of London and it was decided that the Ministry of Supply should be one of these. Initially Nathan was consulted (IoEd N1 D6) as to whether he would like to move or stay, and he opted to stay, especially as, at this time, Susan had just returned to London from Cambridge. However it was decided that the work of his Department was too important to risk and he was sent to Ashow, a village near Leamington Spa in the Midlands where he was billeted in temporary accommodation. He remained there as Head of the Ferro-Alloys Department until the end of the war. Susan returned to Cambridge where she found another flat. Most weekends she travelled to the Midlands (Gardner, 1969, p. 127) to stay with Nathan in a room at a farm near his work. When she was unwell he would come to Cambridge for the weekend to be with her.

Nathan found his prolonged stay at Ashow a less disagreeable experience than he had expected. He worked very long hours often late into the evening and at weekends, taking a good deal of responsibility for maintaining the supply of ferro-alloys to arms manufacturers. In his brief amounts of leisure time he played high-level chess and table tennis at what he described as a much lower level. His Department had a chess team and he sometimes played first board.

Although they rarely met during this four year period, Nathan and Evelyn corresponded frequently and many of Nathan's letters have been preserved (IoEd N1 D6 1 and 2). Some of these letters are very long and one wonders how Nathan found the time and energy to write them, bearing in mind he had an exhausting job and, after the autumn of 1940, often had to commute for meetings between Leamington Spa and London. According to Karina, his niece, he trained himself during the war to need less and less sleep, so that gradually he was able to manage on only about four hours a night (Karina McIntosh, personal communication). The letters, mostly around 8–10 pages long but sometimes longer, are usually dated, but only one or two give any clue as to whom they were addressed. However the recipient is clearly living in Torquay where Evelyn had been evacuated.

The letters are mainly written in a chatty, but otherwise impersonal style. They are full of commentary on the progress of the war, on his colleagues at Ashow, on the people he meets socially (mainly left-wing intellectuals), and on his work. His main task is to ensure the supply of ferro-alloys to Britain, using all the official and unofficial contacts at his disposal. At one point in late 1939 (Letter, Nathan Isaacs to Evelyn Lawrence, 12 November, 1939) he describes how he negotiates a large shipment of ferro-alloys from a small port in Norway. But the Norwegian government embargoes the deal. He goes with the ships to anchor off the Norwegian coast but the Norwegians remained adamant and the ships return without their cargo. He writes that he wishes he could contact the responsible Norwegian minister himself, but this is impossible; he is too lowly a civil servant.

The letters make frequent references to Susan and to the activities that he and Susan do together, holidays, weekends away and so on. They provide some insight into the arrangements in Cambridge as well as his ironic perspective on the psychoanalytic world. In late 1939 Melanie Klein joined Susan Isaacs and Sibyl Clement Brown in the flat they shared together. The three of them shared the flat until the summer of 1940 when Melanie Klein went to Pitlochry for greater safety. After a weekend spent in Cambridge, Nathan reported (Undated letter, probably Spring, 1940, Nathan Isaacs to Evelyn Lawrence):

> Susie tells me that she's written to you, so probably she's told you the latest turn by which the happy family here now consists of her, Clement and Mrs. Klein. It's all very pleasant and amiable, except for the fact that Melanie's coming has, by an unfortunate but unavoidable concatenation, already meant one patient less for Susie and this may prove a small world for two of them. On the other hand, it's a densely populated one, I should think all ripe for psychoanalysis if not now then before

long, so that after a bit they should have little difficulty keeping going. What with the University itself, the LSE and, I believe, Bedford College, Cambridge will presently be one terrific buzz of mutually worked up excited brains and nerves and, I imagine, a whole College of Psychoanalysts won't be enough to cope with them; the prospects seems rather horrifying.

Once Susan and he go to Beacon Hill where it becomes clear from his letter Evelyn and Nathan had also been together before the war. Nathan does not attempt to hide how close he is to Susan. Nor does he wish to exclude Evelyn from the enjoyable times he and Susan have together. In July, 1941 he went down to Cambridge for a sociable weekend with friends including the Poles and Sibyl Clement Brown. He wrote to Evelyn (letter 18 July, 1941, IoEd N1 D6) "I wonder if we can perhaps arrange another such party but *including* you".

Only one of the letters to Evelyn contains any note of affection or intimacy. The exception, clearly one he could be assured would be kept confidential, was written in January 1940 just before one of their rare meetings at this time. Its contents are striking (Undated letter, probably late January, 1940 IoEd N1 D6).

How lovely sweetheart. I had a secret hope that somehow Saturday morning (*as later made clear, he probably meant afternoon*) would be kind and fit in. Of course there wasn't any reason for the hope, but it was just the pleasure-principle working for one, legitimate or illegitimate as is its business. Now you've legiti-mated it and straightaway it's gone off on another expedition. Shall I share the secret with you? It probably won't come off, but now that I'm going to have an assistant who by that time should begin to be good for something, perhaps I can snatch the Saturday morning too. I'll have a good try. I'm very sorry you can't show me all the things you speak of at Torquay and I wish I could share them with you. But I'll make the most of all there'll be to see in less than four weeks time at a flat on the edge of Primrose Hill. We'll share that and be happy again. . . . Goodbye Evelyn darlingest, I love you and want you with all my heart.

Nathan's invocation of the Freudian concept of the pleasure-principle to justify his tryst with Evelyn was an in-joke that Susan would have appreciated although she was probably not invited to share it!

In January 1940 Nathan completed a philosophical work entitled "The Theory and Practice of Knowledge". Routledge and Kegan Paul wrote that their reader had thought well of the book, but in the present publishing climate they regretted they could not publish it. However, shortly after Susan's death, the same publishers did produce a book by Nathan Isaacs with the same theme (Isaacs, 1949).

A little later Nathan and Susan went on a walking and bird-watching holiday in Wales and there is another short break on the Yorkshire moors in July, 1940. But mostly Nathan's letters to Evelyn are about the war, his reactions and those of their friends, for example to the Russo-German entente which split the British left-wing in 1939. At the end of May 1940 he writes (IoEd N1 D6 1/2 Letter Nathan Isaacs to Evelyn Lawrence, 31 May 1940) of Dunkirk.

> The first act ends with our men swimming away from France, whilst the whole nation applauds and almost celebrates a victory. I suppose that in the circumstances to get away with so many whole skins *is* a triumph.

A fortnight later he writes (ibid., June 1940) "Well, the inevitable has happened—the Germans aren't merely in Paris but are there according to timetable". In the same letter he describes how he tried to join the Local Defence Force (LDV), but was turned down because he "doesn't have the right sort of parents". When he told them he had served in France in the last war, they quoted back to him the example of a man with the Victoria Cross who had also been rejected for the LDV as his parents were not British.

Nathan writes a good deal about the latent or sometimes overt anti- semitism he encounters. At one point (ibid., 16 January 1942) he catches sight of a departmental memo referring to "the Jew in charge of wolfram at Westminster" as well as a menacing note written by the same man beginning "If that fool Isaacs at the Ministry of Supply has let the country down for wolfram, he ought to be hamstrung" (Wolfram is an ore yielding tungsten).

Nathan did not have a strong Jewish identity though in the nineteen thirties he was deeply concerned with the Nazi persecution of the Jews (personal communication, Karina McIntosh). He showed a sense of Jewish camaraderie, relishing Jewish self-mocking humour unexpectedly perhaps in the light of his strongly assimilationist views. After the war he joined the Reform Club perhaps because it was known to be the haunt of liberal Jews. Much later he was to write (letter dated mid-September to mid-October, 1956, IoEd N1 D 7/3 to Jack Pole)—"mostly I don't feel like a Jew, but just like a member of a particular civilisation. . . ."

In his letters he makes frequent reference to journeys to London and other parts of the country, occasionally traveling abroad to Holland before it is occupied by the Germans. He reports on his conversations he has on his travels. On one occasion (Letter Nathan Isaacs to Evelyn Lawrence 11 December 1942. N1 D6 1/2) he strikes up a conversation with J M Keynes, the economist, with whom he discusses the changing views of Lionel Robbins, Nathan's economist friend made during the First World War. On another occasion (ibid., 26 February 1942) he bumps into William Brierley and his wife. They talk for an hour or so, but Nathan, who likes William, makes no reference to the fact that this is his wife's first husband.

His references to Susan are solicitous and matter of fact. Bearing in mind this is a man writing to his mistress about his wife one might expect his remarks to be more guarded. There is only one point, in a letter dated July, 1941, when he is critical of his wife. He writes to Evelyn (ibid., 31 July 1941) that his sister Mallie has obtained a job working with evacuated children, but become so appalled with the way those in charge shouted at, hit and generally showed a complete lack of understanding of the children that she had left in disgust. Nathan goes on:

And Susie goes and steeps herself in her handful of analyses, when she, more than anyone else in the whole country, has the position and influence as well as the understanding and power of statement for the leadership of a campaign that would save untold miseries, injustices, injuries and warping.

This criticism seems well-founded. Nathan may have forgotten or not have known that Susan had, at the outbreak of war, written to the Board of Education (Gardner, 1969, p. 127) offering her services in any way it might find useful and had received no reply. She also attended at least one meeting at the Board of Education at which she put her views forcefully about the rigid habit training that many evacuated children were receiving. But it is remarkable (and many would agree with Nathan regrettable) that, having carried out the Cambridge Evacuation Survey described later in this chapter and identified gaps in child care, she did not do more herself to improve the quality of child care in the country. Nathan was right to suggest that she was in a better position than anyone else to take a lead in this matter. In London, for example, Anna Freud and Dorothy Burlingham, though also engaged in analytic work, nevertheless found the time, energy and courage to set up the Hampstead Nurseries for 80 resident and 40 day care children who were victims of bombing and whose family life had been badly disrupted by air raids (Freud and Burlingham, 1943).

In the summer of 1941, Nathan and Susan went on another walking holiday in Scotland. They met up with Melanie Klein who was now living there and seeing a child for analysis. Nathan writes that Melanie reminded him that when he and she had discussed their future a year earlier, they had both expected to be dead or at least in concentration camps before they could discuss the matter again.

In November, 1941, Susan had a recurrence of the cancerous growth in her breast (ibid., 21 November 1941). She was operated upon at the Acland Clinic in Oxford, but microscopic examination of the part removed at operation revealed that some cancerous cells were still present so she had to have another course of radiotherapy. A year later she had some bleeding from her bladder that turned out to be caused by a benign growth, a papilloma, and this too needed treatment.

During the mid-nineteen forties, Susan and Nathan played an increasing part in Karina's upbringing (personal communication, Karina McIntosh). When they were in London, she spent a fair amount of time with them in her holidays from boarding school, and they took her away on holiday with them. After one such holiday (Letter Nathan Isaacs to Evelyn Lawrence 18 April 1941, N1 D6 1/2) in the Easter of 1941, a few months before Susan was taken ill again, Nathan wrote to Evelyn that "Karina enjoyed the thrilling novelty of each sight and sound and we enjoyed her enjoyment". Shortly afterwards, Karina reached the age of 13 years and became a rebellious adolescent (personal communication, Karina McIntosh). In her teen years Karina got into a number of scrapes involving unsuitable relationships from which the Isaacs rescued her. According to her they were remarkably tolerant while quietly steering her towards pursuit of her studies. Karina's memory of Susan during her own adolescence is of a "wonderful companion— wise, witty, immensely knowledgeable, with practical competences (eg rowing) which I esteemed and with a sheer intelligence which impressed even cocky young Karina". At times though Karina found her to be almost inhumanly controlled in her emotions. She remembers a time when she was playing racing demon with her. Susan kept on winning, despite Karina changing the rules to her advantage. Karina got angrier and angrier. Eventually Susan put the cards away and said "I don't think we should go on playing any more" which Karina found made her even more furious. Susan never told her off, and she felt like saying to her "What sort of a psychologist are you? This isn't making me calm down at all". According to Karina, Susan never got angry herself and this superhuman self-control could be intimidating and controlling. Although obviously Susan was generally able to keep her emotions well under control, Karina and many others often saw Nathan and Susan engaged in fierce, intellectual arguments.

Meanwhile Evelyn and Nathan continued to write regularly to each other. In early 1943 the post of Director of the National Froebel Foundation based in London became vacant. Evelyn, with Nathan's encouragement applied. There were other good candidates and considerable doubt whether she would be successful However in June 1943 she was appointed and took up the post in the autumn (Froebel Institute Archive, Roehampton, B9/1072–3). In his last letter dated 29 July, 1943, to her Nathan very coolly concludes (Letter Nathan Isaacs to Evelyn Lawrence 29 July. N1 D6 3): "Now I must stop. But hope to continue soon verbally". The impersonal tone of this correspondence strongly suggests that both Nathan and Evelyn were anxious it might be read by people from whom they wished to keep the secret of their relationship.

Whether Evelyn's return to London made the continuation of her affair with Nathan less complicated is uncertain. Susan also returned from Cambridge, so the pre-war triangular pattern of the relationship continued. Susan's emotions became increasingly engaged with the affairs of the British Psychoanalytic Society but there is no indication that this affected her relationship with either her husband or with Evelyn. Nathan and Susan continued to have an active social life. John Bowlby, many years later, described (BPaS CBC/F09/006) the small evening parties they held where there was much intellectual discussion, for example about the scientific status of psychoanalysis. His recollection was that both he and Nathan were more demanding of evidence than was Susan. But the discussion was "lively and tolerant" and "Susan had a much better sense of humour than first impressions suggested". Her capacity to defend her particular school of psycho-analysis was soon to be tested to the full in a more critical forum.

Notes

1   Interview: Edward Glover by Bluma Swerdloff, Oral History Research Office, Columbia University, 1968.
2   National Archive, Kew ED64. National Training College for Domestic Subjects Record.

CHAPTER TWELVE

Battling for the minds of children

n London at the beginning of 1939 the world of British psycho-
analysis was in considerable disarray. Melanie Klein was furious
with Ernest Jones, still the President of the British Psycho-analytic
Society (BPaS) for having arranged for the Freuds to come to England
rather than the United States. Later, still resentful, she wrote to Jones
(King and Steiner, 1991, p. 228):

> . . . at the time I resented Anna settling here with a large and
> representative part of the Vienna group and thought that you
> had too little considered the disturbance to our work and also
> that you had confronted us with a fait accompli . . . Some of
> those Viennese who since went to USA . . . have very soon
> volunteered the information to me that they had every
> possibility to go to America and would have done so, had you
> not invited them and encouraged them to come to England.

Bearing in mind he had every reason to feel pleased with the
results of his efforts, having saved both the Freuds from the Nazis
in Vienna as well as having helped Sigmund Freud, by now an old
and sick man who was to die a little over a year later, to avoid a long
and exhausting sea voyage to the United States, Jones replied in a
remarkably mild manner. He conceded to Melanie Klein that Anna
was (ibid., p. 229):

> "undoubtedly a tough and indigestible morsel. She has probably
> gone as far in analysis as she can and has no pioneering

originality." Jones concluded: "There are many things I should arrange otherwise if I were God, but I do not happen to be. When the last war broke out, Freud wrote to me that he refused to take on his shoulders the foolishness of the world and I think that was a wise remark".

Melanie remained inconsolable. She continued to see the new arrivals as a "disaster". "It will never be the same again", she confided to Donald Winnicott, one of her strong supporters, though he himself was to be rejected by her for developing independent ideas before too long. She now had to share the centre of the British psychoanalytic stage with her arch-rival, the woman who had attacked her so fiercely more than a decade previously and who was still dismissive of her work. According to John Bowlby the problem was the two of them worshipped different gods. Anna Freud prayed at the shrine of St. Sigmund; Melanie Klein at the shrine of St. Melanie.

The situation grew more serious for Melanie Klein and her group of followers or "disciples" after Freud died in September, 1939. In 1940, as a result of the bombing London became a changed city for the analysts as for everybody else. By now the younger men such as John Bowlby and John Rickman had been recruited into the Emergency Medical Service and were working out of London, dealing with psychiatric casualties. When the bombing became intense, some of the women, including Susan Isaacs, Joan Riviere, and Melanie Klein herself, left London for safety reasons. But the refugees from Austria and Germany were classed as enemy aliens and Home Office regulations did not allow them to leave London.

Despite the air raids on London that continued almost nightly from the late summer of 1940 until the late spring of 1941, and continued sporadically first with conventional bombing, then, after June, 1944, with V1 flying bombs and finally with V2 rockets, many scientific organisations continued to hold meetings in London throughout the war. The British Psychoanalytic Society met at 96 Gloucester Place in Marylebone, about halfway between Euston and Paddington railway stations, both prime bombing targets. Occasionally the sounds of bombing and the response of the emergency services could be heard by those at the meetings and, if an air raid warning was sounded it was agreed to adjourn to the basement. The bombing affected the lives of members in other ways. Seaside towns on the South Coast where Sylvia Payne lived were often targeted. In May, 1943, between the fourth and fifth Scientific Meetings, the town of Reading where Marjorie Brierley lived was bombed with much loss of life when there was a direct hit on a British restaurant. And, while the debates on infant phantasies raged on at the BPaS, many children were actually losing their lives only a short distance away. The Times of 28 January, 1943 carried a report of the burial of 39 children and 5 women teachers killed in an air raid on a school in Lewisham, about five miles away from Marylebone. The Isaacs flat in Primrose Hill Road did not receive a direct hit and survived the war though the house in which it was situated was later knocked down to make room for the development of a block of flats. However it did sustain some damage later in the summer of 1944 when a flying bomb fell just behind it between King Henry's Road and Oppidans Road, destroying a number of houses in both streets. The Isaacs were not in their flat at the time, but their housekeeper, Annie was there and, though she was unhurt, witnessed the collapse of the dining room ceiling (Karina McIntosh, personal communication).

The meetings of the Society took place on the first and third Wednesdays of each month, initially in the afternoons, but later in the evenings. For the first couple of years the attendance was largely made up of refugees from Germany and Austria. Most of the other analysts had either left London for the relative safety of the provinces or had joined one of the armed services (King and Steiner, 1991, p. 28).

Shortly after the war began, decisions regarding the emergency measures that needed to be taken were made by the Honorary Officers of the Institute and of the BPaS (often the same people). These officers were appointed by the Boards and not elected democratically. The Board of the BPaS was elected annually by block vote. There was no limit to the period of office of members of the Board, some of whom had served for very long periods, and some indeed held multiple positions. Ernest Jones, for example, had been President of the Society since 1919. Edward Glover had been on all the main committees of the Society and Institute for many years. He was Chairman of the Training Committees of both the Institute and Society (ibid., p. 31). The Training Committees were key bodies as they determined the suitability of candidates (trainees) for psychoanalytic training and the suitability of members of the Society to become training analysts. They allocated candidates to supervisors of particular schools, Freudian or Kleinian, and, once enlisted, candidates were likely to follow the party line of their supervisors. Edward Glover, increasingly anti-Klein, admitted later that, when chairman of the Training Committee, although he gave the appearance of impartiality, he had deliberately allocated strong candidates to the Freudians and shaky ones to the Kleinians.[1]

At the same time as decisions about emergency measures and training were taken by the Officers, the scientific meetings of the Society, held every other Wednesday, became increasingly argumentative and ill-tempered. Although initially, at the beginning of the war, there was a majority of Viennese analysts in attendance, in 1941 Melanie Klein returned to London from Scotland where she had gone after Cambridge, and she and the other Kleinians, including Susan Isaacs began to attend meetings of the BPaS again. The two sides were now more balanced in numbers and the atmosphere became increasingly unpleasant (King and Steiner, 1991, p. 32). At a meeting of the Training Committee in April, 1940, Anna Freud had claimed that her work and that of her collaborators was Freudian analysis, but that Melanie Klein's ideas were "not psychoanalysis, but a substitution for it" (King and Steiner, 1986, p. 256). In a phone call to Melanie Klein, she made it plain that she would like the Kleinians to form a separate group of their own (ibid., p. 285).

The anger of the Freudians was focused on a number of issues. They thought the public was deliberately being exposed more to Kleinian than to Freudian ideas and were consequently being give a false idea of psychoanalysis; this was giving the field a bad name. The Kleinians, they complained, were organising their own supervisions, poaching patients and re-analysing people who had had a Freudian analysis for purposes of indoctrination. In brief, they accused the Kleinians of empire building.

But the Kleinians were also unhappy. They were particularly concerned at the extent of the power in the hands of Edward Glover, who, as Vice-President of the Society chaired meetings in Ernest Jones's absence and was also Chairman of the Training Committee. With some justice, as his later revelations made clear, they did not see him as in any way independent or fair-minded. According to his own account, Glover had been positive about Melanie Klein's ideas when she arrived in London, but rapidly became sceptical of their scientific value. As early as 1928 he wrote an unpublished paper called "Present tendencies in psychoanalytical research" that called Klein's ideas into question.[2] Glover thought that her ideas represented not just an extension of Freud's ideas as she claimed but a radical revision and that she had little or no clinical evidence to support them. In fact, even as late as 1940, Glover was not wholly negative about Klein's therapeutic approach to children. In a well-regarded monograph (Glover, 1940) on psychoanalytic technique with adult patients he made two references to Klein's work. In discussing patients who speak little or not at all he suggests "adapting the method which has been used so successfully by Mrs. Klein" and later, in discussing what he calls "active therapy" in adults he refers to the possibility of turning "to advantage in adult analysis the findings of Melanie Klein in child analysis". It was her theories on early child development he found unacceptable. In an Appendix to his monograph he attacked the ideas she had put forward in her 1935 paper on mourning and its relation to the manic-depressive state with some ferocity. According to Glover, her ideas led to the rejection of the Oedipus complex, a theory central to Freudian psychoanalysis. He felt that her tendency to discount the importance of real experiences in favour of examining only the meaning of such experiences was unhelpful. He suggested, and here he singled out Susan Isaacs for particular criticism, that the tendency of the Kleinians to infer earlier experiences from current behaviour even in the face of negative evidence was unsound and unscientific.

The Kleinians thought he was strongly under the influence of Klein's daughter, Melitta Schmideberg, whose training analysis he had conducted from 1934 onwards. He and Melitta had a very close relationship though there is no real basis for the idea that they were having an affair. As we saw in the last chapter, in the early stages of her analysis, Melitta had developed a virulent hatred of her mother whose ideas and behaviour she now saw as little short of poisonous. Melanie Klein complained to Ernest Jones about his lack of ability to stand up to Glover and see fair play between the two groups.

In late 1941, as a result of the increasing animosity between the Freudian and Kleinian groups the atmosphere at meetings of the Society reached a new low. Some members, especially Melanie's daughter, Melitta Schmideberg and her husband Walter wanted to exclude Melanie from the Society and Institute because her work did not derive, they maintained, from Freudian psycho-analysis. It was clear that something would have to happen to resolve the situation, either a split or some sort of compromise. James Strachey, generally regarded as a mild and reasonable man, had indeed even as early as 23 April, 1940, written to Edward Glover, giving his views on the best way forward. He wrote (King and Steiner, 1991, p. 32):

I should rather like you to know (for your personal information) that if it comes to a showdown—I'm very strongly in favour of compromise at all costs. The trouble seems to be with extremism, on all sides. My own view is that Mrs. K. has made some highly important contributions to PA (psychoanalysis), but that it's absurd to make out a) that they cover the whole subject or b) that their validity is axiomatic. On the other hand, I think it's equally ludicrous for Miss F. to maintain that PA is a game reserve belonging to the F family, and that Mrs. K's ideas are totally subversive.

These attitudes on both sides are of course purely religious and the very antithesis of science. They are also (on both sides) infused by, I believe, a desire to dominate the situation and in particular the future—which is why both sides lay so much stress on the training of candidates; actually, of course, it's a megalomaniac mirage to suppose that you can control the opinions of people you analyse beyond a very limited point. But, in any case, it ought to be the aim of a training analysis to put the trainee into a position to arrive at his own decision on moot points—not to stuff him with your own private dogmas.

In fact, I feel like Mercutio about it. . . .

Strachey's thought—"A plague on both your houses"—led him to express himself in more extreme terms, for he went on, doubtless ironically—"Why should these wretched fascists and (bloody foreigners) communists invade our peaceful, compromising island?"

The responsibility for achieving greater harmony lay partly, at least, with the President of the Society, Ernest Jones. His own position was balanced in that he agreed with many of Melanie Klein's views but thought she went too far in expressing them. He wrote to Anna Freud in these terms, saying about Melanie that she was "in many ways neurotic and has a tendency, which she is trying to check, to become 'verrannt' (stubbornly attached)" (Grosskurth, 1986, p. 288). Jones acutely observed to Anna Freud that much of the conflict arose from economic insecurity—everyone was worried where the patients were to come from and if there were no patients, there would be no income. Sylvia Payne, Honorary Secretary of the Society and Institute and later President, who was alert to the economic fears that were prevalent, also took a middle view and was an important stabilising force in the dispute.

In any event, by December 1941, the time for the showdown to which Strachey had referred well over a year previously, had arrived. Melanie Klein marshalled her forces. It was agreed that John Rickman, Clifford Scott and Susan Isaacs were to provide the heavy artillery. Paula Heimann would be active behind the scenes. The aim was to show that the Kleinians were working very much in the Freudian tradition, that Freud in any case favoured the development of his ideas and to point out that Edward Glover had himself been a supporter of Kleinian ideas at an earlier stage of the dispute (Grosskurth, 1986, p. 289). Throughout the painful discussions that were to follow, Susan Isaacs and Melanie Klein were in constant correspondence. Although only a fraction of the correspondence survives, an indication of its frequency is contained in a letter from Melanie Klein to Susan dated 25 June, 1942, which begins "Here is my weekly letter regarding our affairs ..." The letter concludes "Much love, Melanie" (Melanie Klein Trust).

In the first few weeks of 1942 four members of the Society called an Extraordinary Business Meeting to discuss the state of affairs of the Society (King and Steiner, 1991, p. 37). All members were asked to send in resolutions to be discussed at this meeting and sixteen were received. Some expressed concern at the exposure of the public to non-Freudian ideas under the guise of psychoanalysis (ibid., p. 34). Another worry related to the feeling that the Kleinians were capturing candidates for analysis. Finally, and this was the focus of a resolution submitted by Susan Isaacs, it was proposed that there should be a change in the constitution of the Society to ensure that power was no longer allowed to remain indefinitely the preserve of a small elite (ibid., p. 38).

In fact, all these constitutional matters could clearly not be resolved at one meeting, and, in all, there were five Extraordinary Business Meetings, thus rather stretching the meaning of the word "extraordinary". Attended by between 25 and 31 members, they occurred over the period from 25 February 1942 to June 1942. The first meeting was held at lunchtime to avoid the evening bombing, but subsequent meetings were held at 8.15 in the evening to make it easier for out of London members to attend. They were all chaired by Ernest Jones, the President of the Society. Susan Isaacs was present at all the meetings and bearing in mind her activities in many other national organisations, she was probably the person most experienced in matters relating to the constitution of such societies. She played a key role as a protagonist of the view that changes to the constitution should be made as soon as possible and should, in any case, not have to wait until the end of the war as others proposed. She argued that the responsibility for the activities of the Society should be the responsibility of all the members and that the Council and Officers should be answerable to the members for all their decisions (ibid., pp. 56–61). She then proposed that, apart from the Treasurer, a small Council should be elected annually, and that no member of the Council, again apart from the Treasurer, should be eligible to hold office for more than two years or hold more than one office at a time.

There were special difficulties, she suggested, in carrying out scientific discussions in the British Psycho-analytic Society that did not exist in other organisations. These arose from the fact that professional relationships between the members were greatly complicated by the fact that they often acted or at least had acted as analysts to each other and were therefore in possession of intimate details of each other's lives. (She must have had in mind Edward Glover's knowledge of Melanie through his analysis of her daughter, Melitta.) Further, in their training analyses, candidates and their analysts often formed strongly positive as well as negative relationships with each other. (In psychoanalytic parlance, strongly positive or negative transferences occurred.) These inevitably spilled over into the transactions in the Society. Further, just because they were so aware of the pull of unconscious feelings towards each other, they became more deeply distressed than in other organisations when they perceived "bias and unscrupulousness" in others.

Although, she argued, the present arrangement of re-election of the Council once a year meant that, in theory, there was much flexibility in its membership, in practice, because everyone was so afraid of causing offence to those who currently held power, no one ever dared to oppose the existing members. What appeared on the surface to be a flexible, democratic system, in fact operated in a rigid, authoritarian manner.

Joan Riviere, who supported Susan's resolution, was well known for her forthright candour. She spoke in characteristically undiplomatic language. She believed, she said (ibid., p. 62), that "the rank and file members of the Society felt as if the officials, the Elect, behave as if they and they only owned the talisman of psychoanalytic truth and as if that ownership presupposed that they could control and dictate, both to the outside world and to the non-elect in the Society, what is and what is not to be done with and done by this magic talisman. . . ."

Both Susan Isaacs and Joan Riviere felt that decisions should be taken about the constitution before there was further discussion of scientific differences. However this was far from a universal view among the members. Edward Glover, in particular, thought that decisions on the constitution should take place last and not first. It was clear matters were not going to be resolved rapidly and further meetings were arranged. Reading the minutes of the next three meetings, one is left with the impression of a thoroughly bad-tempered, highly repetitive discussion that does not bear further repetition here. At the fifth meeting, held in June, 1942, it was agreed by a narrow majority that "a committee should be appointed to investigate the question of tenure of office and the holding of multiple official positions" (King and Steiner, 1991, p. 190).

Setting up a sub-committee to consider a contentious issue is a well-known manoeuvre for postponing a decision, sometimes for ever. Predictably therefore, at the Annual Meeting of the Society held in July, 1943, over a year later, it was reported that the Committee had failed to agree. A large majority, however, then voted in favour of a resolution that the Committee should announce a decision by the following Christmas. Again this deadline was not met, but in June, 1944, at a business meeting at which Susan was present, a proposal that "No member who has served as President, Scientific Secretary or Business Secretary for three consecutive years shall be elected to the same office until two further years have elapsed" was passed unanimously (King and Steiner, 1991, p. 896). Two and a half years after she had proposed her resolution to much disagreement,

Susan Isaacs finally saw it passed without a single dissenting view. She had played a major part in ensuring the power held by the anti-Kleinian Edward Glover was removed from him.

The agreement to change the constitution did not occur without a great deal of pain. Profoundly hurtful remarks were made both at the business meetings and between them among small groups talking in private. Barbara Low, a long-standing member of the Society said at the second meeting that "the discussions which have taken place at our first meeting and the present one have revealed the devastating effect of the animosities, rivalries and unresolved conflicts among members" (King and Steiner, 1991, p. 83). There was much discussion of the way the meaning of the term "psychoanalysis" had been stretched, not only by Melanie Klein, but by the general public. Walter Schmideberg, a staunch Freudian, to illustrate how far the definition of Freudianism had been stretched pointed out (ibid., p. 85) that the judges choosing the Beauty Queen of California had been reported to have made the proud claim that the selection had been made strictly according to scientific principles based on "Freud's own view of sex appeal".

During these discussions (ibid., pp. 92–99), Melitta, supported by her husband, Walter, had launched a powerful attack on her mother and her mother's followers. She complained that the Kleinian group had conspired to attack many members of the Society so forcefully that they had ceased to attend meetings. She herself, she claimed, had been called a "paranoiac" because she had dared to protest against "intrigues and concerted attacks". She claimed that "every member who was not 120% Kleinian had been attacked systematically, directly or indirectly". Kleinians, she alleged, had bribed trainees to leave their non-Kleinian analysts; in return they would be given high fee-paying patients.

Some colleagues had also used emotional blackmail to achieve their ends. For example, she said (ibid., p. 95):

> Another candidate took objection to the behaviour of his analyst over a certain matter, and wanted to change to another one. His analyst, a leading Kleinian, used every conceivable method of emotional appeal to dissuade him: she pointed out that he would wreck his career and there was the danger of him committing suicide as other analysts were probably unable to

analyse his depressive position. Nevertheless he clung to his position. Then suddenly another Kleinian analyst asked him to come to see her. I do not know how she had learned about the matter, but she expressed her concern about it to him and eventually wept over his decision to leave his analyst. This decided him and he stayed.

John Bowlby later revealed it was he who was the candidate in question while he was in a training analysis with Joan Riviere (ibid., p. 294n). The analyst who tried to persuade him not to change was Susan Isaacs. Bowlby could not however remember the weeping and it certainly sounds out of character.

At one point Melitta made what must, to this group, have been the most hurtful accusation of all—a comparison of these Kleinian methods with those used by the Nazis. "In a manner reminiscent of Dr. Goebbels" she said, they (the Kleinians) try to impress us "by repeating time after time the same slogans, by putting forward exaggerated claims and dogmatic statements, by accusing their opponents and intimidating the hesitating, by a constant play on emotions of every sort, instead of presenting and substantiating their theories according to scientific standards" (ibid., p. 98).

After this meeting Susan Isaacs, in an open letter dated 11 April 1942 (Melanie Klein Trust) wrote to many of the senior members of the Society, Ernest Jones, Sylvia Payne, Marjorie Brierley, Ella Sharpe and Anna Freud, expressing deep concern at the tone of the remarks that had been made. "The fact that it was possible for these attacks to be made at all is a disgrace to our Society and a terrible handicap to Psycho-Analysis". She went on to list what she regarded as the frequent lies and distortions in Melitta's contribution. "The present situation", she went on, "requires that the President, members of the Council and members of the Society should openly declare that they will no longer tolerate such behaviour in the Society".

The climate was improved between the fourth and fifth meetings by a letter sent to Melanie Klein by Marjorie Brierley, the wife of William Brierley, Susan's first husband, one of the more independent-minded spirits in the Society. She suggested a "working armistice", an agreement putting a stop to all members making personal attacks on others. At the fifth meeting she, in association with other uncommitted members, proposed (ibid., p. 274):

1) The Society immediately pass a self-denying ordinance in respect of all current charges and counter-charges, and all activities directed against individual members and groups of members.

2) The Society requires all members to refrain from personal attack or innuendo in discussion, but also strongly affirms the right of all Members to complete freedom of speech within the limits of common courtesy.

This resolution was carried unanimously, voting being by a show of hands. The way was then clear for the resolution, described earlier, of the debate about the tenure of elected officers, and, more importantly, for a discussion of the discussion of the scientific differences that had split the Society so acutely.

On 27 January, 1943, apart from the formality of agreeing proposals at the Annual General Meeting later that year, the meetings to discuss the Society's constitution had now been concluded. The first of the series of Scientific Discussions on controversial issues was then held. These and the subsequent scientific discussions focused almost entirely on the mental life of the child in the first three or four years of life. They are not easy to summarise. The proceedings were taken down verbatim by shorthand typists, except during tea breaks when discussion continued but no notes were taken. Not only are the discussions lengthy, but they are sometimes obscure in meaning. This is clearly not just a problem for a non-analyst such as myself, for not infrequently members of the Society involved in the discussions complained they did not understand the points put forward by those taking a different view. Nevertheless, sometimes obscure and frequently repetitive as they may have been, the Scientific Discussions are not only central to the story of Susan Isaacs, they are of vital importance in the history of child psycho-analysis, which, at the time and for some decades subsequently, was probably the most influential theory of child development and child psycho-pathology (the study of emotional problems in childhood) in the western world. Relatively recently the record of these discussions has been called by a leading French psychoanalyst, André Green, "the most important document of the history of psychoanalysis" (quoted.by Perelberg, 2006).

The first two meetings of this series, lasting from 27 January, 1943 until 19 May, 1943, were entirely taken up with the presentation of a previously circulated paper "The Nature and Function of Phantasy" by Susan Isaacs and by discussion of this paper (King and Steiner, pp. 264–384). Many years later John Bowlby gave his impressions of Susan Isaacs at this time (BPaS, CBC/F09/006). He described her as "rather prim and school-marmish", though he thought this was an image she was keen to shed. "She always kept a foot", he wrote, "in the academic and educational world". Although she was a strong supporter of Melanie Klein, he saw her as open to other ideas. Hanna Segal, widely accepted as the foremost exponent of Kleinian ideas from the 1950s onwards, thinks that Susan Isaacs achieved a clear conceptualisation of Klein's ideas at a time when Klein did not have the capacity or perhaps the interest to perform this task herself (Hanna Segal, personal communication). Although the Kleinian group consulted together before Susan gave her papers on the strategy she should take to rebuff the attacks of the Freudians, Segal sees her as having an independent, exploratory mind, in no way merely repeating the views of others. Bowlby thought she knew more academic psychology than anyone else in the Society and this put her in a strong position in debate. In contrast, the tone she took towards the Freudians may have exacerbated their resentment. John Rickman, a member of the Society present at some of the meetings, later (Rickman, 1950) described her manner as one of "strictly controlled condescension", though this does not come through in the verbatim accounts of her contributions.

Right from the start, Susan attempted to pre-empt the line of attack that Klein's writings departed from Freudian doctrine. She quoted (ibid., p. 265) Freud's view, given in the Preface of his Introductory Lectures, that there were gaps in his knowledge and understanding ". . . it has been my guiding purpose to make no sacrifice in favour of apparent simplicity, completeness and finality, not to hide any problems, and not to deny the existence of gaps and uncertainties. . . ." Freud had therefore not only left the way open, but had positively encouraged development of his ideas. She intended to demonstrate "the way in which Freud's most pregnant hints as to further problems with research", not fully explored by Freud himself or followed up by all analysts, have been taken up and made use of by Melanie Klein and those who, during the last 15–16 years have been identified as the "English School". So Freud is credited not just with general encouragement for further work, but for specifically pointing in Melanie Klein's direction. The point was doubtless made by Susan Isaacs in this way as a political attempt along the lines suggested by Melanie Klein to persuade the Anna Freudians that she was respectful to Freud's views, as indeed she was. Contributions to the psycho-analytic literature at this time and indeed for many years afterwards nearly always referred to Freud's work in their introductory paragraphs.

She went on to explain why she had chosen to focus in her talk entirely on the topic of very early phantasy. This was so important because, while some analysts denied even the existence and certainly the importance of phantasies in the early months and years of life, phantasies were fundamental to the ideas of Klein and her followers. She explained that the English translations from German had preferred to use the spelling "phantasy" because this made it clear that the term did not include what was usually described as "fantasy"—mental content occurring in full or semi-conscious day dreaming, but was exclusively used to describe unconscious content. For the analyst, as Freud had often stated, the unconscious was as "real" to the individual as external reality to the conscious mind; indeed Freud had written "in the world of neuroses, psychical reality is the determining factor". But, again as Freud had said, phantasy was not only important in neurosis, but also in normal mental development. The unconscious was a living, active entity in all of us, affecting our pre-conscious, the bridge between our unconscious and conscious mental activity. It was capable of being influenced by our pre-conscious.

In her own view, she went on (ibid., p. 271), the primary content of all mental processes are unconscious phantasies and such a view was, she contended, the only one capable of integrating the known facts "with some degree of clarity and significance". At this point, drawing on her early training in philosophy, she tackled the distinction between percepts and concepts (ibid., p. 273). Melanie Klein had been reproached for relying on perceptual rather than conceptual understanding, on experiences rather than ideas. She suggested that all words, whoever uses them (and, by inference, this must be true of Melanie Klein) stand for concepts. But the mind and mental processes are all directly experienced or perceived. Therefore, whoever we are, when we talk in words about experience, we are using ideas or concepts to describe experiences or percepts.

Initially the infant's experience consists of pure sensation, but as its experience widens, the understanding of time and space becomes possible (ibid., p. 274). The infant first experiences introjection (putting things inside his mind) without a direct, conscious experience of his own mental activity. Later introjection is an experience that can be consciously remembered, felt or imagined. Much, much later, the individual can put his experience into words. In support of this model of mental development, she quoted John Locke, who wrote "We have no ideas at all, but what generally came either from sensible objects or what we felt within ourselves." She quoted Marjorie Brierley (ibid., p. 275) who had written in objection to one of Melanie Klein's central idea that "while one can think of a mother being actually dismembered, one cannot conceive of a mental object being literally shattered—one cannot take a hammer to a mental object". But, replied Susan Isaacs, that is precisely what it feels like to an infant for whom psychic reality is as real or more real than external reality to an adult. The child does indeed feel, she insisted, that he takes a hammer to his imagined mother who is, to him, really in bits, and, she goes on (italics hers), ". . . *when the child feels he has dismembered his mother, his mental life is split and disintegrated*—he shows the most acute anxiety, he is confused and behaves chaotically, he cannot see or hear or control what he does and says, and so on". In other words, the child experiences this anxiety as arising from the phantasy that "my mother inside me is in bits". This part of the argument is worded in such, for Susan, uncharacteristically passionate terms, one wonders if, during her own analysis, she had come to experience her own mother as "in bits" inside her.

Further, Susan Isaacs claims, Kleinians had discovered that when the infant feels anxiety, perhaps stirred up by an aggressive wish, he feels "I shall be bitten or cut up by my mother". When he feels loss and grief, he experiences, as Freud taught us, "My mother has gone forever". He may feel "I want her back" and try to overcome his sense of loss and grief by the phantasy "I shall bring her back by stroking my genital", when he masturbates. When he wants to restore his mother, he feels "I want to make her better, to feed her, to put the bits together again" (ibid., p. 277). Freud, Susan Isaacs claimed, had come to a similar conclusion when he wrote about infants achieving satisfaction of their wishes by hallucinating—"whatever was thought of (desired) was simply imagined in a hallucinatory form, as still happens with dream thoughts every night".

These suppositions about the way the infant mind works, probably surprising to many non-analyst readers and incredible to some, Susan Isaacs justifies by further reference to Freud's own writings (ibid., p. 281). On one occasion when he was explaining a little girl's death wish regarding her mother, he wrote ". . . We find aggressive, oral and sadistic wishes in a form forced on them by early regression, ie in the dread of being killed by the mother—a dread which, on its side, justifies the death-wish against her, if this should enter consciousness." These wishes, described by Freud as "dim impulses which it was impossible for the child to grasp psychically at the time, and which were only interpreted later". Isaacs suggests are exactly the same mental contents that Melanie Klein describes as "phantasies".

How analysts who share Melanie Klein's beliefs obtain their information, beliefs or, as they would see them psycho-analytic insights into the mind of the infant, is the next question Susan Isaacs tackles. She refers to Klein's analytic work with children of two years and over. The play of these children, according to her, reveals the characteristic distortions of "primary process" or dream-thinking in which symbols are confused with reality, two or more objects or people are "condensed" into one, feelings about one person are "displaced" onto another and so on. In any case, it is unnecessary to assume that the infant must have or ought to have sufficient language to describe their experiences before they can be "felt" to be real. Isaacs points out that we can all find implicit meaning in shape, colour, line etc (and she might have added music) without being able to put our experiences into words.

These phantasies, whose existence has been revealed in the play of slightly older children are, Susan Isaacs suggests (ibid., p. 283), the "archaic mental processes through which primary libidinal (pleasure-seeking) impulses are experienced". They have implicit meaning for the child. By the end of the first year when the child's understanding of words has grown significantly (though not yet his capacity to express them), his phantasy life is beginning to make use of verbal images. Isaacs then draws on her substantial knowledge of child development to describe in more detail the observed facts of normal speech development. She draws on a scientific survey carried out by the psychologist, M. M. Lewis to support the fact that by 13 months, young children can respond to a request for an object such as a ball, even when the object in question is out of sight. By 20 months children have a wide range of words they understand, are interested in adult talk, can grasp complex social situations and have considerable memory capacity for relevant information. In fact they can express words (though infants of 20 months do have very limited spoken vocabulary) before they can experience complex phantasies (ibid., p. 286). So, according to her, it is by no means improbable that infants can experience phantasies long before they can speak.

In the final section of her paper on phantasy, Susan Isaacs provides some examples to illustrate and justify her belief that infants sometimes show disturbed behaviour that can be readily explained on the basis of their complex phantasies. She describes (ibid., p. 311) a little girl of 18 months who was terrified by the flapping sole of one of her mother's shoes. When she was 2 years 11 months, fifteen months later, she said in a frightened voice to her mother—"Where are Mummy's broken shoes?" Her mother told her that she had sent them away. The girl replied "They might have eaten me right up!" Another little girl of sixteen months has a favourite game in which she picks off imaginary bits of a brown embossed leather screen and pretends to feed her parents with them. Can this not be explained, Susan Isaacs asks, by the fact that previously she had soiled and smeared herself and put the faeces into her mouth? Was she not trying to prove that her faeces were good and that her parents could eat them too? A little boy aged 16–18 months has a favourite game involving shooing imaginary ducks into a corner of the room (ibid., p. 312). At the same time he experiences night terrors and nightmares, waking screaming in the night. This boy when he had been weaned at 7 months, had refused milk for several years afterwards. At two years he explained his nightmare by saying "White rabbit eating my toes". Susan Isaacs writes that it is hard to resist the conclusion (though some readers might not find it too difficult to resist) that in his imaginary play with the ducks, "he was trying to overcome his fear of the biting retaliatory breast".

There was much discussion of Susan Isaacs's paper, lasting over five scientific meetings (ibid., pp. 322–475). This is not surprising for, although this was not made explicit in the discussion, the establishment of the infant's capacity to experience "phantasy" was central to Melanie Klein's views on the presence of the "paranoid-schizoid" and "depressive" positions she claimed were universally experienced and were of such great significance in the first year of life. Ernest Jones, the President of the Society, opened the discussion and concluded that her ideas and therefore those of Melanie Klein were consistent with those of Freud. In contrast, Edward Glover spoke in hostile fashion, asserting in an uncompromising manner that Klein's arguments were based on several unsound assumptions. In summary, he did not believe Mrs. Klein's views were in any way consistent with Freudian teaching. Anna Freud, of course, agreed. Marjorie Brierley, a more independently minded analyst, suggested that "meaning" was a better word than phantasy to describe what Susan Isaacs wished to convey because it implied that the infant was trying to make sense of both internal and external reality. Sylvia Payne, a senior, similarly independent-minded analyst, congratulated Susan Isaacs, as did many of her colleagues, on her valuable contribution. However she was sceptical of the claim that phantasy is the primary content of all mental processes.

But there were many who objected much more strongly; none more violently than Melitta Schmideberg who noted various omissions and concluded that these were "contrary to scientific tradition and spirit. It is the lack of these", she objected (ibid., p. 340) "that makes it impossible for me to take Dr. Isaacs's paper seriously". And so the discussion proceeded with rather little give or take on either side.

Reading the arguments sixty years after they took place, it is difficult to see how either side could have conceded to the other. From the vantage point of a non-analyst (though both sides might well reject my right to have an opinion in any way worthy of consideration), the situation seemed deadlocked. The Kleinian side was committed to the idea that the inner mental life of the infant in the first two or three years of life was filled with phantasies of envy and hate of frightening proportions while the Anna Freudians could not concede that such immature infants could have phantasies of anything like this degree of complexity and believed that the way external events impinged on infants of this age was of greater significance in their development than their mental lives. As babies do not live in a vacuum and must have experiences that affect their minds and as their mental activity inevitably affects their behaviour, it is surely the case that both are essential to understanding them. Even to a non-analyst it seems likely that only the unconscious motivations and deeply experienced emotions of the participants could have prevented them from realising this. There was clearly a lot going on under the surface.

In fairness, there *was* one concession that the Anna Freudians had made before these discussions took place. They were, unsurprisingly, not gracious enough to admit that their position had changed in this respect but they did now acknowledge and had for some time, that the beginnings of Oedipal wishes take place as early as the end of the first year of life (Klein, 1928). This was quite a major modification of original Freudian teaching. This change of view had however occurred previously and it is doubtful if Susan Isaacs's paper had any impact in either direction. The significance of this change of mind for the Kleinians was that it established their position as academically respectable, capable of robust defence and backed by evidence that satisfied Susan Isaacs, a recognised authority in the field of child development.

After the discussion of Susan Isaacs's paper on phantasy[3] the scientific meetings continued with discussion of a paper by Paula Heimann, another prominent Kleinian, on introjection and projection in early development. The participants then discussed a paper on "Regression" that Susan Isaacs co-authored with Paula Heimann (Heimann and Isaacs, 1943). In this paper they tried to bring their experience of analysis with children to bear on existing psycho-analytic ideas concerning regression, ideas that had previously been derived from work with adults. If anything these stimulated even more forceful defence and rebuttal. Edward Glover (King and Steiner, 1991, p. 711), for example, claimed (his italics):

> *If these distortions of Freudian metapsychology were allowed to pass unchallenged it would be open to anyone to claim that whatever he or she has thought about the unconscious is true. . . . Other child analysts with precisely the same opportunities of observing child behaviour and utterance hold that Kleinian interpretations and reconstructions are inaccurate.*

There is a certain irony in Glover's attack. He is arguing here that it is ridiculous to suggest that one theory of mental activity is as good as another. Yet the post-modernist position he is attacking owes much to Freudian views on the primacy of psychological reality. Glover, the arch-Freudian, is arguing here against a philosophical position that Freud did much to stimulate. Given the forcefulness of his views, it is not surprising that before too long he resigned from the Society. In his letter of resignation (ibid., p. 851) written in January 1944 to Sylvia Payne he claimed that since 1933 and the ascendancy of Melanie Klein the Society had become both less scientific and, by his definition, less Freudian in nature. He predicted that "The Controversial Discussions will end in smoke". At about the same time that Edward Glover resigned from the Society Anna Freud resigned from the Training Committee.

In July 1944 Sylvia Payne succeeded Ernest Jones as President of the BPaS. Under her guidance and that of James Strachey a so-called Ladies Agreement was brokered. In October 1945 Susan Isaacs, together with Sylvia Payne, John Bowlby, and Adrian Stephen, formed part of a training sub-committee to consider proposals made by Anna Freud. But it was not until November 1946 that final agreement was reached (ibid., p. 906).

It was decided that there should be two training courses of which the second, Group B, should be under the supervision of Anna Freud. The other Group A, should consist of Kleinian analysts and of those who felt themselves to be independent of both parties. However after a short period of time the Independents formed a Middle group of their own. It was agreed that trainees should be exposed to both schools to whichever group their training analyst belonged. Lectures and seminars other than those on technique would be common to all students. In their third year all students would attend clinical seminars held by representatives of all groups.

It is notable that Susan Isaacs played a key part both in formulating the changes in the constitution of the Institute and British Psychoanalytic Society and in defending the scientific validity of Melanie Klein's theories and practice. If it had not been for her it is very doubtful if the constitution of the two organisations would have been changed in such a sensible way. More importantly, Melanie Klein's dominant position in British psychoanalysis and, more particularly, child psychoanalysis owes a considerable debt to Susan Isaacs's advocacy skills, scientific authority and capacity to explain the complexity of Kleinian thought. It was her exegesis that made Kleinian theory respectable in the world of psycho-analysis (Hanna Segal, personal communication).

By April 1943 Susan had returned to the Isaacs's flat in London in Primrose Hill. There continued to be bombing with, from June 1944 onwards, flying bombs and later V2 rockets but London was a much safer place than it had been from 1940 to 1941. She continued with her analytic practice but retained an interest in educational matters. She formally resigned her position at the Institute of Education in 1943 and her pupil, student and disciple, Dorothy Gardner, who had only been appointed a year earlier to be an Inspector of Schools in Bolton, was appointed in her place on a full-time basis. Susan supported her during the interview process and was delighted with this turn of events (Gardner, 1969, p. 133). The following year Dorothy Gardner published the results of a study of children in infant schools in which she showed that children of six and seven years of age produced distinctly superior performance if they were educated in schools in which the curriculum was based on the spontaneous interests of the children than in those where the curriculum was of a more traditional type (Gardner, 1944). The design of the study was faulty by modern day standards and it is really not possible to draw such firm conclusions from the findings. All the same, it was unusual at that time for any sort of systematic comparison of different forms of schooling to be made, so Dorothy Gardner was well ahead of her time.

Towards the end of the European war in 1945, Susan and Nathan began to pick up their pre-war work and social life. Nathan returned to London and started working with a commercial firm, Derby and Co. at a senior level. In 1946 he was awarded the OBE for his war-time services as Controller of vital war materials at the Ministry of Supply. Appreciative letters from the Ministry give him a great deal of the credit for maintaining the supply of essential ferro-alloys throughout the war.

In early 1945 the editor of the magazine of the New Era Fellowship magazine, founded to promote progressive education, decided to publish a monograph containing articles relevant to the upbringing of children during and after the war. A number of experts, including John Bowlby and Donald Winnicott were approached and Susan

Isaacs was asked to write an article on fatherless children. One of the most tragic, perhaps the most tragic of the outcomes of the Second World War was the number of children in continental Europe who had lost one or both parents. They were numbered in millions, and there were several tens of thousands of British children who had lost one parent, usually a father who had been killed in military action.

In her article Susan Isaacs (Isaacs, 1948b, pp. 186–205) considers what such a loss means to the mind of a child. Though John Bowlby was writing at the same time of children who had been brought up separated from their parents in emotionally deprived circumstances, her account is probably the first in which the topic of fatherlessness is addressed by an expert in mental health. What she has to say, as with so many of her writings, sounds so familiar, even banal to modern ears that it is difficult to remember that her approach was in many ways radically different from others who were writing at the same time. To begin with she emphasized that even very young children are affected (ibid., p. 187): "Even in the first year of life, before the child can speak, the disappearance of the father from his world awakens feelings of bewildered grief and stirs great anxiety in the child". She describes (ibid., p. 188) in some detail a boy of four whose father had died in his first year of life. The little boy blamed his father for his mother's loneliness and financial hardship. He was a "bad Daddy". The boy longed to help his mother and was burdened by guilt and grief that resulted in moods of unhappiness and neurotic symptoms. Children might be too young to understand what had happened, but they were never too young to suffer painful and frightening feelings. These could result, according to Susan Isaacs, in a variety of symptoms and personality problems. Sometimes her concern appears to be exaggerated; we now know that bereavement is not, as she suggests, the cause of schizophrenia or homosexuality, though certainly, as she correctly observes, children who are bereaved can show severe depression and states of anxiety.

She sounds particularly modern when she discusses what can be done to help fatherless children, emphasizing first the need to treat them as individuals. She firmly discourages denial to the child of the fact that the father has died (ibid., p. 194) and describes a boy of two and a half who had been difficult and distrustful until he had been told the truth about his nanny who had been seriously injured in a car accident and not, as he had been told, gone away for a holiday (ibid., p. 195). It was not, she thought, a good idea for mothers to *demand* that their children should talk about their absent father. They would do so spontaneously when they were ready to do so. Mothers should also beware of idealizing the dead father; he should be talked about as a real, not as a perfect person.

A widowed mother should try to make sure that their children had social contact with male relatives as well as other men friends and neighbours (ibid., p. 199). She should, on no account, allow her children to share her bed in place of their father. Again the threat of homosexuality is waved in front of her if she does this. Though today this would not be seen as a risk, it is still felt that bereaved mothers should be careful to try not to use their children for physical comfort.

There are also ways, Susan Isaacs suggests, in which schools can be helpful to the bereaved child (ibid., pp. 202–4). In 1945 there was likely to be more than one child who had lost a father through military action in the class and such children could provide emotional support for each other. Creative art in school could help such children express some of their deepest feelings in a helpful way. Games and sports could provide "an outlet for the ambition and normal competitiveness which so readily becomes inhibited in the fatherless child".

But perhaps Susan Isaacs sounds most contemporary when she pleads for fatherless boys and girls at the time of adolescence to take part in the real life of the community, as well as at home and in the school (ibid., p. 205). Wanting children to stay on in school should not prevent us from giving them a real place in the world, nor should it stop us from allowing them to contribute to the many forms of social activity that were open to them at that time, such as growing vegetables in allotments and paper salvage. One can think of contemporary alternatives that many young people would find attractive if given the chance to participate.

It is hard to think back to a time when there were many more children who were fatherless because of death rather than as a result of parental separation and divorce. Though children of divorced and separated parents are in a different situation from those who have been bereaved, Susan Isaacs had much of relevance to say regarding children in both sets of circumstances.

She had, throughout her life, from the time of her upbringing and schooling in Bolton been aware that many children in Britain were brought up in great hardship and poverty. But her experience in Cambridge with children evacuated from London brought home to her that there were children living in even worse conditions than those she had encountered in her childhood and adolescence at the turn of the century. These were those who, for one reason or another were deprived of parental care and living in children's homes.

She was not alone in her awareness of the deplorable state of British children's homes. In 1945 the coalition government set up a Committee of Enquiry to make a systematic study of such children and make recommendations as to how their situation might be improved. The Committee, chaired by Myra Curtis, found that many children in Poor Law institutions were indeed appallingly treated. In one place (Home Department, 1946, p. 41):

> The infirmary wards used for children are on the second floor of the institution, one end of which is a ward for senile men, at the other for senile women. Two rooms are used for children on this corridor, one for twelve infants, and one for a family of five "healthy" children of scattered ages and one defective child aged two.

It was a common experience for members of the Committee who visited institutions in which children were housed to find the buildings to be run down and the children unkempt and dirty. Often schooling was perfunctory and there was nothing at all for the children to do outside school. For example in one place it was said of eighteen children, thirteen aged over five years (ibid., p. 44):

> The children never go out to school, even though some of them may be here for months at a time. The children have no outside contacts, they merely play by themselves in the gloomy dayroom or in the yard. They are not taken for walks owing to shortage of staff. There is no opportunity for playing with other children. . . .

Susan Isaacs sent a memorandum to the Committee that focused on the psychological needs of children deprived of parental care (Isaacs, 1948b, pp. 208–238). Again it could have been written today. Institutions like children's homes, she wrote (ibid., p. 219), failed the young because they could not meet the essential needs for affection, security, mild control and the companionship of other children.

The experience of love is just as necessary for the child's mental and moral growth as good food and medical care are necessary for his bodily health and development.

She quoted a number of studies in support of this view including an American investigation that would certainly be regarded as unethical today, but that produced important findings (ibid., p. 220). Two groups of two year old children living in the same institution were separated from each other and both groups were given good physical care. The nurses looking after one group were instructed to show very little tenderness, while in the other, "there was no lack of tenderness and affection". After six months the first group was mentally and physically retarded in comparison with the second.

She was equally modern in her views on discipline. This should involve steady but mild control (ibid., p. 224).

Severe punishments are quite as unwise and unfruitful as indulgence and the lack of control. . . . Harsh punishments, rigid prohibition of natural pleasures and healthy activities serve only to increase the child's hate, aggression and anxiety and are far more likely to turn him into a delinquent than into a useful member of society.

In advocating the abolition of corporal punishment as she had done many years previously, Susan Isaacs was well ahead of her time. The members of the Curtis Committee unanimously agreed with her view. They wrote (Home Department, 1946, p. 168) about discipline:

We have given much thought to this question and have come to the conclusion that corporal punishment (ie caning or birching) should be definitely prohibited in Children's Homes for children of all ages and both sexes.

The Committee evidently did not feel able in an official report to mention the child's need for love, but perhaps love, then as now is not a word that civil servants and members of official committees are able to use comfortably when formulating recommendations for child care. All the same, the spirit of Susan Isaacs's memorandum is clearly present in the Curtis Committee Report—not perhaps surprising in that Sibyl Clement Brown, her former flatmate and a woman with whom she and Nathan often went on holiday, was a member of the Committee.

In early 1946 Susan's health began to deteriorate further (Gardner,1969, p. 136). She had had a surgical operation for cancer of the breast in 1935, followed by a course of radiotherapy. Then she remained in good health until November, 1941 when she had a recurrence of the growth in her breast, again requiring surgery and radiotherapy. She remained reasonably well until the summer of 1946 when illness made it too difficult for her to continue to lecture on the courses Dorothy Gardner organised at the Institute. She also suffered from chronic abdominal pain arising from a duodenal ulcer. In November 1946 this perforated and she required another operation.

The next two years before she died were a constant struggle against pain and further disability. Until her sight deteriorated she continued to take pleasure in reading. She had always read widely, including detective stories; when she was ill she would read as many as two of these a day. Now her reading was confined to crime and detective novels (Gardner, 1969, p. 137). In the year before her death, despite her disabilities, she and Nathan spent a holiday in Switzerland for a final stay in the Alps (IoEd, DC/SI/A/3). They stayed in Montana with, as Nathan reported, its wonderful views of the great Valisian peaks with Zinal right among them. Just a few months before she died they spent a holiday in Kylesku in the western Highlands of Scotland, with views of Loch Glendhu.

In January 1948 Susan was awarded the CBE for her services to education. There was a party and a small gathering of friends celebrated with her at the Isaacs's flat. Evelyn Lawrence and Dorothy Gardner entertained while her friends went in ones and twos into her bedroom to speak to her (Gardner, 1969, pp. 139–40).

The following month news came that Geoffrey Pyke, who in 1923 had recruited Susan Isaacs to run the Malting House School, had committed suicide (Lampe, 1959, p. 206). He had been alone in a room in Steeles Road only a couple of hundred yards from where the Isaacs lived. Pyke's career had remained extraordinary after his bankruptcy in the late 1920s. During the Second World War he had risen from obscurity to become one of the backroom scientists working for Lord Louis Mountbatten, Director of Special Operations. His brief was to come up with inventive ways of beating the enemy. His wildest idea was the building of a ship, perhaps an aircraft carrier, called the Habbabuk, that was to be made of super-cooled ice. Such iceberg ships would attack Genoa, Naples, Hamburg. A block of the new material, ice on a pyrkete cube, was shown to Churchill (who was, of course, in his bath at the time). Churchill was impressed and Max Perutz, later a Nobel Prize winner for medicine, was put to work on it. Churchill and Roosevelt had the new material demonstrated to them, but nothing ever came of the idea. On the other hand a snow plough that Pyke invented at about the same time was used a couple of decades later by Vivian Fuchs, the Polar explorer.

At the end of the war Pyke had been commissioned to work on a project looking at how to meet the increasing needs for nurses and teachers, but he had once again become depressed and been unable to continue. After his death Max Perutz described him as having a brain that was "a firework of ideas, some brilliant, some fantastic, but all new and highly unconventional". The scientist J D Bernal called him "one of the greatest and certainly the most unrecognised geniuses of our time" (ibid., p. 209). Both the Isaacs must have been pleased by the observation of "Critic" in the New Statesman— "Perhaps his most useful activity was to found and maintain the Malting House School at Cambridge, under the direction of Dr. Susan Isaacs. It was a most unusual experiment in modern education." Susan Isaacs made an appreciative broadcast a few weeks after he died, but Nathan never forgave him for the way he had treated her. In a letter to Pyke's biographer written ten years later (IoEd N1D3), he wrote that "the Last Judgement will surprise and discomfit Pyke as much as anybody I know".

Over the next two years Susan's cancer recurred and spread. She developed retinal haemorrhages considerably impairing her vision (IoEd N1 D 3). By June 1948 she was in chronic pain from arthritis and probably had bone secondaries in her spine. She was receiving Pethidine four times a day. According to Dorothy Gardner, who visited her frequently in her last weeks and months and who knew nothing of the affair between Nathan and Evelyn, Nathan continued to give unstinted care to his wife right until the time of her death.

Despite the heavy medication she remained clear-headed virtually until the end. In her last months she prepared two books for publication. "Childhood and After" (Isaacs, 1948b) is a collection of papers and chapters, some published and some unpublished, written in the previous ten years. "Children and Parents: Their Problems and Difficulties" (Isaacs, 1948a) is a collection of letters and her replies written when she was writing her column in The Nursery World under her pseudonym of Ursula Wise.

On the last day of her life, the twelfth of October 1948, Dorothy Gardner visited her in the morning and found her extremely weak but in good spirits (Gardner, 1969, p. 140). She even seemed apologetic for leaving her friends. Her main preoccupation was that Nathan would be well looked after following her death. She mentioned that one of her friends had mentioned the possibility of being bored in Heaven. Boredom would be Impossible, Susan Isaacs said, when one could do research on subjects such as the long-term effects of congenital malformations! By the evening she had died.

There were many friends and colleagues at the funeral, including Peter Fraser, the Prime Minister of New Zealand, who had been so impressed by her when she had visited his country in 1937 and who was in London at the time on official business (ibid., p. 141). She had asked that there should be no speeches. Some favourite pieces of music were played and poems read. As her coffin moved towards the furnace the final stanza of Francis Thompson's poem "To My Godchild" containing the line "Look for me in the nurseries of heaven" was read (ibid., p. 143).

In her last weeks Susan expressed to many people the hope that after her death Nathan and Evelyn would comfort each other (ibid., p. 140). She must have done this to forestall any criticism when, as she must have known would happen, after her death their relationship would become more widely known. In August, 1947 Nathan had sent Evelyn a brooch accompanied by a note on which he had written "To my darlingest Evelyn, in celebration of our first two decades of delectation" The note is dated 31 August, 1947.[4]

Nathan and Evelyn were not married until April, 1950, eighteen months after Susan's death. But three months after Susan died and fifteen months before they married Nathan wrote (letter dated 29 December 1948) to Evelyn who had been away from London for a short time:

Many, many happy returns to my own darlingest wife and by the time of the next one I love to think she will be that in *every* way and to all the world. I was very happy in our little holiday, but happiest in thinking of all those future ones which we shall be able to share freely, openly and fully. . . . Goodbye, sweetest heart, look after yourself and come back to me soon.

Your own,

N.

Notes

1   Interview: Edward Glover by Bluma Swerdloff, Oral History Research Office, Columbia University, 1968, p. 42.
2   Interview: Edward Glover by Bluma Swerdloff, Oral History Research Office, Columbia University, 1968, p. 43.
3   A full, revised version of the paper on phantasy by Susan Isaacs (1948) was published later.
4   This and the following letter are in private hands, but were made available to the author.

CHAPTER THIRTEEN

Legacies

I n the Introduction to this book I outlined some of the main trends in the new radical social and psychological thinking at the time that Susan Isaacs's father died in 1909. When she died almost as the twentieth century reached its halfway point, the forces that were beginning to transform society forty years earlier had largely triumphed. The small group of Labour MPs elected in 1906 had grown to form the first majority Labour government in 1945. The vision of the early Fabians of a welfare state with benefits for the retired, the sick and the unemployed had become a reality. The foundations of a National Health Service with medical care available on the basis of need rather than the ability to pay had been laid. Of all the great social projects under way in 1909, only the disadvantaged state of women remained largely unresolved, though even this would soon be tackled with the first wave of the feminist movement in the fifties.

Underlying, reflecting, interacting with, influencing (the relationships are too complex to be encapsulated in a single word), this quiet social revolution were similar transformations in psychoanalysis (the way people saw themselves), and education (the way they brought up their children). Psychoanalysis began at the beginning of the twentieth century at a time when family ties were loosening and, more importantly, family attitudes were more frequently rejected by individuals who were determined to make their own minds up about what mattered to them. "Psychoanalysis was a theory and practice of this new aspiration for a personal life . . . the idea of a dynamic or *personal unconscious*, reflected this new experience of personal life" (Zaretzky, 2005, p. 5).

While Freud's thinking encouraged "defamilialisation", the cutting of family bonds, his explanations of the mental development of the child were initially couched in terms of the boy overcoming the tyranny of the father, eventually replacing him and taking on his patriarchal role; thus he endorsed a conventional family structure. The nineteen twenties and thirties saw many psychoanalysts, led by Melanie Klein, come to appreciate what parents had known all along, namely that the roots of mental life, behaviour, relationships and personality arise in the early nurturant relationship that infants form with their mothers. The increased needs for nurturance that people feel when they no longer have the ties of family to protect them were reflected both in the enhanced realisation of the needs of babies and children for maternal nurturance and the building of a welfare society, a mother present for the whole of life, to meet the nurturant needs of adults.

If children are to be brought up so that they can live independently from their families, then their education needs to encourage autonomy and self-reliance. In many ways educational theory anticipated psychoanalysis in this emphasis on individual self-determination. Rousseau, Pestalozzi, and Froebel were all faithful to this principle. Children would learn best using child-centred approaches in which teachers promoted their autonomy, responding to their curiosity, to what came from within them, rather than teaching in ways that ignored their individuality.

Susan Isaacs, as a prominent member of the modern educational establishment, wanted to transform the style of teaching in British schools, especially those providing nursery and infant education. To what degree did they, over the following years change and adopt, as she wished, an approach that was more child-centred? How long did any change that did occur last? What were the effects on how well children could read, do arithmetic, express themselves creatively, enjoy their schooling? In any case, to what degree can any such changes be attributed to Susan Isaacs? How accurate is the description of her in the Oxford Dictionary of National Biography as "the greatest influence on British education in the twentieth century" (Pines, 2004)? All these questions are only partially answerable. One is reminded of Zhou Enlai's quite possibly apocryphal response in 1971 when he was asked by Richard Nixon for his assessment of the French Revolution. "It is too early to say", he replied. Even seventy years after the publication of her key texts "Intellectual Growth in Young Children" and "Social Development of Young Children" and her appointment in 1933 to the key position as Head of the Department of Child Development at the Institute of Education, London, it is difficult to assess Susan Isaacs's educational legacy.

She was not, of course, the first to espouse child-centred education and the importance of discovery, play and creativity to enhance the learning of young children, nor was she the first to provide a practical demonstration of their effects. In 1911, while she was at Manchester University studying philosophy, having completed her training as an infant school teacher, Edmond Holmes's "What is and What Might Be" was published (Holmes, 1911). This former Chief Inspector at the Board of Education attacked the current system of mindless classroom lecturing *at* children. Even at that time he was able to describe a school in which children learned by being allowed to discover things for themselves and, in the process, demonstrate a capacity for original creativity beyond all expectation. And "Egeria", the pseudonym for the teacher in Sompting, Sussex who produced these wonderful results was only following, as we have seen, in the footsteps of Rousseau, Pestalozzi and Froebel who had advocated similar methods in the previous century and a half.

During the first half of the twentieth century, these ideas were certainly in the air but they were only practised in that small part of the private sector of education that called itself "progressive", and in that even smaller part of state education that had been exposed to progressive methods as Isaacs taught them in the 1930s to a small number of lecturers of Colleges of Education. The situation had changed by the mid-1950s, and there is no doubt Susan Isaacs had played a major part in the transformation in the education of young children that took place over this period. Gradually over the following two decades, although there was still a great deal of whole classroom teaching in which the teacher stood in front of the whole class lecturing, it became much more common, even standard practice, for teachers in state primary schools to take small groups for basic subjects, but to combine this with some whole class teaching.

This made teaching through interaction with the individual child as Susan Isaacs had proposed much easier.

In 1963 Edward Boyle, the Conservative Secretary of State for Education asked the Central Advisory Council for Education to undertake a review of primary education. The Council, chaired by Lady Bridget Plowden, produced a report four years later (Central Advisory Council for Education,1967). The recommendations in the Report were seen as strongly endorsing progressive over traditional methods of education (Gillard, 2004). This is especially the case as far as nursery and infant education were concerned. A key paragraph,that could have been written by Susan Isaacs, reads (ibid., para 523):

> Play is the central activity in all nursery schools and in many infant schools. This sometimes leads to accusations that children are wasting their time in school: they should be 'working'. But this distinction between work and play is false, possibly throughout life, certainly in the primary school. Its essence lies in past notions of what is done in school hours (work) and what is done out of school (play). We know now that play—in the sense of 'messing about' either with material objects or with other children, and of creating fantasies—is vital to children's learning and therefore vital in school. Adults who criticise teachers for allowing children to play are unaware that play is the principal means of learning in early childhood. It is the way through which children reconcile their inner lives with external reality. In play, children gradually develop concepts of causal relationships, the power to discriminate, to make judgements, to analyse and synthesise, to imagine and to formulate. Children become absorbed in their play and the satisfaction of bringing it to a satisfactory conclusion fixes habits of concentration which can be transferred to other learning.

Susan Isaacs pioneering work was acknowledged in the Report and indeed in 1933 in "The Social Development of Young Children" she had written (Isaacs, 1933, p. 425), thirty years before the Plowden Committee was set up on

> ... the significance of play for the young child's growth in manipulative skill, in imaginative art, and in discovery,

reasoning and thought. . . . Play is not the only means by which the child comes to discover the world; it is supremely the activity which brings him psychic equilibrium in the early years.

Further the report's other recurring themes—individual learning, flexibility in the curriculum, the use of the environment, and learning by discovery—were all foundation stones of the Susan Isaacs approach to education and have stood the test of time (Gillard, 2004).

Developments in child psychology over the decades following Susan Isaacs's death confirmed and extended her view of the importance of active experience for effective learning. During the early and mid-nineteen thirties a Russian child psychologist, Lev Vygotsky, in work that only became known in the west in the nineteen sixties, showed how it is through social experience with other members of the child's community that the child acquires the tools for thinking and learning. Unlike Piaget but like Susan Isaacs, Vygotsky thought the process of language acquisition by young children could be advanced by adult intervention in mutual activities, a process that was at the heart of learning (Vygotsky, 1962).

Ironically, the only part of the Plowden Report to which Susan Isaacs would have brought serious reservations is that placing so much emphasis on the stages that Piaget described. Those drafting the Report were probably influenced in this direction by Molly Brearley, the Principal of the Froebel Institute College of Education, who sat on the Committee and, among others, by Nathan Isaacs, Susan's husband, who gave evidence to the Committee and was, by this time, one of the leading authorities on Piaget in the country. The Report cited Piaget's stages of development in support of the view that children, as they grew older, required different types of experience. Susan Isaacs never changed her view that it was unhelpful to divide childhood up into different stages in this way because she saw children's minds as having the basic equipment for logical thought much earlier on in their lives than Piaget envisaged. Further she saw the advance in their competence as attributable not, as he did, to any acquisition of new mental structures, but largely to their exposure to a wider range of experiences and their gradually increasing ability to handle more complex tasks. In the twenty years after Plowden much experimental work demonstrated the fluidity of development and confirmed the criticism Susan Isaacs made many years earlier that Piaget's methods had made him under-estimate the competence of children (Bryant and Kopytynska, 1976). The Plowden Report cited Piaget as the source of the view that children needed active experience in handling materials if they were to learn effectively, but in fact Susan Isaacs, following John Dewey, had made this a central feature of her educational philosophy well before Piaget considered the educational implications of his work (Piaget, 1971).

Twenty first century views of child development would not however confirm Susan Isaacs's view, implicit if not explicit in her writings, that the language and thought of young children is only immature because they lack experience. Following the work of Chomsky (1965) it is now widely accepted that the human brain is programmed through a "language acquisition device" to develop progressively more complex grammatical utterances during childhood. Children do think differently from adults regardless of the quality of their experience.

For at least some class teachers trained around the time of the publication of the Plowden Report, its contents, communicated in a tone of inspiration, took on almost biblical authority. One educationalist, later a Professor of Education, recalled twenty years later the excitement he felt on obtaining his first copy. He had queued at HMSO to get it (Gammage, 1987). "Here it was; the distilled deliberations of a Committee that had spent over three years collating and reflecting on primary practice. The blueprint for primary education for all (or of the 95 per cent in state schools) had arrived."

Despite the criticism leveled at the Report, heightened at the time of the exposure of the methods used at ultra-progressive schools such as William Tyndale in 1974, more moderately progressive educational methods continued to permeate state primary schools during the 1970s. There was a measurable improvement in levels of literacy and numeracy. Then, in 1976 a reaction set in. James Callaghan, the Labour Prime Minister, seeking a topic on which to make his individual mark, hit upon the education system and made an attack on progressive methods of teaching. There was a widespread belief at the time, shared by at least one member of his inner circle, Bernard Donoughue, who had children of his own, making, as he saw it, disappointing progress in London state primary schools, that, because of their progressive philosophy, they were failing in their duty to ensure that children learnt the basic skills of literacy and numeracy (Donoughue, 2003).

The Thatcher regime, from 1979 onwards, led to a much more radical revision of the education system than James Callaghan had envisaged. By 1981 the Department of Education and Science had replaced Plowden's aphorism "At the heart of the educational process is the child" with "At the heart of the educational process is the curriculum". Successive Secretaries of State for Education, first Keith Joseph and then Kenneth Baker, directed the Department to publish increasingly prescriptive guidance as to what should be taught in primary schools and how it should be taught. The introduction of the National Curriculum in 1988, followed by the establishment of regular testing at every stage of the pupil's career and the publication of league tables all made further inroads on child-centred learning. Under New Labour the centralized directives involving for example, the literacy hour and the Numeracy Hour took prescription even further. Now, teachers were told not just what to teach but how to teach it. Inevitably therefore, over the last twenty years of the twentieth century there was a gradual return to didactic teaching of traditional subjects. In the first decade of the twenty first century, it may be that there is a return to some of the principles that Plowden and, well before that, Susan Isaacs had put forward. There is renewed enthusiasm for emphasizing the value of encouraging exploration rather than rote learning in the teaching of science. Craig Venter, who led an independent team that unraveled the structure of the human genome at the same speed as a worldwide network of collaborating scientists, delivering the 2007 Dimbleby Lecture gave his views on the need to change direction is science teaching:

To begin the process of change we need to start with our children by teaching them in place of memorisation, to explore, challenge, and problem solve in an attempt to understand the world around them, and most especially the world they cannot "see" or feel directly. Perhaps, we can also start by changing the way we teach science in our schools.

The importance of the place of the arts in the curriculum of the primary school has been accepted by Labour ministers. In the first decade of the twenty first century, there are strong indications that there is a return to a more balanced attitude to creativity and the achievement of acceptable standards. In a government document entitled "Excellence and Enjoyment in Primary Schools" (Department for Education and Employment, 2003), one reads:

Primary School is a critical stage in children's development—it shapes them for life. As well as giving them the essential tools for learning, primary education is about children experiencing the joy of discovery, solving problems, being creative in writing, art, music, developing their self-confidence as learners and maturing socially and emotionally.

Official school inspections reflect this new approach. In a letter dated 14 July 2005, sent by Her Majesty's Inspector to the pupils of William Tyndale School (the London inner-city school that in 1974, with its chaotic regime, had played a major part in producing a reaction to Plowden) after his team had carried out an OFSTED inspection.

Dear children,

Thank you for all your help when we inspected your school earlier this month. We enjoyed our visit and everyone was very friendly and polite. Now we want to share with you what we thought about your school. These are the things we thought were good.

- We think you work very hard and do very well. By the time you leave Year 6. you are well prepared for your next schools.
- Your behaviour is good in class and has improved enormously in the last few years. We think the peer mentoring is working extremely well and is helping you all to get on well with each other. Your school council is working hard to help make the school even better for you all.
- You told us you enjoy school and we think you do some interesting work. We were really impressed with your art work and music making. We are sure your end of term production will have been a great success.
- Your head teacher, her deputy and her staff have done a really good job in improving the school in the last few years.

But we know everyone wants to do even better and we have suggested a few things that we think will help.

- We think a good number of you especially in the younger age classes could be learning more and we have asked your teachers to check regularly that this is happening.
- We also think it would help if your teachers told each of you some of the main things that you need to work on to improve your own work.

Mike Sutton,
Her Majesty's Inspector.

PS Thank you for the eggs from the hens which you keep at school. They were delicious.

There is so much in this letter that Susan Isaacs would have appreciated. The fact that the children were formally addressed in a way that made it clear they mattered; the emphasis on the art work and music making; the existence of the school council; the use of peer mentoring; even the postscript at the end with its evidence that the children were gaining experience with real live animals and their produce—all this would have pleased Susan Isaacs mightily and made her proud, perhaps justifiably so. It may be that we are witnessing a return to a more balanced education system in which discovery and creativity are fostered while attention is also given to the acquisition of basic skills.

*   *   *

In contrast to her views on child-centred education, Susan Isaacs's belief in the importance of heredity in determining the level of intelligence and in the use of intelligence tests to assess children's innate ability gradually fell out of fashion in the three decades after her death The decline in belief in genetic influences in the 1950s and the subsequent decades came about partly from the discrediting of the eugenics movement because of its links to the racial policies pursued in Nazi Germany. The use of intelligence tests declined at the same time when it was realised how seriously misleading they could be if, when assessing the abilities of an individual child, they were employed in isolation. By the time the Plowden Report was published, there were serious doubts about their value in any situation. The Report discussed the use of IQ tests in some detail (Central Advisory Council for Education, 1967, paras 56–64) but apart from advising great caution in interpreting the results of such tests, did not come to any definite conclusions about them. During and after the 1980s, with the advent of behavioural and molecular genetics there was a revival of interest in the influence of genetic factors in behaviour and learning and it was realized they were of major significance and could not be ignored. Thus there has been considerable confirmation of Susan Isaacs's views in this respect, though the language she used to "write off" children with quite minor learning difficulties remains unacceptable.

Incidentally there has been an interesting sequel to the study of spelling that she carried out in her year in Cambridge in 1912–13. In the publication of this investigation she noted that there was a tendency for "good or bad spelling to run in certain families". She may well not have been interested in investigating this possibility further but she had identified genetic influences as a possible cause of variation in spelling ability, perhaps a good deal more important than the main focus of her study, which was to do with finding out whether imagery was used or not. It was not until seventy years later that, using a method involving identical and non-identical twins, behavioural genetics studies cast further light on this possibility. It was not applied to spelling ability in any rigorous manner until in the early 1980s a study of 285 pairs of 13 year old London twins drawn from the general population was carried out (Stevenson et al. 1987) Comparing the similarities of identical and non-identical twins it was found that spelling was strongly heritable or genetically influenced. This was much less the case for reading ability where the influence of environment was stronger. So Susan's observation had indeed been valid, and it has been possible to establish just why spelling ability has a tendency to run in families. There is almost certainly no specific gene for spelling; indeed Susan's findings, as well as those of others who have followed her, make it likely that a variety of genes are responsible, some more related to the use of imagery and others less so.

It is often suggested that people who believe in the power of genes are inevitably imbued with the notion that success or failure in academic subjects is determined at birth, and that there is not much that the education system can do about it. Perhaps there are believers in the power of heredity who take this view, but Susan Isaacs was not of their number. She was a great believer in education as a force that could change the fate of individual children regardless of their level of intelligence and this view prevails today.

One of the striking features of Susan Isaacs's career is that she never showed any interest in the sort of quantitative research she carried out in Cambridge in her late twenties. Indeed she showed a highly critical attitude to those who tried to apply the use of statistical methods to educational problems. It might have been expected that she would encourage all types of research, but because her view of research was limited to qualitative studies this was not the case. In fact, in the year of her death, her successor, Dorothy Gardner, did publish a modest evaluative of child-centred education (Gardner, 1948).

In her conduct of qualitative studies she was however, in one respect at least, well ahead of her time. In the nineteen sixties what was then regarded as a new approach to the study of the development of young children was introduced. "Ethology" has been defined as "a field which seeks to study animal behaviour through careful observation of species in their natural habitats". The early ethologists such as Konrad Lorenz and Nikki Tinbergen had studied birds, geese and other animals, developing concepts such as critical and sensitive periods of development, innate releasing mechanisms and so on.

As early as the 1950s John Bowlby advocated the application of such methods to the study of children and indeed used them in his groundbreaking work on attachment (Bowlby, 1957). But in fact Susan Isaacs who had studied the interactions of children in one of their natural habitats, the school, using systematic observations of their speech and behaviour had anticipated him in this respect. Her findings of changes in the nature of group interactions between children as they grew older were very much in the tradition of later ethological studies. Like later ethologists she noted the adaptive value of such development for the survival of the individual. She has not been given credit for this innovation in psychological methodology, although it is more than possible that John Bowlby who knew her and her work well was influenced by it.

From a broader perspective, the research output of the Department of Child Development at the Institute of Education for which she was responsible, was very limited (Annual Reports of the Department of Child Development, Institute of Education, London, 1933–9). Basically Susan Isaacs felt she knew the answers to questions that might be raised about educational methods and pursued what she believed to be right with missionary enthusiasm. This attitude to research in education has, to some degree, persisted to this day. Many teachers, indeed some academic educationalists remain sceptical about an evidence-based approach to what goes on in the classroom. The interactions between children and teachers are often thought to be too complex to be subjected to hypothesis testing research using quantitative methods. One result of this attitude is that the volume of educational research is small compared to the expenditure on health research. Although expenditure on educational research has steadily risen over recent years, the gap between public expenditure on education and health remains vast. In his 2006 budget speech, Gordon Brown, the Chancellor of the Exchequer, for example, announced that £1 billion would be ring-fenced for the research budget of the Department of Health and the Medical Research Council. It is difficult to make a similar calculation for governmental expenditure on education research, but it is probably in the region of £100 million—a ten-fold difference. Of course, the influence of Susan Isaacs on attitudes to educational research cannot be regarded as persisting to the present day. But her generally negative stance on research in education, articulated from a position of considerable authority, probably did set a pattern that persisted for some years.

*   *   *

Like her contribution to the spread of child-centred education, Susan Isaacs's legacy to child psychoanalysis and psychoanalytic child psychotherapy is also difficult to assess. This is largely because while her position among educationalists as an influential figure is well established, in psycho-analytic circles, although her paper on phantasy is still frequently quoted, she is not generally thought of as a figure of great consequence. A biographer is inevitably inclined to exaggerate the importance of his subject. All the same, the story of the Controversial Discussions (King and Steiner, 1991) makes clear that without the advocacy Susan Isaacs provided it is likely that the theories and practice of Melanie Klein would not have flourished as they did in the second half of the twentieth century and indeed continue to flourish today. Had she been expelled from the British Psychoanalytic Society as Anna Freud wished, Klein would have been forced to establish a separate training establishment herself. There would have been no lack of members of her school who would have enabled her to do this successfully. (In fact this is what Anna Freud did at the London Hampstead Clinic when it became clear that Melanie Klein was going to become the dominant influence in the Society.) But Klein would have been working in an isolated situation and it is unlikely that her ideas would have flourished as they did. Indeed, the separate clinic that Anna Freud established in Hampstead expanded over the years but to nothing like the extent of the Klein-dominated Tavistock Clinic. Susan Isaacs was not just a devoted follower of Klein; she articulated Klein's ideas in a manner that persuaded others of their significance. In considering her legacy it does therefore seem relevant to provide a brief description of the development of Kleinian ideas since Susan's death in 1948.

Susan Isaacs was succeeded as an exponent of the ideas of Melanie Klein by Hanna Segal, again an articulate analyst whose expositions have achieved considerable clarification of Klein's views. In her "Introduction to the Work of Melanie Klein" Segal (1964) begins by discussing phantasy, and uncompromisingly states the central idea in Kleinian thought that "unconscious phantasy is the mental expression of instincts and therefore, like these, exists from the beginning of life". The Anna Freudians, as we saw, found it difficult to believe that very young infants experienced phantasies as Klein described them, replete with aggressive, sexual, cannibalistic content in which murderous intent and terror of annihilation were universally experienced. What is the evidence to support or refute this central idea eighty or so years after Melanie Klein first formulated it?

There is a sense in which both Freudians and Kleinians can claim subsequent scientific work has supported their views. In the 1960s it became clear to developmental psychologists that babies in the first few days and weeks of life were active participants in their interactions with their mothers. Simultaneous filming of the expressions of the infant and mother made it clear that babies were by no means passive partners; they initiated mother-infant interactions more often than their mothers (Trevarthen, 1977, pp. 227–270). Further, it is also clear that babies do indeed experience pain, terror and anger. The social awareness of infants is far in advance of anything the Freudians would have allowed. Recent studies suggest that infants as young as two months old can exhibit behaviour that suggests they can feel shy and show off, social skills of considerable complexity (Reddy, 2000). By the age of 3 months infants have been shown to be highly sensitive to three-way exchanges with their mother and another child. Daniel Stern, a psychoanalyst as well as a developmental psychologist has focused for many years on the interaction between mothers and babies to confirm the presence of "inter-connectivity". Looking back at studies carried out in the second half of the twentieth century, he writes (Stern1985) that it became clear that:

> infants schematised interactive patterns well before they could talk. Before events could be verbally or symbolically related, infants' early interactive knowledge was somehow encoded in a non-verbal register. What is more most of the mother's behaviour seemed to be intuitive—that is implicit, not following some easily verbalised rule.

Such pre-verbal encoding is surely very close to the Isaacs view of a phantasy arising before the infant can speak.

On the other hand there is lack of evidence for the existence of the actively destructive, murderous phantasies or unconscious knowledge of the facts of adult sexual intercourse that Klein proposed. It is of course possible that such unconscious knowledge does exist in the infant mind and Kleinians would contend that observation of infants and their clinical experience of the play of older children support its presence. All one can say about this is that today's leading developmental child psychologists, while accepting there is much that one still does not know about the infant's mind would here agree with the Freudians and strongly doubt their validity. The accounts that many Kleinian analysts currently give of their interpretations suggests that they too no longer give them the same degree of credence.

In a way more importantly, the Kleinians have been accused of being so preoccupied with infantile phantasies they have ignored the contribution made by parents, especially the mother, to influencing the mind of the baby and young child. Here one must separate the ideas of Susan Isaacs from those of Klein. Though some of Isaacs's writings do suggest that she too downplayed the way differences in parental behaviour affected the child, it is clear that Susan Isaacs accepted the importance of the way parents behaved towards their children in moulding the behaviour and emotional life of the child. This is especially the case in her replies to letters in The Nursery World and in descriptions of the evacuated children she studied in Cambridge.

In contrast, for several decades Kleinians behaved, in the words of one child psychotherapist (Juliet Hopkins, personal communication), "as if there were no bad parents, only bad fantasies projected onto parents by their children". With graphic descriptions of physical child abuse in the nineteen sixties, of sexual abuse even of young children from the nineteen eighties onwards, and of the subtle and sometimes not so subtle ways in which depression in mothers altered the behaviour of very young children, this position became quite untenable.

The establishment of Melanie Klein within the Society and Institute of Psycho-analysis had a massive influence on the subsequent development of the whole psychoanalytic field but especially that of child psychotherapy in the United Kingdom. Although there were many other major schools and powerful figures in the post Second World War world of psycho-analysis, Kleinians dominated child psychotherapy, in particular, at the Tavistock Clinic, the foremost centre of psycho-analysis in the United Kingdom and some would say, in the world. The infant observation seminars that formed part of the child psychotherapy course were, from the outset, predominantly Kleinian in orientation. The dominant position that Kleinian psycho-analysts and psychotherapists achieved at the Tavistock ensured that Melanie Klein's ideas were widely incorporated into the training of a high proportion of child psychotherapists. Her followers were, for some years, so protective of their students that non-Kleinians were given a very limited place as teachers on the Tavistock child psychotherapy courses. The books and articles in the reading lists that the students were given at least until the 1980s were almost entirely restricted to the works of Klein and her adherents. The contributions of analysts who had opposed her, such as Anna Freud and John Bowlby, or broken with her after a period of adherence, such as Paula Heimann and Donald Winnicott were limited, however eminent they might have been considered elsewhere. So, until about 1985, when there was a significant change in the tolerance given to other psychoanalytic approaches, with even some acceptance and very limited inclusion of attachment theory in the curriculum, the focus of the training of child psychotherapists at the Tavistock Clinic was on mental, intra-psychic events seen from a Kleinian standpoint. This was always supplemented with opportunities for observation of infants and mother-infant observation as well as the study of child development. As examination of the curriculum offered to students at that time revealed, the training was narrowly confined to psychoanalytic contributions to the literature (Graham, 1974).

This meant that social influences and the environment were considerably downplayed. Though they worked in partnership with social workers who saw one or both parents, what was seen as the really valuable part of the treatment was the psychoanalytic psychotherapy. Indeed the word "therapy" was used as if it were synonymous with analytic psychotherapy. Since that time this situation has changed considerably. Though the term "therapy" is still sometimes used in this restricted sense in analytic circles, even at the Tavistock Clinic it would now be used to include other forms of psychotherapy such as family and group approaches and, more recently, cognitive-behaviour therapy.

Not only have analytic child psychotherapists become more tolerant of other approaches, their own practice has, to some degree become more sensitive to the needs of children and parents. There is a new, younger breed of child psychotherapists who are more flexible in their approach (Lanyado and Horne, 1999). The interpretations that are given to children in such treatment are likely to be more readily comprehensible to children, more in line with their actual experiences and delivered with much less certainty, as suggestions rather than as evident truths as was the case in the time of Melanie Klein and Susan Isaacs.

There are now several hundred child psychotherapists mainly trained along Kleinian lines, mostly practising in London and the south of England, but with significant numbers elsewhere in the United Kingdom. Although the use of child analysis (four or five times a week fifty minute sessions sometimes over several years), is now only rarely undertaken, there has been a very considerable expansion of the role of child psychotherapists. Mainly working in the National Health Service, analytic child psychotherapists deliver both short and longer-term treatment, but at a frequency usually of once a week, much less than in classical psycho-analysis. They have found roles in consultation in dealing with child protection cases, in consultation with paediatricians and general practitioners, in running groups of depressed mothers, in the conduct of ante-natal and post-natal groups in special schools for children with emotional and behavioural disorders and in a whole range of other situations. They play a part in contributing to the training of many other professionals working with children with mental health problems. These child psychotherapists remain greatly influenced by Melanie Klein's work. In an edited introductory book based on lectures given at the Institute of Psychoanalysis published as recently as 2005, chapters on the paranoid-schizoid position, on the depressive position, and on envy rely heavily on Kleinian concepts (Budd and Rusbridger, 2005).

Their success in the expansion of their activities represents a considerable achievement for analytic child psychotherapists. However, though a vast amount of clinical experience has accrued over the decades, the scientific evidence that psycho-analytic therapy does more than any other sort of kindly intervention to make children and parents feel better, is limited. To a considerable degree this lack of evidence must be attributed to the missionary zeal of Melanie Klein and her followers, including Susan Isaacs, who, it has to be said, should have known better. They *knew* that they were right and any attempt at evaluation would have been regarded as a complete waste of time.

It is, of course, difficult to carry out systematic studies of the effectiveness of psychoanalytic psychotherapy, in which, for example, children are randomly allocated to groups that are treated differently. There are problems in defining the intervention precisely, in taking account of the variable personalities and skills of the therapists, in agreeing on what are the most important outcomes, but all of these difficulties can be at least partly overcome if there is motivation to do so. Some such studies have been conducted with rather disappointing results. Of course, the fact that there is little scientific evidence for a form of therapy does not mean it is ineffective. Lack of evidence is not evidence of lack. But the result of this lack of evidence is that other forms of child psychotherapy, especially cognitive behaviour therapy for which evidence for effectiveness is modest but stronger than is the case with analytic child psychotherapy, are now more widely recommended (Wolpert et al. 2006).

During the 1990s there was a real change in the willingness of child psychotherapists to engage in research and the volume of research into the process of psychotherapy and outcomes, though still small in relation to the amount that is expended in this field of work, has greatly increased (Roth and Fonagy, 2005).

Since Susan Isaacs's time, especially over the last twenty years there have been massive advances in neurobiology as well as in our understanding of the brain and of mind-body interaction. Some neuroscientists have carried out studies in which they have attempted to bridge the gap between psychoanalytic concepts such as repression and findings using brain imaging (Solms and Turnbull, 2002). Some of the results have been of interest, but there are still large gaps in neurobiological explanations of psycho-analytic processes. Further, non-psychoanalytic explanations of behaviour that, for example, put more emphasis on imitation or role-modelling have gradually come to supersede psychoanalytic explanations. This is especially so for aggressive behaviour, in which there are strong links between family and individual child violence.

Any attempt to make an assessment of the overall benefit to children that Susan Isaacs's contribution to psycho-analysis made possible is bound to be problematic. If one assumes, as perhaps one can, that she was at least partly responsible for the primacy of Klein theory and practice in the half-century after her death, one would have to be cautious in crediting her with a beneficial effect. On the one hand the early recognition that even very young infants have deeply felt emotions has had very positive effects. In the early twenty first century there is much greater sensitivity to the emotional need of babies in the first year of life than was the case even forty years ago. On the other hand, a persistent tendency over decades to discount the quality of child rearing by parents in favour of concern for the inner life and fantasies of the child when assessing the causes of childhood disturbance was clearly not in the interests of children. Further, the acceptance of a situation in which it was possible to continue to practice an intervention without a serious attempt to gather evidence of its effectiveness was, to say the least, unhelpful.

All the same, many mental health professionals, even those who recognise the lack of evidence for the effectiveness of their approach, acknowledge that there is an important positive contribution that the Kleinians and indeed all analysts whose ideas ultimately derive from Sigmund Freud have made. They have all along emphasised how much one can learn by listening to children and observing them attentively and carefully. Having listened and observed it seems to me they then unfortunately went on to make confident inter- pretations to the children they were seeing that were outlandish, at best uninformative and at worst unhelpful or even harmful. But in their insistence on listening, on highlighting the degree to which the feelings of even very young children, for so long dismissed and discounted, really mattered, they were well ahead of their time. Further they were committed to providing a setting in which children and their parents could feel that a serious attempt was being made to understand them by people who would accept even those feelings of which they were most ashamed. If there were some who felt demeaned and blamed by the therapy they received from analysts and analytically trained psychotherapists, there were many others who felt they were understood and cared for. For some of these, especially those who had had an emotionally deprived upbringing, this was their very first experience of loving care and it was much appreciated.

*   *   *

In her obituaries much was made of Susan Isaacs's contribution to building a bridge between education and psychoanalysis. It is difficult to gauge the impact of psychoanalytic thinking in teacher training and teaching practice in the years after Susan Isaacs's death. For many years there continued to be some schools, especially those then called schools for maladjusted children that ran along lines that were at least partly derived from psychoanalytic principles. In these schools children's behaviour and emotional distress were overwhelmingly attributed to unconscious forces and attempts were made by specialised teachers to understand what was going on in the mind of the individual child and to provide analytic help if this were available, as it sometimes was in or around London. But such schools were unusual.

In teacher training until the 1990s most teachers received little instruction that they regarded as helpful when it came to managing difficult or disturbed children (Linda Lefevre, personal communication, Yvonne Connelly, personal communication). Piaget continued to figure largely in the curriculum but he had little to say about emotional development. Teachers were encouraged to learn about some aspects of psychoanalytic theory such as mental mechanisms defending against anxiety and were guided towards some books written by psychoanalysts, especially Donald Winnicott. Most did not regard this instruction or the support they received in schools to be of much use in the classroom. There was a widespread assumption among teachers that all bad behaviour derived from bad conditions in the home, especially bad mothering. A small number of schools were able to employ counsellors, usually using psycho-dynamic approaches, and some teachers trained to acquire pastoral skills they could apply in the schools in which they worked.

At the same time studies of populations of school children established important links between difficult, especially antisocial behaviour and reading ability. In the late 1970s work was carried out in London schools demonstrating that schools could make a difference and reduce rates of behaviour problems (Rutter et al., 1979). This was not however by applying psychoanalytic principles, but by improving the academic ethos, making sure homework was marked on time, that teachers turned up punctually to lessons, that damage to the school premises was rapidly repaired and that prefect-type responsibility was not just accorded to one or two favourite pupils but shared around. At this time Infant and primary school-teachers particularly became involved in the recognition of neglected and physically maltreated children; here the interventions were appropriately focused on child protection with involvement of social service departments rather than the application of psychoanalytic approaches.

In the 1980s and 1990s government ministers, more strongly focused on educational achievement and the National Curriculum, became aware of the devastating effects on learning of the presence of disruptive pupils, not only on their own learning but in the interference they produced in the learning of others. So-called behaviour support initiatives were introduced that encouraged teachers to apply behavioural methods, rewarding good behaviour and, as far as possible, ignoring bad behaviour or using brief time-out procedures. Gradually too, especially in the first years of the twenty first century there was some improvement in the level of child and adolescent mental health services so that at least some schools received more appropriate help than they had in the past when such services were usually inaccessible. By this time the clinics to which children were referred were largely offering the more evidence-based interventions such as cognitive behaviour therapy (Graham, 2005), although some degree of psychodynamic understanding was also applied, especially in the assessment of emotional and behaviour problems.

The bridge that Susan Isaacs was thought to have built between education and psychoanalysis thus turned out to be rather insubstantial. It is however still the case that many teachers find ideas derived from psychoanalysis such as denial, repression and transference very helpful in thinking about the disturbed behaviour some children show. Phrases like "he's in denial" or "he's just shut it out of his system" or "what do you expect, he's frightened of his Dad, so he takes it out on us" are commonly heard in staff rooms. Freudian language that Isaacs first made available in the training of teachers in state schools has now become so much part of everyday discourse as to be barely recognisable as such.

*   *   *

It has to be said too that Susan Isaacs left the bridge between psychology and psychoanalysis in no better state than that between education and psychoanalysis. In the early years of the British Psychoanalytic Society from the time of its foundation in 1919 a number of academic psychologists, such as Cyril Burt, whose main interest was in education and child development, were members. With the arrival of Melanie Klein the discussions moved away from ideas that could be verified by direct observation and experiment. These psychologists left the Society or remained members in name only. At the same time, methods used by academic psychologists in university departments became even more behavioural and statistical. The rift between the two became ever wider. Susan Isaacs firmly joined the ranks of the analysts and though perhaps not as dismissive of experimental methods in child psychology as some of her analytic colleagues, nevertheless did much less to bridge the gap than might have been expected given her training in academic psychology. As Oliver Zangwill, describing the field of psychology between 1918 and 1945 put it (Zangwill, 1972, p. 187),

> ... academic psychologists have seen in psychoanalysis a strange and esoteric system, possibly of some value in psychological medicine, but having little to offer to the systematic study of normal human behaviour. Psychoanalysts, on their side, have seen academic psychology as superficial, trivial and divorced from the realities of human conduct.

Ian Hunter (1972) describing the development of psychology from 1945 to 1965 refers to the explosion in empirical enquiry in that subject and does not even mention psychoanalysis. It took until the early 1990s for links to become established between university departments, not always departments of psychology, and the Tavistock Clinic. These links occurred for a number of reasons. University departments of psychology had come to accept that qualitative research into subjective experience could produce findings of scientific interest; psychoanalysis could be regarded as providing data that fell into this category. Another push came from the insistence on evidence for National Health Service funded therapy. With the passage of time there had been a move too away from the strong bias against the use of non-psychoanalytic approaches to the study of emotional development that Melanie Klein and Susan Isaacs had personified. Finally the renewed interest in the possibility of finding a neuro-biological basis for psychoanalytic mechanisms provided a further impetus. Whatever the reasons for the recent rapprochement between psychology and psychoanalysis, it cannot be said that the Kleinians, including, one has to admit, Susan Isaacs, did anything for many years other than delay its occurrence.

After Susan Isaacs dispensed advice to parents in the nineteen thirties in The Nursery World under the name of Ursula Wise, there was a steady flow of baby books that turned into a flood towards the end of the century. Now, in the first decade of the twenty first century, "any good bookshop" provides a choice of anything up to thirty of forty books on the subject. During the nineteen forties the first edition of Benjamin Spock's book "Baby and Child Care" was published and dominated the baby book field for the next four decades. Indeed, although Spock died in 1998, his book is still in print in 2006. Spock who, like Susan Isaacs, drew many of his ideas from psycho-analytic theory, at first advocated a highly permissive approach to child rearing to such a degree that he was blamed for the permissive, hippy culture, the "flower revolution" of the nineteen sixties. He subsequently changed his advice in the 1970s, advocating firmer discipline and clearer boundaries to behaviour.

It is possible to compare the psychologically understanding, permissive Isaacs approach and Watson's behaviourism in a variety of child-rearing topics with that widely advocated nowadays. For example, if one looks at the advice given on smacking in the Great Ormond Street Book of Baby and Child Care one finds an approach rather balanced between that of Susan Isaacs and that of John Watson. In discussing physical punishment by parents, for example, the Great Ormond Street Book first admits (Hilton and Messenger, 2004) "there are few parents who have never hit their child, some in the belief that smacking or slapping is the best way to correct behaviour, but most in moments of exasperation which they usually regret the next minute". It then goes on ". . . hitting children teaches them only that you are angry with them at that moment, and it may encourage them to hit other children and indulge in the behaviour you have disapproved of the moment your back is turned. . . . If you do lose control and slap your child, it is best to tell him afterwards that you are sorry and that it was wrong, explaining why he drove you so mad. . . ." This is followed by a discussion of other methods of discipline, such as briefly isolating a disobedient child, but, interestingly, no mention of the "function" of disobedience in the development of autonomy. In comparing the different approaches to smacking, it is interesting to note that both Susan Isaacs and the Great Ormond Street Book acknowledge that even the best parents are sometimes so exasperated that they do lose control and smack children in their care.

Modern-day advice to smacking is close to that of Susan Isaacs. But the current emphasis on the need for firm boundaries to behaviour and on the use of behavioural approaches to dealing with disobedience, using rewards and sanctions like time-out when children behave unacceptably, is nearer to that of her detested competitor, John Watson. The popular Supernanny television pro-grammes advising parents how to cope with their wildly disobedient children, owe much more to Watson than they do to Isaacs, though there are many points at which she advocated "the use of control when control is appropriate".

Twenty first century approaches to the understanding of childhood fears are diverse, but are also probably closer to that of Watson than they are to Susan Isaacs. As did Watson, they generally advise a very gradual approach to the feared object is advised. On the other hand, when discussing the best approach to sex education in young children, contemporary baby books such as the Great Ormond Street Book are much nearer to that of Susan Isaacs. Very much in her vein the Great Ormond Street book counsels "be led by your child's questioning and do not burden him with more information than he wants".

So the spirits of both Susan Isaacs and John Watson live on in contemporary baby books. Their relative importance depends on the aspect of child-rearing that is in question. To *understand* behaviour the psychological approach of Susan Isaacs is much preferred. But when it comes to finding the most effective way to *change* a child's behaviour, the reward and sanctions approach for so long advocated by the behaviourists still holds sway.

One idea of Susan Isaacs, not shared with John Watson was her view of the child, even at a very young age, as an inquisitive, persistent enquirer after the truth. In his search for the nature of the real world and the reasons for inconsistencies in adult thinking the infant behaved like the best sort of scientist. This notion of the child as scientist has been recycled a number of times since Susan Isaacs made the comparison. Jerome Bruner, a leading American developmental psychologist, describing the acquisition of language referred to the young child engaging in "an active process of hypothesis formation and hypothesis testing" (Bruner, 1975). Alison Gopnik (1999) and her colleagues, also American developmental psychologists, in their best-selling book titled "The Scientist in the Crib" describe just how much infants and scientists have in common. Young children ". . . make predictions, do experiments, they try to explain what they see, and they formulate new theories on the basis of what they already know". In the article entitled "The Child as Scientist" that she wrote in The Spectator in 1931 (Smith, 1985, pp. 271–3). Susan Isaacs had made this same comparison many years earlier and, like those who came after her, pointed to the need for adults to take children's questioning very seriously. If we do, we shall learn as well. After all, what father or mother would not benefit from being able to work out how to answer the questions quoted by Nathan Isaacs in his wife's first major book (Isaacs, 1930, p. 318). These were all put by children under the age of four and a half to their parents in the early nineteen thirties?

"How can the hippo get down the steps into his tank, when his little front legs are such a long way off his little back legs?"

"Why does the soap look smaller in the water?"

"Why can't we see the stars in the daytime?"

"Why does the glass look different in the water, but it doesn't if you just put water in the glass?"

The children who asked those questions reached their teens in the Second World War and were part of the immediate post-war generation of scientists and creative artists who contributed so much to advance technology and enrich the cultural life of Britain. They had relatively low crime rates and suffered less from depression and anxiety than the generations that followed them. Many of their parents, who brought up their children neither with the Victorian rigidity that persisted well into the nineteen twenties, nor with the laissez-faire permissiveness of the post-nineteen fifties, were at least partly guided in their parenting by the sensible advice given by Susan Isaacs. Those of this generation, as I am myself, should be thankful to her.

References/Bibliography

Abbreviations

BPAS	Archives of the British Psycho-Analytical Association, Institute of Psychoanalysis
FKC	Pearl King and Riccardo Steiner (Eds.), *The Freud-Klein Controversies 1941–1945*
Gardner	Dorothy Gardner, *Susan Isaacs: The First Biography*
Grosskurth	Phyllis Grosskurth, *Melanie Klein*
Hughes	Athol Hughes (Ed.), *The Inner World and Joan Riviere*
IoEd	Archives of the Institute of Education, London
I-Int	Susan Isaacs, *Intellectual Growth in Young Children*
I-Soc	Susan Isaacs, *Social Development in Young Children*
Kl-1	Melanie Klein,*The Writings of Melanie Klein, Volume 1, Love Guilt and Reparation and Other Works, 1921–1945*
KS	Pearl King and Riccardo Steiner, *The Freud-Klein Controversies 1941–45*
NA	National Archive, Kew
SE	Sigmund Freud, *The Standard Edition of the Complete Psychological Works*

Collections consulted

Bolton Library Archive
British Newspaper Library
British Psychoanalytic Society Archive
Froebel Institute Archive

Institute of Education, London Archive
John Rylands Library, University of Manchester Archive
London Metropolitan Archive
London School of Economics Archive
Melanie Klein Trust Archive, Wellcome Institute
National Archive, Kew
National Archive of South Africa, Cape Town

Published works

Abraham, K. (1920). Manifestations of the Female Castration Complex. In: *Selected Papers on Psychoanalysis*. London: Hogarth Press, 1927.

Aldrich, R. (2002). *The Institute of Education: 1902–2002*. London: Institute of Education.

Appignanesi, L., & Forrester, J. (1993). *Freud's Women*. London: Virago Press.

Bancroft, J. (1989). *Human Sexuality and its Problems*. Edinburgh: Churchill Livingstone.

Bartlett, F. C. (2004). *Myers, Charles S (1873–1946)*. Oxford: Oxford Dictionary of National Biography, Oxford University Press.

Bennett, Arnold. (1985). *Anna of the Five Towns*. London: Penguin.

Bifulco, J., Brown, G., Lillie, A., and Jarvis J. (1997). Memories of childhood neglect and abuse: Corroboration in a series of sisters. *Journal of Child Psychology and Psychiatry, 38*, 365–74.

Board of Education (1933). *Report of the Consultative Committee on Infant and Nursery Schools*. London: HMSO.

Bolton Library Archive: Log book of the Central High Grade Board School, Bolton, SLB/8/1.

Bowlby, J. (1957) An ethological approach to research in child development. *British Journal of Medical Psychology, 30*, 230–240.

Bowlby, J. (1971) *Attachment and Loss, Volume 1. Attachment*. London: Penguin.

Bowlby, J. (1991). The role of the psychotherapist's personal resources in the treatment situation. *Tavistock Gazette*, 1–8.

Bradburn, E. (1976). *Margaret McMillan: framework and expansion of nursery education*. Redhill: Denholm House Press.

Brehony, K. J. (2000). *English Revisionist Froebelians and the Schooling of the Urban Poor*. In M. Hilton and P. Hirsch (Eds.), *Practical Visionaries: Women, Education and Social Progress, 1790–1930*. (p. 192). London: Pearson Education.

Bringuier, J-C. (1980). *Conversations with Jean Piaget*. Chicago: Chicago University Press.

British Medical Association (1929). *Report of the Psycho-analysis Committee*. London: British Medical Association.

Brome, V. (1982). *Ernest Jones: Freud's alter ego*. London: Caliban.

Brooks, R. (2004). *Findlay, Joseph John (1860–1940)*. Oxford: Oxford Dictionary of National Biography, Oxford University Press.

Brown, J. A. C. (1963). *Freud and the Post-Freudians*. London: Penguin.

Bruner, J. (1975). From communication to language—A psychological perspective. *Cognition, 3*, 255–87.

Bryant, P. & Kopytynska, H. (1976). Spontaneous measurement by young children. *Nature, 260*, 772.

Budd, S. & Rusbridger, R. (Eds.) (2005). *Introducing psychoanalysis*. London: Routledge.

Calman, M. (1968). Untitled. In: B. S. Johnson (Ed.), *The Evacuees* (pp. 34–5). London: Victor Gollancz.

Campbell, A. (1953). *A Family Life*. IoEd. S1 A1, also IoEd. S1 A3.

Campbell, A. (Ed.) (1938). *Modern Trends in Education: The proceedings of the New Education Fellowship Conference held in New Zealand in July, 1937*. Auckland: Whitcomb and Tombs.

Central Advisory Council for Education (1967). *Children and their Primary Schools*. London: HMSO.

Chomsky, N. (1965). *Aspects of the theory of syntax*. Cambridge: MIT Press.

Cole, M. (1963). *The Story of Fabian Socialism*. London: Mercury Books.

Crampton, C. (1978). *The Cambridge School: The life, work and influence of James Ward, W. H. R. Rivers, C. S. Myers, and Sir Frederic Bartlett*. Ph.D. Thesis, University of Edinburgh.

Creak, M. (1934). Review. *Eugenics Review, 25*, 280–1.

Crichton-Miller, H. (1921). *The New Psychology and the Parent*. London: Jarrolds.

Darwin, C. (1887). Biographical Study of an Infant. *Mind*, No. 7.

Department for Education and Employment (2003). *Excellence and enjoyment: a strategy for primary schools*. London: Department for Education and Employment.

Department of Health (1976). Fit for the Future. Report of the Committee on Child Health Services. London: HMSO.

Dewey, J. (1906). *The School and the Child*. Ed. J. J. Findlay, London: Blackie and Son.

Dewey, J. (1899). *School and Society*. Chicago: University of Chicago Press.

Dixon, C. W. (1986). *A History of the University of London Institute of Education, 1932–1972.* London: Institute of Education.

Donaldson, M. (1978). *Children's Minds.* London: Fontana.

Donoughue, B. (2003). *The Heat of the Kitchen.* London: Politicos.

Drummond, M. J. (2000). *Susan Isaacs: Pioneering Work in Understanding Children's Lives.* In: M. Hilton and P. Hirsch (Eds.), *Practical Visionaries: Women, Education and Social Progress, 1790–1930* (pp. 221–234). London: Pearson Education.

Dyer, R. (1983) *Her Father's Daughter.* London: Jason Aronson.

Ellesley, S. (1975). *Psychoanalysis in Early Twentieth Century England: a study in the popularisation of ideas.* Ph. D. University of Essex.

Eyken, W. van der, and Turner, B. (1969). *Adventures in Education.* London: Allen Lane, Penguin Press.

Flugel, J. C. (1931). Review. *International Journal of Psychoanalysis,12*, 371.

Frankenburg, C. (1922). *Common Sense in the Nursery.* London: Cape.

Freud, A. (1930) Four Lectures on Psychoanalysis for Teachers and Parents. In: *Introduction to Psychoanalysis, Writings, Vol. 1.* London, Hogarth Press.

Freud, A. and Burlingham, D. (1943). *War and Children.* New York: International Universities Press.

Freud, S. (1900a). *The Interpretation of Dreams.* SE., 4 & 5.

―――― (1901). *The Psychopathology of Everyday Life.* SE 6.

―――― (1901–5). *Three Essays on Sexuality.* SE7.

―――― (1907). *The sexual enlightenment of children (An open letter to Dr. M. Furst).* SE7, 1901–5.

―――― (1909). *Analysis of a Phobia in a Five-Year-Old Boy.* SE., 10.

―――― (1927). *The Future of an Illusion.* SE., 21.

―――― (1895b) with Breuer, J., *Studies on Hysteria.* SE., 2.

Fulford, R. (1957). *Votes for Women.* London: Faber and Faber.

Gammage, P. (1987). Chinese Whispers. *Oxford Review of Education, 13,* 95–109.

Gardner, D. (1944). *Testing results in the infant school.* London: Methuen.

Gardner, D. (1969). *Susan Isaacs; the First Biography.* London: Methuen Education Limited.

Gathorne-Hardy, J. (1993). *The Rise and Fall of the British Nanny.* London: Weidenfeld

Geissmann, C. and P. (1998). *A History of Child Psychoanalysis.* London: Routledge.

Gesell, A. (1928). *Mental Growth of the Pre-School Child.* New York: Macmillan.

Gilbert, S. (1957). *Letters of James Joyce*. London: Faber.

Gillard, D. (2004) "The Plowden Report", *the encyclopaedia of informal education*, www.infed.org/schooling/plowden_report.htm.

Gillham, A. (1972) *History of Birtenshaw Methodist Church and Sunday School*. Personal Communication.

Glover, E. (1940). An investigation into the technique of psychoanalysis. *International Journal of Psychoanalysis. Supplement No. 4*.

Godfrey, J. (2004). Perhaps the most important and certainly the most exciting event in the whole history of education in Australia. *History of Education Review, 33*, 45–58.

Gopnik, A., Meltzoff, A., & Kuhl, P. (1999). *The Scientist in the Crib*. New York: William Morrow.

Graham, P. J. (1974). Child psychiatry and psychotherapy. *Journal of Child Psychology and Psychiatry, 15*, 59–66.

Graham, P. (Ed.) (2005). *Cognitive Behaviour Therapy for Children and Families*. Cambridge: Cambridge University Press.

Gregory, B. (2006). *A History of the Artist's Rifles: 1859–1947*. London: Pen and Sword, Military.

Grosskurth, P. (1986). *Melanie Klein*. London: Hodder and Stoughton.

Hardt, J. and Rutter, M. (2004). Validity of adult retrospective reports of adverse childhood experiences. *Journal of Child Psychology and Psychiatry, 45*, 260–73.

Hardyment, C. (1995). *Perfect Parents*. Oxford: Oxford University Press.

Hattersley, R. (2004). *The Edwardians*. London: Little, Brown.

Hearnshaw, L. (1979). *Cyril Burt: Psychologist*. London: Hodder and Stoughton.

Hemmings, R. (1972). *Fifty Years of Freedom: A Study of the Development of the Ideas of A. S. Neill*. London: Allen and Unwin.

Hilton, T. & Messenger, M. (2004). *The Great Ormond Street New Baby and Child Care Book*. London: Vermilion.

Hinshelwood, R. D. (1995). Psychoanalysis in Britain: Points of Cultural Access, 1893–1918. *International Journal of Psycho-analysis, 76*, 135–151.

Hobsbawm, E. (1987). *The Age of Capital:1875–1914*. London, Abacus.

Holmes, E. (1911). *What is and what might be*. London: Constable.

Holt, L. E. (1894). *The Care and Feeding of Children*. New York: Appleton.

Home Department. (1946). *Report of the Care of Children Committee*. London: HMSO.

Horney, K. (1924). On the genesis of the castration complex in women. *International Journal of Psycho-analysis, 5*, 50–65.

Hughes, A. (2004) *The Inner World of Joan Riviere*. London: Karnac Books.

Hunt, J. McV. (1969). *The Impact and Limitations of the Giant of Developmental Psychology.* In: D. Elkind & J. Flavell (Eds.), *Studies in Cognitive Development: Essays in Honor of Jean Piaget.* (pp. 3–66). Oxford: Oxford University Press.

Hunter, I. (1972). *Psychology.* In: CB Cox & AE Dyson (Eds.), *The Twentieth Century Mind. 3. 1945–1965.* Oxford: Oxford University Press.

Isaacs, N. (1949). *The Foundations of Common Sense: A Psychological Preface to the Problems of Knowledge.* London: Routledge and Kegan Paul.

Jenkins, C. (1989). *The Professional Middle Class and the Social Origins of Progressivism.: a case study of the New Education Fellowship.* Ph.D. Thesis, London: Institute of Education.

Jones, E. (1934). Review. *International Journal of Psychoanalysis, 15,* 86–7.

Jones, E. (1959). *Free Associations.* London: Hogarth Press.

Jones, E. (1962). *The Life and Work of Sigmund Freud.* London: Hogarth Press.

Kahr, B. (1996). *D. W. Winnicott: A biographical portrait.* London: Karnac Books.

King, F. T. (1924). *The Expectant Mother and Baby's First Months.* London: Macmillan.

King, P. & Steiner, R. (Eds.) (1991). *The Freud-Klein Controversies 1941–1945.* London: Routledge.

Klein, M. (1921). The Development of a Child:The Influence of Sexual Enlightenment and Relaxation of Authority on the Intellectual Development of Children. In: M. Klein, *The Writings of Melanie Klein, Volume 1, Love Guilt and Reparation and Other Works, 1921–1945.* London: Hogarth Press, 1975.

Klein, M. (1923). The role of the school in the libidinal development of the child. In: M. Klein, *The Writings of Melanie Klein, Volume 1, Love Guilt and Reparation and Other Works, 1921–1945.* London: Hogarth Press, 1975.

Klein, M. (1925). A contribution to the psychogenesis of tics. In: M. Klein, *The Writings of Melanie Klein, Volume 1, Love Guilt and Reparation and Other Works, 1921–1945.* London: Hogarth Press, 1975.

Klein, M. (1928). Early stages of the Oedipus Conflict. *International Journal of Psychoanalysis, 8,* 340–384.

Klein, M. (1935). A Contribution to the Psychogenesis of Manic-Depressive States. *International Journal of Psychoanalysis, 16,* 145–174.

Klein, M. (1975). *The Psychoanalysis of Children.* London: Hogarth Press. (1st Edition 1932).

Laird, J. (2004). *Alexander, Samuel (1959–1938)*, revised Michael Weinstein. Oxford: Oxford Dictionary of National Biography, Oxford University Press.

Lampe, D. (1959). *Pyke, The Unknown Genius.* London: Evans Brothers.

Lanyado, M. and Horne, A. (1999). *The handbook of child and adolescent psychotherapy.* London: Routledge.

Lawrence D. H. (1923) *Psychoanalysis and the Unconscious.* London: William Heinemann.

Lawrence, E. (1961). *Friedrich Froebel 1782–1852 and English Education,* London: University of London Press.

Lawrence, E. (1931). An investigation into the relation between intelligence and inheritance. *British Journal of Psychology Monographs,* 1–80.

Lee, L. (1962). *Cider with Rosie.* London: Penguin Books.

Lieberman, E. J. (1985). *Acts of Will. The life and work of Otto Rank.* New York: Free Press.

Litten, J. (1991). *The English Way of Death.* London: Robert Hale.

Locke, J. (2000). *Some Thoughts Concerning Education.* Oxford: Oxford University Press.

Lowe, R. (2004). *Sadler, Michael Ernest (1861–1943).* Oxford: Oxford Dictionary of National Biography, Oxford University Press.

Maddox, B. (2006). *Freud's Wizard: The Enigma of Ernest Jones.* London: John Murray.

Manchester University Magazine (1909–1912). Manchester: John Rylands Library Archive, University of Manchester.

Marwick, A. (1976). *The Home Front.* London: Thames and Hudson.

McCarthy, D. (1934). Review. *Journal of Educational Psychology, 25,* 234.

McIntire, M. (2000). *Researching the British Sporting Press.* London: British Library Newsletter, No. 28.

Meisel, P. & Kendrick, W. (Eds.) (1986). *Bloomsbury/Freud. The letters of James and Alix Strachey, 1924–1925.* London: Chatto and Windus.

Moffitt, T. (1993). Adolescence-limited and life-course persistent antisocial behaviour: a developmental taxonomy. *Psychological Review. 100,* 674–701.

Montessori, M. (1912). *The Montessori Method.* London: Heinemann.

Myers, C. (1911). *Textbook of Experimental Psychology: with laboratory exercises.* Cambridge: Cambridge University Press.

Myers, C. (1913). Letter to Professor Samuel Alexander. ALEXA/A/1/1/ 208/1. Manchester: John Rylands Library Archive, University of Manchester.

Neill, A. S. (1973). *Neill, Neill, Orange Peel.* London: Weidenfeld and Nicholson.

Nethercot, A. H. (1961). *The First Five Lives of Annie Besant.* London: Rupert Hart Davis.

Nunn, P. (1920). *Education: its data and first principles.* London: Edward Arnold.

Nursery School Association of Great Britain (1937). *The Educational Value of the Nursery School.* London: Nursery School Association of Great Britain.

Oppenheim, J. (1988). *The Other World: Spiritualism and Psychical Research in England: 1850–1914.* Cambridge: Cambridge University Press.

Perelberg, R. (2006) *The* Controversial Discussions and Apres-coup. *International Journal of Psychoanalysis, 87,* 1199–1220.

Piaget, J. (1926). *Language and Thought of the Child.* London: Routledge and Kegan Paul.

Piaget J. (1928). *Judgement and Reasoning in the Child.* London: Routledge and Kegan Paul.

Piaget, J. (1931a). Le developpement intellectual chez les jeunes enfants. Etude critique. *Mind, 40,* 127–160.

Piaget, J. (1931b). Retrospective and prospective analysis in child psychology. *British Journal of Educational Psychology, 1,* 130–9.

Piaget J. (1971) *Science of Education and the Psychology of the Child.* London: Longmans. Tr. D. Coltman from *Educational Principles and Psychological data* (1935) Chapter 2.

Piaget, J. (1973). *An Autobiography.* In: Richard Evans (Ed.), *Jean Piaget: The Man and His Ideas.* London: Duckworth.

Pires, M. (2004). Isaacs, Susan Sutherland (1885–1948). *Dictionary of National Biography,* Oxford: Oxford University Press.

Quinton, A. M. (1972). *Social Thought in Britain.* In: C. B. Cox & A. E. Dyson (Eds.), *The Twentieth Century Mind: 1: 1900–1918* (pp. 113–135). Oxford: Oxford University Press.

Rapp, D. (1988). The Reception of Freud by the British Press: General Interest and Literary Magazines: 1920–1925. *Journal of the History of Behavioral Sciences, 24,* 191–201.

Ratcliffe, C. (1997). Mutual Improvement Societies and the Forging of Working Class Consciousness in the nineteenth century. *Journal of Lifelong Education, 16,* 141–55.

Reddy, V. (2000). Coyness in early infancy. *Developmental Science, 3,* 186–92.

Richards, G. (2000). Britain on the Couch. The popularisation of psycho-analysis in Britain, 1918–1940. *Science in Context, 13,* 183–230.

Richards, G. (2004). *Flugel, John Carl: 1884–1955.* Oxford: Oxford Dictionary of National Biography, Oxford University Press.

Rickman, J. (1950) Obituary: Susan Sutherland Isaacs. *International Journal of Psychoanalysis, 31:* 1–7.

Riviere, J. (1921). Review of C. W. Valentine: Dreams and the Unconscious. *British Journal of Medical Psychology, 2,* 244–6.

Riviere, J. (1929) Womanliness as a masquerade. *International Journal of Psychoanalysis, 10,* 303–313.

Riviere, J. (1932) Jealousy as a mechanism of defence. *International Journal of Psychoanalysis, 13,* 414–424.

Riviere, J. (1936). On the genesis of psychical conflict in earliest infancy. *International Journal of Psychoanalysis, 17,* 395–422.

Robbins, L. (1935), *The Nature and Significance of Economic Science.* London, Macmillan.

Robbins, L. (1966). *Address at Memorial Service for Nathan Isaacs.* London: Institute of Education.

Robbins, L. (1971). *Autobiography of an Economist.* London: Macmillan.

Robertson, A., B. (1990). *A Century of Change: the Study of Education in the University of Manchester.* Manchester: University of Manchester.

Rogerson, D. (1957). Letter to Nathan Isaacs. IoE NI D10/2.

Roth, A. & Fonagy, P. (Eds.) (2005). *What Works for Whom? A Critical Review of Psychotherapy Research.* London: Guilford Press.

Rousseau, J-J. (1991). *Emile or On Education.* London, Penguin.

Rutter, M., Maughan, B., Mortimore, P. & Ouston, J. (1979). *Fifteen Thousand Hours.* London: Open Books.

Segal, H. (1964). *Introduction to the Works of Melanie Klein.* London: Heinemann.

Silber, K. (1960). *Pestalozzi: The man and his work.* London: Routledge and Kegan Paul.

Skidelsky, R. (1969). *English Progressive Schools.* London: Penguin.

Smith, L. A. H. (1985). *To Understand and To Help.* Cranbury, NJ: Associated Universities Press.

Solms, M., and Turnbull, O. (2002). *The Brain and the Inner World.* London, Karnac Books.

Spock, B. (2005). *Dr. Spock's Baby and Child Care.* New York: Simon and Schuster.

Stern, D. (1985). *The Interpersonal World of the Infant.* New York: Basic Books.

Stern, W. (1924). *Psychology of Early Childhood*. London: George Allen and Unwin.

Stevenson, J., Graham, P., Fredman, G., & McLoughlin, V. (1987). A twin study of reading and spelling ability and disability. *Journal of Child Psychology and Psychiatry, 28,* 229–248.

Stewart, W. A. C. (1968). *The Educational Innovators. Vol. 2, Progressive Schools 1881–1967.* London: Macmillan.

Stoughton, R. H. (1963). Obituary: Professor William Broadhurst Brierley. *Annals of Applied Biology, 51,* 509–10.

Sturt, M. (1934). Book Review: Social Development. *British Journal of Educational Psychology, 3,* 291–4.

Sully, J. (1895). *Studies of Childhood*. London: Longman.

Titmuss, R. (1950). *Problems of Social Policy*. London: HMSO.

Tizard, B. & Hughes, M. (1984). *Young Children Learning*. London: Fontana.

Tosh, J. (2005). *Manliness and Masculinities in Nineteenth-Century Britain.* London: Pearson Longman.

Trevarthen, C. (1977). Descriptive analyses of infant communicative behaviour. In H. R. Shaffer (Ed.), *Studies in mother-infant interaction.* London: Academic Press.

Turner, J. M. (2005). *Wesleyan Methodism*. Peterborough: Epworth Press.

Valentine, C. W. (1931). Review. *British Journal of Educational Psychology, 1,* 106.

Vygotsky, L. (1962). *Thought and Language*. Cambridge: MIT Press.

Watson, J. B. (1928). *The Psychological Care of Infant and Child.* New York: W. W. Norton.

Weitzmann, C. (1950). *Trial and Error.* London: East and West Library.

Wells, H. G. (1943). *Ann Veronica.* London: Everyman Edition. J. M. Dent.

Williams, B. (1994). *Education with its eyes open: a biography of Dr. K. S. Cunningham.* Melbourne: Australian Council of Educational Research.

Willoughby, R. (1931). Review. *Journal of Genetic Psychology, 39,* 417–20.

Wolpert, M., Fuggle, P., Cottrell, D., et al. (2006) Drawing on the Evidence. London: Evidence-Based Practice Unit, University College, 21, Maresfield Gardens, London, NW3 5SD.

Wooldridge, A. (1994). *Measuring the Mind: Education and Psychology in England, c.1860–c.1990.* Cambridge: Cambridge University Press.

Zangwill, O. (1972). *Psychology.* In: C. B. Cox and A. E. Dyson (Eds.), *The Twentieth Century Mind, 2, 1918–1945.* Oxford: Oxford University Press.

Zaretsky, E. (2005). *Secrets of the Soul.* New York: Vintage Books.

Books by Susan Isaacs

Brierley, S. (1921). *Introduction to Psychology.* London: Methuen.

Isaacs, S. (1929). *The Nursery Years.* London: Routledge and Kegan Paul.

—— (with Victoria Bennett) (1930b). *Health and Education in the Nursery.* London: Routledge.

—— (1930a). *Intellectual Growth in Young Children.* London: Routledge and Kegan Paul.

—— (1932). *The Children We Teach.* London: University of London Press.

—— (1933). *Social Development in Young Children.* London: Routledge.

—— (1936). *Psychological Aspects of Child Development.* London: Evans Bros.

——, Oliver, R., and Field, H. (1936), *The Educational Guidance of the school child: Suggestions on Child Study and Guidance Embodying a Scheme of Pupils' Records.* London: Evans Brothers.

——, Clement Brown, S., & Thouless, R. H. (Ed.) (1941). *Cambridge Evacuation Survey.* London: Methuen.

—— (1948a). *Children and Parents: Their Problems and Difficulties.* London: Methuen.

—— (1948b). *Childhood and After.* London: Routledge and Kegan Paul.

Main articles by Susan Isaacs

Fairhurst, S. (1912/13). A Manchester Girl. *Manchester University Magazine, 9,* 113–4. Manchester: John Rylands University Archive.

Brierley, S. (1918). Analysis of the Spelling Process. *Journal of Experimental Pedagogy, 4,* 239–254.

Brierley, S. S. (1920). The Present Attitude of Employees to Industrial Psychology. *British Journal of Psychology, 10,* 210–227.

—— (1921). Science and Human Values in Industry. *The Co-operative Educator, 5,* 11–12.

—— (1923). A note on sex differences from the psychoanalytical point of view. *British Journal of Medical Psychology, 3,* 288–308.

Isaacs, S. (1927). Penis-Faeces-Child. *International Journal of Psychoanalysis, 8,* 74–76.

—— (1928). The Mental Hygiene of the Pre-School Child. *British Journal of Medical Psychology, 8,* 186–193.

—— (1928b). Review. *British Journal of Medical Psychology, 8,* 237–9.

—— (1929a). Critical Review. Jean Piaget, The Child's Conception of the Mind. *Mind, 38,* 506–513.

—— (1929b). Critical Review. Jean Piaget, Language and Thought of the Child. *Journal of Genetic Psychology, 36,* 597–697.

—— (1929c). Privation and guilt. *International Journal of Psychoanalysis,* 10, Parts 2 and 3.

—— (1932). Some notes on the prevalence of neurotic difficulties in young children. *British Journal of Educational Psychology, 2,* 71–91.

—— (1934). Property and Possessiveness. *British Journal of Medical Psychology, 15,* 64–78.

—— (1939). Criteria for interpretation. *International Journal of Psychoanalysis, 20,* 148–60.

—— (1943). An acute psychotic anxiety occurring in a boy of four years. *International Journal of Psychoanalysis, 24,* 13–32

—— (1948). The Nature and Function of Phantasy. *International Journal of Psychoanalysis, 29,* 73–97.

Heimann, P. and Isaacs, S. (1943). Regression, in J. Riviere (Ed.), *Developments in Psychoanalysis,* London: Hogarth Press and Institute of Psychoanalysis, 1952, pp. 169–97.

Index